Maria Bellonci was born and ⟨...⟩ the distinguished critic Goffredo Bellonci she wrote and sponsored literature throughout her life, through the Strega Prize and the Italian PEN society, of which she was Vice-President. With the publication of *Lucrezia Borgia* in Italy she won the Viareggio Literary Award and the Galante Prize. It was then published throughout the world to great acclaim. She wrote numerous distinguished works of history and also wrote for newspapers and radio.

By Maria Bellonci

A Prince of Mantua:
The Life and Times of Vincenzo Gonzaga
The Travels of Marco Polo
Lucrezia Borgia

THE LIFE AND TIMES OF
LUCREZIA BORGIA

Maria Bellonci

Translated by Bernard and Barbara Wall

PHOENIX

A PHOENIX PAPERBACK

First published in an abridged translation
in Great Britain by Weidenfeld & Nicolson in 1953
This paperback edition published in 2000
by Phoenix Press
an imprint of Orion Books Ltd,
Orion House, 5 Upper St Martin's Lane,
London WC2H 9EA

Fifth impression 2003

A CIP catalogue record for this book
is available from the British Library.

Printed and bound in Great Britain by
Clays Ltd, St Ives plc

TO MY FATHER

CONTENTS

PART ONE

THE CONQUEST OF
THE VATICAN

On the night of July 25, 1492, Pope Innocent VIII lay dying. He was a benign old Genoese of the Cibo family who for years had been criticized by his contemporaries for slackness and neglect.

But the worst thing about him was his attitude to his family. Friar Egidio of Viterbo, in his severe Latin *Historiace*, reproached him for flaunting his relatives before the public, celebrating his children's marriages in the Apostolic Palace and breaking the rules of canon law by sitting down to meals with women. When the humanist, Marullo, attributed sixteen children to him he was exaggerating for the sake of his epigrams. But, as always happens with the relations of people who enjoy transitory power, the children the Pope did have were restless and very acquisitive. He had protected and favoured the two most famous of them, indeed the only ones known to history – Teodorina and Franceschetto. Wealth and favours had been showered upon them; and in 1488 the whole of Rome had witnessed the public processions and heard of the sumptuous ceremonies at the Vatican on the occasion of the political marriage between Franceschetto and Maddalena, daughter of Lorenzo de' Medici. In 1489 came another marriage, that of Teodorina's daughter with Luis of Aragon. The celebrations were meant to testify to the peace reigning between the Pontiff and the King of Naples, and once again the marriage took place in the Vatican.

Even on his deathbed Innocent VIII had his children around him. Now that death was at hand, the Pope felt free from guilt, or at least felt that his errors should be pardoned, and he may well have been right. Franceschetto stood by his pillow or in the adjoining room (later he was to write that his father breathed his last in his arms) when the Pope made his public confession in the presence of all the Cardinals, urging them to choose a worthy successor and begging their pardon for not using the office entrusted to him to nobler ends. And then, gently, he wept. The Pope hoped that his last days might be passed in peace, but by July 21 stories of new and ferocious rivalries between the bellicose Cardinals reached his ears. Amongst the Vice-Chancellors of the Church was the Catalan, Rodrigo Borgia. He was a man who sugared his suggestions with persuasive and charming manners, and he now proposed that the Pope should entrust the Castel Sant' Angelo to the College of Cardinals. The interview was interrupted by Giuliano della Rovere who made a timely entry as in a play, and drily and factually pointed out that, as Borgia was the strongest force in the College, to hand the Castel Sant' Angelo over to him would be tantamount to giving him Rome and the Papacy on a platter. An angry argument developed and foul language was used. The two churchmen called one another 'Marranos' and 'white Moors', as Antonello da Salerno informed the Marquis Gonzaga. But della Rovere got the best of it and the Castel Sant' Angelo remained in the hands of its Governor who was instructed to hand it over to the new Pope and no one else. Four days later, on July 26, 1492, the succession to the Papacy was open.

As is well known, the situation in Italy at that time was riddled with difficulties. The peninsula was divided up into small states and dukedoms amongst which peace of a kind was preserved by arms and diplomacy, though it was continually being broken by guerrilla activities. The precarious but necessary balance of power had been maintained so far by clever navigation between the rocks of contention on the part of the princes and the lay and ecclesiastical administrators who were well aware that the division of forces and parties in the peninsula would lead in the end to disaster. Towards the end of the fifteenth century there were threats of foreign invasions, not only from the East but also and more dangerously from the North, from France. France had been pacified and welded into a powerful kingdom by Louis XI, and now her claims to the Kingdom of Naples, which she considered had been usurped by the Aragonese from the House of Anjou, were no secret. Furthermore, though less publicly, the French considered that the Duchy of Milan should by rights be theirs since Valentina Visconti had married into the House of Orléans. Hence the young King Charles VIII, who succeeded Louis XI, tried to bring pressure to bear on the conclave so as to have a Pope favourable to his aim of conquering Naples; and with this end in view he supported the strongest enemy of Naples, namely Ludovico Sforza, 'il Moro', who at that time was uncle, tutor and factotum to the young Duke of Milan. Sforza was wealthy, his presumption knew no bounds, and at that time he was utterly fearless. His hand was felt in all the political affairs of the peninsula, and his henchmen, informers, friends, men of business and spies were to be found everywhere. Moreover, in the Vatican, awaiting his orders, was his brother Ascanio, an ambitious young Cardinal, intelligent rather than subtle, liberal and inclined to take risks – a typical Milanese. Cardinal Ascanio Sforza became the centre of the anti-Neapolitan party which included all the enemies of King Ferrante of Aragon; and by way of defence the King of Naples formed an alliance with Giuliano della Rovere and his faction. Neither marriage alliances nor attempts at peacemaking had been able to compound the fatal enmity between Naples and Milan, and it was now on the point of developing into a struggle in which the two contending parties might easily destroy the freedom and independence of all the Italian States.

Thus the two parties, representing Milan and Naples, assembled as many Cardinals as possible around their respective leaders – Ascanio Sforza and Giuliano della Rovere. Ascanio – as is shown by the recently published scrutiny of the conclave of 1492 – had no hope of being elected as he was barely thirty-seven years old and hence too young; moreover he was convinced that no one would tolerate the idea of the Papacy falling to a power as aggressive as that of Ludovico il Moro. Giuliano della Rovere was not so young but his time had not yet come and he knew it, quite apart from the fact that he was the bitterest, prickliest of all the Cardinals and aroused the greatest number of hatreds and enmities. So both of them served as important electors, Giuliano for the Portuguese Cardinal Costa, a man of eighty with a bold majestic air, and a favourite because his great age made it likely that there would be another conclave in the near future (though actually Costa lived for another fifteen years); while Ascanio became supporter of a Neapolitan who was hostile to King Ferrante – Cardinal Oliviero Carafa – with Rodrigo Borgia, Vice-Chancellor of the Church, as second string.

Rodrigo Borgia's name was not taken very seriously in the forecasts; contemporary commentators spoke of his candidature as that of an outsider who had few chances. We do not know what went on in his elegant Catalan head – possibly he fostered these views so as to have more play for his manoeuvres. This was certainly not the first time that his desires and ambitions had been fixed on the throne, for at the conclave of 1484, when Innocent VIII was made Pope, he had intrigued in vain to get elected. Now, after a lapse of eight years, he was richer and in a better position, for he represented, in the struggle between the extremist parties, a group that was neither Neapolitan nor Milanese; so, once more, doggedly but unobtrusively, he set to work. Ascanio, whose main interest lay in the election of a Pope under an obligation to him, began to think that at worst – not to mention the benefits of wealth he would gain – even a Borgia Pope might have his points. But Ascanio's calculation was mistaken, not on grounds of reason but of psychology: he foresaw everything except the fact that he would never be able to use such a clever fox as Rodrigo Borgia.

On August 6, 1492, after a courageous address by Bernardino Carvajal on the evils afflicting the Church, the conclave began. They came to the first scrutiny. Rodrigo Borgia obtained seven votes, Carafa nine, Giuliano della Rovere five, Costa seven, and Michiel, Cardinal of Venice, seven. Those were the most important results. Ascanio Sforza did not receive a single vote –

a sign that he had given precise injunctions to his faithful followers. The vote was null, and the people who had been waiting in Piazza San Pietro went back home. At the second scrutiny Rodrigo obtained eight votes, Carafa retained his nine, Giuliano della Rovere had five, and Michiel again seven. It was nine o'clock on a summery morning and everything seemed at a standstill. The conclavists attending on the Cardinals kept themselves aloof, but even so the news began to seep through. Hour by hour messengers left Rome and spread the latest reports all over Italy. Was it Carafa? Or Michiel? Or Costa? Meanwhile, despite the semblance of order, the conclave was in turmoil. The struggle between the two parties was bitter but vain, for neither side managed to penetrate the other's armour. Ascanio would not yield; nor would Giuliano. Rodrigo Borgia's hour had come. A little longer, and the world would be his. What really happened on that day – the Vice-Chancellor's great day? How did he manage to insinuate his case into the minds of all the Cardinals? There is no need to go into the long and intricate account of the negotiations and contracts, some of them verbal, that were made between August 10 and August 11. By the evening of the 11th Borgia could count on seventeen votes which was more than the two-thirds necessary for a majority. When Giuliano della Rovere heard the news he saw that there was nothing more to be done. 'Then,' as the Ferrarese ambassador later related, 'seeing that he could neither win nor get even,' he 'swiftly and with good grace' joined the enemy side. For his capitulation he was rewarded with an abbacy, various other benefices, the extremely important legation at Avignon, and the fortress of Ronciglione. Ronciglione, which lay on the road to the North, was complementary to the Rovere castle at Ostia that looked out to sea. Now that he could watch the ways that led to and from Rome, the Cardinal hoped at least to establish a close control over the new Pope's movements.

Day and night Rodrigo Borgia pursued his secret strategy. At dawn on August 11 there were few Romans in the Piazza San Pietro to see the bricks falling from the walled-up window and to hear the voice joyfully announcing that the Vice-Chancellor, Rodrigo Borgia, had been elected and would take the name of Alexander VI. At the fourth scrutiny he had been chosen unanimously.

How far the voting was lawful, or to what extent the sin of simony played its part, would take too long to discuss and would side-track us from our main story. As La Torre has recently shown, Rodrigo Borgia's greatest debt was unquestionably to the political intransigence of the two major contendents at the conclave. But there can be no doubt that he won the hearts of the majority of the Cardinals with generous gifts and that everyone had a look in when the spoils were distributed. Money changed hands so feverishly that the Spannocchi bank where the Borgia wealth was deposited nearly crashed. And if Infessura's description of mules loaded with silver driven from Rodrigo's residence to Ascanio Sforza's must be looked on as a colourful legend, it is nevertheless certain that simony did take place. Morally speaking this was only to be expected, given the precedents in Rodrigo Borgia's life.

'Our enterprising Pontiff,' wrote Giannandrea Boccaccio, Bishop of Modena and correspondent of the Duke of Ferrara, on August 31, 'is already showing himself in his true colours.' These correspondents, foxes of the Curia, whose eyes penetrated events with a ruthlessness that came from habit and experience, knew what to expect of the Spaniard, given the pattern of his life so far.

The Borgia family had its origins in Yativa near Valencia in Spain, a small town of white houses low against a blue sky with inhabitants of mixed Spanish and Arabic blood. The Borgias were an ancient family of the locality and down the centuries had yielded their crop of soldiers and governors. They were provincial grandees, looked on with moderate favour at the courts of Castile and Aragon, energetic and restless, with family ties as strong as a tribe of Israelites. When they did not make noble matches to add splendour to their name, they usually married one another. But the great Borgia fortune began only when Alonso became Pope Callixtus III. His is a good luck story. He was the youngest in his family and had four elder sisters. He had a vocation for the ecclesiastical career, chose the study of jurisprudence, and took a passionate interest in the intricate formulas of canon law – that perfect embodiment of the legal mind. On hearing him preach, the Dominican Vincenzo Ferrera foretold that he would have a great future and called him the glory of his family and of the nation. Doubtless this prophecy struck him as a lucky omen. Anyway, from these beginnings, Alonso Borgia never looked back. He was chosen as secretary by King Alfonso of Aragon and was then sent as ambassador to Pope Martin V. His clever diplomacy was of great service to the Pope, for he even managed to persuade the Anti-Pope, Clement VIII, to renounce his usurped dignity. He was rewarded by being given the Bishopric of Valencia which thereafter remained with the Borgia family as hereditary demesne. He won his Cardinal's hat by his merits and good behaviour. Finally, on April 8, 1455, when he was seventy-seven and gouty, though still unwearied of intrigue between rival camps, he was unexpectedly made Pope. He himself was as surprised as anyone.

Callixtus III was an honest man, a good priest, and a sincere believer in his own actions and intentions, but he never really understood the problems of high politics, still less the life of art and culture. The obstinacy and obtuseness of his temperament, his lack of taste for classical literature in a century passionately devoted to Latin and Greek, caused the Italian humanists to look on him as a barbarian. They accused him, not without reason, of removing gold and silver from illuminated manuscripts in the Vatican so as to get money for the crusade against the infidel. The only valid excuse for his behaviour was the extremely critical state of the war against the Turks. Indeed, the scimitar of the Turk and his love for his family were Callixtus III's life-long obsessions. Like Innocent VIII, he fell for the temptations of nepotism, and all those feelings of kindness and understanding that he normally lacked rose to the surface the moment he saw someone of his own race and felt the call of the blood. He had no children, for it is doubtful whether he was the father of Francesco Borgia who later became Archbishop of Cosenza; but he made up for this lack with sisters, nephews, cousins, relations of every kind who poured into Rome despite the hatred of the people. His greatest affection was for his nephews, Pedro Luis and Rodrigo, the sons of his sister Isabella. She was the wife of Jofre Borgia and hence these nephews were Borgias twice over, both on their mother's and father's side.

Thus when Rodrigo set out on his ecclesiastical career, he was very well placed. He became a Cardinal at twenty-five, and with his uncle's influence had been given the rank of Vice-Chancellor of the Church, a position which constituted what a jealous contemporary called 'a second Papacy'. Rodrigo was a magnificent prelate: eloquent and extremely likeable, he was the only member of his family who managed to get every advantage out of life without being hated. In this he was the very opposite of his brother, Pedro Luis, who held down an extraordinary number of posts and offices – amongst others those of Captain-General of the Church and Prefect of Rome – but was immediately and invariably loathed by everyone who set eyes on him.

Then one day Pope Callixtus fell ill. His agony was long and magnificently lugubrious in the Spanish style. Surrounded by relations, chaplains and the most loyal of his compatriots, by candles that burnt night and day and the recitation of psalms, he lay dead to this life while rumour and tumult spread in the city. Pedro Luis did not feel safe: he realized that the hour for settling accounts had come and thought up grandiose plans for countering the moves of his enemies; but Rodrigo, whose prudence now showed itself for the first time, had other ideas. On the last day of Pope Callixtus' life, Pedro Luis, Prefect of Rome and Captain-General of the Church, fled with the help of Cardinal Rodrigo and the Venetian Cardinal Barbo. These two accompanied him as far as the road to Ostia and there abandoned him to struggle on alone. Pursued by the Orsini, deserted by his own soldiers, Pedro Luis played his last card with characteristic energy and challenged his fate. He managed to shut himself up in the fortress of Civitavecchia with a few faithful followers and there waited until he could get back to Rome. He died an obscure death on September 26, 1458.

Meanwhile Rodrigo remained calm and active amid the popular tumult, and went to St Peter's to pray for the dying Pope. He was protected by his purple but still more by his prestige. He allowed his palace to be sacked, judging that the turbulent elements in the crowd would be satisfied with robbery; and he was right, for beyond that he suffered nothing, though even Italian friends and mercenaries of the Borgias were persecuted and killed. When the last spark of life was flickering on the face of Callixtus, his household, including relations, friends and even sisters, abandoned him in the general panic. But Rodrigo stayed behind and was present when the old Pontiff breathed his last.

The next Pope was Aeneas Sylvius Piccolomini who took the name of Pius II. He was an artist, a thinker and a polished humanist, and had every reason to be grateful to the Borgias, for it was Rodrigo who had cast the decisive vote at his conclave. Piccolomini was not a man to forget those who had helped him, yet his famous letter of admonition to Cardinal Borgia is one of the most outspoken documents we have about Rodrigo's life. The letter was written in June 1460, in the Pope's own hand, when the Cardinal was at Siena.

'We have heard that three days ago a number of Sienese women were gathered together in the gardens of Giovanni Bichi and that you, forgetful of your high office, were with them from one o'clock until six in the afternoon. Your companion was one of your colleagues whose age, if not his respect for the apostolic see, should have reminded him of his duties. We have been informed that there was unseemly dancing, that no amorous allurements were lacking, and that you conducted yourself in a wholly worldly manner. Decency forbids us to go into the detail of what happened, for they were things whose very names are unworthy of your rank. The husbands, fathers, brothers and other kinsmen who had accompanied the girls were forbidden entrance so that you and a few intimates could be more free to indulge your pleasures. They say that in Siena this is the main topic of conversation and everyone is laughing at your vanity . . . We leave it to you to judge whether paying court to girls, dispatching fruit and delicate wines to the woman of your choice, spending the whole day watching every kind of folly and finally sending away the husbands so as to have all freedom for yourself, are compatible with your dignity. We are blamed on your account, and your late uncle Callixtus is blamed too for entrusting you with so many offices and honours . . . Remember your dignity and do not try to win the reputation of a vain gallant among men and girls . . .'

Various attempts have been made to prove that the reports giving rise to these reproaches were actually founded on a gross piece of gossip. But this is absurd as the affair was obviously notorious, and the aggrieved Pontiff added: 'Here at Bigni there are many ecclesiastics and laymen among whom you have become a byword . . .'

To confirm the justice of these reproaches Luzio has published a letter from the Mantuan ambassador at Siena to the Gonzagas, written in July 1460, which also recounts the episode. The occasion, he informs us, was a baptism. His words are these: 'I have nothing else to write to your lordship save that a baptism was celebrated here today . . . for a gentleman of this region at which the sponsors were Monsignor de Rohan and the Vice-Chancellor (Rodrigo Borgia). They were invited into a garden by the godfather, and the god-daughter was taken there too. The cream of society was to be found there and a fine party there was, but no one entered save the ecclesiastics . . .' A witty Sienese who was unable to gain access said: 'My God, if every child born within the year came into the world with its father's clothes on, they would all be priests and Cardinals.'

In all the glory of his thirty summers, Rodrigo Borgia attracted women as, to quote the chronicler Gaspare da Verona, 'a magnet attracts steel'. Pius II's letter hit the mark and we can well imagine how unwelcome it must have been. But Rodrigo answered immediately with clever excuses, and even if he could not deceive the Pontiff, he induced him to mitigate his severity. Pius II wished for nothing better than to absolve his Cardinal Vice-Chancellor from all charges, and in his reply we can see the desire to forgive at odds with his anger at what had occurred. 'What you have done,' he wrote, 'cannot be blameless, though it may be considerably less blameworthy than I was given to understand.' In future the Cardinal should be more circumspect: as for himself he forgave him and assured him that as long as he behaved well he, the Pope, would be father and protector to him.

Yet we can sense that the Pope had a melancholy foreboding as to the future, while knowing himself to be powerless to do anything about it. Rodrigo made a show of repentance by leaving Siena for the solitudes of Corsignano where he pretended to do penance; but far from mortifying his exuberant vitality he gave it full rein by organizing furious hunts through the woods and over the hills of Tuscany and the Apennines, for which his friend the Marquis of Mantua sent him well-trained hawks and hounds. In thanking the Gonzagas the Cardinal confessed that but for their generosity he would have had 'to live in idleness and without any pleasure' and 'endure the tedium of living in these rough and wild valleys'. We get a glimpse of his idea of a penitent's idiom.

Rodrigo was barely sixty when he ascended the Papal throne – an age which for men of sound constitution is the summit of maturity. Though he had all the majesty and confidence of one privileged by fortune, I do not think that we can ascribe true political genius to Alexander VI. But he was endowed with a good brain, an outstanding physique, and a strong power of attraction, to which must be added his intelligence in affairs of state, his mastery in matters ecclesiastical and juridical, and his quick and accurate intuition in politics. He never learnt the Ciceronian oratory that was common among the Cardinals of the age, but his Latin was remarkable for its liveliness, vigour and excellence, and whether he spoke in Latin, Italian or Spanish, what he said always had a native grace. It is beautiful in its variety of accent, and in its unexpected cadences of melody and pathos; and it is persuasive in that it suggests or imposes a personal truth which contrives to replace the need for absolute truth. In appearance and bearing he was consciously theatrical. He was a wonderful actor, imposing and dignified, and this was accentuated by the purple and jewels that suited him so admirably. He was handsome but not in the sense of having regular features. His attractiveness lay in the expression of virility at once brilliant and insolent that shone in his face, burst from his full lips, and found completion in the ample curve of a nose which gave the full measure of his force and sensibility. At the age of sixty he still loved women openly. He had a passionate affection for his children: the more handsome and vigorous they were the more he saw himself in them, and as he watched them blossoming he felt a deep inner satisfaction. As his contemporaries said: 'Such a carnal man was never seen.'

In 1492 Rodrigo's eldest son Pedro Luis, for whom he had created the Duchy of Gandia in Spain, died. Jeronima also died, who had married into the noble Roman house of the Cesarini. Another daughter, Isabella, was happily married to the Roman nobleman Pietro Matuzzi. We do not know the names of the mothers of these three children. But the younger ones, those of whom Rodrigo was most fond – Cesare, Juan, Lucrezia and Jofre – were borne by Vannozza Cattanei, the woman whom Rodrigo loved longest and always protected. Though she lived in obscurity and seems to have had no direct influence on her great protector, she loved and was loved, and her children grew like graceful poplars on the river banks of their father's care. Cesare was getting on for eighteen and wore ecclesiastical dress: perhaps his father already thought of him as the third Borgia Pope. Juan, aged sixteen, had inherited his brother Pedro Luis' Duchy of Gandia and was marked out for a military career. Twelve-year-old Lucrezia was in the charge of one of the Pope's nieces,

Adriana Mila Orsini, who was responsible for her education, while little Jofre, though at eleven his career was still undecided, had the title and revenues of a canon and archdeacon of Valencia.

Vannozza, who had had much happiness and lived in comfort, thanks to Cardinal Borgia's lasting devotion, saw the children often but did not live with them. Her life was regulated by social obligations and she needed to be conventional and dignified. She always lived in a separate house of her own and, except for short periods, had always been regularly married – first to an 'officer of the Church', Domenico d'Arignano, and subsequently, in 1480, to Giorgio de Croce, a Milanese, to whom she bore a son, Ottaviano, and with whom she lived in an imposing house, next to the Cardinal's, in Piazza Pizzo di Merlo.

The house had a façade looking on to the piazza; it was light and sunny – uncommon in the narrow streets of medieval Rome – with numerous rooms, a water cistern and a garden very dear to Vannozza's heart as she loved her fresh suburban vines.

Here Vannozza lived for a number of years; but when her second husband died, followed shortly afterwards by her son, Ottaviano, she married yet again and went to live in Piazza Branca in the Arenula district. Her third husband, Carlo Canale, from Mantua, came from a Cardinal's court and had enjoyed a limited regional celebrity among a group of literary friends, including Politian who dedicated his *Orfeo* to him. Among the wedding presents for her third marriage Vannozza received a dowry of 1,000 gold ducats and a post for her husband at the Papal court.

Very probably Vannozza originally came from Mantua herself, because the Venetian chronicler, Marin Sanudo, who had accurate information about everything that happened in the Marquisate of the Gonzagas just over the frontier, refers to her in his diaries as a Mantuan. Cattanei is a common family name everywhere in Italy but was particularly widespread in Mantua at this time and is always cropping up in correspondence. Vannozza was not only beautiful but also must have had a power of feminine seduction that challenged the Borgia exuberance, for she was loved by Rodrigo for many years and was still loved by him at an age that in those days was considered old – forty. It was then that Jofre, Rodrigo's last son, was born, and by then her relations with the Cardinal certainly dated back more than ten years and had become a sort of marriage. Like a morganatic wife, Vannozza had her quiet but well-supplied court that accompanied her wherever she went – for instance when, in the summer or at the first hint of the epidemics that were an annual event in Rome, she betook herself to the well appointed and fortified castles of the Borgias, to Nepi or preferably Subiaco. Rodrigo, like all strong men who believe in the future, had a taste for building and at Subiaco had reconstructed the great stronghold above the medieval monastery walls on which the ferocious and quarrelsome abbots had lost and won so many battles. In this airy and roomy domicile Vannozza would install her court and wait for the Cardinal to join her. When on the look-out from the summit of the fortress, she could see the monastery just below her with its memories of saints and emperors, of peaceful and warlike monks – a holy labyrinth whose history was told in paintings on the walls. Callixtus III had given the revenues to Rodrigo in 1471.

It appears that the fair baby who was destined to bear the name of Lucrezia Borgia was born at Subiaco in April 1480. The place is mentioned in the *Storia Sublacense* of the learned don Alessandro Tummolini who based his work on the monastery archives and made use of a manuscript of 'Memoirs of Stipendiary Cardinals' which is also referred to by other historians and is now lost. There is no reason to question Tummolini's story, especially as, when he speaks of the birth of Cesare Borgia, which also took place here, he begs pardon of the citizens of Subiaco for attributing to their city the dishonour of giving birth to such a monster, and indulges in naïve effusions to show that they were not responsible for this historical fact.

The child Lucrezia had light hair and gentle grey-blue eyes, and she melted her father's heart. When he held her in his arms and looked at her little laughing face, he must have seen himself, so dark and strong, as a bulwark defending her frailty. It is not known whether little Lucrezia was educated at a convent, but she certainly loved the convent of the Dominican nuns of San Sisto on the Appian Way, and it may well be supposed that she at least made retreats there in preparation for the great religious feasts; and there can be no doubt that a sense of dignity was implanted in her within the walls of this convent that was to save her from shipwreck in the days when she went farthest astray. Doubtless, too, she derived from it the unquestioning sincerity of her religion and her love of prayer, incense and sacred music. The cloister was her anchor in the tempests of her life. To Lucrezia it meant not so much a return to faith in the abstract as a return to her own childhood faith, and she always felt safe when surrounded by the whispers of gentle voices in a world stripped of sensuality.

As the daughter of a very powerful Cardinal, Lucrezia must have been held in high esteem. She can never for a moment have felt the need to reflect on the singularity of her position except to feel pleased with her privileges. She saw the women of Innocent VIII's Papal household coming and going in the Vatican, respected and honoured like legitimate princesses. The children of Cardinals were to be met with on all sides and they were much like the children of other princes. She was certainly proud to belong to a family that counted a Pope among its forebears and was so bound up with the things and personalities of the Church as to seem superior to all others.

Lucrezia resembled her father in his cheerful way of believing that the future was full of promise. Like her father she had a receding chin, but this was so prettily shaped that it gave her an appearance of perpetual adolescence. She was fair with light eyes, and graceful. In spite of her slenderness, her thick Spanish blood gave her a certain colour and robustness. Educated as she was by Adriana Mila Orsini, Rodrigo Borgia's niece, who must have spoken of the land of Catalonia as of a legend, she felt herself to be Spanish. When she listened to Adriana she re-created a lovely fable that took the form of her own dreams. Like all noble women of the epoch, she followed a course of humanistic studies, but possibly she preferred to learn the Spanish language and to dance the dances of her country with the light steps of the girls of Valencia. And so the overtures which were initiated in 1491 for her marriage to a young Spanish nobleman must have seemed to her the natural outcome of all this preparation.

For the first official act in Lucrezia's life was an engagement. On February 26, 1491, the notary, Camillo Beneimbene, who was expert in all the affairs of the Borgias, drew up the matrimonial agreement between the Borgia child and Don Cherubino Juan de Centelles, Lord of Val d'Ayora in the kingdom of Valencia. The contract was written in Catalan and promised a dowry of 30,000 'timbres' partly in money and partly in ornaments and jewels, as a gift to the bride from her father and brothers. Within a year she should be sent to Valencia and the wedding would take place six months after her arrival. So it seemed as if Lucrezia's destiny was already settled and she would shortly be off to Spain. But less than two months after this first marriage contract a new agreement was drawn up engaging Lucrezia to the fifteen-year-old Don Gaspare Aversa, count of Procida, who was also a Valencian. Cardinal Rodrigo probably changed his daughter's betrothed for reasons of ambition.

It is almost certain that Lucrezia knew neither of these claimants, though she did know – there being no reason to keep it from her – that she was betrothed. But whether it was the name of Cherubino or of Gaspare that coloured the dreams of her adolescence, or indeed infancy, we do not know. Perhaps there was no name, for girls of eleven, however precocious, dream about the future without much reference to reality. But Lucrezia's thoughts probably dwelt mostly on the two women with whom she lived, Adriana Mila and Giulia Farnese, for they were both extraordinary women who played an important part in the love life of Alexander VI.

Adriana Mila was the daughter of Pedro de Mila who came to Italy at the time of Callixtus III with the wave of Catalans who then invaded the apostolic palace. She was probably born in Rome as her classical name suggests, and in Rome she became established as the wife of Ludovico Orsini of the great house of that name, lord of the little domain of Bassanello near Viterbo. By 1489 she was a widow living with a young son called Orsino after his family. Orsino had a squint – '*Monoculus Orsinus*', as the Vatican book of ceremony describes him – and it was his fate to go down in history as a cuckold. His wedding took place on May 21, 1489, when the Borgia notary, Camillo Beneimbene, in the presence of Cardinal G. B. Zeno, titular of Santa Maria in Portico, of the Vice-Chancellor Rodrigo Borgia, of prelates, nobles, witnesses and relatives of the houses of Orsini, Farnese and Borgia, united him in holy matrimony with 'the magnificent and unaffected girl', Giulia Farnese.

Giulia belonged to an ancient family of the provincial nobility who were lords over estates round Lake Bolsena, Capodimonte, Marta and Isola Farnese – fine fertile land yet not such as permitted its owners to live like grandees. In the castle of Capodimonte the splendour of an illustrious name was tempered by an almost patriarchal simplicity. But the generations of the Farnese had by now reached a point of maturity in which all the gifts of nature – beauty, intelligence, grace, astuteness and good fortune – had combined, and the only thing still wanting for the family to rise to greatness and renown was opportunity. In 1489 there were four surviving children of the late Pier Luigi Farnese. Angelo was the head of the family, and like all lords he was dedicated to the arts of war. Alessandro was a protonotary who had set out on the path that was to win him the papal tiara (later he became Paul III). Girolama was married to a Pucci of Florence. But the guiding star of the family was the young and ravishing Giulia who, as soon as she arrived in Rome, became known as Giulia Bella. Her beauty was the mainspring of the glory of the Farnese family, for Cardinal Rodrigo Borgia, as he then was, fell passionately in love with her. It is difficult to say whether the celebration of Giulia's marriage with Orsino in the Vice-Chancellor's orientally luxurious palace can be taken as evidence that a love relationship already existed between the fifteen-year-old Giulia and the Borgia. Rodrigo may have been present at the ceremony merely out of kindness to his niece Adriana, Orsino's mother. In a letter of 1494 Alessandro refers unequivocally to the conjugal intimacy between Giulia and Orsino, and this shows that the marriage was a regular one and not a mere blind used by the Cardinal so as to have the girl for himself. The Borgia's passionate feelings were more probably aroused after Giulia's marriage when he met her in Adriana's house where he was a frequent visitor – for he was fond of his niece and had great faith in her judgment. So it remains uncertain at what precise moment Adriana got to know that the Borgia's sensuality had her son's wife as its object, nor do we know how or why she decided to act as an accomplice, and still less how she made her decision known to her daughter-in-law. This must have been difficult for Adriana, as she should have been the first to be horrified by what was happening.

As things turned out, the astounding and monstrous collusion between mother-in-law and daughter-in-law seems to have been smooth, if not entirely candid. The two women lived harmoniously together. Visitors found them at one on all questions, whether on a matter of recommending friends or relatives to the Pope or about receiving envoys and ambassadors in court affairs. Giulia's business was to be loved. Adriana's was to use her lively and secretive intelligence to safeguard the intrigue. She was a practical woman and prepared to sacrifice her son if the Pope would pay him well in material goods. For this reason she never wearied of recommending Orsino in the Vatican. Presumably she took it for granted that Rodrigo's infatuation was bound to end one day and that then her attitude would prove to have been worthwhile all round.

So in November 1493 Giulia was the Borgia's semi-official favourite. When ambassadors and princes wanted favours and privileges from the Pope they had recourse to her as much as to

Adriana and little Lucrezia. All three were living in the newly-built palace handed over to them by the Cardinal of Santa Maria in Portico, next to the Vatican on the left of the entrance to the Papal residence, and there was access into St Peter's from the private chapel of the palace thanks to a door that led into the Sistine Chapel. The palace was very beautiful, with a loggia on the first floor, windows with round arches or trellis work, and suites of airy and regular rooms. It housed the female court that Alexander VI loved, together with all the maids and ladies-in-waiting. There he could find the women who appealed either to his fatherly tenderness, or to his sensual desires, or to the special needs of friendship which in his case involved complicity. His body heaved with great laughter at the mere thought of it.

Crowds of Borgias invaded the Vatican. First came those who were already in Rome or Italy. They were followed by Borgias from Spain; men, women and children, whole families, made greedy by the fortune that the earlier Pope had brought to their house, insignificant people who set whole spirals of relationships in motion around the chief of their clan.

Alexander VI got to work quickly. As soon as he was elected Pope he transferred his Archbishopric of Valencia to his son Cesare; and in the secret consistory held on August 31 he created his nephew Giovanni Borgia, then Archbishop of Monreale, a Cardinal. 'He managed things so cleverly,' Giannandrea Boccaccio comments, 'that all the Cardinals were loud in their insistence on this promotion.' The College of Cardinals was as yet not too distrustful of the new Pope; and anyway, as Borgia rewards were being showered on the Cardinal electors, it would be going too far not to expect the Pope's kinsmen to come in for some of the spoils. The new Borgia Cardinal took up residence in the apostolic palace. One of our informants describes him as 'an outstanding man and very competent' – in other words, able to lend the Pope a hand in all eventualities. Two months later, yet another Borgia settled in the Vatican; for the new Pope's cousin, Rodrigo, succeeded Domenico Doria as captain of the palace guards. These Borgias were meant to restrict the power of Ascanio Sforza, and it was because Giuliano della Rovere had seen the point at once that he had so warmly applauded the promotion of Giovanni Borgia. As for Cardinal Sforza, it did not take him long to see that he would have to have all his wits about him to hold his own against the Pope. It was already generally felt that Alexander VI was going to be 'a Pontiff who will do what he wants without regard to anyone'. Ascanio was living in the Vatican near the Pope and keeping a close watch on him; he felt uneasy and smelt danger in the air. The rumours that spread were not reassuring. 'Here many are trying to establish a relationship to the Pope by marriage with his niece' – in the first months of her father's Pontificate this way of referring to Lucrezia was not unusual – 'and hope is extended to all: even the King (of Naples) is in the running'. But Cardinal Ascanio left no way open to the King of Naples. He knew the Pope's love for his young daughter well enough to make it worthwhile trying to tie her to the Sforza party.

The reigning Duke of Milan was the wretched Gian Galeazzo Sforza who, though young, was worn out by pleasures and dissipation which his uncle and tutor, Ludovico il Moro, permitted if he did not actually encourage. Ludovico himself was one of those men whose hunger for power is even stronger than life itself, and his wife, Beatrice d'Este, who belonged to the ducal house of Ferrara, added her own almost ferocious ambitions to his. Though she was not twenty when Alexander VI became Pope, Beatrice d'Este already had clearly established aims and knew the path she intended to follow. She was a very capricious woman who combined rare grace with refinement of intellect and obstinate pride, and above all else in the world she hated the woman who had robbed her, as she thought, of the position of first lady of Milan – the generous Isabella of Aragon, wife of Gian Galeazzo. Though one woman can hardly be held responsible for the great events that were to follow – and that were perhaps inevitable at that moment of history – it is certainly true that only a woman of Beatrice's calibre could have urged il

Moro to invite the foreigner into Italy so as to crush and rout the hated Aragonese dynasty. Indeed Beatrice was the 'genius' of the struggle between the Sforzas and the Kingdom of Naples; and though she may have felt pangs of jealousy (as far as I know no letter exists from Beatrice to Lucrezia) she certainly agreed to Ascanio's project so as not to let such an important hostage as a Pope's daughter slip through her fingers.

Ascanio immediately began reviewing his family tree – both the direct and the collateral branches. Amongst the latter he came across a Sforza of the second rank, Giovanni, who bore the title of Count of Catignola and was Lord of Pesaro, a little papal domain on the boundary between the Marches and Romagna. Giovanni seemed to have all the necessary qualities. He was twenty-eight years old and the widower of Maddalena Gonzaga. He had received a humanist education, and if his appearance was almost insignificant – the word 'almost' is putting it mildly – he was not without elegance in his bearing and mode of life and was extremely sensitive to all the promptings of vanity and still more to those of self-interest; to the overbearing pomp of his kinsmen in Milan his attitude was almost servile.

So Giovanni Sforza was immediately summoned to Rome. He arrived incognito towards the middle of October 1492. Bishop Boccaccio spotted at once what was in the wind, but no more quickly than one of Lucrezia's fiancés, Don Gaspare d'Aversa, whom the Pope no longer bothered about, for he already saw his children powerfully allied with princely families and founding dynasties. When Don Gaspare d'Aversa heard about the project of the Sforza marriage his gorge rose and he went at once to Rome. But Sforza, Lord of Pesaro, was on his guard. He stayed indoors all day and went out only at night. The Spaniard's behaviour was quite different from that of the wary favourite. With his contract in his pocket and his father's backing, he persisted in asking for audiences that were never granted, and with Catalan bravado he told all and sundry that he was determined not to give way and that the King of Spain was on his side. If justice was not done, he said, he would appeal to all the princes and potentates of Christendom. His listeners were people toughened by years of tight-rope diplomacy who merely wondered how much Don Gaspare's rebellion would cost the Pope. We cannot be certain on this point, but the price seems to have been 3,000 golden ducats. What we do know is that Alexander VI tied up the two Spaniards, father and son, in a web of hesitating refusals and feigned concessions and that on August 8 a contract was drawn up that postponed but did not dissolve the marriage contract. A clause in the deed bound the young Valencian not to marry for a year so that 'when a more propitious moment occurred' he could marry Lucrezia. We cannot be sure what Alexander VI had in mind when he drew up this clause, but it was probably a ruse to liberate Lucrezia for the time being. Don Gaspare was stubborn – he fell into the trap, but not easily. As for Giovanni Sforza, when people spoke to him of the affair, he said he felt perfectly confident, and as soon as he got back to Pesaro he dispatched his procurator, messer Niccolò da Saiano, to Rome to draw up the contract – Niccolò was a doctor of law at Ferrara and as cunning as they are made. Lucrezia's destiny was henceforward settled: she was to be Countess of Pesaro.

So the Count of Pesaro, feeling very important, devoted himself to wedding preparations. Through the Pope's intervention he had been granted a high-ranking post with good pay in the Milanese army. People envied him his future wife, not only because she had been the centre of such rivalry but also because she was fresh and young and held her father's heart in her small hands. It was known that she possessed fabulous dresses and jewels – her wedding-gown alone cost 15,000 ducats – that she would receive magnificent presents, and that her brother, the Duke of Gandia, was the most elegant and spendthrift young man in Rome who would flaunt superb jewellery: so Giovanni, in courtesy to his new relations, prepared to cut as fine a figure as they. But his money-bags were not so well-lined as theirs and this he found humiliating, especially as he needed above all

things an elaborate gold necklace, one of those masterpieces of
Renaissance goldsmiths that were the hallmark of the wearer's
wealth and good taste. So he decided to ask the Marquis of
Mantua, his first wife's brother, for the loan of his necklace.
Gonzaga was delighted to comply with this request and sent him
several of his richest jewels as well, for Giovanni's goodwill and
favour were important now that he was to become 'the dear son
of Alexander VI'.

Meanwhile, on February 2, 1493, in Rome, messer Niccolò da
Saiano had betrothed him to Lucrezia by proxy and had signed
the marriage contract. Lucrezia immediately began receiving
visitors, ambassadors from the princely houses who came to
congratulate her. She was helped by Saiano and, of course, by
Adriana Mila who found scope in these discussions for her
Spanish magniloquence and her genius for intrigue. When the
Bishop of Modena came to compliment the fiancée on behalf of
the Duke and Duchess of Ferrara, and profited by the occasion
to ask for a Cardinal's hat for Ippolito d'Este, the Duke's second
son, it was, as usual, Adriana who answered. She said she had
spoken on this subject with the Pope and that the prospects were
excellent; and then added: 'in any case, *we* will make him
Cardinal' with all the majesty and complicity of the language of
favourites. Her brilliant tutorship probably went far to obliterate
the fact that Lucrezia was only thirteen. At one moment it
looked as though Lucrezia's destiny was going to be changed yet
again, for a rumour spread that the Pope was carrying on
negotiations in Spain to marry her to the Count of Prada. But
this was only another clever manoeuvre to humour those
opposed to the Sforza marriage. Various contemporary chroniclers were taken in, however, and so were later historians
including Gregorovius who thought the Pope must have
genuinely changed his mind. In a recently discovered letter
Giannandrea Boccaccio informs the Duke of Ferrara of what
Cardinal Ascanio had told him in confidence, under the seal of
the confessional: 'So as to achieve a specific purpose and for
many sensible reasons, this thing (the marriage) is being kept

secret, and they have let it be believed that they intend to marry her in Spain.' The wedding was first arranged for April 24, the feast of St George, and then put off until May. The date finally decided on was June 12.

In Rome the summer is hot but not stuffy; for when the sky is a deep blue expanse and there is not the faintest hope of a cloud, up blows a sudden breeze, swift and penetrating, that reaches every hot corner of the city streets, lifting up people's hearts as well as anything that may be lying in its path. Such must have been the setting for the wedding cavalcade that arrived under the walls of Rome on Sunday, June 9. It was led by squires in coats of brocade followed by files of pages dressed in variously coloured silks; and an atmosphere of levity and carefreeness was introduced by the clownings of a jester, Mambrino 'the priest', in a suit of velvet and a golden cap. Outside the Porta del Popolo the bridegroom was met by members of the Cardinals' households, and the Venetian ambassador delivered a little speech of welcome so as to show the paternal benevolence of the Republic towards the little State of Pesaro that lay on its borders. Then, to the merry music of fifes and trumpets, the vivid procession moved on. It glittered in the hot sunlight as it passed under the palace of San Marco and through the Campo dei Fiori, over the bridge by the Castel Sant' Angelo, and through the Borgo, going a little out of its way so as to pass under the bride's palace.

We can imagine Adriana Mila's busy pre-nuptial hands getting Lucrezia ready well in advance. The girl had already received the good wishes and congratulations of the Roman gentlewomen and had experienced, perhaps for the first time in her life, the heady intoxication that comes from being the centre of all eyes. As soon as the first blast of trumpets was heard from afar, all the women and children took up positions at the windows leaving the bride alone in the place of honour in the loggia. In a moment the piazza was seething with people; the squires and pages came first, then the households of the Cardinals and finally the ambassadors with the bridegroom in their midst. The gaze of all, from the smallest page to the most portentous ambassador, was turned to the Palace of Santa Maria in Portico, the palace of the Pope's women, the home of Giulia Farnese (much whispered about – *de qua est tantus sermo*), of the relatives of Innocent VIII, of well-known noblewomen of the Orsini, Colonna and other families. There little Lucrezia, whom the Pope loved 'supremely', was to be seen with the sun shining on her long fair hair that fell over her delicate shoulders to her waist, like serpents of fine gold. Giovanni Sforza drew his horse to a standstill under the loggia. His glance met Lucrezia's, and for a second their problem was that of any man and any woman. But the bridegroom knew his part. He had to bow like a courtier towards the window where he saw the bejewelled head. Lucrezia responded with a conventional curtsy. Then the company proceeded on its way to the Vatican where the Pope was waiting with five Cardinals. The Count of Pesaro entered, fell on his knees before the majesty of his extraordinary father-in-law and made a short Latin speech in which he dedicated himself, his State and all his possessions. The Pope made an affectionate answer. When this official reception was over, the Count of Pesaro and his suite repaired to the palace of the Cardinal of Aleria near the Castel Sant' Angelo where they lodged while awaiting the wedding ceremony.

At this point I must stop to say a few words about Giovanni Burchard, master of ceremonies at the Papal court and a first-hand witness of events. He was a German from Strasburg who had bought his post for four hundred gold ducats and spent his time in the cameras and anticameras of the Vatican. He owes his importance to the fact that he kept a diary – written in a kind of dog-Latin – in which he noted all the significant incidents that came his way in the course of his work. Though psychologically blinkered, he is generally recognized as one of the major witnesses for the life of the Borgias in Rome, though historians exist who question the validity of his evidence. It is certainly true that he sometimes gives the impression of wanting deliberately to confuse our judgment. The pages of his diary, the *Liber Notarum*,

are crammed with the minutest descriptions of various ceremonies and details of pontifical etiquette, so it seems at first only
reasonable to trust him and see in his pedantic and orderly mind
all the reliability of the painstaking civil servant. But we
occasionally come across inflammatory passages that provide
evidence for the worst accusations against the Borgias and
Lucrezia. Burchard never indulges in gossip, nor does he discuss
or give his own opinion. His malignity lies precisely in an
ostentatious restraint. Yet it is almost impossible to disbelieve a
man who for over a thousand pages patiently shows us that he
knows how to keep his place. Obviously his narrow and
Puritanical views were bound to misrepresent certain events in a
milieu such as that of the Borgias, but to say this does not
disprove his veracity. For he does not accuse the Borgias; he only
provides cold, accurate and even toned-down descriptions of
obscenities at which he may well have been present as master of
ceremonies. A further objection to omitting Burchard from a
history of the Borgias is that nowadays the majority of historians
have been forced to admit that in almost every instance the
accounts he gives are echoed in the correspondence of contemporaries who were unaware of his diary. I shall have cause to
take up this point later. Throughout the period we are dealing
with now Burchard merely planned the processions and receptions and, in June 1493, he was occupied with the marriage
ceremony of the Pope's daughter.

The wedding took place in the new apartment in the Vatican
in which Pinturicchio had already begun to paint his landscapes
and gardens. The rooms were splendidly ornate but not cluttered
with furniture. Apart from the coloured walls, gold ceilings, and
stuccoes and marbles of the brackets and frames, the decoration
consisted of oriental carpets and silken hangings below the
paintings. There were chairs, stools and velvet cushions, but
most important of all rose the throne of the Pope, or rather the
two thrones, one in the great hall where the reception took place
and the other in the small room reserved for the ceremony. The
Duke of Gandia was given the decorative task of fetching the

bride, and he was well fitted to perform it. In his sister's honour he had put on an extraordinary Turkish robe *à la française* that swept the ground and was made of curling cloth of gold with sleeves sewn with enormous pearls. He wore a necklace of rubies and pearls and a cap adorned with a resplendent jewel.

The day – June 12 – and the hour of the ceremony arrived at last. The first people to press into the apartment were the gentlewomen who were so excited that in the rush many of them forgot to kneel before the Pope – a fact duly noted by the shocked Burchard who thought it a sign of moral anarchy. A flock of prelates had been sent to fetch the bridegroom 'and all his barony', and eight Cardinals were awaiting him with the Pope. He too arrived in a Turkish robe *à la française* with curling gold, but unlike the Duke of Gandia he had no enormous jewels – only the necklace which the Duke of Mantua had lent him and the Mantuan ambassador recognized with a smile. Immediately after Sforza's arrival came the melodramatic entry of Juan and Cesare, the Pope's two eldest sons, who slipped into the room through a secret door that opened in the wall – Juan having rejoined the others after conducting his sister into the Vatican. Cesare was wearing episcopal vestments in striking contrast to his brother's clothes, the luxury of which caused much comment; for even in those days it was unusual to see anyone wearing precious stones worth 150,000 ducats. The rooms of the Borgia apartments are not large and on this occasion, given the extraordinary circumstances, they were packed; there were all kinds of military and civil representatives, famous names were bandied about, and there were many rumours and feverish curiosity. Even the eyes of the ambassadors were not sharp enough to see everything.

The bride was now announced, and she entered in her jewelled dress. She was beautiful and even a little touching, for she was playing the grown-up woman in a way that showed what a child she really was. In accordance with the fashion of the time, her sumptuous train was held by a gallant little negress, black and shining. On one side of Lucrezia was Giulia Farnese on whom rested the inquisitive and dazzled eyes of all present, and on the other was Lella Orsini, daughter of the Count of Pitigliano, who had joined the Farnese family by marrying Giulia's eldest brother, Angelo. Next came Innocent VIII's niece, Battistina d'Aragona, Marchesa of Gerace, who was famous for her elegance and known as the 'foundress of all women's fashions in her time'; she, too, had a little negress to hold her train. There followed other noblewomen, making a hundred and fifty in all. The rooms, already crowded, were overflowing. All the Borgias were there, of course, and Ascanio Sforza – triumphant – with his faithful Sanseverino by his side, and Cardinals and archbishops and Roman barons and senators and archivists; Spanish and Italian noblemen, the Captain of the Church, the Captain of the Palace, officers and guards. Lucrezia advanced with a light rhythmical step (as a chronicler later put it, 'she carries her body so gracefully that she hardly appears to be moving'), and Giovanni Sforza came forward in his turn. The betrothed couple knelt down on golden cushions at the Pope's feet, there was a silence, and immediately after, the voice of the notary, Beneimbene, was heard asking the ritual questions. 'I will, with a good heart,' answered Sforza; 'I will,' echoed Lucrezia, and the Bishop of Concordia – his name seemed of good augury – put on the rings. The Count of Pitigliano held the naked sword above the heads of bride and groom, and the Bishop made an excellently turned little sermon on the sanctity of marriage. And then came the time for merry-making.

Even at the best-conducted marriage-feast sensuality can lie heavily in the air, and with people of the Borgia temperament and habits the atmosphere must soon have become stifling. The man responsible for selecting the play – the *Menaechmi* of Plautus in the original Latin – obviously failed to grasp the situation, and it was obvious that the comedy was a flop. The Pope interrupted the players halfway through, prompted to do so because he noticed a woman who preferred modern plays to 'classics' suppressing a yawn. The performance of an eclogue composed by Serafino Aquilano in honour of the married couple was well received, however, and was described by a chronicler as 'very elegant' – meaning that it had all the classical adornments and symbolic and mythological allusions as well as the lyricism that we still feel in the poet's best verse today. Serafino was a court favourite towards the end of the fifteenth century, and, from experience gained in moving from court to court, he acquired the trick of spinning allegories about the names, families and aspirations of his princely employers; and he propounded flattering riddles that were easy to solve and always to the point. Finally, and it must have been high time, came the refreshments which were described as being ample but not unduly lavish, that is without gastronomical masterpieces. Sweetmeats were passed round amid the laughter of women who were delighted to come into their own at last. According to the prevailing etiquette the first to be served were the Pope and the Cardinals, and then the newly-married couple, the women, the prelates and the other guests. Instead of being returned to the kitchens, the remains were then thrown out of the windows to the applauding populace below. Over a hundred pounds of sweetmeats were thus wasted, lamented Burchard.

In the evening the Pope gave a private dinner in honour of the couple, and the list of guests had an especial interest for ambassadors, less because of their personal curiosity than because of the dispatches that had to be sent home: it was enormously important for them to find out who most enjoyed the Pope's favour. The dinner was served in the pontifical hall which was still decorated for the morning's ceremonies. There were Cardinals; there were Teodorina Cibo with her famous shoulders, Giulia Farnese, Lella Orsini and Adriana Mila. Ascanio Sforza was there with the Duke of Sanseverino, and also the new Cardinal Borgia; Giulio Orsini Lord of Monterotondo, Cardinal Colonna with his younger brother the Count of Pitigliano, Lucrezia's brothers and the newly-wedded couple, together with about twenty other guests. The 'festive' supper came to an end at about midnight and the chamberlains entered with the wedding-presents. The gifts of the Sforzas of Milan to their new kinswoman included pieces of world-famous Milanese brocade and two magnificent rings. Cardinal Ascanio's present was useful, solid and almost middle-class – a complete '*credenza* set', that is to say a complete silver dinner service including cups, bowls, plates, a large dish for sweetmeats, two chalices, all of the finest craftsmanship. There were also gifts from Lucrezia's brothers, from the Duke of Ferrara, from Cardinal Borgia and from the protonotary, Lunati. The festivities began after the display of presents: there were comedies, music and dancing, and possibly the music included something by the greatest composer of his time, Josquin de Près, a Fleming in the service of Alexander VI. As the hours passed the merriment grew louder and broader until it became licentious, and all the contemporary commentators are at one in stressing the 'worldly' character of the party. The story of how dainty confections were dropped down the bodices of the women's dresses has appealed to the imagination of biographers and novelists, and was told originally by the Roman chronicler Stefano Infessura. But all Infessura says is that the Pope amused himself by throwing these delicacies *in sinu mulierum*, which in my opinion ought to be translated 'into their laps', and in that case the game seems to have consisted in tossing the sweets from one person to another, which is a childish occupation, true enough, but not indecent. If this was what happened it is not improbable that some of the chocolates fell into the wide decolleté of the women's dresses and this may have given rise to a freer game, but even this does not justify the insinuation that there was an unbridled and collective orgy.

We can imagine Lucrezia gazing around her with fascinated and laughing eyes, a little apprehensive about being a bride and at the same time enjoying it. There was plenty to marvel at in the loose vivacity of Giulia Farnese who was the real queen of the feast, in the superb vitality of her father, in her handsome and elegant brother Juan, and in the dark and fascinating power of her other brother Cesare. But what was her impression of her husband in whose honour the party had been organized? And what did she think of herself? No historian sitting in judgment upon her has asked himself whether her interior life was in harmony with the life she played in public. I shall deal at greater length later with an unpublished document in the Pope's own hand by which we know that the couple were married only in name – at least until the middle of November 1493 (the reason for the delay in the consummation of the marriage was doubtless due to Lucrezia's physical immaturity). There was every reason for Lucrezia to have complicated feelings when the twenty-four hours of feverish merry-making drew to an end at dawn on June 13 and she withdrew to the bed of her childhood. As she got out of her wedding dress she must have rejoiced at the rich wardrobe that was henceforth to be hers, for she loved clothes dearly. She had already had a glimpse of surprises in store, but how did she stand up to them? In the days that followed she must have felt a tremor of emotion on discovering that she had become important, that she was the object of homage and supplication, that the unsuspected gift of power was in her hands. Possibly all these surprises, and her anxiety to live up to her position, left her with no time for self-recollection, and when she found herself married before she knew what it was to be a woman, and sent to live a parody of marriage in the palace of Santa Maria in Portico, she must have felt some of the moral and physical uneasiness that Giovanni Sforza was unable to conceal. This *marriage blanc* marked the beginning of the oscillating existence imposed on Lucrezia by circumstances and the ambitions of her relations, an existence she accepted and continued to accept with ever-increasing readiness. Lucrezia's real drama lay not in weakness but in the fatality of her acts of consent, each of which amounted to a capitulation. Her tactic of ignoring what was going on around her is shown in this light to be a form of woman's instinctive self-defence which, though escapist in a way, also has pathos and courage. If Lucrezia was never able to rise to the point of making a judgment on her father and brothers, it was not because her powers of judgment were at fault, nor merely because she was soft-hearted. The explanation is more violent and elemental. She, too, was a

Borgia; she, too, had the impetuous Borgia blood that combined brutality and splendour and was free from morals. Her normal state was one of disordered tension between religion and sensuality, between the longing for a disciplined life and the burning anarchy of her desires, and only on very rare occasions was she able to rise above this and rebel against her father or brother or future father-in-law, the Duke of Ferrara. Yet these occasional acts of rebellion enabled her to be what she was – the only Borgia who saved herself. But all that was in the future. At the age of thirteen she was still a child who bowed before the potent males of her house and enjoyed life as it came. Hence she did not feel the burden and falsity of the title of Countess of Pesaro.

2

'THE MOST CARNAL
OF MEN'

From his royal seat at Naples, King Ferrante of Aragon had watched with uneasiness the festivities celebrating the alliance between the Sforzas and the Pope. He had sent no ambassadors to the Vatican. When the Count of Pesaro informed him of his wedding with Lucrezia, he had answered merely with an official note. In the hope of getting his own back, he waited anxiously for news from Diego Lopez de Haro, the ambassador whom Ferdinand the Catholic of Spain had sent at his request to Rome with extensive powers and the avowed intention of lodging complaints and threatening the Head of the Church.

The Catholic King's interest in the reigning House of Naples, on which Diego Lopez laid much emphasis, soon began to have a visible effect on the attitude of the Pontiff, who began to look on the House of Aragon with a more friendly eye. As soon as this good news reached Naples, the King thought he should make good his advantage by dispatching his son Federico to Rome to renew a proposal to marry Jofre into his House (for it was known by now that Cesare was to be made a Cardinal, *omnino cardinalabitur*), and to persuade Alexander VI to abandon the alliance against the Kingdom of Naples. Federico found the Pope well-disposed towards him and managed to conclude a marriage agreement for the Pope's youngest son. At that time Jofre Borgia was not yet twelve years old but, in the words of the Florentine ambassador, 'was truly handsome and of pleasing aspect'. A question-mark, however, hung over his head, for the Pope had confided to his intimates and even to his not-so-intimates, that he did not think Jofre was his son though he had recognized him as such by Bull. He must have had his own private reasons for believing Jofre to be the outcome of an act of infidelity committed by Vannozza with her husband. Presumably the King of Naples was unaware of the Pope's reservation about his paternity in Jofre's case, or if he knew of it he didn't believe it, for otherwise he would never have been so pressing about marrying Jofre to his lovely niece, Sancha of Aragon, a natural daughter of Alfonso, the heir to the throne.

The marriage of Jofre and Sancha was celebrated by proxy. Prince Federico represented Sancha, and, while the legal formulas were being read and the rings exchanged, he made such a comic parody of the virginal shyness of a young bride that the whole assembly, led by the Pope, broke into roars of laughter. At the end the new relative embraced all the Borgias and everyone present made those demonstrations of friendship which sometimes create a bond of personal sympathy but leave the political situation much as it was before. The little bridegroom gave the impression of being more grown-up in age and in everything else, and that day probably marked the end of his childhood.

But the Pope's most ambitious manoeuvres were on behalf of the handsome and beloved Juan, who was the apple of his eye. As Carlo Canale, Vannozza's husband, said to the Gonzagas of Mantua when he appealed for horses from their famous stables for Juan, 'no better nor more sure' intercessor for Papal favours could be found than his 'stepson', as he wittily called the boy. Juan could look forward to a great future, for he had inherited not only his elder brother's Duchy of Gandia but also his fiancée, Maria Enriques, who was a cousin of the King of Spain and brought royal protection with her. Pedro Luis died too young to leave a mark on history: all we know about him is that he conducted himself bravely when serving in the armed forces of the Catholic King and that he may have had military gifts. Unfortunately Juan was not endowed with the qualities of a condottiere, as his father dreamed, nor even of a good commander. He was young, handsome and rich, and all he wanted was to enjoy his advantages and pass his time in the company of his favourite women. The women he liked best were either courtesans – who appealed to his undisciplined temperament – or else young girls and brides who were well guarded and therefore satisfied his lust for adventure and gave him the illusion of winning a battle – the only kind of battle he was suited for. He liked shocking people and he liked admiration from no matter what quarter; in other words he was as vain as a peacock and had a strong dash of snobbery. He found someone after his heart in the Turkish prince Djem, the most picturesque person in the town, who was the Pope's hostage at the time and lived in the Vatican. Perhaps Djem's face was not really as diabolical as it appeared to Mantegna, but it certainly betrayed a slow, sleepy but cunning Asiatic cruelty. The contrast between his brown skin and light eyes that were usually half-closed, between his indolent attitudes, yet agile limbs that were ever ready to spring, between his inclination for and yet resistance to orgies and sensual pleasures, so appealed to Juan's fantastic and vicious ideals that he felt he must at least dress like Djem. But when the Romans saw the Pope's cortège on its round of church-visiting, with the Duke of Gandia and the Grand Turk in front of the Cross on two identical horses and in oriental costume including the turban of the enemies of Christendom, they were not so much shocked as ironically amused. Arms and ornaments glistened in the sun as the Pope traversed the city whose churches, palaces, houses and medieval towers dating from the feuds of the Middle Ages were bathed in the warm deep ochre that had matured with the centuries. The women came to their balconies to see the exotic cortège, knelt down to receive the Papal blessing and pretended to be horrified when they saw the Turk (for it was rumoured that he indulged in debauches of cruelty); but they smiled upon the handsome figure of the sixteen-year-old Duke of Gandia who felt more glorious than ever when he caught their glances.

The plan, then, was that Juan should marry the King of Spain's cousin and so become a member of one of Europe's greatest reigning Houses. To ensure the pomp and splendour of the marriage, the Pope opened all his coffers. 'In the shop under my house,' wrote Giannandrea Boccaccio, 'there is a famous goldsmith who for months has done nothing but set jewels in rings and necklaces and buy every kind of precious stone. He showed me everything. There are great pearls in infinite numbers, rubies, diamonds, emeralds and sapphires, all in perfect condition.' Everything went to the Duke of Gandia – not only jewels but furs of lynx, sable and ermine. There were whole chests of brocades, clipped velvets, tapestries, silverware and carpets, and the chests themselves were decorated with paintings. The Pope himself took charge of the wedding presents and also of his son, body and soul. He gave him two trusted advisers, Don Ginès Fira and Mossen Jayme Pertusa, who were told to keep a close watch on the young man and to report on his behaviour to the Pope under pain of excommunication. In Spain he recommended him to the care of the Bishop of Oristano and also gave everybody instructions with a view to organizing Juan's life from the first moment he set foot on Spanish soil, and the minuteness of these were a proof of Alexander VI's knowledge of Spanish life and customs as well as of his common sense and balance.

These measures make it quite clear that the Pope did not trust Juan at all. He ordered that he should not go out at night, should not play at dice, should not touch the revenues of the Duchy of Gandia without the consent of his advisers, and he insisted that he should treat his wife well and keep her company. Juan's farewell to his father on August 2 was proud and uneasy, and before he reached Civitavecchia he was overtaken by a Papal messenger bearing further instructions dealing, *inter alia*, with attention to dress, the care of skin and hair, and an order to put on gloves immediately and not remove them until Barcelona was reached. Salt harms the skin, explained Juan's father, and in our country beautiful hands are highly prized.

The marriage took place at Barcelona in the presence of the King and Queen of Spain. After the wedding the couple spent a short while in Barcelona and thence went to Valencia and, eventually, Gandia. But it was not long before gloomy accounts of Juan's behaviour as a husband reached Rome. He showed such indifference to his wife that he had never even consummated the marriage, and instead of staying with her went out on nightly prowls with young profligates: moreover within two months he had spent 2,600 gold ducats in gaming and debauchery and had already tried to lay hands on the revenues of the Duchy. When the Pope heard these accounts he was naturally furious for he feared, and rightly, the anger of the King of Spain who would never tolerate Juan's contempt for a woman of royal blood. And so, with this fear in mind, and with his usual concern about the behaviour of his children in society, Alexander VI wrote to Juan from Viterbo on October 30, upbraiding him bitterly. He told Cesare to write a second letter on the same theme to which he added, as I discovered in the Vatican, several further lines of his own. He also made Cardinal Borgia write to Don Enrico Enriquez, the bride's father; but this letter of protests, assurances and guarantees remains so far untraced.

Juan was perhaps rather afraid of his father's anger and he answered at once with a long explanatory letter. He said that his father's attitude caused him 'the greatest anguish he had ever suffered'. He could not understand how the Pope could have believed in 'sinister reports written by malicious people without regard for truth'. As for his marriage, it had been more than consummated, as reliable people such as the Archbishop of Oristano, Mossen Pertusa, Fira and others could bear out: had the Pope forgotten that he had been told the day and the hour (why not the minute?) of the consummation? He admitted that he had been out prowling at night, but he did not think he had done much harm, for he had been in the company of his father-in-law, Don Enrico, and relations of the King and other knights, honest and honourable people, and he had 'only strolled along the promenade, as was the custom in Barcelona'. This reference to the 'customs' of his native land must have done more to soften Rodrigo's Catalan heart than any explaining-away, and that is why Juan made it. 'What worries me most of all is that Your Holiness should have believed in rumours that were not even probable.' His protestations of calumniated virtue deceived no one and least of all Alexander VI, and yet the Pope did not worry unduly as he felt sure that now that Juan had received his scolding he would obey and be, if not a good, at least a regular, husband.

The correspondence between father and son continued. Juan's letters display egoism, an extravagance lacking any grandeur, and a vacuous superficiality, while Alexander VI's show an enlightened kind of fatherly indulgence. Despite Juan's repeated assurances the Pope never felt altogether satisfied and he must have breathed a sigh of relief when, in February 1494, he received news that an heir to the Duchy of Gandia was shortly expected. Then only were his doubts removed, and he turned his attention to his eldest son.

No one could have had less vocation for the religious life than Cesare Borgia, and he was the first to admit it. But after the collapse of the marriage negotiations with King Ferrante of Aragon, his hopes of escaping from the ecclesiastical life evaporated, and it looked as if he was prepared to accept the career that his father had planned for him. What mattered to him most in any career was to avoid servility and mediocrity and to direct his energy towards the immediate acquisition of some position of authority. Cesare was well aware of the gulf between his aspirations and reality and he had learnt the art of dissimulation. From infancy he had been destined to follow a career to which he knew he was unsuited, just as he knew Juan was ill-suited to his destined career of arms. And so, twenty years earlier than most men, he had had to face the reality of a solitary existence, and he experienced either burning ambition or icy pessimism. His rancour doubtless played a large part in alienating him from the rest of the world, and he passed his complicated youth in that silence which is the first and last refuge of the frustrated. His sensitiveness got twisted into cruelty and made him monstrously lucid; he understood his father's weaknesses, but the second-sight by which he infallibly got his own way was diabolical. His solitude was his fortress, and he used his inhuman courage and self-sufficiency to serve his idolatry of power.

Yet though his bold spirit could aspire to a throne, he was frustrated even about becoming a Cardinal, for there was an ancient law prohibiting bastards, even royal ones, from joining the Sacred College. So a compromise had to be made. In the Bull of Sixtus IV which legitimized him, Cesare had been described as the offspring of a Bishop and a married woman. Now the child of a married woman was, in law, the offspring of her husband. Hence, so ran the argument, Cesare's father was a man called Domenico d'Arignano, a Church official, who had been Vannozza's husband at the time of his birth. In the Bull that revoked the defect of his birth, the Pope benevolently allowed Cesare to adopt the family name of Borgia. Alexander VI established a precedent – which was to serve again – when he signed another Bull maintaining that he was Cesare's father, and had it kept secret.

The two Bulls in question established the order of birth of the Borgia brothers. For in his Bull of September 19, 1493, Alexander VI asserted in so many words that after d'Arignano's death, which took place at the end of 1474 or the beginning of 1475, Vannozza gave birth to Juan, which is as much as to say that Cesare was the elder.

The subject has given rise to some controversy, but modern historians have come to accept the second Bull of 1493 as genuine. It is now generally agreed that Cesare was born in 1474 or 1475 and Juan in 1476. But we must not suppose that, merely because he was the elder brother, Cesare had no grounds for being jealous of Juan. Far from it. If Cesare was the eldest son he had an even greater justification for his irritation and hatred of Juan, for Juan had robbed him of the rights of primogeniture and seized for himself all the worldly advantages at the Pope's disposal. As everyone familiar with family life will agree, nothing causes more ill-feeling in elder sons than to see their juniors preferred to themselves, particularly if the favouritism is misplaced. As long as Pedro Luis was alive everything seemed fair enough. As the eldest of the Borgia sons he was given the main family property and Cesare, as the second son, was marked out for power in the Church, and the third and fourth sons had the prospects usual to their condition. It was the death of Pedro Luis that caused the confusion. When the incompetent Juan was given pride of place, Cesare's jealousy must have been immediately inflamed. Even the Bull which declared that he was the son of an obscure person such as d'Arignano must have been a deadly blow to his pride.

The consistory was summoned hastily to approve Cesare's legitimization. Of course there was no question of anyone daring to oppose it. As soon as he had won his point, the Pope announced in his sonorous voice and in his most amiable pontifical manner: 'My Lord Cardinals, be disposed and ready: tomorrow, Friday, we wish to elect the new Cardinals.'

It was difficult to argue about a proposal made in such a natural tone, especially as it was also an order. But Cardinal Carafa made so bold as to ask the Pope whether he had given due consideration to the usefulness of making these nominations. The Pope answered that the question of their usefulness concerned him alone, and he stood by his idea, unshaken by those who dared to say that they did not want Cardinals 'of the sort the Pope desired' as colleagues. In referring to his opponents the Pope's rage waxed: 'I will show them who Alexander VI is, and if they still persevere I will annoy them by making as many new Cardinals as I can at Christmas, and even then they will not drive me from Rome'; and after he had threatened anyone who dared to protest, the tiny group of Cardinals present proceeded to nominate the new Cardinals. At the head of the list was Cesare Borgia, followed by Alessandro Farnese, Giulia's brother, Ippolito d'Este of Ferrara, Lunati of Pavia, Cesarini, a Frenchman, a Spaniard, and a handful of others making thirteen in all – men who would strengthen the Pope's hand and infallibly diminish the power of the older members of the college, who in

their turn, led by those who had abstained from travelling to
Rome, protested that they would never recognize the new
nominees. However, once they had recognized the Pope's son,
which they could see no way out of doing, they were more or less
obliged to recognize the others and thus bow in all things to the
will of Alexander VI.

After his happy and hopeful summer, old King Ferrante fell into
a state of despondency. He stayed awake at night trying to
fathom some purpose in the moving waters of the Pope's mind.
He knew that Charles VIII had sent an ambassador to Rome to
ask to be invested with the Kingdom of Naples, and the
ambassador had returned to France empty-handed, but nevertheless he felt that there was an understanding between the Pope
and the Sforzas, and he was ill at ease. Ascanio was still powerful,
and though the decline of his influence was already perceptible
this could not be seen by those outside Vatican circles.

The King of Naples had charged his ambassador to offer gifts
and concessions to the Pope so as to urge that Jofre should come
to Naples to marry Donna Sancha. But though the ambassador
made the suggestion with all possible tact and grace, the only
answer he got was words. Worse, Cesare – whom everyone now
called Valentino or Valenza owing to his Archbishopric of
Valencia – began negotiating directly with the worst enemy of
Naples, Charles VIII. Moreover the position of the Sforzas
seemed immeasurably stronger than before owing to the
marriage of Bianca Maria Sforza with the Emperor Maximilian
of Austria. In this depressing atmosphere King Ferrante died, *sine
luce, sine cruce, sine Deo*, as Burchard put it. He certainly lacked all
consolation.

Ferrante of Aragon had been vicious and violent, but there
was something magnificent about him and with all his vices he
encouraged the arts and literature. His son Alfonso, Duke of
Calabria, who succeeded him, was of a coarser and rougher fibre
altogether and his ferocity was not tempered by magnanimity.
Yet the reign of Alfonso II began favourably enough.

Alexander VI, won over by the many gifts and privileges the new King promised to all his sons, became suddenly friendly. Two orders were issued from the Vatican: one charged Cardinal Giovanni Borgia with the mission of bearing to Naples the pontifical Bull investing the new King and crowning him in the Pope's name, while the other order was for Jofre to go off and marry his princess. Both set out. The little Borgia was accompanied by Virginio Orsini, Captain-General of the Aragonese army, and by his newly-formed court in which a Spaniard, Don Ferrando Dixer, had of course been given pride of place. The Pope entrusted the tutorship of his son to Don Ferrando as well as two caskets of jewels, one for Jofre and the other for his prospective wife.

Sancha of Aragon had obvious grounds for feeling discontented, and only by the use of her reason could she find consolation. Though barely sixteen years old, she was already famous for her beauty. She had a dark complexion, black hair, and eyes that were sea-green and of that peculiar southern clarity that has a fatal power under strong eyebrows – rather like the sea under the violet rocks of Capri. Sancha's mother was a Neapolitan of noble birth called Madonna Tuscia, or Trusia, Gazullo, who also had a son by King Alfonso: he, too, was extremely handsome and had been brought up in the royal palace like a legitimate child. Sancha was hot-blooded and tempestuous and shuddered when she thought of the bridegroom they were sending her from Rome. What could a woman of sixteen, above all a woman like her, do with a thirteen-year-old boy? One does not want to indulge in mere hypotheses, but one cannot help wondering whether Sancha had already been to bed with Onorato Caetani, nephew of the Count of Fondi, and her first betrothed. Even if she were not in love with him she had probably got accustomed to the idea of marrying a man and not a child. All she could do to deflect her thoughts from disillusionment was to form ambitious schemes, or rather – since ambition meant too little to her fiery temperament – form secret plans for revenge. She had no lack of councillors, both male and female, to put ideas into her head, but probably her own lively sense of reality made her think of better ones herself.

Jofre was met by Federico of Aragon and Sancha's fourteen-year-old brother, Alfonso. The Pope's young son was charming and gay and even Sancha, for all her ill-will, cannot have had such a very bad impression of him. The Neapolitans took him to their hearts. He was received like any royal prince, and on May 7, 1494, he was married at Castel Nuovo, in the presence of the King, of Prince Federico, uncle of the bride, the Cardinal of Monreale, twelve of Sancha's women and girls, and a few noblemen. When the Bishop of Tropea asked the question imposed by the ritual, the boy's answer was so childishly precipitate that it caused a smile. But the smile of amusement changed to one of admiration when Don Ferrando Dixer brought in the princely presents which included lovely pearl necklaces, an ornament composed of rubies, diamonds and oblong pearls and a string of rings, fourteen in all, set with all kinds of precious stones. The gold brocades, velvets and silks that followed had obviously been chosen by a connoisseur, and all Sancha's profoundly feminine instincts must have been touched when she saw these beautiful objects. She liked nothing better than cutting a fine figure at social functions and loved to be admired and excite passion or desire, and she knew there were to be plenty of festivities, beginning with her father's coronation.

This was indeed a magnificent ceremony. No imagination, however over-weighted by symbolism, could have thought up more glorious references to heroism and chivalry than were in common usage at the Court of Aragon. Each object used at the coronation – the crown, the sceptre and the sword – had its own proper ceremonial, and Burchard, who went to Naples with Cardinal Borgia, so enjoyed describing this that he became almost lyrical with pedantry. Alfonso II was solemnly anointed and crowned at the Vescovado, and after the indulgences granted by the Pope had been read out, he mounted the throne near the high altar. By his side, but one step lower, was the white-haired, serene-faced Pontano who pronounced the royal allocution which was transmitted word for word to the crowd by a herald who carefully weighed all the syllables.

The King made immediate use of his royal prerogative so as to nominate grandees. The Duke of Gandia was the first to be favoured and he received the titles and ranks of Prince of Tricarico, Count of Chiaramonte and Laurea, and Royal Lieutenant for the Kingdom of Sicily. Next came Jofre Borgia. Jofre advanced, bent his knee at the foot of the throne and the King knighted him by touching him on the left ear with a jewelled sword while saying the words of traditional investiture: 'May God and Saint George make you a good knight.' Jofre was made Prince of Squillace and Count of Coriata and he received the order of the Ermine with its motto: 'Better die than betray'. Virginio Orsini was rewarded for his many proofs of loyalty – the ones of disloyalty were for the moment forgotten – and made Grand Constable of the Kingdom. Finally came a grand cavalcade of honour for the benefit of the waiting crowds.

The religious ceremony for Jofre's wedding took place on May 11 in the Royal Chapel at Castel Nuovo. The Mass, which included many special ceremonies, was said by the Bishop of Gravina. After Communion the Bishop kissed the deacon on the lips, the deacon passed the kiss on to the bridegroom and the bridegroom to the bride. When Mass and benediction were over the company attended a concert of 'music singular and perfect' and then had a long lunch. In the evening Jofre went to await his bride at their new dwelling not far from Castel Nuovo. She arrived soon afterwards in the company of the King and of Cardinal Borgia, and together they mounted the stairs to the nuptial chamber.

The setting for the nocturnal ceremony was prepared by Sancha's court of women and girls. There followed a task which, one hopes, was reserved for the older women – that of undressing Sancha and Jofre and laying them together in bed, uncovered as far as the waist, as the ceremonial prescribed. At this point the women left and the King and the Cardinal of Monreale entered the bridal chamber. As was the custom of the age, these two distinguished personages began teasing the young couple and admiring the prince for being, in Cardinal Borgia's words: 'gracious and full of spirit ... and I would have paid heavily for others to see him as I saw him'. By the time the bed had been blessed, dawn was approaching and the King and the Cardinal Legate went away under a heavy rainstorm.

Meanwhile another bridegroom married into the House of Borgia was growing uneasy. This was Giovanni Sforza. After two months of playing at marriage he seized on the plague epidemic in Rome in the summer of 1493 as an excuse for begging permission to return to the shores of the Adriatic. This he obtained, and he left on August 2 or 3, leaving little Lucrezia alone in the Palace of Santa Maria in Portico. The adventure with the Borgias already looked as though it was going to turn out badly for him, at least financially, for in the early days of September he wrote to the Pope asking for an advance of 5,000 ducats on the grounds that he was being pressed by tradesmen to pay off his wedding expenses. The Pope discussed Giovanni's letter at length with Cardinal Sforza – '*super hoc ad longum locuti sumus cum dilecto filio nostro Ascanio*', as he wrote to his son-in-law on September 15, 1493. They decided that when the air became cooler and healthier towards the middle of October, Giovanni should return to Rome and become Lucrezia's husband in fact as well as in name. '*Convenimus quod, postquam X aut XV die futuri mensis octobris, quando aer erit frigidior et salubrior, ad nos venturus es pro totali consummatione matrimonii cum eadem uxore tua.*' When he had done this he would receive not 5,000 ducats but the whole 30,000 of his dowry and in addition the Pope would help him to set up house. Would he please answer immediately.

This Papal brief was known to Feliciangeli but so far it has never been published. It is written on parchment and was sent to the Florence Archives from Urbino. It proves without the shadow of a doubt that until then the couple had not had physical relations. But why not? One obvious reason is that though in the marriage contract Lucrezia had been described as ripe for matrimony, in reality she was still too immature for it; and yet there is something about the wording, despite its apparent clarity, that gives ground for thought. To begin with Sforza could have been informed of the desirability of an effective marriage more discreetly by a secret message. And if we suppose that Alexander VI deliberately wanted to use his son-in-law's return as an official recognition of his standing as a husband, then his promise to pay the full dowry sounds like an encouragement or reward. In fact the situation deteriorated. In spite of this explicit invitation calculated to appeal to a man who wanted to clarify his position if only for reasons of human respect, Giovanni remained at Pesaro for the whole of October and did not set out for Rome until after November 10. As Vatican circles were well aware, Giovanni Sforza went to Rome to 'pay his duties to his Holiness and to establish his full position with his illustrious wife'. But we have no evidence for what happened when Giovanni reached Rome. There must have been some kind of private celebration, but Giovanni cannot have found it very amusing for after Christmas he went back again to Pesaro, and it was only at the end of January that he decided to put an end to the going and coming and set up house with his wife in the palace of Santa Maria in Portico.

Giovanni Sforza was plainly the victim of an inferiority complex in a very trying period of history. He was frightened of the Pope and frightened of his own relations in Milan. He trembled whenever he felt the wind of discord between them and breathed again at every sign of concord. His authority was as restricted as that of a prince consort and he even lacked the 'go' to impose and uphold it to that extent. So whereas his status seemed outwardly important it was really quite insignificant.

But to return to Lucrezia. Of all human affairs marriage is the most mysterious and the hardest to penetrate, and hence it is far from easy to say what happened between her and her husband. At a later date they were said to have lived in harmony, the proof being the honour Lucrezia paid her husband in public; yet this might well show nothing more than Lucrezia's sense of duty and respect. Anyway, however her nights were passed, her days were fully occupied, for there were innumerable parties and receptions and ceremonies. The court of Santa Maria in Portico was active and brimful of intrigues, and the ambassadors and henchmen of the princes made it their habit to gather there for business reasons. 'The greater number (of those) who seek advantage in that quarter (i.e. from the Pope) pass through this door', says one of our informants, and we know that Lucrezia had whole chests full of appeals and memoranda, and presumably Giulia and Adriana were in the same position. The three women passed their days together tranquilly and harmoniously; they all enjoyed the Pope's favour without feelings of rivalry, and the Pope, for his part, always remembered them and shared with them the choicest gifts that were sent to the Vatican.

Giulia had her daughter, Laura, with her in the palace. Laura, aged two, was rumoured to be the Pope's child, and in view of the expectation that the Pope would give her a good dowry, her marriage was already under discussion (though later we shall come across evidence from the Pope himself which casts doubt on this relationship). Giulia's beauty was by now legendary throughout Italy. All the biographers of the Borgias quote the well-known description of her by her brother-in-law, Lorenzo Pucci: 'I called at Santa Maria in Portico to see Madonna Giulia who, when I found her, had just been having her hair washed, and she was with Madonna Lucrezia, the daughter of Our Lord, and Madonna Adriana beside the fire . . . Madonna Giulia has broadened and become most lovely to behold. In my presence she undid her hair which fell down to her feet, and then had it put up again . . . Thereafter she covered it with a sort of net as light as air and interwoven with gold threads that seemed like the sun . . . She was wearing a Neapolitan wrap and so was Madonna Lucrezia, but after a little while Madonna Lucrezia went to take hers off and returned in a gown lined almost entirely with purple satin.'

Halfway through the year 1494 the whole household got ready to leave Rome and accompany Lucrezia to her home in Pesaro, for Giovanni Sforza was frightened by the policy the Pope now seemed to be pursuing – pro-Neapolitan and anti-French and anti-Milanese. Indeed the Pope was showing undeniable signs of standing by King Alfonso, and he was doing his best to dissuade the King of France from attempting to conquer Naples. But Charles VIII had other intentions. In March he had written to the Pope telling him of his decision to enter Italy and conquer the Kingdom of Naples, and in that event he would lodge at the Vatican and 'make his home' there. Alexander VI was still manoeuvring to canalize his dynamic projects when a new factor arose, namely that Giuliano della Rovere was won over to the French side by Ascanio Sforza and ceased to support Naples and the Aragonese. He left his fortress at Ostia and took ship for his legation at Avignon – in other words he went to France.

This new move was decisive. King Charles VIII, encouraged by the Cardinal's imprudence, realized the extent of the disorder in Italy and the incurable weakness of the Kingdom of Naples, and he began assembling an army. The Pope, on his side, began preparing resistance. Giovanni Sforza was terrified by all these war preparations and despite the Pope's assurances he felt the ground in Rome slipping from under his feet. Fear, as is well known, intoxicates timid people and gives them a certain recklessness: it caused Giovanni to call every day at the Vatican and, with a look on his face as eloquent as his words, ask what would happen to himself and his family in the impending struggle. How, he asked, could he get out of his dilemma as a relative and salaried captain of the Lords of Milan and at the same time as the Pope's son-in-law? He bewailed his plight so insistently and cross-questioned the Pope so minutely that one day the Pope lost his temper and accused Giovanni of wanting to find out decisions before the event. Giovanni was silenced, but as the storm from France grew nearer he was tortured by feeling cut off from his niche in Pesaro. Finally, perhaps on the advice of someone cleverer than himself, he changed his tactics and told the Pope that the people of Pesaro were longing to see their Countess and the time had come for her to be seen there. The argument sounded so flattering and reasonable that the Pope had to agree to it, and in any case the plague was again causing havoc in Rome. Thus it came about that Lucrezia obtained permission to depart, and Giulia Farnese and Adriana Mila were sent too, perhaps because the Pope wanted his women to get away from the plague, perhaps for other motives. They were accompanied by their feminine court which included Lucrezia Lopez, the daughter of the Datary, and Juana Moncada, who was in waiting on Giulia Farnese. The Pope bade an affectionate goodbye to his women and with Adriana had a serious discussion about their journey and the date and itinerary of the return journey in July. The company left Rome on May 31.

The journey was long but it cannot have been dull in view of the women who were travelling: Giulia was beautiful, Lucrezia was gay, and Adriana was intense. The cavalcade had to pass through Umbria and the Marches and the Duchy of Urbino where the gentle humanist Guidobaldo di Montefeltro shone like a star against the pale heraldic beauty of his wife Elisabetta Gonzaga. The Duke and Duchess and their family did not meet them – perhaps they feared the Roman plague – but their subjects welcomed the travellers. When the fourteen-year-old Countess at last reached Pesaro on June 8 she found it triumphantly beflagged and filled with inquisitive crowds who hoped to gain great advantages from the Pope's daughter. The weather was horrible. The cavalcade was drenched in a springtime rain that extinguished the glow of gold and silver and ruined the splendid pageantry. They pressed forward between one storm and the next, while the flowers that were thrown were trampled in the mud. As soon as she reached the palace Lucrezia retired to her room and had her trunks opened by the fire. In all the confusion and wetness, 'that evening we cared for nothing but getting dry', as Giovanni Sforza wrote in the account he sent to the Pope the following day. But the rain was not very important after all. On the morrow the sun shone clear and bright and the women's good humour was restored in a frenzy of merry-making. They drew up programmes of dances and plays and had the fun of making the provincial public gape at the luxury of their clothes.

Among the women who attended the balls and parties was Caterina Gonzaga di Montevecchio, in all the pride of her ancestry and famous beauty. Giulia and Lucrezia had no need to fear rivalry from the provincial nobility, but this Lombard woman gave them a pang and they began wondering if they were going to have to share their triumph with her. Accordingly they put on their most elaborate clothes and dressed 'pontifical-ly', helped by Adriana who was not competing. Giovanni Sforza came to collect them, dressed magnificently too, and the three of them gazed at one another with joy, and their eyes shone with the expectation of social success. As Giulia wrote in her lively dialect: 'It looked as though we had ransacked Florence for brocade, and everyone was amazed.' There was a huge crowd at the party. The noblewomen of the vicinity were presented, and when Caterina Gonzaga came forward, Lucrezia and Giulia adopted a worldly air while they looked her over, and congratulated her between a conversation and a dance, feigning a laughing interest. Was she beautiful? Lucrezia smiled to herself and glanced at Giulia who answered with an almost impercept-ible gesture. Lucrezia described her impressions the next day in a letter to the Pope: 'I must tell Your Beatitude something about her (i.e. Caterina Gonzaga's) beauty, because I am sure her fame must have predisposed you to think her beautiful. To begin with, she is six inches taller than Madonna Giulia, with a fine white complexion, and beautiful hands and figure. But she has an ugly mouth and horrible teeth, big pale eyes, a nose ugly rather than beautiful, a long face, ugly-coloured hair ... She speaks easily and well. I was anxious to see her dance, but I was not very much impressed. In short, in all things she does not come up to her reputation (*presentia minuit famam*).' So Caterina Gonzaga has passed down to history, in a portrait less flattering if more critical than her description of Lucrezia which she also sent to the Pope at round about the same time. Lucrezia, she said, was exceedingly like her father, 'all wit and cleverness with princely manners and a true woman of rank'.

The others present put Lucrezia first owing to her position, but about the rival merits of Giulia and Caterina they were divided, and it is to this division of opinion that we owe a precious and unpublished pen-sketch of Giulia made by Jacopo Dragoni, a doctor to the Holy See. When the festivities were over he wrote to his patron, Cesare Borgia, describing the contest in detail. He contrasted Giulia's 'dark colouring, black eyes, round face and particular ardour (*quidam ardor*)' with the fair complexion and blue eyes of Caterina Gonzaga.

Giulia, in writing to Rome at this period, used a term of address that was rather too worldly for the Pontiff: 'To my only Lord'. This letter, like Lucrezia's, was unearthed and published by Pastor. In describing the celebrations and festivities Giulia adopted an air of feigned modesty which was intended to be provocative. She assured the Pope that he could rest at ease; his Lucrezia was very well married and was comporting herself marvellously; the city of Pesaro was even more civilized than Foligno and all and sundry were affectionately disposed towards the Sforzas. There was dancing and singing, music and acting every day. Yet His Holiness must not imagine that this made her and Adriana happy. Alas, 'as Your Holiness is not here, and as my every happiness and well-being depends upon Your Holiness, I am unable to take delight and satisfaction in these pleasures, because where my treasure is there is my heart'. Neither Giulia nor Alexander VI thought for a moment that there was anything ridiculous in calling a Pope 'my treasure'. 'All is a mockery save being at the feet of Your Holiness,' she continued, 'and whoever says the contrary is a fool ... Do not let Your Holiness forget us,' she went on, 'now we are confined here, but bring us back soon and meanwhile write to us sometimes'; and having recorded her 'faithful servitude' she goes on to thank the Pope for the new favour he had shown her brother Cardinal Farnese, and then draws to an end 'so as not to bore him'. But she was far from boring him. Alexander VI answered passionately, saying that the longer and more effusive her letters were the more he liked them and the longer it took to read them. The phrases he used are more normal for a man of twenty than a man of sixty-two.

Giulia also wrote describing Caterina Gonzaga, but that letter has not come down to us. It appears that she did nothing but make malicious praise of her rival, for the Pope's answer shows a grasp of this form of coquetry: 'In devoting so much space to describing the beauty of a woman who is not fit to unlace your shoe, you are motivated, as we know, by great modesty, and the reasons for it are obvious. You were fully aware that everyone who has written to us says that when you were beside her she looked like a lantern to your sun. When you make her seem so very beautiful your own perfection becomes the more apparent, about which, to tell the truth, we have never been in doubt. And we would wish that, just as we know this clearly, so you should be attached *totally and without division* to the person who loves you more than anybody else in the world. And when you have fully realized this, if you have not done so until now, we will know that you are as wise as you are beautiful.' Here we see both love and jealousy at work. We are not told the name of the rival that prevented Alexander from possessing Giulia 'totally and without division', but later developments suggest that it was almost certainly her husband, Orsino Orsini, who was chafing in his exile at Bassanello.

Adriana Mila also wrote affectionately from Pesaro to protest that her one thought was to live 'under the shadow' of the Pope, and she said: 'I again recommend Orsino to Your Holiness'. Detailed news from Pesaro was completed by Francesco Gacet, a Borgia intimate, who was dispatched after the Papal women for that express purpose. Gacet was a canon of Toledo and conversant with many Vatican secrets and had been present at Giulia's marriage with Orsino Orsini. Gacet was a yes-man – he needed to be to fulfil his task – but he was also quick and penetrating and he could use logic to unravel the complicated whims of women while yet retaining respect and consideration for them. Hence women made a great fuss of him. 'In view of my knowledge that he is the loving slave of Your Holiness and because of the merits of his behaviour towards us, I feel obliged to recommend him with all the warmth in my power to Your Beatitude, that you should deign to know the fervour of his service and do well by him.' So wrote Lucrezia to her father.

Unfortunately nearly all Gacet's letters have been lost. Alexander VI was hungry for news and every time he wrote he complained that the women were indifferent to him and had forgotten him. Hence the storm when, towards the end of June 1494, news spread through Rome that Lucrezia had a mental illness. Alexander VI's paternal instinct was aroused and he tremblingly dispatched letters and missions one on top of the other until he received a letter from Pesaro in Lucrezia's own hand telling him about her condition. The Pope answered immediately: 'Donna Lucrezia, beloved daughter: You have given us four or five days of deep distress; (we were) overwhelmed with anxiety at the evil and bitter news rife in Rome that you were dead or else in such infirmity that there was no hope for your life. You can imagine the sorrow that this rumour caused in our mind in view of the heartfelt and immense love we bear for you as for no one else in the world. And until we saw the letter sent us in your own hand, which was badly written and shows that you are not well, we never had any peace of mind. We thank God and Our Glorious Lady that they have removed you from every danger, and rest assured that we shall never be happy until we have seen you in person.'

In order to hasten the return to Rome and put some order into Sforza's affairs which were drifting towards disaster, the Pope proposed to Lucrezia that the Count of Pesaro should quit service in Milan – where his salary was being paid him with less and less regularity, 'since the State of Milan will be reluctant to give him his money, seeing that we are allied with King Alfonso and Giovanni has no choice but to follow our will' – and accept the command of a Neapolitan brigade. The Pope asked for an immediate answer, but the Count of Pesaro was placed in a very awkward position. True enough, he was dependent on Alexander VI both as his liege lord and his father-in-law, but the Pope railed to take into account the close ties between Giovanni and his family in Milan which made it difficult for him to take a decisive step. When faced with the either-or, Sforza behaved without dignity. He accepted the command of a Neapolitan regiment and the pay that went with it, and at the same time began the perilous game of keeping the Milanese Sforzas informed as to the strength and movements of the army in which he was campaigning. This was worse than espionage; it was high treason, which has been considered a capital offence throughout all history. Sforza's letters reveal how terrified he was at what he was doing. In one, written on August 2, 1494, he tells Ludovico il Moro that he has given all available information about the movements of the Duke of Calabria's troops in Romagna to the Milanese envoy Raimondo de'Raimondi, and points out that if even a shred of this information were to leak out he would be in the gravest danger now that he was in the employ of the Pope.

Lucrezia cannot have had the faintest idea of what was going on. As for Alexander VI, it is probable that he sensed something of what was afoot but, if so, he thought it inopportune to do more than make occasional allusion to it. His main concern at the time was the avalanche approach of the French, yet his affectionate longing for his women was undiminished, for he wrote to Adriana Mila to see if she could do something to hasten their return. 'Madame Niece' was charged with finding out discreetly whether Giovanni Sforza intended to return to Rome. 'If he has not so far mentioned it to you,' wrote the Pope, 'act cautiously and discreetly in conjunction with Messer Francesco Gacet . . . to find out what he has in mind; because should the aforesaid Signor Giovanni be willing to allow Donna Lucrezia to accompany you while himself remaining at Pesaro to look after his men and safeguard his State – especially now that the French are arriving by land and sea – we will write and send for you to come sooner because it does not seem advisable to us that you should be at Pesaro at a time like this when there are multitudes of men-at-arms in that country.' Alexander awaited the reply impatiently, and when it came he arranged to modify the date and duration of a journey he himself had to make in the Rome area to meet the King of Naples. This was the important meeting at Vicovaro when the Pope and Alfonso II made an alliance on July 14, 1494.

This letter to Adriana was written on July 8 and, if it reached her at all, it did so at a time when she was not in a mood for complicity and obedience. Meanwhile in those early days of July Giulia was receiving frequent letters from her native Capodi-monte telling her that her brother Angelo, the head of her family, was gravely ill and likely to die, and urging her to return immediately if she wished to see him. She decided to set out at once though her decision must have been against the Pope's orders for Lucrezia and her husband appeared to be extremely upset by it and did everything to keep her back. They managed to delay her until more detailed information arrived, but when it did it was of such a grave character that Giulia refused to listen to their arguments or even heed the authority of the Pope. At dawn on July 12 she set out for Lake Bolsena with Adriana Mila, Francesco Gacet and a few others.

When Alexander VI heard of their departure he fell into a great rage, and reproached Lucrezia and her husband severely for allowing them to leave. This is bewildering, to say the least, in view of the reasonableness of Giulia's motives. As Giovanni Sforza was at that moment in Urbino spying on Duke Giudobaldo Montefeltro and his Aragonese forces, Lucrezia wrote back to describe how it had all come about, but she was unable to write with her own hand as she had injured her arm, and her letter was not well received by the Pope. He thought he saw through her excuses: she was indifferent, deceitful, and was sending false news in contradiction to what she had written to Cesare. Above all he suspected a lack of filial love for she showed no desire to return to her father. He dispatched his brief to Pesaro with Messer Lelio Capodiferro, who also had to deliver by word of mouth a very stern and detailed message that put

Lucrezia into 'a very great melancholy'. Relations with a father who manifested his affection in such a sombre way were not easy, as can be imagined. Lucrezia proffered excuses in her own graceful and reasonable manner, pointing out to the Pope that if her last letter had struck him as unlike its predecessors there was no cause for surprise for it had been written by a chancellor and a chancellor's style was obviously unlike a woman's. If he read her words again calmly and coolly and compared them with what she had written to Cesare he would see that there was no real discrepancy. He should trust in her affection for she desired nothing save 'to be at the feet of Your Beatitude, and humbly and with all my power I beg you to make me worthy of this for as long as I fail I shall never be satisfied'. The caress of her tenderness tamed even the Borgia bull; it is not difficult to see why Lucrezia was immediately forgiven and put back in the Pope's good books.

But Giulia fared very differently. She arrived at Capodimonte in time to be at her brother Angelo's deathbed and comfort his last hours. Then she had to comfort his widow, Lella Orsini, who later became a nun at the Murate convent in Florence. But even when her family duties were over Giulia made no sign of leaving her birthplace, but stayed on in the company of her mother, her sister Girolama Farnese Pucci, Cardinal Alessandro, Adriana Mila and Francesco Gacet – a happy prisoner who paid no attention to the Pope's repeated summons to return to Rome. We do not know her motives for behaving in a way so contrary to her general attitude and to the tenor of her recent letters. It has been said that her reasons were political, but what could they be at such a time – when the Orsini were reputed to be the most staunch allies of the King of Naples and the Pope? Pastor's interpretation of this episode is far too simple: the conflict of passions may have been strengthened by politics, but it cannot be explained in terms of politics alone as I shall try to make clear.

Bassanello, a demesne of the Orsini, lies between Orte and Viterbo looking north-east. It is an impoverished little village on a low hill and its origins are ancient and military. It is defended by a fine rectangular castle rounded off at each corner with smooth and powerful towers which dominate the stone houses below. There is also a Romanesque church with a six-storied campanile and medieval walls that testify to a past of war, suffering and discomfort for the sake of ambition. The valley spreads out majestically beneath the high castle windows and through it the Tiber silently flows. Beyond the horizon stretch the roads on which Orsino Orsini kept his gaze fixed in 1494 – watching out for travellers from Capodimonte or from Rome.

The love affair between the Borgia Pope and Giulia had been common knowledge in Italy for at least two years and Orsino could not stand it any longer. He had been crushed beneath the weight of the Pope but he chose an excellent moment to revolt. He, like all the Orsini who were fighting in their markedly detached way in the service of Alexander VI's ally, the King of Naples, had received orders at the beginning of September to proceed with his troops to Umbria and join the Aragonese camp under the command of the Duke of Calabria. As at that moment Giulia was with Adriana Mila at Capodimonte under the protection of her brother the Cardinal, it might be supposed that Orsino had no immediate grounds for uneasiness. But he had been told by one of his informants that Alexander VI was busy trying to get Giulia sent back to Rome. Thus, when he arrived at Città del Castello, Orsino feigned illness, sent his soldiers ahead, and himself stayed behind under the pretext of convalescence. Then, silently nursing his fury, he returned home.

Now as long as Orsino was at Capodimonte he constituted a serious obstacle to Giulia's return to Rome – one of a moral kind, for Alexander VI was embarrassed by public opinion. The Pope's desire for her remained the same, but he tried to storm the fortress through some third party. He knew the position to be very delicate. The King of France was in the process of invading Italy with the avowed intention – suggested to him by Alexander's many enemies – of deposing the Pope from the pontifical throne. At a moment such as this a scandal would do no good at all, so the Pope had to devise a way of bending either Orsino, or Giulia's brother, Cardinal Farnese, to his will.

Meanwhile Orsino had given up all idea of waging a military campaign and was lying low at Bassanello. There he balanced the protection of his castle walls against the Pontiff's distant authority and decided that he could afford to go into revolt. He told his mother, his wife, and Cardinal Farnese that at all costs he wanted Giulia to leave Capodimonte and come to Bassanello. If she failed to do so the whole world would hear of the scandal even if he lost his life and his possessions ten times over in the process. His language was not in keeping with his strength, but it gave his family pause and thoroughly upset Adriana Mila who could not overlook the fact that Orsino was her son; it may even have won over the gentle and voluptuous Giulia to her squint-eyed husband. It was Fra Teseo Seripando, Orsino's loyal adviser, who informed her of her husband's fury in letters that he said were written in the interests of both husband and wife. 'I see Signor Orsino,' he wrote in pointed but unpolished phrases, 'waiting in torture of mind and great displeasure at your non-arrival, and half-imagining that you may have straightway set off for Rome instead of coming here; and if you were to commit such an error, rather than endure it he would throw away a thousand lives had he so many, and all such goods as he has; so that I see him very discontented and raging and doing abnormal things. I, from my sense of obligation to both of you, am seeking to placate him and turn him from these projects. Yet for the life of me I cannot do so for he has decided (that) you shall not go to Rome, but shall come here, as I have said (and) should anything else befall he will be like the devil . . .'

There was no one to argue with Orsino and thus his 'devilries' fed upon themselves. At the same time Alexander VI was attempting with ever-increasing fervour to recall Giulia to Rome, going to such lengths that Cardinal Farnese, in his shame at the discreditable affair, sent Adriana to Rome to try to save some shreds of honour for Orsino and the Farnese family. But she achieved nothing and on October 14 returned to Capodimonte – 'God knows how tired', as she herself put it. She brought the Pope's inexorable answer: Giulia must go to Rome. At this Cardinal Farnese was duly indignant and refused to comply with the Pope's wishes: he had too much fundamental dignity not to be revolted by the whole situation (and this although he was a victim of interest and ambition, and although Pasquino called him 'the Cardinal of the skirts' and made an obscene play on his name. He was later to become Pope Paul III).

A few days earlier Cardinal Farnese had written to the Pope saying that he would always serve him 'in things that were possible'. He now let him know, through Adriana Mila, that he was ready to do anything he asked except this. 'It would be a blot on your honour to subscribe to this grave fault, which would end in a break with Orsino *for a thing of this kind, and so public*.' On the very same day Francesco Gacet, who lived in Giulia's shadow and kept watch on behalf of his employer, wrote a similar report. The Cardinal, said Gacet, would not mind offending Orsino so as to serve His Holiness, but he was not prepared to subject his family to scandal and infamy. Would it not be better, he advised, to summon Giulia's husband to Rome to attend on Virginio Orsini rather than order him to take the field? It would be easy to do because by now the Orsini had become the tools of the Pope. As soon as Orsino was out of the way it would be easy to deal with the women. But in Heaven's name let His Holiness act speedily, for at Bassanello requests were rapidly becoming commands and soon there would be no excuses left to make.

Meanwhile Alexander VI dispatched an archdeacon, possibly Pietro de Solis, with a brief explicitly ordering Orsino to let his wife leave for Rome, but when the archdeacon arrived at Capodimonte he was stopped and sent back to Rome whither, on October 19, he was followed by Navarrico, another henchman of the Borgias, who bore letters to the Pope from Adriana, Francesco Gacet and Giulia. These letters make it plain that the Cardinal was determined to defend his family against moral ruin and would not consider allowing his sister to go to Rome without her husband's consent. Adriana was plainly upset but could not see any solution, while Giulia adopted a capricious attitude. She was annoyed by the struggle to possess her, and she was possibly touched or fascinated by the fervour of her husband who still dared to resist his powerful enemy although betrayed by wife, mother, relations and even his own councillor. If Giulia was really the sweet and sensitive woman she was said to be, she may well have thought she should bestow her beauty on the man who showed courage rather than on the man who abused his power. Perhaps too she was going through that slight fever of revolt that drives a woman, at least once in her life, to make a stand. At any rate she informed the Pope that she would not leave Capodimonte without Orsino's consent.

Reading between the lines of the letters he received on October 19 and 20, the Pope realized that his adversaries had formed an alliance against his desires, which hence increased until they grew into a burning craving for Giulia. He wanted to fight. He seized one of the letters on his desk, tore off the part that bore only the address – 'Sanctissimo D. N. ppe' – and penned an answer on that.

It was to Giulia. 'Thankless and treacherous Giulia, Navarrico has brought us a letter from you in which you signify and declare your intention of not coming here without Orsino's consent. Though we judged the evil of your soul and that of the man who guides you, we could not believe that you would act with such perfidy and ingratitude in view of your repeated assurances and oaths that you would be faithful to our command and not go near Orsino. But now you are doing the very opposite, risking your life by going to Bassanello with the purpose, no doubt, of surrendering yourself once more to that stallion. We hope that you and the ungrateful Adriana will recognize your error and make suitable penance. Finally we herewith ordain, *sub pena excommunicationis latae sententiae et maledictionis eternae*, that you shall not leave Capodimonte or Marta and still less go to Bassanello – this for reasons affecting our State.'

As his appeals and orders had been of no avail, Alexander VI was obliged to resort to these drastic methods. But the interest of this letter for the historian is the implied reference to an earlier intimacy between Giulia and her husband from which, it would seem, a child had resulted. As the only known offspring of the marriage was little Laura, who was said to be a child of Alexander VI, we must suppose either that Giulia had another child who was stillborn or died soon after birth, or that little Laura was a genuine Orsini. In the latter case Giulia must have passed Laura off as a daughter of the Pope – as that tradition is so strong – in the hope of providing a better marriage for her.

The Pope's next letter was to Madame Adriana and she received even rougher treatment than her daughter-in-law. 'You have laid bare your malignity and the evil of your soul', wrote the Pope, and then expressed the hope that she would repent and do penance – under pain of excommunication. In his third letter, addressed to Cardinal Farnese, the Pope expressed himself with formal dignity, saying that the Cardinal had forgotten all too soon the favours he had received, and enclosing a brief forbidding Giulia to go to Bassanello, thereby providing Farnese with an excuse *vis-à-vis* Orsino. But the longest of all his letters was to Francesco Gacet, and it has never been published until now. The Pope wrote in his own unique and peculiar language which was a mixture of Latin, Italian and Spanish. He complained at length about everyone, beginning with Gacet himself and going on to Adriana who, after so many promises 'tota si es voltada', 'declarant nos expressament que ella non vuol menar aci a Giulia contro la voluntat de Ursino'.[1] How could she possibly prefer that monkey to us? – 'prepone quella zimia de Ursino a Nosaltres'. But they would soon see who they were dealing with. The Pope informed Gacet that he had also read the letter from Fra Teseo Seripando at Bassanello to Giulia (which explains why the letter is still to be found in the Vatican

---

[1] 'She has entirely changed', 'declaring expressly to us that she is not willing to bring Giulia here against Orsino's will.'

archives) and had seen through the malice by which it was animated. If Giulia and Madonna Adriana chose to please Orsino rather than him they would be excommunicated, and so would Orsino and Giulia's cousin, Renuccio Farnese. Having vented his fury, the Borgia commanded Gacet to let him know without delay what the women had decided to do. With all the briefs and intimations of excommunication that were hurled around, Giulia la Bella was giving the Vatican Chancellery a great deal to do!

Meanwhile the cause of all the trouble remained in the tall castle at Capodimonte that stands on a crest dominating the banks of the lake of Bolsena. At first she must have been very upset, but she was a woman of good sense and must soon have consoled herself. Once she ceased to look on herself as an exotic fugitive from male desires and returned to everyday life, she reconciled herself gracefully to the abrupt and arbitrary end of her romance with her husband. She may have been helped in this by Orsino's spiritless character. Once he had dared to defy the Pope he might at least have ridden over to Capodimonte with a suite of bravoes and commanded the Farnese family, as was his right, to hand over his wife – which they could not have refused to do. But such an idea never crossed his mind. He must have soon grown weary of his rebellion, for the archdeacon whom Alexander VI dispatched once again to Bassanello was well received at the castle and stayed for a long interview. He returned to Rome with a note from Orsino to the Pope saying: 'The archdeacon, bearer of this present letter, has given me Your Holiness' brief and by word of mouth has told me certain things as from you. And I have well understood the tenor of the brief in question' – a short note which suggested the bored surrender of a coward who had lost his nerve: for the rest the Pope would receive through the archdeacon assurances of his 'entire goodwill'. This was, or rather it foreshadowed, a capitulation, and in the following month Giulia and Adriana set out for Rome. Orsino even tried to make his defeat profitable and, forgetting all he had said about preferring to lose all his possessions rather than suffer humiliation, he asked the Pope on November 28 for a substantial sum of money so as to pay his troops and pointed out that they had refused to march until they had been paid. At this time all the troops of the Orsini were faced with serious difficulties, and the general lines of the great Orsini treason which was later to make it impossible for the House of Aragon to hold out were already clearly perceptible.

The women were now free to go to Rome and Giulia's sophisms vanished as easily as Orsino's resistance. At the end of November they were still at Capodimonte but an informant made clear they were there 'at the disposal ... of the Most Reverend Legate' and were merely delaying until the arrival of messire Anichino, a Borgia henchman, who was to escort them 'where they shall want to go' – in other words to Rome. Meanwhile Lucrezia continued to live a quiet provincial life at Pesaro.

It was at this time that Italy began to experience the terrors of a foreign invasion. The King of France had already arrived at the head of a well-trained army which had fought in hard climates and was avid for conquest. France as a whole, however, was not keen on this war, but even the beautiful queen, Anne of Brittany, had failed to deflect the King from his purpose. Charles VIII was a deformed little man and the Italians immediately nicknamed him 'Re Petito'. His advisers had persuaded him of the existence in Naples of a powerful Angevin party that was longing for French domination, and in addition there had been the appeals for help from Ludovico il Moro and Giuliano della Rovere. The cause appealed to his quixotic love of adventure and glory and leaving his Queen at Grenoble, he was in Italy by September 3.

3

THE COUNTESS OF
PESARO

The news was serious and soon became disastrous. The French fleet, commanded by Louis of Orleans, defeated the Aragonese fleet at Rapallo, and the gathering of Italians at Aix who paid homage to the King of France included Giuliano della Rovere, Duke Ercole of Este, Ludovico il Moro with his wife Beatrice, and their brilliant courts. A few days later a tragic meeting between Charles VIII and Isabella of Aragon took place at Pavia. Isabella threw herself at the King's feet and, though she knew he had come to Italy to wage war against the family to which she belonged, she implored him to protect the legitimate branch of the Sforzas – her husband and her son – against the usurper Ludovico il Moro. Charles VIII appeared to be impressed both by her appearance and her words. But scarcely a month later Gian Galeazzo suddenly died. Whether his death was natural or violent is not known, but Ludovico ascended the throne of the Dukes of Milan with his triumphant wife at his side.

The French army began marching on Naples, passing through Piacenza, Sarzana and Pisa. At Pisa Savonarola appeared before the most Christian King and said he was a messenger of God sent to reform the Church. The French entered Florence amid general jubilation and prepared to march on to Rome.

But notwithstanding his successes – or perhaps because of them – Charles VIII did not feel he dared attack the Head of Christendom. Cardinal Giuliano della Rovere's urgent and repeated suggestion that he should call a General Council and depose the Pope did not appeal to him at all. He had reason to fear the other European powers, and he knew that his wife Queen Anne would disapprove and that she would be followed by the whole of Catholic France. It would be best, he thought, to keep to the ways of peace and obtain the Pope's authorization for transit through Rome. But Alexander VI still talked of resisting and when Cardinal Ascanio Sforza went to Rome to negotiate, he seized him as a hostage. Meanwhile the French army was advancing so rapidly that among his other preoccupations the Pope became gravely concerned about Giulia Farnese.

Now that Orsino had changed his mind and submitted to the Pope's demands, Giulia could at last set out. She was accompanied by her sister, Girolama Farnese Pucci and, needless to add, Madame Adriana. The three women began their journey on November 29 in a carriage escorted by thirty horsemen. The cavalcade made rapid progress through the mild early winter morning only to be unexpectedly halted by a squad of men-at-arms who barred the way. Attempts to put up a defence would have been useless and dangerous and the travellers had no choice but to surrender. The aggressors were French reconnaissance troops under the command of Yves d'Allegre, a man who seemed marked out by destiny to conquer beautiful women. The French gallants were overjoyed and fascinated by the beauty of the ladies and conducted them to Montefiascone where, as Giulia was gracious enough to testify, they were excellently received. But when a French envoy arrived in Rome to ask for their ransom according to custom, the Pope took the news very badly. No horse on earth seemed to him swift enough to deliver the 3,000 scudi that the envoy demanded. For safety's sake he dispatched his trusted chamberlain, Giovanni Marraves, with the money, and feeling even this was not enough he also appealed to the Sanseverino family (who were of Sforza allegiance and at this time suspect), and made Cardinal Federico, who was then in Rome, write to his brother Galeazzo di Sanseverino who was campaigning for Charles VIII, while he himself wrote to the King. Galeazzo Sanseverino has left an account of how he approached King Charles. Pastor has published one of Galeazzo's letters addressed (though Pastor does not say this) to his brother the Cardinal; but more to the point is the account

written in his own hand to Alexander VI that has remained
completely unknown until now. As soon as the Papal brief
arrived, says Galeazzo, 'I presented myself before the aforesaid
most Christian King and after reminding His Majesty of the case
of the arrest of the aforesaid ladies . . . I prayed him with such
words as I judged expedient to be good enough to please Your
Beatitude by their liberation: which (Majesty) . . . answered me
benignly that not only was it his will that they should be set free
but before evening he thought to send a trustworthy man of his
company to escort them to Rome . . .' When Alexander VI
heard that the prisoners had been set free and would soon be
arriving, he threw off all thought of politics like a twenty-year-
old. He began preparing to receive them and set about making
himself look as gallant and handsome as he possibly could for the
evening. He selected a cloak of black velvet trimmed with gold,
which concealed and hence diminished his girth, fine Valencia
boots, a rich Spanish scarf and a velvet cap. Finally he girt
himself with sword and dagger partly for defence but primarily
so that the pretty women would not find the change too sudden
from the brilliant military company they had been keeping. The
women for whose sake he indulged in such follies at last arrived
at the gates of Rome with an escort of four hundred Frenchmen.
Through the darkness and the torchlight the Pope saw Giulia's
brown face greet him with a smile that was full of love. The
chroniclers say that she spent the night in the Vatican.

Given Alexander VI's outstanding abilities and temperament,
we do not find it surprising that he managed to hold his own and
avoid humiliation in the grave period that followed. The French
were drawing nearer every day. The fall of Civitavecchia cut off
the possibility of flight by sea – which had at one time been
considered, when trunkfuls of tapestries and precious ornaments
were packed at the Vatican. But the final blow was dealt by the
Orsini who in December suddenly and treasonably deserted to
the French and offered the King their castle at Bracciano for his
military headquarters. The voice of Giulia's husband weighed
but little in the councils of the Orsini family, or we should

presume him to be a ringleader in the plot that proved so fatal to the Pope's projects of resistance: but as it was, it is doubtful whether the urge for revenge was so much as felt at Bassanello. Anyhow, Alexander VI was now left with a mere handful of Aragonese and Spanish soldiers in the midst of an apathetic people, and as he had no allies worthy of the name, he had no alternative but to allow the French army to march through Rome on its way to the Kingdom of Naples. It was in vain that King Alfonso offered the Pope the fortress of Gaeta and the possibility of flight. The Pope refused: the only fortress he trusted was the Castel Sant' Angelo, whence, from the windows of the Belvedere, he could see the French King's horses at pasture in the great fields below him. Sforza was set free and an agreement was patched up.

Charles VIII entered Rome unopposed on the last day of December 1494 and his army took six hours to march past – with its 2,500 noblemen dressed in luxurious cloth and wearing Italian jewels, Florentine for the most part; with its bands of Gascon arbalests, little men, lively, all nervous energy; with its crossbow-men, mace-bearers and gun-crews. When it emerged from the narrow Via Lata and accompanied the King to his lodging in the Palace of Saint Mark, now known as the Palazzo Venezia, the army seemed enormous indeed. Cannon were drawn up in the Piazza by the main entrance to the palace, and meanwhile in a city whose inhabitants were hardly more than double their number, 30,000 young men obviously upset the equilibrium. The French troops felt that the city lay unarmed at their feet and they had no scruples about sacking houses and palaces, raping women and stealing everything they could lay hands on. The King of France had scaffolds erected in the piazzas which were intended as an eloquent warning, but the eloquence was academic and the plundering went on. Vannozza's house in Piazza Branca came off very badly; it was luxuriously furnished and yielded first-class booty of every kind, and the plunderers must have had the additional satisfaction of stealing from a very unusual favourite.

And what was Vannozza doing at the time? There is a

spurious tradition that the French soldiers discovered and violated her in her house and that she exhorted her son Cesare to avenge the deed. But this story is confirmed neither by documents nor by the logic of things. The more likely assumption is that she had left her house and been put into safety by her husband, possibly on the advice of Alexander VI. She may even have taken refuge in the Castel Sant' Angelo as she had done on other occasions when life was stormy for the Borgias. Three short letters discovered by Pastor in 1831 in the Secret Archives of the Vatican prove that the Pope never forgot the mother of his children but continued to see her even after his accession to the Papal throne. Pastor found them in a group of Borgia letters of 1493 and 1494 which had been re-classified by Confalonieri in 1627, but no effort has been made to date them exactly. Now since all the letters in this group belong to the years 1493 and 1494 Vannozza's letters obviously belong to the same period, and the second of them contains a reference that leaves no room for doubt. It is a request for an audience. In it Vannozza asks the Pope to receive her because she has to tell him 'many things about which I am sure Your Holiness would take pleasure in hearing' and, first and foremost, she wishes to join him in rejoicing 'at the good news of the Lord Duke and the fine son that has been born to him'. Now in the House of Borgia at that time there was only one Duke, Juan of Gandia, and, as his wife Maria Henriques bore a son and heir in November 1494, the letter must obviously refer to this event and therefore must have been written at the end of November or the beginning of December. These fugitive glimpses show us a Vannozza more full of life than ever, an active and practical woman. 'Pater santo,' she says, 'I am displeased (because) Your Holiness does good on my behalf and others profit by it.' There was nothing of the beggar in her, and when she asked for an audience she did so as one who knew she would get it. In this case the day and hour of the meeting was arranged by Carlo Canale who was always ready to carry messages between the Pope and Vannozza.

In dealing with people so well versed in the arts of

dissimulation it is obviously unlikely that we will catch them off their guard and in the open. However it does seem to me that the first of Vannozza's letters, written from Rome and, unlike the others, in the third person, may throw light on the problem under discussion. 'Vannozza is humbly suppliant at the feet of His Holiness that he should deign to give her audience tomorrow evening because her heart is beset with fear and at all costs she wishes to leave as soon as may be.' It looks as if the 'fear' in question refers to the avalanche of the French invasion. But even if this letter does not prove beyond doubt that Vannozza was away from Rome at that time, it at least shows that she was on the defensive as soon as there was threat of plague or war. And thus we have an additional reason for supposing that the attack on Vannozza's palace in Piazza Branca was an affair of plunder rather than of rape.

Our next problem concerns Giulia Farnese whom the Pope held even dearer than Vannozza. She does not seem to have taken refuge in the Castel Sant' Angelo; but did she stay in Rome concealed in one of the Farnese palaces? In this connection I have had the good fortune to discover in the Vatican Archives a letter that casts light on some of the conflicts of character and emotion at the time. It is written by Jacobello Silvestri, Bishop of Allatri, and is addressed to 'his Lord' Mariano Savelli, who was a close relation of the Farnese family and at that moment campaigning in the French army. The Bishop wrote in the nervous and agitated style of a man who has measured up all the possible dangers, and he tells Savelli that Carlo Farnese has ordered him to get Giulia away from Rome at the first possible moment. Though at first Giulia had been 'obstinate' and had not wanted to move, she had finally yielded to his exhortations and said she was ready to leave as soon as they had enough horses and a good escort. 'Wherefore,' adds Silvestri, 'I pray your Lordship to act quickly and satisfy her, for in truth it seems to me unfitting that she should remain here, and things might occur that would bring small honour to all, as the most reverend monsignor (Cardinal Farnese) is well aware, for he is eating his heart out while she stays in Rome. For the love of God let your Lordship send her the means whereby she can leave here.'

If Orsino had not admitted defeat, neither did Giulia's brother, the Cardinal, who was more powerful than Orsino. In this as in other relevant documents, none of which can be suspected of bias, we see the future Pope Paul III tormented about the relationship between Giulia and Alexander VI, and he is hence fully cleared of the complicity with which some historians have charged him. He yielded to force. But his deep suffering – 'he is eating his heart out' in the words of the Bishop of Allatri – is a moral vindication. It was at this time, or shortly afterwards, that a Florentine informant noted: 'I understand that they are making rings worth 1,000 ducats for Madonna Giulia and the poor Cardinal has nothing to live on.' And this, too, speaks for Farnese. He had more solicitude than Orsino, for he had people of trust ready to seize his sister from the Borgia at the first possible moment. In addition he must have been inspired by feelings of fear and horror at the thought of what might happen if the French in Rome came into conflict with the Pope, for almost anything could be expected of men-at-arms in such great numbers. He had been deeply wounded by the quips that had been repeated throughout the country when Giulia had been taken prisoner. We do not know what Savelli's reactions were or even if this letter ever reached him: the fact that it is to be found in the Vatican Archives suggests that it was intercepted by pontifical officers and handed to Alexander VI. Anyhow the Bishop, who was Cardinal Farnese's supporter, was shortly afterwards accused of anti-Borgia and pro-Sforza activities and was imprisoned in the Castel Sant' Angelo there to be forgotten until the death of Alexander VI. Even if this letter was not the immediate cause of his long imprisonment, it at least shows the Bishop's party spirit and his readiness to use every opportunity for opposing the Borgia's wishes. We do not know for certain whether Giulia left Rome or not, and I have not succeeded in finding any traces of her either in Rome or at Capodimonte during this period. But the very fact that nothing was heard of her during the French occupation suggests that she was placed in safe keeping.

And now we must return to the Pope in his great fortress on the Tiber. He was well aware of the dangers that lay in the French occupation of the city and knew that they must be dislodged by some means or other at the first possible moment. He therefore began urgent negotiations which resulted in agreeing to give the French King and his army the right of transit through the Papal States. The Pope handed over the fortress of Civitavecchia, the Turkish Prince Djem and the Cardinal of Valencia, Cesare Borgia, as hostages, Cesare's nominal task being to accompany the French army as Cardinal Legate. On January 6 Alexander VI received the King in the Vatican with that radiant and charming manner which was his outstanding quality both as politician and man. The King was paid many compliments and given a Cardinal's hat for his faithful Briçonnet. Then he was taken to the new Borgia apartment where the walls were still fresh with frescoes by Pinturicchio and his school.

The Borgia apartment faces north and when we visit it today it seems pleasant enough, but dark and sombre. The light is dull even on bright June mornings owing to the overhanging cornice above the windows, and it is kept out still more by the two wings to the right and left of the great courtyard. But in those days the windows had no cornices and there were no high buildings in the vicinity, and therefore there was a vista of green gardens right as far as Monte Mario and a stretch of fragrant orange trees and pines that did nothing to prevent the afternoon sun from making its own contribution to the gold and enamel of Pinturicchio's work. Great windows with cross frames cut up the landscape into clear geometric spaces. The doors were small and narrow, and when he entered the apartment, the figure of the Pontiff in his vast golden mantle must have filled the whole aperture as though framed by the marble arabesques – for all the world as if a painted figure had been detached from the walls by supernatural power so as to move among mortal men. But the mortal men from beyond the Alps showed no sign of being intimidated by the supernatural dignity of the spectacle. They expressed their admiration, of course, but, with the rational curiosity that is peculiar to the French, they wanted to take in everything while having no respect for the rules of ceremonial. Burchard was amazed to observe that they went in to kiss the Pope's slipper in a most disorderly way and with 'the greatest hurry', and as he found it impossible to enforce discipline and establish any rule about the precedence of noblemen and captains, he finally decided to ask the advice of the Pope who merely shrugged his shoulders.

The French left Rome at the end of January. On the 26th the King went to the Vatican to be solemnly received by the Pope and Cardinals. The Turkish Prince Djem was summoned and handed over to the King who welcomed him affably with expressions of friendship. When the army finally began to march southwards the light-headed romantic King seems to have been delighted and exhilarated to be travelling at the head of a victorious army through a land in which the flowers were already out in February; and the thought that he was to conquer a kingdom and already held hostages – a prince from the East and a Cardinal who was the Pope's son – gave him further joy. Fresh gratification lay ahead: at Marino he received news that the King of Naples, Alfonso II, had fled to Sicily leaving the throne in the hands of his son, Ferrandino, Prince of Capua. 'A brave man is never cruel', people commented, remembering Alfonso's atrocities; and his flight, which was a public declaration of cowardice (he took the crown treasures with him), was a clear indication of the imminent collapse of the House of Aragon, and provided new fuel for French arrogance. Then, at Velletri, a theatrical event upset the army: Cesare Borgia silently showed his hand.

The Cardinal of Valencia had been riding in the King's following and had made a demonstration of affability and ecclesiastical reserve that could give no ground for suspicion. But he was certainly aware of the stratagem that was soon to turn the fortunes of the French and was merely awaiting an opportunity to get away. This opportunity occurred at Velletri where some noblemen showed him a secret passage. He managed to escape and, passing through Rome, made his way to Spoleto where he waited on events. The French protested furiously to the Vatican. 'The Cardinal has behaved badly, very badly', Alexander VI was heard to say, shaking his head. When the French tried to get their own back by sacking Cesare's baggage-train they found that the coaches contained only rubbish under their luxurious trappings, and Charles VIII, who disliked being fooled by a little Cardinal of twenty, bitterly resented the practical joke. Out of a primitive desire for reprisal the army would willingly have sacked the city of Velletri had not the Bishop, Giuliano della Rovere, managed to pour oil on the troubled waters. The French pushed furiously on, meeting no resistance. The only serious opposition came from the fortress of Monte San Giovanni, where the inhabitants tried unsuccessfully to defend themselves and were cruelly massacred for their pains. Capua flung open its gates in terror; while the lily-livered King Ferrandino, seeing the uselessness of resisting with the army he had to hand, fled to Ischia. The French soldiers could hardly believe in their good luck as they entered Naples.

But while they were basking in the shadow of sunny Vesuvius and growing lazy and sybaritic, the Pope was busily preparing his revenge. He formed a grand alliance: with Ludovico the Moor who was disappointed to see that the Borgia Pope had not been deposed; with the Republic of Venice which foresaw the threat of French domination in Italy; with the King of Spain and with the Emperor Maximilian, both of whom had the same danger in mind. The alliance between these powers was proclaimed on April 12, 1495, and the outlook began to change very rapidly.

As he did not want to become a prisoner in the Kingdom he had conquered, Charles VIII ordered an immediate retreat to the Alps and began a forced march northwards, leaving a French garrison behind at Naples. Yet he failed to by-pass his enemies and on the Taro near Fornovo a famous battle took place that still divides historians to this day. The opposing commanders, the King of France and the Marquis of Mantua, Francesco Gonzaga, displayed outstanding gallantry, but there was not a decisive victory. Charles VIII managed to get through, but he left large numbers of prisoners in the hands of the enemy as well as the booty he had gathered in Italy. The battle of Fornovo was on July 6, 1495. Charles VIII halted at Asti to re-organize the remnants of his army and shortly afterwards recrossed the Alps into France. His adventure in Italy had lasted less than a year.

Alexander VI did not stay in Rome to await the transit of the retreating King: he retired prudently to Perugia where he was cheered by the arrival of Lucrezia. But after the French retreat over the Alps, the Pope returned to the Vatican and Lucrezia returned to Santa Maria in Portico where she was rejoined by Giovanni Sforza who seems to have been well received. Lucrezia gave a series of elegant receptions, and amongst other visitors were the four newly-elected Cardinals and also Francesco Gonzaga, the victor of Fornovo, who was fêted wherever he went and had a cheerful and gallant Lombard character. Lucrezia enjoyed listening to the Marquis' sallies, but she had not the faintest idea that this tall lithe man with prominent features and brown beard was destined to play a major part in her personal life later on.

In March Giovanni Sforza left Rome for a month, and dark and mysterious rumours concerning him were to be heard in the Vatican. 'The Lord of Pesaro perhaps finds something at his home that others do not imagine,' wrote the Mantuan inform-ant, G. Carlo Scalona, on April 28, 1496. And on May 2 he added that Sforza had gone away 'in despair, leaving his wife beneath the apostolic mantle', and giving out that he would never return to Rome. And at Pesaro he remained, despite the Pope's attempts to entice him back with expressions of affection, flattery and offers of posts. So summer gave way to autumn and autumn to winter.

Lucrezia may have been unhappy, but she had the resilience of girls of sixteen and was successfully distracted – especially when the Pope decided to summon his youngest son, Jofre, and his wife, Sancha, to Rome.

At first Lucrezia was uneasy about Sancha. She lacked experience of life and, above all, of court life, and everybody noticed her malaise. 'This (i.e. Sancha's arrival) is beginning to make the (Pope's) daughter jealous,' and 'The Countess of Pesaro is anything but pleased', the informants tell us, adding maliciously that she was obviously afraid of rivalry. We can well imagine the care that Lucrezia took over her clothes on the morning of May 20 which was the day she welcomed her sister-in-law. She selected her escort, too, with an eye for detail: it consisted of twelve girls in beautiful dresses, two magnificently-mantled pages, and mounted attendants clad in gold and red brocade. The meeting of the two cortèges on that May morning was a brilliant spectacle enhanced by the Cardinals' households, the palace guards, and the presence of Italian and foreign ambassadors. The princess, with a royal retinue that included six jesters, arrived at ten o'clock. She was mounted on a parade horse caparisoned with velvet and black satin in alternating bands, and she was wearing the city dress normal in the south of Italy – black with large sleeves. Lucrezia's horse was caparisoned with black satin. The two young women met with a solemn embrace, and the cortège moved on. Jofre rode ahead with his customary gracious and insolent air, his glance made lascivious by his wife's caresses, his long well-combed hair with copper high-lights, his skin bronzed by the southern sun. Sancha rode between Lucrezia and the Spanish ambassador. Her blooming face was well made-up and it glowed as she threw lively and arrogant glances around her. Those who had swallowed the legend of that 'most beautiful creature' too readily, may have felt disillusioned, but, as a chronicler put it, 'be this as it may, the sheep will look and behave exactly as the wolf wishes'; and referring to Sancha's ladies-in-waiting, Loysella, Bernardina and Francesca, he added: 'They are not unworthy of their mistress, and people are saying openly that they will make a fine team.'

Pope Alexander VI was waiting with all the impatience of a young man dreaming of the arrival of a pretty woman. He was scanning the piazza from an open window and only when he caught sight of the head of the procession did he take his proper place among his Cardinals. After a few minutes had elapsed they heard the sound of arms in the nearby hall, the rustling of silks and the voices of women, and then Sancha boldly entered – she was the daughter and sister of a King and would not be intimidated. She and her husband knelt, and she bent her dark head to kiss the Pope's foot. There followed Sancha's court of women who paid reverence to the Pope with a mixture of worldly and sacred pomp and then everyone took the places assigned to them – Jofre next to his brother Cesare, and Sancha and Lucrezia on two red velvet cushions on the steps of the pontifical throne. When the Pope looked down from his throne and saw the fair head of Lucrezia on one side and Sancha's dark one on the other, he felt satisfied that they were surrounded with the respect and consideration that enhances the beauty of young women. Moreover he was in his element as their master and arbiter and displayed his aptitude for gay conversation and made them laugh. His joyful pagan humanism was quite at home under the golden vault painted with the story of Isis and with the myths and symbols of the East.

Sancha was accorded a sovereign rôle in the Papal court but her sovereignty was not direct, like Lucrezia's. Her title and her royal relatives made her position higher than that of a favourite but it was still lower than that of a daughter-in-law in the normal sense. Though she realized her predicament better than anyone, she never visibly hated or ill-treated her husband, the little prince; on the contrary, she defended him, spoilt him and caressed him too much. Of course she did not love him, as she was the kind of woman who could love only someone more violent and dominating than herself. And with the passage of time she grew to be aware of just such a man, one who had all these qualities to excess – her brother-in-law Cardinal Cesare Borgia. Two such misfits could hardly be expected to hesitate for long before reaching an understanding. Sancha threw herself into the love affair as if it were a vendetta. Indeed from her very first day in Rome she exhibited the disturbing attributes of her Aragonese blood.

On Whit-Sunday, May 22, the Pope and his court of Cardinals and all the women of the House of Borgia, led by Lucrezia and Sancha, were present at a ceremony in St Peter's. The Spanish prelate who officiated must have felt very important to be preaching to the most outstanding congregation of the whole Catholic world. While he was engaged in slowly picking off the petals of his theological rose, the women, who had been standing, began to feel tired, and the whole congregation, including the Pope, became so bored and impatient that they could hardly bear to listen a moment longer, despite their reverence for the sacred place. Suddenly, against this grey backcloth of boredom, there was a movement: Sancha and Lucrezia, in clothes whose folds did not conceal their agile young bodies, were climbing up to the stalls customarily assigned to the canons of St Peter's for the singing of the gospel. All the girls of the court followed, clambering after them, and then there followed the huge business of settling down again, putting clothes straight, laughing and smiling at one another, pretending to pay exaggerated attention to the sermon while their eyes and faces were bright with the joke. The Pope was amused by this act of revolt – after all it involved only young girls. But those were days of rigid formality, and Burchard said that the incident occurred 'magno dedecore, ignominia et scandalo nostri et populi'.[1] When wild-eyed Sancha came to stir up still more the already troubled waters of the Vatican, Burchard did not know where to turn. It was only too obvious that the idea of usurping the sacred

---

[1] 'With great impropriety and to the disgrace and scandal of ourselves and of the people.'

seats was Sancha's, and that Lucrezia imitated her and behaved like a child invited to play and very ready to do so, but who, left to herself, would never have taken the first step because of her timidity and respect for ecclesiastical custom.

So Lucrezia and Sancha became friends. True, their relationship was governed and tempered by natural reserve, but there was never any misunderstanding, for they both, fortunately, grasped from the start the great difference between their two rôles. Thus Lucrezia's fears of rivalry subsided and she felt her enjoyment of Vatican festivities was heightened by the imperious authority of Sancha's character. At this time there was a whole succession of balls and concerts. In vain from his pulpit in San Marco in Florence did Savonarola hurl the warning of the prophet Amos against the Pope's women: 'Audite verbum hoc, vaccae pingues quae estis in monte Samariae;'[1] neither Alexander VI nor his family allowed his austere language to touch them: the great friar was powerless against the Borgia fortress and he was to perish in his attempt at an impossible reform. When we compare the fiery blast of Savonarola's eloquence with the life and character of the Pontiff we understand why no bridge could ever be built between the two parties and, as the greater power lay with the Pope, and as Savonarola would never agree to negotiation, we see why he was burned at the stake on May 25, 1498.

Members of the Borgia family continued to assemble round the head of the House and it was said in political circles that the Pope was gathering his relations around him so that he would not be cut off from them if the French again invaded Italy, as they had threatened. Rumour was confirmed when the Pope recalled the Duke of Gandia from Spain in the summer of 1496.

It is not easy to define Alexander VI's character as a politician. Even if we say that, like all men, he had many distinct

---

[1] 'Hear this word, ye kine of Basham, that are in the mountain of Samaria.' (Amos, iv, 1.)

personalities, we cast no light on the real motive that set the multiple forces of his spirit in motion – forces so active that, as contemporaries said: 'The Pope has ten souls'. The French invasion had taught Alexander VI that trusty allies were hard to come by. Hence the idea of founding a powerful Borgia dynasty adequate for defence on a wide front had a logic of its own, and shows that his nepotism was not caused solely by immoderate affection. Recalling the disaster that had occurred when the House of Orsini went over to the French, the Pope decided to give that family a lesson – which would also be the first episode in a large-scale project for liquidating the Roman barons whose turbulence was a constant threat to the State. The Duke of Gandia was recalled to Italy with the enterprise against the Orsini in mind.

Alexander VI had no illusions about Juan's moral qualities and, as we have seen, could lecture him severely. Yet he thought that magnificence and ribaldry were the excesses of a robust temperament and should be tolerated in a young military man, granted that the rights of the family were safeguarded. The Pope took an extremely optimistic view of Juan's valour and military capacity and indeed it was for the sake of these that he had recalled him at the time of the French invasion in 1494 and 1495 (a summons Juan had not obeyed) – as if the Duke of Gandia's mere presence in the camp would win the day. After the departure of the King of France the Pope's summons became so imperious that Juan felt it only proper to take ship. He left the Duchess Maria Henriques, who was again pregnant, and his little son Juan II in the castle of Gandia, and set sail for Italy, the land of all adventure, at the end of June 1496.

Juan Borgia entered Rome from Civitavecchia on August 10, the feast of St Laurence. The Cardinals' households turned out to meet him with the usual ceremonial; Cesare met his brother at Porta Portuense and accompanied him with all honours to the Apostolic Palace where the Duke was to reside. The Borgias were pastmasters at organizing solemn entries and on this occasion the pomp of the Papal retinue vied with the even greater display of luxury on the part of the Duke. Juan was mounted on a bay horse that had 'golden ornaments and little silver bells' – as the humanist Bernardino Corso tells us in a bad sonnet: he wore a red velvet cap adorned with pearls, a waistcoat of brown velvet with sleeves and front embroidered with pearls and gems, and even the Roman public, accustomed as it was to luxury, was amazed.

The intended liquidator of the Orsini was accorded his fill of triumphs in advance, while the Pope was busy building up army and artillery for him. Duke Guidobaldo of Urbino was made lieutenant of the forces, a man expert in the arts of war and without any ambitions that would clash with the aims of the Borgias: moreover his name was a guarantee of seriousness. By October 1496 all was ready and the Duke of Gandia, now Captain-General of the Church, took the field, girt with a jewelled sword, with standards bearing the arms of the Church and those of the Pope, and with the white stick of office. With the high disdain of a great commander he sent out his first dispatches, and it so happened, either by chance or because of deliberate tactics on the part of the enemy, that the news at first was good. Ten castles fell to the Papal troops with very little resistance and spirits were high. But when the army came within sight of Bracciano it stopped.

The defence of the powerful castle at Bracciano was in the hands of a warlike woman, one of a number who flourished in the Italian Renaissance. She was Bartolommea Orsini, the sister of the great Virginio. She was assisted by her husband, Bartolommeo Alviano, the ugliest, most misshapen and bravest man in Italy. From the tall battlements the French flag streamed in the wind in defiance of the Pope. Juan Borgia examined the pentagon of towers from afar. They were a monument of human pride and he must have reflected how uncomfortable it would be to camp in the rain without golden finery on his clothes or gaily plumed caps. He sighed impatiently and set about making absurd or childish plans of campaign and drew up edicts urging the enemy ranks to desert or betray their leaders. Besieged though they were these veterans laughed at such ingenuous methods. The echo of their mocking laughter was heard throughout Italy and though this did not worry Juan, it made the Pope tremble with bellicose feelings and shower messages on his lazy troops. Finally the Papal army moved on to attack Trevignano to the north of Bracciano. But when they had taken the castle there, the Duke of Urbino's mercenaries fought Juan's so fiercely over the booty that they had to be separated by force. Meanwhile an army mustered with French money and commanded by Giulio and Carlo Orsini attacked the Papal forces and a battle was fought in which the Duke of Urbino acquitted himself with characteristic loyalty until he was taken prisoner. The Duke of Gandia was slightly wounded and used this as an excuse to announce that he could not carry on, and he had himself removed to safety. Bereft of its leaders the Papal forces withdrew while the enemy quickly relieved the besieged.

When news of these events reached Rome, the Pope was moved to transports of fury; he raged, he denounced, and he declared that he would throw even his tiara into the war. But on reflection he realized that the moment was not opportune for challenging the course of events and that the best plan would be to agree to peace and accept what the Orsini offered – namely Cervatelli and Anguillara and 50,000 golden ducats. He pretended to forget the Duke of Urbino and left him a prisoner in the castle of Soriano where the Duke proudly and patiently waited for his family to pay his ransom.

Though in Rome ironical posters appeared urging anyone who had any information concerning a certain army of the Church to impart the same to the Duke of Gandia, the Duke himself, without a care in the world, reverted to his programme of merry-making and love adventures. By good luck the end of the war had synchronized with the beginning of Carnival, so why waste such a favourable time for pleasure? It would have been a pity, too, to fail to notice the bold and laughing eyes of Sancha of Aragon, which were just the thing to encourage an unscrupulous man to try to make a conquest. It is not clear what really happened between the in-laws. Possibly Sancha had grown tired of having the Cardinal of Valencia as lord and master, or she may have been prompted by her love of playing with fire, or she may have thought it a good revenge on a father-in-law, who had only wished to have her as daughter-in-law in part, to make herself his daughter-in-law three times over. Whatever her motive may have been, she certainly seems to have responded to Juan's advances. Meanwhile the Pope was so infatuated with his son that he did not even blame him for the recent and ruinous defeat; it was an unfortunate business, of course, but Juan would soon make ample amends.

Thus, if Cesare had hoped that the humiliating campaign would make Juan smaller in their father's eyes, he must soon have seen his mistake. Cesare, it is true, was receiving more appreciation and affection than before, but Juan remained 'the beloved', the one expected to make the Borgia name resound with military glory in future ages. And if Juan's passion, or rather whim, for Sancha was a fact, we can see why Cesare's proud heart should harden with his intention of making himself felt somehow, anyhow, even by the use of force. In the year 1497 many tragic events were brewing in the Pontifical Court.

From May to December 1496 the Pope made repeated efforts to persuade Giovanni Sforza to return to Santa Maria in Portico. Though he failed he still considered Sforza to be in his service, for his allowance was paid, and in November 1496 the Pope asked him to put his troops in contact with those of the Duke of Gandia then operating against the Orsini. Giovanni Sforza had recourse to his well-tried principle: he gathered together a few soldiers but instead of stirring from Pesaro he sent a chancellor, Geromino, to the Pope to explain the reasons for his immobility. Alexander VI played up to this; he accepted the excuses and explanations and, on December 30, 1496, he answered that he had given the matter his full consideration and quite understood. This letter is a clear indication that his main concern was that his son-in-law should come back, and he obviously hoped to disarm him by benevolence. When the moment seemed ripe – on January 5, 1497 – he sent him a brief intimating that he should present himself in Rome within fifteen days. Giovanni Sforza was in a tight corner, as he wrote on January 15 to the Duke of Urbino, and was afraid that he would 'cause His Beatitude greater indignation'. So at last he set out.

When he reached Rome great efforts were made to make him welcome, and the Pope and the Borgia brothers outdid themselves 'in demonstrations of kindness and in endearments'. As one of the correspondents expressed it, Lucrezia herself was now 'very happy and quite crazy about him'. I am sure that the word 'crazy' is exaggerated, but she must have behaved as a 'most worthy Madama' – for it is thus that the contemporary records least well-disposed towards the Borgias describe her. She must have rejoiced in her husband's return for it restored her to the rank that was her due, and at parties and ceremonies her husband was placed almost as high as Juan and Cesare. Giovanni Sforza was seen at Papal functions, as for instance on the feast of the Purification (February 2) and he participated in ceremonial cortèges such as the one organized for the official reception in Rome of Consalvo de Cordova. On March 22 he was amongst those who received the blessed palm from the steps of the Papal throne, being placed immediately behind the Duke of Gandia. If he was keeping his eyes open, the peaceful atmosphere must have given him food for thought – and he had every reason to be on the watch and distrustful, given the developments in the political situation. The power of the Sforzas in Rome was now definitely waning, for the Pope could not forgive them for the alliance they had made with the French and the separate peace that followed it. And though Cardinal Ascanio fought in public and private to conciliate the Pope and was even sometimes deluded into thinking that he had won back his position as Vice-Pope, it became increasingly plain that the interests of Borgias and Sforzas were divergent and incompatible.

On the morning of Good Friday the Count of Pesaro rose at

dawn and went to call on his wife. In the course of their short conversation he told her that he planned to go to confession at San Crisostomo in Trastevere or at Sant' Onofrio on the Janiculum, and then make a pilgrimage round the seven churches in honour of the solemnity of the day. Instead of doing so, however, he mounted on horseback, headed for the Roman campagna with a small escort, crossed the Apennines and arrived home at Pesaro in a state of terror and – to use his own words: 'worn out by an early start'. In a word, he had fled. Gossip immediately seized on the idea of poison. Poison was rumoured to have been concealed in some presents he had received, and these suspicions are borne out by what we find in the chronicles of Pesaro in which both Bernardo Monaldi and Pietro Marzetta refer to a Borgia plan to remove Giovanni Sforza. Monaldi, who is quoted by all Lucrezia's biographers, tells the story of how a certain Giacomino, a retainer of Giovanni Sforza's, was in Lucrezia's room when she told him to hide behind a chair so as to overhear a conversation between herself and Cesare, a conversation which left no doubt that the Borgias had decided to murder Giovanni; and as soon as Cesare had departed Lucrezia instructed Giacomino to report the whole affair to his master. The story sounds specious and theatrical, but we cannot reject it on those grounds, for all kinds of theatrical things have occurred in history. There is another difficulty, however. Lucrezia saw her husband at all times of the day and he visited her just before his flight, so what earthly reason had she for using this complicated way of warning him that his life was in danger? Courage was not the Count of Pesaro's strong suit and he hardly needed to be pressed to run away. The story of the other chronicler is less dramatic. He says that the Pope had made up his mind either to withdraw Lucrezia from the Count of Pesaro or else kill him, 'but he, having heard this from his wife, returned here on horseback'. The importance of the two chroniclers lies in their agreement that it was through Lucrezia that Giovanni heard of the Borgia conspiracy, and this shows that both chroniclers – writing some years after the events described and after weighing up the evidence – retained their conviction that Lucrezia was innocent in the affair and even took her husband's side. 'Regarding the suspicion of poison I have found no other basis for it and do not think it is true,' wrote Archdeacon Gian Lucido Cattanei, one of our most reliable informants, some days after the Count's flight. The incident turned the whole Roman court upside down and it looked as though it were going to cause a lot of unforeseen developments. Observers followed the manoeuvres of the Pope's attack and of the Count's defence and the ablest were convinced that Giovanni Sforza would never again return to Rome. But if we set aside the question of poison, what was the real reason for the Count's sudden departure?

On Holy Saturday Sforza's secretaries, who had stayed behind in Rome, paid an official call on the Milanese ambassador, Stefano Taverna, and informed him of their master's departure which they explained in general terms of his 'dissatisfaction' with his father-in-law. On the same day, when Taverna wrote his account of the conversation to the Duke of Milan, he added that, speaking for himself, he had the impression that something more serious lay beneath this explanation, something to do with 'his wife's lack of modesty' which had already put the Count of Pesaro into 'a state of grave discontent . . .' He ended up with yet a further piece of news. On his departure the Count had left a letter to Lucrezia strongly urging her to join him in Pesaro in Easter week.

Once home in Pesaro Giovanni Sforza felt restless and lonely in the very palace that the little Countess had enlivened with her presence only two years earlier when there had been no shadow in her life. He expected her, for he wanted to believe that she would come. When Ludovico the Moor wrote asking for further explanations of his flight from Rome, he answered that he would send them shortly by confidential messenger, but not before he had had an answer from Rome – by which he meant Lucrezia's answer. It was indeed very unbalanced of him to put his trust in

such an improbability as Lucrezia's arrival, for it was unthinkable that the Pope would allow his daughter to follow her
husband and leave him alone and outraged in the Vatican.
Instead of Lucrezia, there arrived on April 1 Messer Lelio
Capodiferro bearing a measured but firm Papal brief dated
March 30. 'Your wisdom can tell you how deeply we are stricken
by your unexpected departure from the City,' it read, 'and since
in our opinion there is no other reparation for a deed of this
nature, we appeal with all our strength to your noble feelings,
and if you are anxious to safeguard your honour, to make ready
to return immediately.' Sforza felt that there was safety in
distance and answered brusquely that his wife should be sent to
him. The Pope informed him perfectly calmly that he had no
hope of ever seeing his wife again unless he returned to Rome,
and warned him not to attempt resistance as he had reached an
understanding with both Cardinal Ascanio Sforza and Ludovico
the Moor.

The Count of Pesaro had also been sending letter after letter
to Duke Ludovico of Milan and to Cardinal Sforza, fully
confident that they would help him, for he failed to realize that
the exigencies of politics would oblige his relations to act
unjustly. The Sforzas found the situation thoroughly embarrass-
ing and fell back on verbal assurances to hide their desire and
determination to remain as neutral as possible, and to gain time
they both continually asked for still further explanations about
their cousin's mysterious departure – on which point the Count
of Pesaro remained persistently silent. But on May 12 he wrote to
Duke Ludovico saying that when Ascanio came on pilgrimage to
Loreto, as he had promised to do, he would confide the whole
matter to him; 'and I do this in spite of my unwillingness to make
this matter public'. What was there about this 'matter' that made
it so very private? His reticence and obstinate silence suggest that
he had already arrived at certain appalling convictions but
feared the consequences if he breathed a word about them.
Possibly this links up with what Taverna said about his wife's

'lack of modesty' and we should also refer back to the hints made by Scalona in May 1496.

Meanwhile Alexander VI, seeing the uselessness of his appeals and orders, sent Fra Mariano da Genazzano to Pesaro to resolve the situation once and for all. Fra Mariano, who was General of the Augustinians and Savonarola's great enemy, was an eloquent and moving preacher, too much a lawyer to be a good churchman, and the very man needed in this case. As soon as he set eyes on this new ambassador, Giovanni Sforza guessed what the Pope's latest idea was – namely, the annulment of his marriage with Lucrezia. To make things easier the Pope pointed out to Sforza that he had two alternatives: one was to declare that he had never consummated his marriage, the other to maintain that the marriage was invalid because Lucrezia had never been formally released from her earlier matrimonial contract with Gaspere da Procida. The Pope's aim, as he declared to Ascanio Sforza, was that 'the aforesaid gentleman should in no manner rejoin the aforesaid Madonna Lucrezia whom he wished to send to Spain'.

While Giovanni Sforza was listening to the words of his sentence, Lucrezia suddenly realized the cruelty of what was being done. We do not know what she thought or planned or whether she envisaged rejoining her husband or acting as intermediary between him and her father and brothers. Perhaps she came to the conclusion that the lesser of two evils for herself and her husband would be to agree to the divorce. She must have given her consent, for on May 26 the Pope signed the briefs and dispatched Fra Mariano to Pesaro to suggest the annulment; yet she unquestionably went through a crisis, for on June 6 she rode out unexpectedly with her women in the direction of the Circus Maximus and towards a convent of Dominican nuns – it still exists – whose air of repose was a refuge for young noble-women wishing to renounce the pomp of the world. If the young women were delicate they ran the risk of renouncing life itself, for in those days this part of Rome was extremely malarial, but the fear of death does not seem to have weighed on the nuns.

The inhabitants of San Sisto were serene and, better still, convinced that it was their duty to be serene, and with the help of work, music, meditation and prayer they achieved that spiritual order that women can find in a convent. San Sisto was one of the rare communities of women organized on a strictly hierarchical pattern. As the prioress was to point out later, the arrival of Lucrezia and her court upset the quiet daily routine and introduced worldly passions and thoughts. But it was impossible to bar the door to the Pope's daughter.

And so it was bruited around that Lucrezia wanted to become a nun. People said that she had entered the convent without telling her father – 'insalutato hospite', as Donato Aretino put it. But Alexander VI told Ascanio Sforza, when asked for an explanation, that he himself had sent his daughter to San Sisto 'because it was a religious and very proper place', and he wanted her to stay there until her husband had made up his mind. If this is true, why, on June 12, did he send a troop of men-at-arms and the sheriff to remove her from the convent? 'The Pope sent the sheriff for her so as to have her himself', Cattanei tells us. The hearts of Sister Serafina, Sister Paulina, Sister Cherubina and Sister Speranza must have beaten faster when they heard the noise of arms, but the prioress of that year, Sister Girolama Pichi, was a practical and courageous woman and it was she who spoke with the soldiers. We have no idea what she said or did to get round the Pope's command; all we know is that Lucrezia remained in the convent.

A life of prayer helped her to forget her tensions and struggles with the hot-blooded men among whom fate had placed her. Possibly the calm of her place of exile encouraged her to hope that she might be forgotten. But while she was inside the convent walls, the secrets of her life were the chief subject of diplomatic correspondence and busied the minds of courtiers.

4

MYSTERIES AND CRIMES

Fra Mariano da Genazzano had a long and arduous task arguing with Giovanni Sforza so as to prepare him for the dissolution of his marriage. The Count of Pesaro stuck desperately to his guns, but the friar's icy dialectic frightened and irritated him and he lost ground step by step. Finally he asked for a week's grace to think things over and rode off to Milan to ask Duke Ludovico's advice.

It must have been at this time that Lucrezia addressed to the Pope her appeal for a divorce drawn up in accordance with a decree of Gregory IX who laid down that a woman could appeal for a divorce after the lapse of three years if the marriage had never been consummated. Lucrezia's appeal was written in Latin and all we know of it are the few phrases quoted by the interested parties: but those phrases are enough. It said that she had been 'in eius (that is Giovanni's) familia per triennium et ultra translata absque alia sexus permixtione steterat nulla nuptiali commixtione, nullave copula carnali conjunxione subsecuta, et quod erat parata jurare et indicio obstetricum se subiicere.'[1] Lucrezia signed the painful declaration with her own hand. It is tempting to think that she signed it so as to be left in peace.

In the Vatican Cardinal Ascanio Sforza was bombarded with protests and recriminations against his kinsman, not only by the Pope who swore that he was prepared to suffer 'the very worst' rather than restore Lucrezia to Giovanni, but also by the Duke

[1] She had been 'transferred to his (Giovanni's) family for over three years and was still without any sexual relation and without nuptial intercourse and carnal knowledge, and that she was prepared to swear and submit herself to the examination of midwives'.

of Gandia and the Cardinal of Valencia who both 'indulged in the severest words, maintaining that they would never consent to their sister being restored to the hands of the Lord of Pesaro'. Ascanio Sforza endured it all with the cold patience of a politician who has decided that endurance is the best policy. In any case both he and Ludovico the Moor had already abandoned their provincial cousin, sacrificing him to their need to be on good terms with the Pope. They made a pretence of supporting his arguments, but this was principally so as to impress on the Borgias that other people had wills too.

At this time Alexander VI was in a very strong position and was pursuing with his usual energy the dreams of glory he had in mind for his son Juan. In a Consistory held on June 7 he announced that he intended to hand over the city of Benevento and the fortresses appertaining to it to his son as a domain for himself and his descendants. All the Cardinals except Piccolomini agreed for they knew how useless it would be to do otherwise. But the Spanish ambassador was not of the same mind. A prey to religious scruples, he pathetically threw himself at the Pope's feet and implored him not to alienate Church property, and though Alexander VI's face darkened he was condescending enough to explain benignly that the domain involved was not large and that the self-same land had already been sold once into private hands in the reign of Nicholas V. When the ambassador insisted that the donation would set a 'bad example,' the Pope flared up and said 'Get to your feet', and adjourned the discussion until the insolent Spaniard, who had dared to champion ecclesiastical affairs against the Head of the Church, had departed.

As the Pope's favouritism for Juan had no limits it was only to be expected that the political parties should attempt to make use of the young Duke, and the enterprising Cardinal Ascanio was the first in the field. It would be a wonderful *coup* for the Milanese if they could win Juan over to their side and one not to be missed. If Cardinal Sforza's efforts were unrewarded it was not for any lack of ability on his part nor as a result of any direct resistance on Juan's, but because the Duke's behaviour was so coarse and infantile that no reasonable man could possibly have been expected to foresee what he would do. Whereas Cardinal Ascanio spoke the political language of adult people, the Duke of Gandia knew only a language of egotism and vanity without a single ray of intelligence. What happened between the two is well illustrated by an episode in the Vice-Chancellor's Palace in early June 1497.

One evening Cardinal Sforza held a great reception to which he invited many guests of high standing including the Duke of Gandia. As he had a ready tongue and was convinced that he himself was immune, Juan began to make fun of the other guests and even went so far as to call them 'lounging gluttons'. One of the guests so abused answered with a brief reference to the Duke's bastard origin. Juan immediately leapt to his feet, but, instead of beginning to fight as everyone expected, he walked straight out and went to see his father. Alexander VI dealt with the affair in a stern and terrifying manner. Regardless of Cardinal Ascanio's immunity, he dispatched a band of soldiers to break into the palace and seize the luckless guest who was hanged forthwith.

This primitive spirit of revenge and purely instinctive reaction cannot be easily explained in Alexander VI, whose tolerance of the current gossips and libels about him was proverbial. Rome is the land of the free, he used to say. But when the Duke of Gandia was insulted through himself, the Pope's pride and paternal love must have undergone intolerable humiliation which could be offset only by a devastating display of supremacy. After this exhibition of strength Juan's high spirits returned and he became intoxicated with his own importance, blindly involving himself in endless love-intrigues despite his father's recommendations of caution. Quite apart from his friendship with Sancha, there was a rumour that he had fallen in love with the daughter of Count Antonio Maria della Mirandola, a noble and lovely girl from Ferrara, and that he was out to win her by fair means or foul. We do not know whether he succeeded: the girl was well guarded. Yet it seems significant that a gentleman called Jaches in the household of Cardinal Sforza, to whom she had been offered in marriage with a large dowry, refused to marry her although he was in love with her.

Juan's round of gaiety and love adventures went on until June 14. By then Lucrezia had been in San Sisto for a week. One evening Vannozza Cattanei gave a large party for her sons. We know about this particular party because of the events that followed it, but presumably it was not an exception; Vannozza must have gathered her children round her table often enough. As summer was beginning Vannozza did not prepare the banquet in her Roman palace but in a vineyard she owned between the churches of San Martino ai Monti and Santa Lucia in Selce, and she invited Cesare, Juan, Cardinal Borgia of Monreale, and a few close relations. There were still traces of commanding beauty in Vannozza's face, and the supper party must have been very enjoyable. Cesare was dressed as a layman and displayed his usual velvety manners. The Duke of Gandia, with his boasting and bravado to which his courtiers and household played up, was the hero of the evening; until suddenly, at his side, there appeared a masked man. Nobody seemed to take this new arrival seriously – the guests went on with their tales of love affairs which, like all such stories, were secret. It was late when the supper party broke up and the guests took their leave of Vannozza and set off home. They left in groups, each with its little suite, making towards the Vatican. Near Cardinal Sforza's palace in the Ponte district the Duke of Gandia stopped and, taking a groom with him, and accompanied by the masked man, made off into the night to some tryst, heedless of the advice of the others to take armed men with him. The echo of the young man's laughter was the last thing his relations and household heard of him. In Piazza degli Ebrei he stopped his groom and instructed him that if no one turned up within an hour he was to return home. Rome lay dark and deserted; all the houses were bolted and silent. The dense shadows were broken here and there by a lantern which threw out a yellow circle of light, almost more frightening than the darkness. The groom waiting in the deserted little piazza cannot have felt at all comfortable for no one who wandered around at night alone was safe. The Duke of Gandia had disappeared into the darkness to meet the summons of death.

Dawn brought another day. The Pope's mind was taken up with thoughts of the new royal coronation in Naples caused by the untimely death of King Ferrandino (who was said to have died on account of his excessive love for his wife and aunt, Giovanna of Aragon). The morning hours passed in routine business and the Duke of Gandia made no appearance. As the day wore on and his Spaniards told him of Juan's absence, the Pontiff became slightly uneasy but consoled himself with the thought that this was not the first time Juan had woken up in broad daylight in the house of some well-known professional beauty and stayed on there till nightfall so as not to be seen leaving – a precaution that the Pope was the first to approve. But the Pope found the bright June day long and tedious, and by evening when darkness fell he began to be seriously worried. The Spaniards patrolled the streets with drawn swords, but this served only to terrify the citizens and bring the Orsini and the Colonna clans, who were always ready to take advantage of any disorder, out of their strongholds. A search began. The first discovery was that of the groom who was mortally wounded and unable to speak. This was proof positive that the Duke of Gandia was dead. The search went on, the city was turned upside down, and at last a Dalmatian boatman spoke up. His name was Giorgio and he spent his nights on a boat tied up amongst the reeds of the Tiber so as to guard a woodpile that stood more or less on the site of the church of San Gerolamo degli Schiavoni by the Ripetta bridge. On the night between June 14 and June 15, he said, he had seen two people cautiously approaching to explore the road and area round the Schiavoni hospital; they had disappeared and reappeared and repeated their examination inch by inch. Then, after a while, he saw a man approach mounted on a white horse and bearing a body across the saddle behind him, held in place by two grooms, one on either side. The horseman advanced nervously to the river, turned his horse and gave an order – whereupon the grooms with a certain bravado slipped the body from the crupper and cast it into the water. The boatman had heard the 'plop' and then the distinct voice of the horseman who asked whether they had thrown it in properly. 'Yes, my Lord,' they answered. The horseman then turned, glanced down at the river slowly flowing beneath him, and distinguished something in the water: it was the dead man's cloak swollen with air like a funeral sail hoisted to waft the corpse to the shores of Acheron. He ordered this trace to be eliminated and watched while his men threw stones at the target. When everything was under water the men disappeared and the night was quiet once more. When the Dalmatian boatman was asked why he had not made an immediate statement, he said that he hadn't given the matter a thought: from his boat he had seen at least a hundred bodies thrown into the river and no one had made a fuss about them. Even if we allow for the element of bravado that we would expect to find in a man who was being listened to for the first time in his life, we cannot help feeling that his little boat was a terrifying observation point.

The Pope was now beside himself. Though everyone else took it for granted, he was unwilling to believe that Juan was dead and waited for more conclusive proof. The Tiber was dragged with a hundred nets and scrutinized by thousands of eyes, and that very evening it yielded up the corpse of the Duke of Gandia disfigured with wounds – one of which had cut his throat – and filthy with the mud and refuse that clung to it. It was carried to the Castel Sant' Angelo, undressed, washed and re-clothed in ducal robes, and by night it was conveyed by a disordered and tragic crowd composed of the Duke's household, priests, noblemen and Spaniards, to be interred at Santa Maria del Popolo. The fantastic cortège hurried out of the Castel Sant' Angelo in the light of a hundred and twenty flares, and witnesses inform us that above the moans and prayers of the crowd, the Pope's cry was heard from the dark windows of the castle, calling for his lost son. At Santa Maria del Popolo the body was possibly laid in a chapel on the right of the transept where the first Duke of Gandia, Pedro Luis, already reposed. In the reign of Julius II both were transferred to their final resting place at Gandia.

The Pope behaved as if he had been in the torture chamber. For two days and nights he neither ate nor drank nor slept, but lived in lonely communion with his grief, and moaned from the very depths of his being. But such an acute state of sorrow had to have a reaction and when this came it was the thirst for justice that prevailed. The Pontifical Palace immediately began an investigation. The first suspect – one that was pleasing to the Pope – was Cardinal Ascanio Sforza, and as the body had been found in the neighbourhood of a country house belonging to the Sforzas a perquisition was made there. The Cardinal displayed much endurance and resourcefulness: he handed over to the inspectors the keys of all his palaces and praised the measures they were taking, whereupon he retired with all the dignity of his purple to the residence of the Milanese ambassador, Stefano Taverna. Not unnaturally Cardinal Ascanio was suspected of trying to avenge the hanging of his quick-tongued guest, but at this period the Sforzas had too many preoccupations to run the risks of private vengeance. The Duke of Gandia had many enemies – in fact he had nothing but enemies. The man who had planned the assassination knew this and had counted precisely on the multiplicity of likely-sounding suspects to cover his own tracks. Ascanio Sforza was soon exculpated. Indeed Alexander VI sent him an apology for the threats that had been made him by the Cardinal of Valencia and some of the Duke's henchmen, and explained that these were motivated by sorrow. Other suspects included Guidobaldo da Montefeltro, Giovanni Sforza and Giovanni's brother Gian Galeazzo – but they too were soon exculpated, as Alexander VI made clear in a public declaration before the consistory held on June 19. On that occasion tragedy nearly gave way to melodrama, for it was perhaps the first and only example in history of a Pope, in all his pontifical regalia, before an assembly of Cardinals and in the presence of

ambassadors, publicly weeping for the death of a son. 'A worse
blow,' he said in his grave and sonorous Spanish voice, 'could
not have been dealt us for we loved the Duke of Gandia above
all else in the world ... We would willingly give seven tiaras to
recall him to life ... God has punished us for our sins, because
the Duke of Gandia did not deserve such a terrible and
mysterious death ... The rumour has gone round that the
perpetrator was Giovanni Sforza, but we are convinced that he is
innocent, and even less guilty are Gian Galeazzo Sforza and the
Duke of Urbino ...' These phrases were followed by expressions of repentence and resolves to live a holy life in future. The
Pope announced that the whole Vatican would be reformed,
that the sacred offices would be carried out with scrupulous
attention, and that a rigid watch would be kept to see that
worldly interests did not cross the threshold of the apostolic
palace. 'Henceforward benefices will be conferred only on those
who merit them: we intend to renounce all nepotism and begin
our reforms in our own house.'

Alexander VI must have been touched on the raw to make
such a confession and to dismiss as negligible the things to which
he had held most strongly – his family and his tiara. But however
idiosyncratic his declaration, it must be recognized that the
Borgia Pope rose for a moment to the heights of a Church
reformer. He nominated a commission of ecclesiastics of
outstanding virtue, headed by Cardinal Costa, in order to study
details for a great reform. He received a letter of mixed
condolence and warning from Savonarola which was possibly
the only piece of writing by the Dominican that he ever read or
felt at all deeply. And meanwhile, as time passed and the
ordinary daily routine returned, the first spasms of anguish
diminished. The search for the perpetrators continued. The
mystery was profound, and hypotheses and conjectures were
formed only to be abandoned. The contemporary chroniclers lay
their wagers on the names of the Orsini and the Sforzas, and
even return to the accusation against Cardinal Ascanio – or they

hint darkly at some master plot involving risks for anybody who dared to speak up.

At this point we must ask the question well-known in logic: 'Cui prodest', who benefited by the murder? And there can be only one answer: Cesare Borgia. With his flair for estimating causes and effects with accuracy while feigning indifference to the affairs of government, Cesare had managed to win first the affection and then the confidence and esteem of his father. He had worked exceedingly hard for this and everyone had observed his progress. During the campaign against the Orsini when Cesare had gone hunting in the direction of Tre Fontane at the risk of falling in with wandering bands, one writer said that if he had been taken prisoner there would have been a new Pope in Rome – implying that Alexander VI would have died of grief. But Cesare knew his real situation too well to be deluded by hope; he knew that he could never have first place in his father's heart as long as the Duke of Gandia, who had been singled out by their father for a worldly career, still lived. If Cesare was esteemed and beloved, Juan was idolized. The Cardinal of Valencia could plan a triumphant future and work out his ideal form of government; but between him and his longings there was always the obstacle of a brother who, though with innate inefficiency, would prevent his conquests and ruin his plans. There was a logic, if a monstrous one, in Cesare's resolution to remove his brother from his path. The question is whether he did so or not.

'I have heard once more that the cause of the Duke of Gandia's death was the Cardinal, his brother ... and the aforesaid view of the aforesaid death I have had from an excellent source.' So Giovanni Alberto della Pigna wrote to the Duke of Ferrara from Venice on February 22, 1498. This document seems to take Cesare's guilt as certain, and certain it seemed so to public opinion and to contemporaries such as Sanudo and Giucciardini in the years that followed. But it is still an open question to historians. Villari, Gregorovius, Piccoti, Leonard and Gebhart all think that Cesare was unquestionably guilty; Woodward, Fester and Schintzer are doubtful, while Pastor, Luzio and Höfler reject the theory entirely. There are no certain proofs, say the latter, and this is true. But Cesare's burning ambition, his indifference to crime, his rancour at being in the second place, his contempt for his brother's cowardice, and his overpowering hunger for power, are pointers that seem to be as convincing as proofs. But it is above all the uncertainty and confusion of the various hypotheses, the complex chain of circumstances that no one has been able to unravel, which seem to me to reveal the hand of Cesare Borgia – the man who always made use of a thousand studied circumstances so as to turn a crime into a complete and convincing work of art in its own right. The culprit was never found because he could not be found; as the chroniclers put it, he was too much of a *maestro*. It is perhaps even more difficult to arrive at what the Pope thought about it all. On July 5, scarcely twenty days after the crime, he ordered the police investigation to stop, and this action gave ground for supposing that he knew perfectly well what had happened. The chroniclers say that this may have been a ruse; but might he not have already found out too much? Cesare exhibited all his skill in choosing the right moment. Early in June he had been nominated Cardinal Legate for the coronation of the new King of Naples (between 1494 and 1498 four successive kings had been crowned in Naples; the new King was the brother of Alfonso II, the Federico who had functioned at the marriage by proxy of Sancha of Aragon and Jofre Borgia). Cesare set out for Naples on June 22, and he may have calculated that by the time the clues pointed to him and the Pope had begun to suspect his guilt, he would not only be a long way away, but would be filling a position of such importance that to accuse him – should the Pope's anguish urge him to this extreme – would involve the dishonour of his family and the Church. By August 1 he had reached Capua and there fell ill of a fever. On August 7 Sancha and Jofre were dispatched from Rome to their principate at Squillace – evidence that the Pope was being true to his pledge and no longer wanted to be surrounded by children and relatives. We can well imagine that Alexander VI now found the sight of Sancha, who had made Juan fall in love with her and arouse Cesare's malignant jealousy, quite intolerable. His attitude to his children was now one of bitterness and disgust: he had loved them too much and they had betrayed him. So away with all the women. Lucrezia was included in the list and the old plan of marrying her off to some Spanish nobleman was revived. The only people allowed free entry into the Vatican were the prelates engaged in the new reforms.

> Away with musicians, actors and young people,
> Games and hunting parties are things of the past,
> The Pope will not alienate Church property,
> Singers must be decent.

The difficult points of the new order were drawn up slowly but surely, but by the end of August the Pope began to feel that the work in progress was less urgent than he had thought, and it was soft-pedalled. By September – only two months after he had written to the King of Spain saying he wanted to abdicate from the Papacy and shut himself up in a convent – the Pope had already put aside all idea of leading an austere life. The Duke of Gandia's murderer was sought only to keep up appearances. The Borgias picked up again.

As soon as he heard that the Pope was showing signs of worldliness, Cesare set out from Naples and returned to Rome. There was a gathering of Cardinals and Cardinals' households at the city gates to meet him with the honours due to a Papal legate of his standing. But when the cavalcade arrived at the apostolic palace a consistory was found to be in progress and the Pope would not allow the discussion – which was about an ordinary trial for insulting behaviour involving the Rector of the University and the Bishop of Vienne – to be interrupted. The Cardinal of Valencia was kept waiting half an hour in the ante-chamber. Observers also remarked the Pope's chilly greeting, a mere ritual kiss without a single word of welcome. What was the meaning of his attitude? But if some people entertained hopes that the Pope's nepotism was at an end, Cesare himself knew that the victory would be his, and very soon everyone knew it.

The death of the Duke of Gandia did nothing to revive Giovanni Sforza's hopes of getting back his wife. Though the Pope had acquitted him of the murder, no one came forward with better proposals concerning Giovanni than those already made, and five days after the assassination Alexander VI, still weeping for the loss of his son, summoned Cardinal Ascanio and recommended that he should act quickly in the matter of his kinsman in Pesaro and enable the divorce to go through immediately and without scandal. He reminded Cardinal Ascanio that agreement was preferable to the course of justice though even the latter could be speeded up. But these were empty threats. It was not for nothing that Giovanni was surrounded with learned jurists such as Niccolò da Saiano of the renowned University of Ferrara. As he was fully aware, unless he gave his consent to the divorce it could never be pronounced legally, and if it were effected by force with recourse to an arbitrary sentence, it would dishonour Lucrezia. It was with this knowledge, yet driven desperate by the difficulties of struggling against an enemy too strong for him, that Sforza had gone in disguise and incognito to Milan. Ludovico the Moor was no fool and knew that the Pope was not short of spies, so he insisted on his kinsman making a public appearance with all the insignia of his rank so that his visit should be given an official character. In the days after Giovanni's arrival it became increasingly clear that Ludovico the Moor intended to make as little as possible of his kinsman's unfortunate adventure so as not to give the Pope a handle for coming out against the House of Sforza; for this would benefit the French, who were now determined to make good the claim they had inherited to the Duchy of Milan. So Ludovico's first thought was to tell as many people as possible, including diplomats and ambassadors, that Giovanni had not come to Milan for political reasons but merely to seek advice and help about his marriage.

Once he had made up his mind to look on the whole affair as a joke, the Duke of Milan began to enjoy it thoroughly, showing an amused curiosity which he tried to pass off as interest and concern. He asked his cousin how much truth there was in the Pope's statement about his failure to consummate the marriage, whereupon the Lord of Pesaro answered with the coarse boast that his marriage had been consummated over a thousand times, and then, at the end of his tether and his self-control, he blurted out his conviction that the Pope was taking Lucrezia back because he wanted her for himself. This, obviously, was the dreadful and unspeakable thing that Giovanni had hinted at in his letters and had not dared to name. Once it had been said, and by someone who had lived in intimate Vatican circles and had every reason to be privy to its secrets, how could it be refuted? Duke Ludovico seems to have felt this bald statement to be enough; he asked for no more details, possibly on grounds of prudence. He made no outward sign. But as he felt bound to suggest something, he made a proposal to his cousin that was at once practical and ridiculous. It was that Lucrezia should be got to go to the estate of Cardinal Ascanio at Nepi where Giovanni should join her with an escort of guards of the Sforza allegiance. If this could be managed, Giovanni and Lucrezia could have a demonstrative honeymoon on neutral territory under the observing eye of both Borgia and Sforza forces. Giovanni refused, but whether he did so because he feared that the test might prove fatal to a man of his nervous temperament, or whether he was afraid of being stabbed or poisoned, we do not know. Then Ludovico produced a second suggestion, which was that Giovanni should make some 'try-outs with women' in Milan itself in the presence of the Cardinal Legate, Giovanni Borgia. But the Count of Pesaro declined this too. If he felt nauseated we cannot help agreeing that he had some justification. Finally Ludovico asked him how on earth the Pope could accuse him of impotence when, as was well known, his first wife, Maddalena Gonzaga, had died in childbirth. 'But only consider,' answered the Count of Pesaro, 'they say that I had her made pregnant by someone else.' The discussion was as coarse and comic as a scene in *Mandragola* or *Calandria*. Ludovico's humour was remorseless. He showed how little he really cared for his provincial cousin when he told Antonio Costabili, the Ferrarese ambassador in Milan, about his proposals and Giovanni's answers, and added that, in his opinion, if Giovanni were given two twists of the rope he would confess 'that he had never had intercourse' either with his first wife or with Lucrezia; 'for if he were not impotent he would have given some proof to rebut this accusation'. He said furthermore that were the young fellow 'not afraid of being made to hand back the dowry, he would not make any great difficulty about agreeing to the divorce'.

All this may well have been untrue, for Ludovico was at pains to show even in his private relationships that he was on the Pope's side. And the gift of Lucrezia's dowry was a very small indemnity in view of the insults Giovanni Sforza had received from the Pontiff. He had one consolation for his wounded pride: the relations of his first wife, the Gonzagas, chose this moment to offer him a fresh marriage into their family 'with which he (i.e. Giovanni) will have every reason to be content'. Giovanni answered with profuse expressions of thanks and put off the discussion until after the dissolution of what he called his 'Papal marriage' from which he hoped shortly to 'emerge in a way that would not soil himself or others'. In the meantime he begged the Gonzagas of Mantua to keep their intentions very secret because, as they knew, he was dealing with people who oscillated 'between violence and poison'. When Giovanni returned home to Pesaro he felt more insecure than ever as a result of the galling disappointment of his useless visit to Duke Ludovico. But on one point he took a firm stand: he refused to agree to the divorce.

As he wrote to Cardinal Ascanio: 'I do not want to agree to this dissolution for no man, under God, could do so; and even were I to give my consent it would be invalid owing to the things that have passed between me and the said Madonna Lucrezia, as I explained at greater length to his Excellency the Most Illustrious Lord Duke (of Milan) – things that I do not care to repeat here (and that) I shall not repeat at all unless I am obliged to . . .' 'But,' he went on more energetically, 'if our Lord (the Pope) intends to employ force and not justice, as he seems to be trying to do, I would prefer to lose my estate and life itself rather than my honour, and I would say without respect for persons, though unwillingly, *all that on one occasion I said to his Excellency the said Lord Duke which is truth itself*, so that it should be plain to every man that justice is on my side.'

Sforza was here alluding yet again to the accusation that he had involuntarily uttered in Milan and it is plain that he genuinely believed it. Historians of the Borgias who reject the abominable suspicion view Giovanni Sforza's words as a wild piece of calumny invented when he was in a fury and wanted to avenge himself on the Borgias. But they do not seem to have paid sufficient attention to Sforza's behaviour as a whole, including the mystery of his reticence in the first place down to his confession in Milan and his continual references afterwards – all of which points to the fact of his nursing a deadly certainty. Now what were his grounds for certainty?

Alexander was a man of instinct who expressed his paternal love too ardently. His love was not limited by any kind of spiritual interposition: he seemed to be moved only by the physical images of his children – their appearance, their behaviour, their voices, their personalities. His delirium about the Duke of Gandia recalls the blindness of a lover and the same thing occurred again in the case of Cesare. His feelings for Lucrezia had the additional tenderness that sensitive fathers are bound to experience when they compare their daughters with their hardy male offspring. If all this is so, the Pope's love for his daughter must have made a cold man such as the Count of Pesaro feel quite dizzy. Or was he in the possession of certain knowledge – something more than mere hints and suspicions: had he seen an unmistakable gleam in the eyes of his father-in-law? But the fact that, while maintaining his accusations against the Pope, Giovanni went on desperately trying to get his wife back, implies that he had reasons for thinking she was innocent, either because nothing had actually happened between father and daughter or, in the worst hypothesis, because she had consented when out of her mind. In that event everything – the conscious act, the desire, the responsibility and the infamy – was to be laid at the door of the other party.

Alexander adopted an attitude of complete innocence. He kept imploring the Sforzas of Milan to help him to deal with their kinsman, and wrote to them discussing the whole question, twisting and turning between rules, legal arguments, excuses and evasions (he went so far as to pretend that it was possible to ascribe Giovanni's physical deficiency to a 'particular malpractice', with a deftness and facility that would have queered the pitch of people cleverer than the Sforzas). In the end Giovanni yielded on the question of the validity of the earlier marriage contract between Lucrezia and Don Gaspere D'Aversa, and the whole Vatican heaved a sigh of relief. Once assent on this point had been obtained everything else followed as a matter of course and there was no escaping a total surrender.

The formal divorce proceedings were judged by Cardinal Alessandrino Giovanni Antonio San Giorgio, Cardinal of Santa Prassede, Antognotto Pallavicino, and the auditor of the Rota who was a Ferrarese humanist, Felino San Dio. As soon as he received Giovanni's answer the Pope summoned Cardinal Alessandrino and, in the presence of Ascanio Sforza who was one of the shrewdest and most distinguished canonists in the Vatican, handed it over to him. The Cardinal read it and shook his head. The proposals contained in Giovanni's declaration, he said, were 'neither just nor honest nor in accord with the terms of the law'. The marriage could be dissolved in only two ways, either by a sentence delivered by the Cardinals on the Commission or else, if both parties were in agreement, by means of a Papal Bull. Alexander VI sighed and said that such words were offensive to his delicacy and then held forth at length about his honour and that of his daughter, about how the divorce must be so contrived as to leave no blot on the Borgia name. For the love that he bore the Duke of Milan and Cardinal Ascanio, he urged them patiently to return to the question of which of the two alternatives his son-in-law would select. And, as Cardinal Sforza reported in a letter to Giovanni, 'to extend his supreme clemency and to demonstrate the high esteem and goodwill he feels for our House, he (the Pope) was pleased to make over to your Lordship (Giovanni) the payment of the whole dowry and to make it a gift'. Should he refuse, this great clemency would turn into severity. Nothing more was to be heard of the pre-existing promise of marriage between Lucrezia and Don Gaspere D'Aversa as motive for the divorce: it was better left unmentioned now that Cardinal Alessandrino had condemned it as unjust and dishonest.

Giovanni Sforza opted for the course that was least hard on him, namely procedure by sentence which dispensed him from confessing to conjugal unfulfilment. At this point the Pope began to register surprise and displeasure at what he considered calculated delay, and he complained that Sforza was deliberately trying to upset Lucrezia's re-marriage which was already being planned. Sforza insisted that nothing would ever induce him to sign a declaration that contained the nightmare phrase 'quod non cognoverim Lucretiam'. He was so emphatic that the Milanese ambassador, Stefano Taverna, desisted from the practice of allowing Giovanni's letters to be read in the Vatican, in deference to the Pope's feelings. The Pope, wrote Taverna, desired nothing as much as the divorce, and he wished to establish that his daughter had been left *virgo intacta* by the Count of Pesaro, 'for if this impression prevailed he could give her to another husband'. Finally, after months of comings and goings, embassies and protests, Ludovico the Moor dispatched a henchman to warn Giovanni that if he did not fall in with the Pope's wishes he, too, would withdraw his protection from the State of Pesaro. That would have meant collapse, and Giovanni lacked the 'guts' to carry on any longer. Worn down, he capitulated.

On November 18, 1497, a large gathering of doctors and theologians met in the palace at Pesaro. The Count appeared in the hall where they were assembled and probably repeated the phrase that he had written to Ludovico the Moor: 'If His Holiness wishes to establish his own kind of justice I cannot gainsay it. Let him do what he wishes, but God is higher.' Though it went much against the grain he signed his name in the presence of all these witnesses. The substantial memorandum sent to Ascanio Sforza contained the vital phrase that attested to the non-consummation of the marriage and it empowered the Cardinal to take all necessary steps for the annulment on those grounds. Now that Giovanni had given in, his letters to the Duke of Milan in the days that followed, reiterating that he had signed only because forced to by others more powerful than himself, served merely to relieve his own feelings. In Rome Cardinal Alessandrino, the Cardinal of Santa Prassede, and Messire Felino San Dio sifted out impeccable formulae to clothe the sins and lies.

But while her youthful personality was the subject of so much discussion, and claimants to her hand were springing up all over Italy, Lucrezia was quietly straying from the straight and narrow path on her own account.

News of Juan's death had reached her in the Convent of San Sisto and, given her passionate feelings about her family, she must have been prostrated with grief. She had always harboured the conviction that, whatever befell, she could count on her stylish and brilliant brother. After the Count of Pesaro's flight Juan had intended to take her to Spain – always a land of dreams to the Borgias – but his brutal death had put an end to all that, and what had made things worse was the Pope keeping her at a distance and not letting her share his sorrow. She was lost in sombre thoughts, and in view of her age it is hardly surprising that she snatched at the first straw of distraction that came her way. As luck would have it, it was the wrong straw.

The Pope selected personally the messengers who were sent to and fro between the Vatican and Lucrezia, and most of them were Spaniards. One of these, Pedro Caldes, who was familiarly known as Perotto, came more often than the others. His daily presence awakened feelings of trust and friendship in Lucrezia which developed into affection and finally into passion. The testimony of contemporary witnesses is fragmentary but unanimous: Pedro and Lucrezia fell in love. The affair was steeped in secrecy and is difficult to reconstruct, but it seems to have been of great importance in that it shaped Lucrezia's character.

If it is true that Lucrezia gave herself entirely to this young Spaniard, she must have known from the outset that there was not the slightest hope that she and Pedro would be able to spend their lives together. What is more melancholy and yet exhilarating than a love in which each meeting is an end in itself and has no bearing on the morrow? And yet there was indeed a morrow in this case. According to contemporary accounts the young lovers were so imprudent that one day Lucrezia became aware that she was expecting a child. We can well imagine her youthful alarm. Possibly with the help and advice of her devoted girl-in-waiting, Pantisilea, she contrived to hide her condition under the fullness of her winter clothes. For a time she was successful, but it is difficult to conceive of the courage that must have been needed when she was summoned to the Vatican on December 22 for the promulgation of the sentence of her divorce, and she had to hear herself solemnly referred to as *virgo intacta*. Yet she went, she listened and she smiled. Stefano Taverna describes how she made a speech of thanks in Latin 'with such elegance and sweetness that had she been Tully himself she could not have spoken more to the point or with greater grace'. To compare Lucrezia with Cicero is absurd, yet it shows that her efforts must have been successful. Even if we suppose that she had learnt her little speech by heart before she set out, it is remarkable that she was able to string her Latin periods together so faultlessly and with such calm and ease. Either she possessed all the Borgia qualities of courage and dissimulation in a high degree, or else not a word of what our witnesses relate about her clandestine love affair is true.

Yet we can deduce a good deal from the fact that Perotto was a thorn in the flesh of the Borgias and still more from the fact that it was Cesare who finally did away with him. The Cardinal's rage upon discovering the facts had this to be said for it: he had freed his sister from the Count of Pesaro so as to make her serve his political plans, and to see her compromised by an inferior was almost as bad as being burnt alive. So one day, as Polo Capello the Venetian ambassador tells us, when he came across Perotto near the Pope's apartment, he leapt upon him with a drawn sword. Perotto took to his heels and Cesare chased after him through the length and breadth of the Papal apartments with his sword at his rump, until both reached the steps of the pontifical throne. There under the eyes of the Pope who vainly stretched out the hem of his garments to protect his servant, Cesare thrust at him; 'and the blood spurted into the Pope's face,' adds Capello. We do not know if Perotto's wounds were mortal. A further piece of information comes from Cristofero Poggio, the informant from Bologna who wrote on March 2, 1498: 'Perotto, the first *cameriere* of our Lord, who was no longer to be found, I now understand to be in prison for having made His Holiness's daughter, Madonna Lucrezia, pregnant'. And there is a note in Burchard's diary which says that the Spaniard's corpse, bound hand and foot, had been found in the Tiber. On the very same day the river yielded up the body of Lucrezia's lady-in-waiting, Pantisilea. According to our informants, Lucrezia's baby was born in March. 'From Rome it has been ascertained that the Pope's daughter has given birth.' The dispatch is dated March 18, 1498.

Lucrezia's tears are not a part of history; but the candidates for her hand are, and they presented themselves at the Vatican even before the sentence of divorce from her first husband was announced. The Pope and the Cardinal of Valencia weighed and examined each offer. Not for nothing had they battled with the Count of Pesaro and overcome all obstacles. Now Lucrezia was free they needed her for their new ambitions. It was Cesare who provided the impulse and set the tone of their aims. During his sojourn in Naples he had had an opportunity of seeing that pleasant land at close quarters, and had found the Neapolitan

court, though on the decline, still splendid. He had observed the
civil and military weakness of the Kingdom of Naples, divided
against itself and at the mercy of rebellious barons, and bastard
though he was, he had conceived the idea of seizing part or all of
the realm. There had been a persistent rumour that Cesare had
renounced his Cardinal's hat and married Sancha of Aragon and
that Jofre had been given the Cardinal's hat in his place. But
there were grave obstacles to changing Sancha's husband, for, as
readers will remember, a Cardinal and a King had been present
at the consummation of her marriage. Moreover the ambitions
of the Borgias had swollen enormously in the meanwhile and
they may have reflected that Sancha, after all, was illegitimate
too and would not bring her husband within sight of the throne.
In due course gossip about her ceased. Cesare's thoughts and
plans were now fixed on Carlotta of Aragon, a legitimate
daughter of the King of Naples, who was completing her
gentlewoman's education at the chaste court of Queen Anne of
Brittany, and had the escutcheon the Borgias needed for their
aims. Cesare got busy, and the Pope began a tactful correspondence with the Court of France to test the feelings of the new
King, Louis XII (Charles VIII had died prematurely on April 7,
1498).

The new Borgia policy involved steering between Scylla and
Charybdis. Cesare's pretensions to Carlotta's hand presupposed
at least a surface friendship with her father, the King of Naples.
But the friendship of the King of France was still more
important, for the marriage would probably depend even more
on what he said than on Carlotta's own parents. There were two
reasons for this: one was that Carlotta was on French soil under
the protection of the Queen Mother, and the other was that
Louis XII had made his own intentions perfectly plain and at his
coronation had been proclaimed King of France and Naples. So
Cesare embarked on the dizzy and perilous enterprise of
obtaining the favour of opposing parties who were disputing
their claim to a Kingdom, while at the same time struggling to
seize at least part of it himself. Meanwhile with all his customary

skill Alexander VI wove diplomatic intrigues that became so subtle and tenuous as to be always on the point of snapping, but in the matter of winning the friendship of the Aragonese, while retaining the power to intimidate them should need arise, he played the trump of Lucrezia.

The number of proposals and requests to marry Lucrezia, now a *divorcée* at the age of eighteen, go to show that Giovanni Sforza's insinuations had caused no feelings of repugnance even if they had been believed. One of the first to enter for the marriage stakes was Antonello Sanseverino, the brave and intelligent son of the Prince of Salerno. His candidature displeased the King of Naples intensely for Antonello belonged to one of the most powerful families of the Kingdom but, like the rest of his family, was a pure Angevin and extremely well-disposed towards the King of France. As soon as King Federico had ascertained that practical steps were being taken and that the intended bridegroom was to be nominated Captain-General of the Church and live in Rome under the Pope's protection, he sent off an envoy to Milan to ask the Sforzas to use their dwindling influence at the Vatican to undo a project which threatened to give both the King of France and the Pope a hold over the Kingdom of Naples. Naples and Milan, once so hostile, had by now formed a tardy alliance against the French peril. Cardinal Ascanio was well stocked with cunning arguments, and the Sanseverino marriage plan fell through. Further projects followed immediately.

Other suitors included Francesco Orsini, Duke of Gravina; the Lord of Piombino, a member of the Appiani family; and Ottaviano Riario, a son by her first marriage of Caterina Sforza, Countess of Forlì (it would seem that Ascanio, who proposed Ottaviano, had learnt nothing from Lucrezia's first experience with the House of Sforza). But the suitor the Borgias really fancied, though they did not want to show too much interest in him, was a member of the House of Aragon. This was Alfonso, an illegitimate son of Alfonso II and of Donna Tuscia Gazullo, and brother of Sancha. The Pope gave out that he admired 'neither his mind nor his qualities' at the very moment when he was backing him to the hilt. On the subject of the Pope's apparent duplicity Gian Lucido Cattanei comments with his usual insight: 'The Pope was keeping everyone guessing both in this matter and in another of greater importance' for, before reaching a decision, he wanted to get an answer from France as 'he is fishing for many things there in accordance with his plans'.

His tenacious fishing brought what looked like a good catch. Louis XII seemed ready to help the Cardinal of Valencia if the Pope would in his turn help him. First and foremost the King of France wanted to be granted a divorce from his wife, the pious and plain Jeanne de France with whom he had been saddled by his father, and he swore that he had never consummated his marriage with her. On this basis of mutual understanding there were no obstacles to an early agreement. As soon as the Cardinal of Valencia had been given adequate grounds for hoping he could marry Carlotta of Aragon, Lucrezia's marriage was also arranged: she would become the first link with Naples by marrying Alfonso of Aragon who would receive the title of Duke, the estate of Bisceglie, and a substantial allowance from the King. Lucrezia herself was granted a dowry of 40,000 ducats, more than the sum left with her first husband. The agreement stipulated that the married couple should reside in Rome in the palace of Santa Maria in Portico.

Lucrezia had every reason for feeling fairly happy about it. She had heard Sancha talk about her brother and he had already entered into her study of imagination. She knew that he was one of the most handsome young men in Italy, with charming manners, and a pleasing character, and it was fun to be given a high ranking title that would give her a position in the household of the King's sons and brothers. She suffered under the burden of her background, followed by the scandal of her divorce and the love affair with Perotto, and she knew that popular legend held her life at the Vatican to be shameless. This opinion of her was growing as we can see in the writings of the Venetian chronicler, Girolamo Priuli, who called her the greatest whore in all Rome, and the Umbrian chronicler usually known as Matarazzo refers to her as the leading fallen woman and standard-bearer for all the others (only the chroniclers use much worse language). Both Priuli and Matarazzo lived far from the Vatican court and hence are concerned with rumour rather than with things seen, and rumour was generally hostile. Lucrezia's private life may have had a darker side than even her detractors describe, but she certainly did not enjoy the easy passions and materialistic life of a great courtesan. Moreover as the Neapolitans, who were particularly well-informed and shrewd, realized very well, Lucrezia's only problem in Rome lay in her relations with her family – so much so that the poets who supported the House of Aragon turned their elegant Latin arabesques on one point only – the monstrous accusations made by Giovanni Sforza. Pontano asked:

> Ergo te semper cupiet, Lucretia, sextus?
> *Will then the sixth one always desire you, Lucrezia?*

and Sannazaro composed a famous epitaph summing up every kind of obloquy:

> Hic jacet in tumulo Lucretia nomine, sed re
> Thais: Alexandri filia, sponsa, nurus.
> *Here in her grave lies Lucrezia in name, but Thais in truth:*
> *daughter, bride and daughter in-law of Alexander.*

But all that happened later. For the moment we must return to Alfonso's arrival from Naples in the middle of July 1498. He was at that time a lad of eighteen, about whom a Roman humanist, Evangelista Capodiferro, had prophesied that neither his name nor his royal stock would safeguard him from harm if he made this reckless marriage. Lucrezia was ready for him and the wedding was celebrated in the Borgia apartments. This time there were only a few guests – including the Vatican household, Cardinal Sforza, who was delighted at the Pope's new alliance with his Neapolitan friends, Cardinals Giovanni Borgia and Giovanni Lopez, and Bishop Marrades. During the ceremony the Spanish captain Juan Cervillon held a naked sword over the heads of the couple. The celebrations that followed began unluckily for when Cesare's suite met Sancha's they began quarrelling about precedence, venting all the ill-feelings of their masters and mistresses. Insults were bandied about in both Spanish and Neapolitan, and two bishops received 'many punches'. The Pope himself ended up 'in the thick of the fray', and the struggle was so keen that his servants fled and it took some time to pacify them and bring them back again. Peace was made at last and sealed by a very long supper followed by dancing and theatricals that lasted till dawn. Cesare appeared on the stage disguised as a unicorn, the symbol of purity and loyalty, and was much admired. As for the Pope, he joined in the activities 'like a young man'. The days that followed showed clearly that Alfonso and Lucrezia had taken to one another. The Pope was all smiles.

Louis XII called Cesare Borgia cousin and promised him wonders. He was badly in need of the Pope, for he wanted to marry the woman he loved, Queen Anne, the widow of Charles VIII, who was beautiful and wise and would bring him the province of Brittany as dowry. On July 29, 1498, Alexander VI set up a commission to examine the case for a divorce from Jeanne of France, though, as King Louis was well aware, he had only to help Cesare to carve out a state for himself and everything would be considered settled from the start. Cesare's plans, however, now exceeded the limits of his ecclesiastical status, for even the Borgias did not dare to speak of matrimony in connection with a Cardinal who was still wearing his purple. So, donning his cardinal's regalia for the first time for months, Cesare attended a consistory held on August 17, and begged the handful of Cardinals present – all more or less prepared to participate in an 'unheard of' thing – for permission to speak. He made his address from notes perhaps prepared in collusion with the Pope. He began by saying that he had never had a vocation for the religious life but had been forced into it, and went on to beg permission to return to the lay estate in the interests of the salvation of his soul. If his request were granted, he would place himself entirely at the service of the Church and would go in person to France in an attempt to save Italy from yet another French invasion. The Cardinals referred all power and responsibility in the matter to the Pope, and Alexander VI used all the sonority and pathos of his beautiful voice in adducing numerous considerations about the gravity of the case and the wisdom required for solving it.

Now that the most difficult part was over, Cesare must have breathed again. Casting off the red robes he had found such an intolerable burden, he went off to meet the French ambassador, Louis de Villeneuve, Baron of Trans, who had arrived in Rome that very day bearing a royal decree. By this decree Louis XII conferred on Cesare the title of Duke of Valence – 'a lovely city on the Rhône in Dauphiné where there is a university . . . near Lyons, and at two days' journey from Avignon, and it would bring him 10,000 *écus* (of revenue) . . .' (as his informant wrote to the Marquis of Mantua). So the Cardinal of Valencia became the Duke of Valence and in Italy he was still called 'il Valentino'. As Cattanei noted, not without irony, the change was made 'so that his first title should not be forgotten'.

Cesare, it was decided, would leave for France accompanied by Villeneuve and the most distinguished Spanish nobles available. His personal preparations have become famous. He sacked the Roman shops so that no cloth of gold or silver remained, he collected gold chains and magnificent horses brought from the renowned studs of the Gonzagas. At the sight of all this splendour Alexander VI rejoiced: 'the Pope is more delighted about it than words can express', said the ambassadors. Now that he felt he had powerful support, the Pope took insidious pleasure in being very nice to the Sforzas to whom his pro-French policy was such a menace. While Cesare spent money like a madman, the Pope rejoiced at the thought of the arrival of

his spectacular cavalcade in France. Both he and his son had a
Spanish feeling for pomp and solemnity and the idea of ridicule
never entered their minds. Moderation was the last thing that
occurred to them. With more experience and control of their
feverish desire for an apotheosis they would have avoided the
temptation to dazzle the King of France.

Cesare was a real Borgia and fine clothes suited him. His body
was muscular yet lithe and his agile supple limbs were
harmonious. Unfortunately his face was disfigured by periodical
returns of 'the French evil', or syphilis, which he had caught
when he was in Naples, and he had to put off his journey to
France because of one of these visitations: he did not want to be
seen with the pox by the girl he needed to conquer. He set out at
last on October 1 by way of the Vatican gardens. He was dressed
in white and gold damask and wore a French-cut cape of black
velvet. Curls of 'false hair' framed his face (probably he wore a
wig so as to hide his Cardinal's tonsure). He was mounted on a
bay horse, and with him he carried two Papal Bulls, one
conceding his divorce to the King of France and the other
nominating Georges d'Amboise a Cardinal.

His journey was the talk of Italy and his silver-shod horses
became a legend. But when he reached the French frontier he
did not find things as plain-sailing as he had hoped. Scandal had
gone ahead of him and the provincial and austere Catholics of
medieval France were dazzled yet frightened at the sight of him,
as though, with his cortège and his coffers containing the wicked
divorce of the pious Queen Jeanne, he were a sort of evil genius.
When the cavalcade reached Chinon, where the King and court
were residing at the time, and effected a solemn entry with the
splendour of golden trappings, of multi-coloured clothes, of
precious stones and cloths, the common people stared open-
mouthed and the courtiers decided that 'it was really too much
of a good thing for a little Duke of Valentinois'. Cesare was
received with all honours and invited to court, but when the
subject of marriage to Carlotta of Aragon came up, the words
used were so vague that he refused to hand over the Bull of

divorce to the King unless some definite decision about his own marriage were reached first. However finally he had to hand it over, and he was present at the King's marriage with the reluctant Queen Anne of Brittany who, whether out of coquetry or genuine scruples, had put up a resistance for months saying, among other things, that she was of too good a family to become a courtesan of France. She at last became Queen for the second time on January 6, 1499. Meanwhile Cesare seized the opportunity provided by the merry-making to pay court to Carlotta of Aragon who was one of the Queen's ladies-in-waiting, and the graceful affability that he knew how to display at need seems to have made some impression on her – though up till then she had maintained that for nothing in the world would she be called 'la cardinale'. She was reported to have given him to understand that so far as she herself was concerned she would consider giving her consent only on condition that her father gave his, which may well have been a way of escaping from her suitor's insistence without recourse to a direct rebuff (she may already have been in love with the French baron whom she married a few months later). Her ruse worked well for King Federico flatly refused his consent and his ambassadors were in consequence dismissed and given 'an unpleasant farewell' by the King of France.

But although Louis XII appeared to be upset we have no reason to believe that he really was. Anyone who follows the details of Cesare's sojourn in France with a critical eye can see what one of the Cardinals in Rome meant when he said that the King was holding Valentinois as a hostage so as to have the Pope on his side during his coming campaign in Italy. Now that Cesare was isolated and away from the land of his birth, the French indulged in witticisms at his expense: they said that the 'son of God' would not be able to slip through their fingers this time as he had done at Velletri, and the reference to his position as hostage at the time of the previous invasion was a significant comment on his sojourn in France. Soon Cesare became bitterly aware that he had been caught in a spider's web but he tried manfully to dominate events and himself, whereas his gentlemen-in-waiting, lacking his will-power, could not disguise their anxiety. One of them, 'a man of great ability', wrote to Rome describing the honours paid to Valentinois by the King, but concluded: 'let us hope that in a few years they will not turn out to be like the honours paid to Christ on Palm Sunday when on the Friday they crucified him.' The comparison may be irreverent but that does not diminish its significance.

Playing the part of the Betrothed who had come from afar to no purpose was galling to Cesare's pride. March came without bringing any change in his situation. He was offered one French princess after another without any decision being reached, and the Pope now began to adopt a tone of bitterness with the King of France. Alexander VI, as a good politician, realized that Cesare's journey could run the risk of becoming a moral defeat for the Borgias. There was a rumour that no less than five crowned heads had stooped to write to the King to say that Carlotta's royal blood 'should not be violated' – meaning by an adventurer. The Pope was so annoyed that at one moment he planned to call Cesare back and give him an Italian princess for wife, thereby binding up his destiny with Italy. He said that he 'wanted him (Cesare) to marry in Italy and to be with her (Italy)'. Alexander VI's leanings towards Italy at this time are corroborated by various informants, and it is easy to imagine what effect a nationalist Pope prepared to defend Italy against foreign invasion would have had on the country. But really the Pope lacked the authority to recall his son – the French would not have let him go. So as things stood it was best to pretend to think their game amusing.

Meanwhile Lucrezia was living peacefully in Rome with her husband who was gay and attentive and Neapolitan enough not to bother about politics unless he had to. He held court, he received poets, men of letters, cardinals and princes, and under his quiet but enthusiastic protection the little Aragonese party, which later gave umbrage to Cesare, began to thrive. Ascanio

Sforza, meanwhile, took to visiting Lucrezia in moments of serious political tension, even before being received at the Vatican, so as to be better equipped for defence against the French. Like most women, Lucrezia had no love of politics, yet she had lived long enough among people in command to have learnt the art of looking after her own interests in the agitated interplay of family ambitions. The assiduity with which Ascanio Sforza cultivated the Duke and Duchess of Bisceglie is a proof that, through her husband's relatives and the allies of the House of Aragon, Lucrezia tried to help the Milanese and the Spaniards who, for their part, were anything but docile.

The Portuguese ambassador had not minced his words when he complained about the Pope's pro-French behaviour and nepotism at the time of the arrival of a large Spanish embassy headed by Garcillaso de Vega, a man ready to adopt a tone of violent insolence in the name of his King, and to threaten the Head of the Church with a General Council to depose him. In this head-on clash, Alexander VI was not outdone for a moment, but parried insult with insult and countered the accusations of simony brought against him by declaring that Ferdinand and Isabella were reigning as usurpers. And when it was put to him that the death of the Duke of Gandia might have been an instance of divine punishment, he answered by drawing attention to the still graver punishments that afflicted the offspring of the Spanish royal family. In the end the Spanish and Portuguese proclaimed that they no longer considered Alexander VI to be Head of the Church, and one of them used such irreverent expressions that he was threatened with a dip in the Tiber. These brutal exchanges enraged the Pope but at the same time stimulated him, as if the process of quarrelling with his fellow-countrymen in his native tongue gave fresh scope to his energies. But oil had to be poured on the troubled waters, and the Pope racked his brains for a gesture of conciliation. As the Spaniards had a chronic mania for declaring themselves defenders of the territorial integrity of the Papacy (which also concealed the political aim of opposing French claims in Italy), the Pope solemnly took the Duchy of Benevento away from the heirs of the Duke of Gandia and restored it to the Church; though in view of his lack of interest in his grandchildren the gesture looked almost like a slight on the King of Spain. With this and other minor concessions to religion Alexander VI played for time; and meanwhile he lost none of his taste for amusement and provided gay parties for Lucrezia and her young husband. Towards the end of January and in the company of Cardinal Borgia, Cardinal Lopez and Alfonso of Bisceglie, he took part in a great hunt which was centred on Ostia and its nearby wooded countryside, in those days as rich in game as the area round Castel Porziano is today. The company returned on February 1 in a fine huntsmen's procession of quivering hounds and servants bearing the booty of 'stags and wild goats' in triumph. That same month the Pope appeared with Lucrezia on the balcony of Castel Sant' Angelo to watch the masquerade as it passed and enjoy the popular jokes. But that year the carnival cannot have been very lively for, as a correspondent says, 'the Pope and Madonna Lucrezia stand as long as they like on the castle and let themselves be seen, but nobody passes save an occasional guttersnipe'.

Lucrezia could always find something to laugh about. She was enjoying the happiness of being in love and in this mood naturally wanted air and light outside the huddled houses of the city. February 9, 1499, must have been one of those sunny days of the Roman winter whose Apollonian splendour makes one restless, for on that day Lucrezia and her ladies-in-waiting set out on a pleasure trip to Cardinal Lopez' vineyards. Lucrezia was two months gone with child, but she must have forgotten about that when she suggested to her companions that they should have a race along the pathways. Off she flew, the others in pursuit, regardless of the sloping ground; she stumbled, her slipper caught, and she fell to the ground bringing the next girl down on top of her. She was taken back to the palace in a faint, as Cattanei says, and 'that night at nine o'clock she lost one knows not whether a boy or a girl'. The Pope was very upset but probably comforted himself with the thought that Lucrezia and Alfonso were young and passionate and in love. As things fell out Alexander VI's fatherly heart was warmed barely two months later by the hope of another birth.

During the spring there was good news from France. Cesare's messenger – Garcia – arrived in great haste on March 16, 1499, to report that Cesare had already married and consummated his marriage. His wife was Charlotte d'Albret, 'the most gallant young lady of her country', daughter of the King of Navarre and kinswoman of the King of France. She had the reputation of being a beauty though an Italian who saw her some years later said that she was 'more human than beautiful' by which he meant that she had charm rather than classical beauty. She may have faded early as sometimes happens with delicate skins. The marriage had not been easy to arrange because the girl's father, the rough and austere Alain d'Albret, was loath to admit that a churchman and an ex-cardinal had the right to marry, and the business of showing and explaining the Papal Bull that declared Cesare free from all ecclesiastical bonds took time. And there had been other obstacles and misgivings all finally overcome, however, by Cesare's extravagant gifts and his promises of honours and advantages in store, but above all by the firm will of King Louis who took it upon himself to promise a Cardinal's hat to Charlotte's brother, Amanieu d'Albret.

The marriage was celebrated at Blois on May 12, and on the dawn of the 13th, as soon as Garcia had learnt what the newly-wedded couple had achieved during the night, he leapt on his horse taking only four days to reach Rome. He was so worn out that he could not remain on his feet even in the Pope's presence, and was given permission to sit, on condition that he told the story as quickly and with as many details as possible. He talked for seven hours. He began with the marriage negotiations and left nothing out – the exchange of rings, the festivities, and the night of love during which the sacrament was consummated six times, on which the King had congratulated Cesare amid broad laughter, saying that he had more than beaten him in that field.

Then the description of the great party that Cesare had given for the King and Queen, the Duke of Lorraine and all the nobility of the court of France: there had been so many distinguished people present that the halls of the palace were too small to contain them all; the party had been held in a great meadow divided for the purpose by hangings into 'halls and rooms', so for ceiling they had had the gentle May sky, for carpet the springtime grass, and for walls tapestries embroidered with flowers.

There was much good cheer and gaiety at the Vatican. Cesare was the happiest man in the world and had given his wife jewels, brocades and precious silks worth 20,000 ducats. The Pope embellished the theme of Cesare's wedding with fresh variations for each visitor, whether friend or enemy, so that all should either rejoice with him or be made frightened. He ordered some jewel caskets to be brought to him and he fondled the stones with his fat sensitive fingers, demonstrating how rubies were shot with blood, how emeralds were like cold, cutting lightning, how pearls fluctuated like the eastern sky. All were to go to his new daughter-in-law. He quite forgot the things he had said against the King of France. He laughed at the Duke of Milan and Ascanio Sforza when they said they did not believe in an imminent French invasion despite the recent proclamation of a League between Louis XII and Venice for partitioning the Duchy of Milan. 'Let him (i.e. Ludovico) beware,' laughed Alexander VI, 'lest he be caught like that good man King Alfonso (of Naples)' – who, at the time of Charles VIII's invasion, had refused to believe that the French would arrive until he saw them at the gates of Naples.

For the Aragonese the outlook was black once more and this might be the final storm. Lucrezia began to feel uneasy and Sancha was already very worried, a fact which she displayed at every opportunity. Jofre seemed to be doing everything in his power to show that he was a genuine Borgia – the Pope had denied him this status on a number of occasions – by imitating the turbulence of his brothers. Accompanied by his Spaniards he

went out at night on noisy prowls through the city and as often
as not molested the guards on their rounds. One night, when
with twenty-five Spaniards he was crossing the bridge at Castel
Sant' Angelo, he insulted the sheriff and received a wound in the
thigh from the rusty arrow of a soldier on guard; and, as a
contemporary witness puts it, he all but went 'to join the Duke of
Gandia in the Tiber'.

When Sancha saw her husband brought home with his life in
danger all her rancour against the Pope's family revived. She ran
to the Vatican to lodge her complaints against the little prince
her husband or against the Pope for allowing common soldiers to
use arms against his own son. The Pope appears to have replied
that Jofre had got what he deserved for molesting the police; but
this did not satisfy Sancha. Her Neapolitan violence, her
Aragonese pride and her woman's temper were unleashed. The
tussle between Alexander VI, so massive and strong in his great
papal robes, and the dark little woman with the brilliant blue
eyes went on for a long time and there was an outpouring of
words 'from one and the other party' which was 'very bitter and
did little honour to either'. The Pope told his confidants
afterwards that his distress was for the honour of his House and
not because Jofre was his true son. Possibly while quarrelling
with Sancha he let slip some kind of denial of his paternity – in
which case Sancha would have found no difficulty in making a
cutting reply.

In the meantime the Pope's alliance with the French and the
satisfaction he was showing about it became more and more
riling to Ferdinand the Catholic's ambassadors, and they became
so suspicious as to accuse the Pope of receiving gunpowder and
cannon-balls in wine barrels from France. Seeing that their
protests made no impression on the stubborn Pontiff they
decided to go back to Spain and give a full account of the
situation in Italy to the King, so that he would be able to judge
for himself and take the necessary steps. On the eve of their
departure they had an audience with Alexander VI which ended
like this: 'Holy Father,' said Garcillaso de Vega, 'I am leaving

and going to Spain. I hope that you will have to follow me as a fugitive, not in a ship with honourable escort, but on a barge if you are lucky enough to find one.'

Garcillaso was brief and to the point and his words could hardly have been more disrespectful, but Alexander VI was clever and countered with promises and protests. He could barely conceal his satisfaction at seeing the last of these people who had bound him hand and foot and deprived him of the freedom necessary for weaving his web of plots with France.

As these plots grew thick and fast and their outcome became more obvious, Alfonso of Bisceglie began to ruminate. He must have been kept in touch with developments by Ascanio Sforza, the Spanish and Neapolitan ambassadors and his sister Sancha. Though the Pope was at pains to make an outward show of neutrality and kept saying that King Louis had his eye only on the Duchy of Milan and would never be allowed to touch Naples, it was common knowledge that he said this to gain time – 'per temporezar', as Cattanei put it. At the end of July Cardinal Ascanio Sforza left Rome to join his brother Duke Ludovico in his fight against the French. He had the strength of mind to appear to be – and he may really have been – 'in gay and in good spirits', and to be entertaining the hope of returning soon in triumph. Perhaps his optimism was reinforced by the thought that something highly displeasing to Alexander VI was about to happen. Given his friendship with the Duke and Duchess of Bisceglie it is extremely likely that he had warned Alfonso of the snares and dangers he was running with the Borgias and had reminded him, as he had reminded others, of the fate of Giovanni Sforza. In any case he must have been very relieved to hear that on the morning of August 2, 1499, Alfonso of Aragon had taken horse with a small following and fled from Rome. The Pope's police had followed him until nightfall. He sought refuge at Genazzano, a property of the Colonnas who were friends of King Federico. From there he set out for Naples, having dispatched letters begging his wife to join him.

When Lucrezia was told the news she gave a long nervous

laugh. It seemed so utterly absurd that husbands should flee from her submissive, tender devotion as if she had the death-dealing head of a Gorgon. 'The Count of Pesaro will laugh still more,' it was said. She was already six months gone with child and felt shame and humiliation. The Pope hurled thunderbolts at King Federico and the whole House of Aragon and as a revenge ordered that Sancha should return to Naples immediately, on the grounds that if the King didn't wish to leave any of his property with the Pope, the Pope on his side didn't want anything belonging to the King. The return of the princess meant that each would have his own property. The Pope behaved 'with very little grace' and when Sancha did not want to leave he threatened to have her 'thrown out', which gave her royal blood good reason for resentment. Possibly she urged Jofre to follow her as Alfonso had urged Lucrezia.

Even Cesare Guasco, the Milanese envoy, had to endure the Pope's complaints against Alfonso and against King Federico who had made him flee. The Milanese envoy answered that it was Alexander's business as Pope to remove the causes of flight and, in his opinion, sending Sancha back to Naples was adding insult to injury. But Alexander was adamant and Sancha left. Lucrezia was dissolved in tears – 'she does nothing but weep' say our witnesses – and the Pope in his efforts to console her gave her the post of Governor of Spoleto and Foligno, a position normally reserved for Cardinals or other high prelates. Historians have missed the psychological connection between Lucrezia's tears and her new nomination. But we can see what was going on in the Pope's mind if we reflect on her condition and character. As a witness puts it, the Pope was afraid that his children would be 'led astray or stolen' and moreover he wanted to prove to the King of Naples that he could manage perfectly well on his own. He did not want to humiliate his beloved daughter, but he did want virtually to imprison her and, as she was sensitive to dignity, he would do this in a very special and grandiose way. He knew she would never dare to slight the majesty of her office by running away; she would come to see herself not as an abandoned wife wanting to rejoin her husband, but as a responsible officer of the State at a time of imminent war. The Pope also took into account the fact that Spoleto is a hundred and fifty kilometres north of Rome and hence that much farther from Alfonso. As Governor of the city Lucrezia would have to live behind the fortress walls and would have no means of sending secret messages to her distant husband. Jofre followed his sister to Spoleto accompanied, apparently, by six pages who had taken an oath not to let him out of their sight. He was a prisoner, and that is a further corroboration that his sister was a prisoner too, though in a disguised and honourable way.

Lucrezia and Jofre set out on the morning of August 8 followed by a magnificent cortège that had been personally supervised by the Pope. It consisted of forty-three coaches – most of them were Lucrezia's – a company of noblemen that included the young Fabio Orsini, women, ladies-in-waiting, soldiers and attendants – or rather prison-warders. In view of Lucrezia's condition the Pope had provided a litter with mattresses of crimson satin embroidered with flowers, two white damask cushions and a canopy, and in case Lucrezia felt a desire to travel seated he had added an ornamented palanquin upholstered with satin and furnished with a footstool – and the whole contraption was ingeniously fitted upon the saddle. When Lucrezia and Jofre set forth from the palace of Santa Maria in Portico at the head of their cortège, the Pope went out on to the Benediction loggia to salute Lucrezia as Governor of Spoleto. His large face radiated affection in the August sun when the brother and sister below him removed their wide sombreros and bent in respectful homage, their hair, Lucrezia's fair and Jofre's chestnut, caught in the same ray of light. The Pope raised his hand three times in blessing and stood watching them until they were out of sight.

Lucrezia was engaged in deep conversation with the Neapolitan ambassador as far as the bridge of Castel Sant' Angelo, deluding herself that she was thus somehow in touch with her husband. Thenceforward she was alone, accompanied only by her suite and her factitious title that disguised very thinly the humiliation of being an abandoned wife. Yet if anything kept her courage alive it must have been the realization of her political position and her determination to play the part of a man. Only by actively exercising her power could she prove to others and to herself that she had been nominated to a governorship not as a family expedient but for the well-being of the State. Her thoughts turned to Alfonso, and she cheered herself up by telling herself that the parting words of the Neapolitan ambassador had been optimistic. Her motives for good spirits were strengthened by the loveliness of the landscape through which she was passing, at times Arcadian and at times austere. The road she took stretches through meadows and chestnut woods, and the first glimpse of Spoleto is of its castle which stands alone above the city, anchored in a tide of green leaves. It was built by Matteo Gattapone and can be seen in its square massiveness against the delicate Umbrian sky only from this one point, for the road then descends and the fortress disappears to be seen again from the city itself, crowning it, the houses sweeping up and converging towards it, built in terraces as if following a military plan.

Lucrezia stopped for lunch at the castle of Porcaria a few miles from the city where she was met by four hundred infantry led by four commissioners who welcomed her as Governor on behalf of the citizens. Escorted by them and her own suite, Lucrezia entered Spoleto in the early afternoon borne on the golden seat under the canopy of damask and gold. It was August 14. An inquisitive and festive crowd cheered as she passed under the triumphal arches amid banners and standards and flowers. She smiled when the magistrates made speeches. Finally she reached the castle just before sunset. She entered the garrison forecourt on horseback, and crossed the geometrical space bounded on one side by the Spiritata tower and on the other by the Torretta. Next she passed beneath the archway embossed with the arms of Cardinal Albornoz and Urban V, and thence finally reached the highest point of the fortress. Here, out of earshot of the acclaiming crowd, she was received in the magnificent court of honour with its great brick portico supported by the octagonal pillars that separated the arcades.

Lucrezia, now invested with her powers, handed the briefs from the pontifical chancellery to the notables of Spoleto. She gave audience to the magistrates in the hall of honour whose windows looked down over the two courts where the men-at-arms and castle servants spent their time. She listened to speeches about the affairs of the municipality and its surroundings and, with grace and patience, examined petitions and heard complaints. But we can be sure that in her heart of hearts she was thinking about the messengers coming from the South. Things, as she knew, were looking brighter. On August 20 a Spanish commander, Juan Cervillon, of whom both the Borgias and the Aragonese thought highly – he had been a witness at the Borgia-Bisceglie marriage – left Rome for Naples on a mission from Alexander VI to King Federico to negotiate for the return of the Duke of Bisceglie, and he set out with high hopes and excellent promises concerning Alfonso's future. Though the King of Naples was not convinced by his speeches, he at least gave him a hearing and possibly got a better impression of the Pope's sincerity when expounded by a loyal soldier. After much haggling and many guarantees, it was decided that Alfonso should rejoin his wife towards the middle of September. This was the last attempt made by the House of Aragon to regain the Pope's friendship and protection, and it was to result in a sacrifice.

5

THE TRAGIC DUCHESS
OF BISCEGLIE

The French began their conquest of Milan in the summer of 1499. They traversed the cool Alpine heights in July and marched straight on the city, where Ludovico the Moor, having faced reality at last, was trying to raise help and draw up plans of defence. In both he was unsuccessful. His first card had been his alliance with Maximilian of Austria; but the Emperor, who was engaged in warfare with the Swiss, let him down, and this to Ludovico spelt ruin. He was not a man who could face war alone, for his interest lay in politics and he depended on others for military tactics. His wife Beatrice, the little Este princess with an iron character, would certainly have inspired him with the strength needed to hold out, but she had died two years earlier. Hemmed in on both East and West by the alliance between the French and the Venetians, he could think of no better plan than flight to join Maximilian in the Tyrol, whither he was followed by Cardinal Ascanio whose determination and fervour, like his famous Damascus armour, were useless. Milan opened its gates to the French and the populace acclaimed the King of France as his army marched proudly through the streets in easy triumph.

The King was escorted by many Italian princes who hoped that their proffered friendship would spare their States from ruin. They included representatives of the House of Savoy, of Monferrat, of Saluzzo, of Mantua and of Ferrara. And the King was followed by Cesare Borgia whose authority and self-confidence were given fresh impetus now that he had left his uneasy sojourn in France behind him and was breathing the air of Italy. Even so he must have still raged when he recalled the comedies satirizing his marriage that had been acted by the

students of the University of Paris. He and the Pope had been
portrayed in such an ignominious light that Louis XII had
dispatched the grand chancellor and the Comte de Ligny to
Paris to put an end to the scandal, and when those two envoys
were faced by 6,000 students in arms threatening revolt, the
King himself had to hurry from Blois to restore order – though
privately he may have considered the demonstrations more
inopportune than silly.

Alexander VI now felt safe again. He knew that Cesare was at
hand and he said he hoped that dear King Louis would come to
Rome to attend the Christmas Mass in St Peter's. When the
Cardinals pointed out with some asperity that the Kings of
France were not the kind of visitors one should most look
forward to seeing, and reminded him of how he had had to leave
Rome at the time of Charles VIII's invasion, the Pope merely
smiled. On the subject of the fugitive Sforzas he laughed outright
and pretended to be sorry for them. 'Poor people,' he said, 'they
should have had Duke Francesco (the founder and great general
of the House) for he would not have been chased away like that.'
But all the same he had not refused the gift of Nepi offered him
by Ascanio (Nepi, it will be remembered, had been among the
rewards given by the Pope to Ascanio for serving as his chief
elector). His attitude to the Sforzas was now one of 'kind words
and hostile deeds'. The King of Naples was bitterly distressed
when he heard of the flight of his ally and the French entry into
Milan, and in his despair invoked every expedient he could think
of to involve the Pope, even threatening that if the Pope failed to
protect him he would seek help from the Turks. If he did this he
would place the Church in very serious danger, as Alexander VI
knew full well, so he was on his guard not to appear too closely
allied with the French in Neapolitan eyes; indeed at times he
gave the impression of being deeply devoted to the House of
Aragon, Spain and Naples, and sowed so many seeds of illusion
all round that he gave everyone a ray of hope.

It was with illusions of this kind that Alfonso of Bisceglie
returned from Naples in the second half of September. He
travelled with an old favourite of King Ferrante's, one of the

Pignatelli, and by-passing Rome at a distance of a few miles, he rode straight on to Spoleto where he arrived on the evening of September 19. The first moments of the meeting between husband and wife must have been difficult, but Lucrezia's smile dispelled all uneasiness, and her joy in her restored security spread to the whole household. Both husband and wife were happy that September, wandering from loggia to loggia, from courtyard to courtyard, roaming the surrounding countryside on horseback, and returning in the evening heralded by a flourish of trumpets and the clatter of their galloping horses' hooves – young and weary and ready for the pleasures of repose.

During this same period the Pope finally drew up the precise geographical limits of the future Borgia Kingdom – Romagna; and he also drafted a Bull declaring that the Lords of Pesaro, Imola, Forlì, Faenza and Urbino had forfeited their title-deeds for failing to make regular payment of tithes to the Church. As soon as the Bull was promulgated, Cesare, who had been awaiting the signal, set his army in motion, and reinforced by French troops, descended on Romagna from Milan.

Lucrezia, accompanied by her husband, returned to Rome on October 14 to enjoy the quiet triumph of being a satisfied wife. Their household was kept busy preparing for the festivities that customarily celebrated births in princely houses. About fifteen days later, on November 1, the luxurious cradle was occupied by a baby boy. Arrangements had to be made for the baptism. Lucrezia's son had to be baptized if not by the Pope at least by a Cardinal, and with enough pomp and ceremony to satisfy the Borgia taste. On November 11, when all was ready, sixteen Cardinals gathered in the chapel of the palace of Santa Maria in Portico where all the furnishings and tapestries and carpets did not distract Burchard's meticulous eye from noting a hole in the altarcloth. Lucrezia, though a little pale, had the ethereal beauty of happy young mothers. She was propped up in a bed decorated in red satin and bordered with gold, in a room hung with velvet of that blue anemone colour which in those days was called 'Alexandrine'. An air of muted happiness pervaded the palace where the halls were carpeted and hung with tapestries and arrases and there were magnificent silken hangings covering the staircases and the entrance. Renaissance art and exotic Spanish memories were combined in the system of decoration.

Noblewomen, ambassadors, prelates and friends filed past Lucrezia's bed. In spite of the fatigue of the ceremony Lucrezia realized the importance of having friends and tried to pick them out among the guests. At the hour fixed for the baptism the Cardinals passed directly from the palace chapel into the chapel of Sixtus IV next door, in other words, the Sistine Chapel. Michelangelo had not yet given life to its walls and ceiling with the figures of his great drama, but Botticelli had already painted the diaphanous daughters of Jethro there, and Perugino's fresco of the handing-over of the keys resembled musical intervals recorded in space. For the baptism the far wall, where today we see Michelangelo's Last Judgment, was hung with a golden banner with a tribune draped in gold brocade against it. The floor was carpeted.

Preceded by Papal guards and chamberlains dressed in rose-coloured cloth and musicians with drums and fifes came Juan Cervillon, the brave Spanish soldier, friend of the Aragonese and the Sforzas, who had acted as intermediary between the King and the Pope. He bore the baby covered with splendid golden brocade edged with ermine. There followed two by two the squires bearing sacred objects of gold. Then came the Governor of Rome, the Imperial Governor, the ambassadors and, also two by two, a long procession of prelates. When Cervillon reached the altar he handed the baby to Francesco Borgia, Archbishop of Cosenza, who carried it to the silver baptismal font where it was baptized by the austere Cardinal Carafa. It was named Rodrigo like its grandfather. Burchard notes with his customary fault-finding that many women at the ceremony who wanted to get a better view of the baby occupied the first row in the Cardinals' stalls, and the Cardinals, seeing their places taken, had to sit in the back benches and rest their feet on the icy floor. After the ceremony the baby was entrusted to the hands of Paolo Orsini as a gesture of renewed friendship between the Pope and the Orsini family. Baby Rodrigo, who had been quiet until that moment, began to cry lustily and continued as long as he was in Paolo's arms, which the superstitious interpreted as a bad omen. The baptism was a triumph and testified to the Pope's affection for his daughter and through his daughter for Alfonso and the whole House of Aragon. The illusion of confidence was restored.

A week after the baptism Cesare Borgia arrived in Rome incognito with the Pope's favourite gentleman of the bedchamber, Morades. He dismounted in the Vatican where the Pope was awaiting him and there he spent three extremely busy days discussing recent events and future plans. He must certainly have seen Lucrezia, Alfonso and the baby who were at that time idolized in the Vatican, and when he heard his father speaking dotingly about his baby grandchild he must have felt great irritation. Cesare could not stand the House of Aragon. He could never forget the disdain of Carlotta of Aragon and Prince Federico and, what was more, Louis XII was quite set on conquering the Kingdom of Naples and had made Borgia assistance the first condition of his help to Cesare. If we look for first causes of the feelings that were later to lead to tragedy, it would be reasonable to suppose that it was now that Cesare began to entertain, if not a definite plan, at least a vague design of eliminating the Aragonese element as being an obstacle to Borgia ambitions. If Lucrezia remained devoted to her husband and the Pope himself shared her affection, this would, obviously, serve to hinder a total defeat of the House of Aragon. Cesare had too many enemies and there were too many obstacles in his way as it was; it would be unwise to fight a battle within his own family.

At this time the Borgia terror reached a peak that was to last right up to the death of Alexander VI. Even in normal times, as we have already seen, the Tiber served as a sinister depository for corpses, but during these years it swallowed and then, in due course, cast up again, Spaniards, churchmen, captains, soldiers and, very often, Borgia favourites. Even while the Duke of Gandia was still alive, Cesare had proved his ability for removing what stood in his way, but now that fortune had smiled on his plans he felt more need than ever to forge ahead regardless of the victims he left by the wayside. In the year 1499 the Tiber had yielded up the corpse of the Spanish Constable of the Guards who had once been Cesare's favourite. The body was tied in a sack with the hands bound, and the simple cause of his horrible death was that 'he knew too much'. That was only the beginning.

Towards the end of the same year, a few days after he had carried little Rodrigo of Bisceglie to the baptismal font, Juan Cervillon asked the Pope's permission to leave Rome and return to Naples where his wife and children lived and where he hoped to put himself at the service of King Federico. Permission was reluctantly given. But Cervillon was privy both to personal Vatican secrets and to the military secrets of the Pontifical State. He had shown that he was not afraid of plain speaking – he appears to have publicly deplored Sancha of Aragon's conduct, probably regarding her affair with Cesare – and hence his friends feared for him and repeatedly urged him to be on his guard. Cervillon merely laughed. But his rash courage served him badly for on the evening of December 2, as he was coming away from a supper party given by his nephew, Don Teseo Pignatelli, he was sabred to death before he had time to draw his sword from the scabbard. He was hastily buried at dawn next morning in the church of Santa Maria in Traspontina in the Borgo Nuovo and, according to Saludo, no one was allowed to see his wounds.

An even more mysterious death occurred in Cesare's camp in Romagna. The victim was the Portuguese Bishop of Ceuta, Ferdinando d'Almaida, a mean, ambitious man with a bad reputation who had helped Cesare in France with his marriage and had followed him closely in Italy – though more from vigilance than friendship. We don't know quite what he was doing – spying for the King of France, blackmailing, or both.

Anyhow one day excitement was to be observed outside the Bishop's quarters, and an almost ostentatious display of doctors and surgeons and nurses with bandages and ointments. It was announced that Almaida had been wounded in battle; but really he was dead. Had he been poisoned? people asked. We wonder whether there was already talk of the famous Borgia 'powder'.

Meanwhile Cesare's military operations were forging ahead. Imola had fallen though Dionigi di Naldo, who commanded the town in the name of the Countess of Forlì, had put up all possible resistance before parleying with the French and pontifical troops and going over to Cesare's side. The Pope was heard telling 'with much delight and pride' how his son had been under the walls of Imola with the foremost assailants, defended only by his shield, and how in the whole war he was proving his courage and clear-headedness, and how all his troops adored him because he was so rich and generous. Cesare was next involved in the difficult enterprise of laying siege to Forlì. The fortress and city were defended by Caterina Sforza who was reputed to be the bravest woman in Italy – in an epoch when there were many warlike women. One contemporary described Caterina as 'extremely cruel, almost a virago' but even in that description there was a shade of admiration, for the mantle of her ancestor, the great condottiere Francesco Sforza, had certainly fallen on her. When her first husband, Gerolamo Riario, had died, she married a simple gentleman, Giacomo de Feo, and when he in his turn was assassinated by a faction, she had ridden at the head of a squadron of soldiers to the murderers' headquarters and ordered as a reprisal that every man, woman and child of the enemy party should be wiped out.

The descriptions of her left by those who knew her, as 'a woman of good temper and gay' with hands 'as soft as fur' – she kept them soft with sweet ointments – and a face which, as her portraits show, expressed resolution and self-centredness, and tended to fat (an informant of the Marchioness of Mantua described her around 1502 as 'so fat that I can think of no parallel') – these descriptions would certainly never lead us to suspect the tireless energy and strength of muscle that made her seem the personification of war as she stood high on the walls of her city. As soon as Cesare began advancing on Forlì, Caterina got her defences ready. She inspected her strongholds and once she had got her children safely out of the fief, she played out the last act of her feudal power with the cold passion that was characteristic of her. But Cesare's overwhelming army could not be resisted for long. Amidst the smoke and the light of the fires, the Countess of Forlì stood directing and inspiring the defence. When she was captured by the enemy who had forced an entry elsewhere, her frenzy did not impair her lucidity for an instant, for without a moment's hesitation she admitted she was a prisoner and demanded to be handed over to the King of France. Nothing more was needed to fire the French with enthusiasm for they already admired her valour, beauty and dignity. The French commander, Yves d'Allègre, who had imprisoned an exceptional woman in Charles VIII's time – namely Giulia Farnese – would have taken the Countess under his wing and then set her free. But Cesare insisted on having her himself and in the end she had to be left to him though with guarantees of good treatment. It was said – and the story is not improbable – that Cesare wanted to inflict all the ills of captivity upon his intrepid prisoner including that of his lust. We know that he kept her with him for a while and then sent her to Rome, not in chains as legend has it, but honourably escorted by the Papal captain, Rodrigo Borgia. She was housed by the Pope in the Belvedere under a strong guard, and in that cheerful villa among pine trees and orange groves she was well treated. Later she was lodged in the Castel Sant' Angelo as an economy. In both places she maintained her proud bearing and though 'heart-sick with rage' she was in no way subdued: indeed she appeared to be 'possessed by a devil'.

Even his enemies had to recognize that Cesare Borgia had strong qualities of generalship, and he needed them to lead his disorderly troops, who after the fall of Forlì, seem to have snatched at every excuse for quarrelling and dispute. The

Italians and French were at daggers drawn. We are told that the French refused to recognize the authority of the Italian commanders and behaved very arrogantly, as if each man wanted to play the part of 'the King of France in the field'. Cesare performed 'miracles in view of the difficulties of the time, the diversities of outlook and other obstacles' – the quotation is from Cattanei who cannot be suspected of sympathy for the Borgias. And besides his military gifts, Cesare showed great administrative ability for he governed the conquered territories with justice and tried to save the inhabitants from robbery and pillage; moreover his published edicts have a fine and free sense of civilization that could almost be called humanist. For centuries Romagna had been accustomed to greedy and aggressive feudal lords, and the Romagnols observed the beginnings of good government with something akin to stupefaction. That explains why, when Cesare later fell upon unlucky days, Forlì and Cesena remained loyal to him.

A few days after the capture of Forlì there was another death in the entourage of the Borgias. This time it was a member of the family, Cardinal Giovanni Borgia, known as 'the Less'. He set out to join Cesare and congratulate him on his latest victory but at Fossombrone was seized with a violent fever and died within a few hours. Though the Pope and Cesare made a great display of grief, people at the time were suspicious. No contemporary witness suggests any grounds for suspicion, and yet it hardly surprises us as the tribe of Borgias was lavish with deadly secrets. If the Cardinal's death was not accidental it cannot have been caused by money motives, for though he was well provided with revenues he had even bigger debts. His revenues, his debts and his Cardinal's hat were passed on immediately to his brother, Ludovico Borgia, a knight of Rhodes with gallant habits and, so Cattanei says, a dishonest face. The dead Cardinal was hurried off to Rome and buried in Santa Maria del Popolo without a tombstone. After that he was hardly mentioned, for references to him – as to death generally – were 'very disagreeable to the Pope'.

There still remained plenty of thorns. Aided by Maximilian's army, Ludovico the Moor re-entered Milan amid the cheers of the citizens who by now had come to realize that any sort of native government was preferable to government by foreigners. Cardinal Ascanio wrote a fervent letter to the Pope announcing the restoration of the Sforzas and displaying a natural delight in revenge beneath formulas of respect and filial devotion. The Pope read this with itching fingers.

The change in the political scene effected by the return of the Sforzas called a halt to Cesare's war of conquest; he had now turned on Pesaro where he had begun treating with his ex-brother-in-law, Giovanni Sforza, in the hope of gaining the city by agreement. By now Giovanni was very poor and anxious to save whatever he could of his little fief; but even his anaemic heart was given fresh life by the news from Milan, and he withdrew from all negotiations. Cesare, brought to a standstill, had dumbly to watch the departure of the French who abandoned him in Romagna and hurried by forced marches to Lombardy, venting their fractious feelings by leaving a train of pillage and disorder in their wake. When Cesare saw that there was nothing for it but to accept a truce, he announced his intention of returning to Rome and making a triumphal entry with a large force of soldiers.

'The only thing lacking is the four prisoners on the triumphal car, as if a Kingdom had been conquered,' murmured the Romans as they watched the preparations the Pope had ordered and became more and more satirical. Nevertheless, prelates, nobility and ambassadors were at the Porta del Popolo to welcome Cesare on February 26, 1500. The entry was solemn and took an unexpected form. With a film-director's inventiveness Cesare had dramatically set the whole show in a key of mourning – mourning the loss that the House of Borgia had recently sustained (the one that had been so suspicious). The hundred carriages preceding the troops were covered with black draperies that fell down their sides like funeral palls. The troops marched without the sound of drum or fife in a strange, savage silence broken only by the hurried clatter of the horses' hooves and the hollow rumble of artillery. The soldiers, marching five abreast, included the Papal lancers, Gascons and Swiss and their banners fluttered above them. There were two hundred Swiss, wearing black velvet coats and caps adorned with the dark plumes of night birds, and fifty squires also in black velvet and cloth forming a compact group. Then came Jofre Borgia, drunk with admiration for his brother, and Alfonso of Bisceglie, who broke all women's hearts; and finally Cesare in a suit of plain black velvet with a simple collar but of perfect cut and material. Members of the household followed, including bishops, priests and others connected with the nobility and the curia, and at the end of the procession came the mercenaries of Vitellozzo Vitelli whose shining armour was hidden under cloth jerkins. When the sombre cortège arrived at the Castel Sant' Angelo fireworks were let off. The rockets had been so arranged that the ones that shot into the sky from the top of the tower were answered by others and all formed gigantic shapes of armed warriors against the background of the massive fortress walls. Then all the various firework patterns were caught up in one final explosion. Shutters fell from nearby houses and walls shook as Cesare Borgia entered the Vatican.

Lucrezia was passing through a happy period of her life. She was still quite unsuspecting, or rather she trusted the Pope to come to some agreement that would spare the Aragonese. She was now strong in her own right and more than ever beloved. Her father had made her acquire the city of Sermoneta with the castle and the grounds belonging to it – all of which had recently been taken away from the Caetani who were friends of King Federico of Aragon. The Church needed money, the Pope had said, and Lucrezia had paid 80,000 ducats to the Papal camera for the domain. Lucrezia's properties now included the duchies of Bisceglie, Nepi and Sermoneta and, of course, the lands around Spoleto. After the birth of Rodrigo she had regained her brilliance, though perhaps in a slightly quieter key. It was with an emotion of pride that she went on January 1, 1500, with an armed cavalcade under her command, to inaugurate the jubilee year at St John Lateran. The road was cleared for her by fifty outriders followed by her private chaplain, the Bishop of Carinola, who rode between a Roman baron and the last person we would have expected to find in such company – Orsino Orsini, Giulia Farnese's cross-eyed husband.

Between 1494 and 1500 the relationship between Giulia Farnese and Alexander VI had become more discreet and it is not easy to follow in our documents. We know that she was still in favour in 1497, and in August 1499 the Milanese envoy, Cesare Guasco, noted that 'Madonna Giulia has come back to the Holiness of Our Lord'. Does this refer to a return after absence or to a return of love? Whichever way we understand it, it is certain that Giulia had to undergo, like all lights of love, the wretched experience of seeing the passion that had given her so much power gradually diminish. In 1500, when the Pope had an attack of fever, a satirical poem entitled *Dialogo fra il Papa e la Morte* was much quoted in Rome, and in it Alexander VI invoked his 'Sweetheart'. But between 1499 and 1500 there was unquestionably a break, for in references to her in 1500 all our correspondents call her 'Madonna Giulia, former favourite of the Pope', which shows that her reign as a star in the Borgia heaven was by then over. Yet Cardinal Alessandro Farnese remained to the fore in Borgia ceremonies and fêtes, and Orsino became an intimate of the House of Bisceglie, so we must suppose that Alexander VI retained tender feelings of affection for Giulia just as he did for Vannozza, thus proving over again that his memories stayed green. As for Adriana Mila, her influence with the Pope had been largely ousted with Cesare's overbearing ascent to power, but she still remained in favour up to a point and her views were heard with attention. She must have had some part to play at the delicate juncture when the Pope began soft-pedalling his relationship with Giulia, and she must have helped him to bring it to an end without any unpleasant words being used. So – to return to the description of the suite of honour that escorted Lucrezia for the jubilee of 1500 – Orsino is mentioned, but not Giulia. Probably Giulia was at Bassanello or Capodimonte, for she only reappeared in Rome later, and when she did so she still looked very beautiful and was very much a centre of attention. Poor Orsino saw an ironic end to his conjugal life. The very year his wife returned to him and he might have hoped to enjoy her company unshared, the advantages for which he had been waiting so long were nullified by his own sudden death as a result of a ceiling collapsing on him in his sleep. No one regretted the mishap. In Rome the news was greeted with the comment: 'His wife will have a chance to change her board.'

Nobody took Giulia's place and the Pope's favourites were henceforward kept in the background. On the first day of the new century it was Lucrezia who occupied the centre of the stage with her beloved husband by her side and 'served' by noblemen and courtiers to the utmost of Spanish chivalry. Alexander VI went to Castel Sant' Angelo to watch the cavalcade as it rode by, if not, as Burchard put it, 'to the glory and honour of the Holy Roman Church, at least to his own personal satisfaction'.

The degree to which the Pope bore his daughter in mind is illustrated by the gifts and messages conveyed from the Vatican to the palace of Santa Maria in Portico. Lucrezia was the first and most welcome guest at all receptions, balls, plays and sermons. And now she was beginning to experience the delight of gathering around her in her own court people whom she herself liked, including churchmen, politicians (of her Aragonese party), writers and artists who flattered her in poetry and prose, both Italian and Latin, as was the custom during the Renaissance.

Our ideas about Lucrezia's intellectual life in Rome depend on a few clues and our own deductions. Documents are lacking though not to the extent that Gregorovius thought. The lack of documentation is not surprising if we remember that the period of her premature marriage with Sforza was unsettled and uncertain, that between 1497 and 1498 she lived in retirement, and that the first months of her marriage with Alfonso had been taken up by pregnancy and her distress about her husband's flight. Thus she had hardly had time to gather a literary court around her. But her education cannot but have been influenced by the great forces of classical literature and contemporary humanism, even if she transposed such influences onto a romantic plane. She knew enough Latin if not to converse easily and spontaneously, at least to read, compose speeches and understand allocutions. She also knew a little Greek. Her deep love for poetry was of a very feminine kind – her appreciation being entirely emotional rather than intellectual or artistic.

Petrarch, alas more valued for his love poetry than for his pure lyrics, was the presiding deity for Renaissance women. It goes without saying that Lucrezia, like all other women, had her copy of the *Canzoniere*, and it is described in the inventory of her little private library as being written by hand on parchment, bound in red leather and with copper clasps and decorations. She loved Petrarch not merely because it was fashionable to do so; she felt the attraction of the melodious flow of his verse and still more, perhaps, of his restless and sensitive temperament. Similar reasons explain her enjoyment of other contemporaries such as Serafino Aquilano who imitated Petrarch, and she never fully understood the difference. This Abruzzi poet's graceful turns of phrase and limpid diction touched a chord in Lucrezia's heart.

Something must be said, too, of the Roman academician, Evangelista Maddaleni Capodiferro, known poetically as 'Fausto'. He was the nephew of that Lelio Capodiferro who made so many journeys from Rome to Pesaro and back in the service of the Pope and his women in the years 1494 to 1497. Evangelista Maddaleni Capodiferro had a strange way of celebrating his relationships with the Papal family. We find very conflicting feelings in his verses preserved in manuscript in the Vatican library, only part of which have been published. On the page immediately following poems in praise of the Borgias, including Lucrezia, we come across venomous epigrams against them. The praises were written to be read in the Vatican and the epigrams doubtless circulated elsewhere. This humanist seems to have nursed rancour against Alexander VI because he had once asked him for some benefices and had been told that his work was adequately rewarded by his glory as a poet. It would have been an ungracious reply if Capodiferro had not had private means.

But often in writing about Lucrezia Capodiferro's tone softens. A note of tenderness (*O nimium cilio lenem: nimiumque potentem*), or a comparison with the wife of Collatinus (*altera nobilitat virtute Lucretia Romam*), or sorrow for the miscarriage of February 1499 which he attributed to the fatal jealousy of Venus – we find these alternating with allusions to long nights visited by incestuous phantoms and with not very clear references to Myrrha, Byblis and Pasiphae who loved the Bull.

We are unable to establish with certainty that Lucrezia had contact with other Roman humanists, though when, later on, a discussion was held in their circle concerning the respective merits of Lucrezia and various other women, we see that a strong party of the Roman literati were on her side. It is even more difficult to establish what contact she had with the artists then in Rome, such as Pollaiuolo, or Michelangelo, or even Pinturicchio, the Borgia's favourite painter. Pinturicchio must have made some drawings of her so as to paint her portrait and those of her brothers in a series of frescoes at Castel Sant' Angelo which are now unfortunately lost. But we cannot be certain that the famous St Catherine of Pinturicchio's *Disputa* in the room of the Saints in the Borgia apartments in the Vatican, which both tradition and many historians hold to be an idealized portrait of her, is a real likeness. St Catherine's lovely head framed in long golden hair has characteristics we also find in other heads of women by Pinturicchio, and moreover the more critical art historians are not prepared to admit that a fifteenth-century painter could have indulged in an idealization. Yet there is something in this figure that brings Lucrezia immediately to mind. When we compare it with medals representing her and the pictures at Como and Nîmes, both of a later date, we cannot possibly deny the resemblance. Her figure became fuller as she grew older, but we see the same oval face with its regularity broken by the retreating line of the chin, the same soft mouth, the same open and wandering glance. Indeed in the medallion known as the Amorino Bendato we even observe the same way of arranging and binding the hair. The slim young figure, its composure seeming slightly rigid when surrounded by people in easy and lively attitudes, is characteristic of a child who has grown up and been dressed too early in elaborate adult styles; and hence her rich woven red velvet dress and blue mantle seem almost unsuited to her tender age. In other words if this is not a portrait of Lucrezia done from the life it is certainly an allegory of her, just as, in the same fresco, we have a figure of the Emperor Maximilian that looks like Cesare – not only because the profile resembles Cesare's profile in the Jove collection which is the basis of our knowledge of his face-structure, but also because the body is lightly resting on a throne with limbs ready to spring. Possibly Pinturicchio already had the extraordinary models of the Pope's handsome children in his mind's eye and, when he painted, translated them into images without even being aware of it. Or perhaps he deliberately set out to paint portraits from memory so as to flatter his protector, the Pope, whose love of family was known to all. In the latter case those who have recognized yet another likeness in the group – that of the young man dressed in oriental fashion on a horse at the extreme right to the Duke of Gandia – would be quite correct; Lionello Venturi has, however, found a possible sketch for this portrait and is convinced that the figure is the Turkish prince Djem who, as readers will remember, had been a hostage at the Vatican.

We are equally short of documentary evidence about the musicians who, during her residence in Rome, helped to form Lucrezia's musical culture and awoke the passion for music which she inherited from Alexander VI and later manifested at Ferrara. But at the Vatican she heard the admirable compositions of the Fleming Josquin des Pres, who was in the Pope's service until 1494 and directed the music for all Borgia ceremonies both sacred and profane, without, it must be admitted, receiving much in the way of remuneration, for he suffered deeply from having to dress very modestly in a court where gold seemed part of the normal livery.

Lucrezia, like all people of princely rank at the time of the Renaissance, had a taste for fine oratory and the fact that she was Spanish gave her an additional cause for this liking. At her father's court she had the opportunity to hear the famous orators and humanists who were invited there, such as Inghirami, Marso and Sabellico, or the preachers Fra Mariano da Genazzano, Fra Egidio da Viterbo or the famous blind brothers, Aurelio and Raffaele, who belonged to the noble Florentine family of the Brandolini and had joined the eremitical Augustinians. One of the regular frequenters at the court of the Bisceglie family was Vincenzo Calmeta, a friend of Aquilano, who was first and foremost an intriguing courtier and only secondarily an artist as he proved at the Court of Duke Ludovico in Milan and later in Rome and Urbino. We should also include one other poet whom Borgia biographers have overlooked, namely Bernardo Accolti who has left us a rare piece of evidence about Lucrezia's private life in Rome. Bernardo Accolti, who came from Arezzo and was known by the pompous title of 'l'Unico Aretino' or simply 'l'Unico', 'the Unique', was a less than mediocre poet whose felicity as an improviser was his claim to fame both in courts and among the common people. In Rome, when he furrowed his brow and his smooth face took on an intent expression as he declaimed his improvised verses, the crowd that ran to listen was so big that the shops had to be closed. Being anything but modest, he became so proud of his popularity that he gave himself third place amongst poets after Dante and Petrarch. Not only was he brazen in character, but he lived, wrote and worked himself up in cold blood. He had two actor's gifts – a power of swift communication and a wonderful talent for amusing courts which meant, first and foremost, amusing women. A wary Tuscan, he took care to be inspired only by the most powerful women, fell in love with them, platonically of course, and, adopting the airs of his model Petrarch, gave them the illusion that they were playing in life the lovely rôle of Laura. He acted the part of the rejected lover, suffering torments, shedding tears, grasping at any straw of hope, and he expressed all these experiences in his verse, so that his poetry reads like a profanation of Petrarch's *Canzoniere*. Naturally his profession was a profitable one as the court ladies paid him for his ability to make them laugh by gifts and protection, and he subsequently defended the advantages thus gained by extremely brutal methods, as was proved on the occasion when his enemies assaulted him in his house and he defended himself with such diabolical energy that he wounded a hundred people.

This literary filibuster spent the years 1499 and 1500 in Rome and he saw Lucrezia so often and was on such familiar terms that he was able to write that he made love to her – meaning, of course, chivalrous and platonic love. One day when he saw her setting out – most probably for a reception at the Vatican – between the ambassadors of the two rival nations, France and Spain, he composed a sonnet on this theme. Lucrezia must have found it very welcome for she was always dreaming that peaceful agreements could be brought about and preferably under her auspices.

This short composition was known to Vittorio Cian who quotes it. It is to be found in a manuscript in the Biblioteca Nazionale in Florence and, perhaps owing to the copyist's indifference and carelessness on certain points, its meaning seems obscure. The dedication, which speaks for itself, and the first two stanzas, run as follows:

Messer Bernardo Accolti to the ambassadors of France and Spain having between them the daughter of Pope Alexander VI to whom the poet makes love:

> Regi invicti e accorti, or chiaro parmi
> ch'a tutta Italia dominar volete,
> poi che quella che in mezzo a voi tenete
> vince co' gli occhi piu che noi con l'armi.

La spesa e la fatica or si risparmi
di macchine fatal che conducete,
che, dove volge lei sue luci liete,
romperà 'l ciel non che ripari e marmi.

Unconquered and able Kings, it now
seems clear to me that you desire to
dominate the whole of Italy, for she
whom you have between you conquers more
with her eyes than we do with our arms.

Let the expense and fatigue of
the fatal machines you are bringing be spared:
for where she turns her gay glance
she will break down not only ramparts
and marbles but even heaven itself.

His Petrarchan love for Lucrezia was the talk of the Roman humanists and became one of those stories about men of letters of which everyone understood the point and allusion. Evangelista Capodiferro was acting in conformity with the strictest etiquette of academic custom when he wrote a love poem about Lucrezia in which he copied the accent and passion of the 'Unico'. Capodiferro headed his work: 'De Lucretia Borgia Alexandri Pont. Max. F. loquitur Unicus', and he began, 'Once upon a time there was born a Lucretia more chaste than the Lucretia of ancient days; she is not a daughter of man but born of Jove himself.' If we remember that the humanists referred to the Pope as Jove we realize that the poet is glorifying a fatherhood that should at least have been left to be understood. It must seem strange if not repulsive to many people to see Lucrezia proclaimed the most chaste of women when she had such a heavily charged past at the age of only nineteen. Yet though this form of praise obviously did not suit her it cannot be called low and ignominious. Lucrezia was highly strung, but she was not subject to whims like Sancha of Aragon and she had always been contented with her husbands as long as she was able to keep them. While married to Alfonso of Bisceglie who was as kind and gentle as a shepherd from Pontano's or Sannazzaro's Arcadia, she naturally felt that fate had smiled upon her. If behind the scenes of the well-directed play there lurked an obscure threat, as the Count of Pesaro appears to have guessed, it was a mystery that she wanted to shut her eyes to.

Milan fell once more into French hands after a battle that spelt disaster for the Sforzas. Ludovico the Moor tried to escape in disguise but was captured and taken to the castle of Loches in Touraine where he died in unknown misery in 1508. Ascanio, once the Vice-Pope, was also captured and imprisoned in Bourges whence he emerged only after the death of Alexander VI. Now that the fortunes of the House of Sforza had collapsed, the Borgias were more dependent than ever on France. And it was common knowledge that the French were preparing a drive southwards to conquer Naples.

When she heard this news Lucrezia must have been plunged in despair. But events would not perhaps have moved so swiftly towards their conclusion had it not been for a new factor that diminished her vigilance and made Cesare more determined than ever to cut free from all commitments other than those to the French in whom he placed all his hopes.

The year 1500 was a Jubilee year, as we have seen. Multitudes of pilgrims came to Rome, among whom was the man who was to bring about the great split in the Western Church, Martin Luther. The Pope was lavish with receptions, ceremonies and missions, and though his robust constitution had not spared him a stroke – he had one in the early days of June – with his usual optimism he was the first to make light of it, and on St Peter's day, June 29, fully restored to health, he was awaiting a visit from his children in the hall of the Popes, the last in the Borgia apartments. He was feeling cheerful at the thought of passing the afternoon with them and had already taken his seat on the throne under the canopy. There were only two people with him, the Bishop of Capua and a chamberlain of the name of Gasparre – possibly the unlucky Perotto's successor. Suddenly a great gale blew up followed by rain and hailstones – a typical summer storm. Bishop and chamberlain rushed to close the windows and as they were struggling to do so they heard a terrific crash behind them followed by a sound of things collapsing, and when they turned they saw a black cloud of dust and a mass of masonry that seemed to have swallowed up both Pontiff and throne.

The palace was in an uproar. 'The Pope is dead, the Pope is dead' the shout went up, and the rumour rapidly spread through the city causing a clatter of arms, while people shut themselves up in their houses and the Vatican gates were closed and closely guarded. Meanwhile workmen and members of the household were trying to unearth the Pope with spades and shovels. The cause of the disaster had been a thunderbolt striking through the apartment above which was usually occupied by Cesare, but he happened to be absent, and three floors had collapsed in a pile of rubble. The men worked in silence broken only when someone cried out 'Holy Father' and everybody listened for an answer. But there was dead silence. It was not until they had cut a way through the rubble that they caught sight of the pontifical throne and an edge of the Pope's cloak. 'Holy Father' they cried once more, convinced that they would never hear the Borgia's voice again. They frenziedly cleared away hangings and plaster and finally discovered him upon his throne dazed but perfectly sound except for some superficial cuts on his face and hands. They carried him to bed and he was bled. A fever developed bringing with it the fear of an infection. Lucrezia was at her father's bedside to nurse him at his request, and otherwise he wanted to see only Cesare and the faithful Cardinal of Capua.

By the end of the week the Pope had forgotten his fright and all thoughts about a divine warning, and had started discussing and planning the future. He summoned the Venetian ambassador with the double intention of having him bear witness that the Pope was thoroughly alive and of recommending Cesare to the Republic. The Venetians were being watchful and suspicious about the affair in Romagna, and apparently even considered sending their own troops to reinforce the defences of Faenza and Pesaro. Doubtless Cesare had suggested the idea of this visit to his father, and he made use of all his blandishments and protestations of devotion in the attempt to diminish the ambassador's cold and distant manner. But for all his wiles on this occasion he received a snub. When the Venetian ambassador took leave of the company which, besides the Pope, included Lucrezia, Sancha (now forgiven and restored to favour), Jofre and a lovely young girl who had taken Giulia Farnese's place as the Pope's favourite, Cesare saw him through the pontifical apartments, taking his arm with an affability that he tried to make confidential and dignified, and murmuring: 'Ambassador, I now realize the risk I have been running. I don't want to be dependent on the fate and will of the Pope any longer; I have decided to hand myself over entirely to the signory of Venice.' The Venetian answered that it was an excellent idea to put things under the protection of the Republic, but – as if exchanging confidence for confidence – 'without the Pope your affairs couldn't last four days'. Which, if cruel, was pungently true.

After this experience with the Venetians who, at best, could be expected perhaps to remain fairly neutral, Cesare inevitably turned his eyes northwards again. If it had to be France after all, he would need to sever every thread that tied him to Naples and Spain, and avoid giving ground for the slightest shadow of distrust on the French side. His uneasiness increased from day to day. It was aggravated by his continual meetings with Alfonso whose handsomeness and kindness made him an ideal figure of youth and whetted his brother-in-law's political jealousy and spite against the House of Aragon. Finally he developed a kind of animosity that it is not easy to define – a feeling brothers sometimes have about husbands with whom their sisters are in love, which can turn into passionate hatred. What at first had been the merest skeleton of a plan began to take a clear form in Cesare's mind and, by its own interior logic, became necessary and then urgent. Before Alexander VI had recovered sufficiently to return to the helm, Alfonso was doomed.

In the Vatican Lucrezia was helping her father over his convalescence and playing up to his domestic tyranny, assisted by Sancha of Aragon, whose concern with the cause of the Aragonese meant that this period of retirement was fraught with worries, discussions and Palace and State affairs. July 15, 1500, was an evening like any other. Alfonso of Bisceglie went to visit his wife and sister, stayed to dinner with his father-in-law and ended the summer day in the heart of the family circle. As night began to fall, he bade his family goodnight and left the Vatican by the door under the loggia of Benediction, accompanied by a gentleman-in-waiting, Tomaso Albanese, and a squire. They strolled quietly towards the palace of Santa Maria in Portico, scarcely bothering to glance at the muffled figures lying on the steps of St Peter's who looked like beggars or pilgrims. Such spectacles were a daily occurrence that year, for the Jubilee had brought Christians to Rome from all over Europe, seeking forgiveness; and many of them, either because of a vow or out of poverty, slept out of doors in the shadow of St Peter's.

But scarcely had the Duke of Bisceglie entered the piazza than at a quickly-whispered signal several of the sleepers suddenly leapt up, surrounded the three men, cut off all means of flight, and hurled themselves on the Duke with upraised swords. Alfonso immediately drew his sword and made to defend himself. He was brave and well-trained. His defence displayed the excellent technique of the Neapolitan school of fencing and infuriated the assailants who were pressing him closely. Swords crossed, clashed and bent. The young Duke lost his mantle and the gold embroidery from his elegant doublet, his shirt was cut and he began to bleed. At last overcome with wounds in head, shoulder and thigh he fell, and his enemies plunged upon him and tried to drag him to the horses stamping impatiently nearby, with the intention perhaps of taking him to the Tiber in repetition of the Duke of Gandia's tragedy. But the squire and Albanese had to be reckoned with. They were shouting for help while the former drew his master's bleeding body towards the palace of Santa Maria in Portico and then, on discerning threatening shadows in that direction, towards the Vatican, and the latter covered the retreat 'like a paladin', fighting with the fury that comes from being in the right, with the precision of a fencing master and the determination of despair. Moments of anguish passed while the swords still clashed and there were shouts, groans and desperate cries for help. At long last, though not too late, the Vatican gates were opened and as soon as the great portals began to creak the shadowy assassins took to their heels. When the Papal guard emerged all that could be heard was the distant galloping of horses.

Contemporary chroniclers tell us that the soldiers bore Alfonso of Aragon in their arms and appeared with their bleeding burden at the threshold of the room where Lucrezia was still conversing with her father and Sancha. With the little breath he could muster, Alfonso denounced his aggressors. 'He said that he had been wounded and he said by whom', reports Sanudo. Lucrezia fainted. But at some moments the slightest sign of weakness is shameful and she realized this as soon as she had been brought round. Alfonso was unconscious from loss of blood and it was impossible to carry him out of the Vatican. Lucrezia obtained a room in the Papal apartments from the horror-struck Pope, as well as sixteen trusty guards, permission to summon the Neapolitan ambassador at once, and facilities for bringing King Federico's doctors and surgeons from Naples. With Sancha by her side and trembling as though with fever, Lucrezia set about preparing her defences as best she could. Perhaps she already had forebodings of darker days ahead.

On the following morning Rome was turned upside down. In the early rays of dawn a page in the service of the court poet, Vincenzo Calmeta, crept into Piazza San Pietro and under the eyes of the Vatican guards gathered up the clues of the duel – Albanese's slashed cloak, the golden embroidery from Alfonso's doublet. As he slipped along under the walls he must have been very excited by his adventure – the early hour, the danger, the blood-stained bundle. Albanese had taken refuge under the protection of Vincenzo Calmeta so as to recover from his wounds.

The fact that Albanese chose the poet's house as his refuge is significant for two reasons. First it shows the relations existing between the Bisceglie household and Calmeta, for the latter would not have undertaken such a grave responsibility, even if he were a personal friend of Albanese, had he not been influenced by his friendship for Lucrezia and known that he would be rewarded. Secondly it proves Albanese's feeling of insecurity about convalescing in his own house or, worse, in the palace of Santa Maria in Portico. In both places he would have been within reach of the man who had prepared and directed the ambush and who might well be brooding over the failure of his plans. Albanese knew perfectly well 'who' had struck the blow for he had seen him, and for this very reason his life was no longer safe. But in Calmeta's house it would be difficult to get at him, for Calmeta was a friend of princesses and lords and men of letters throughout the whole of Italy, and busy tongues would soon be set wagging and epigrams penned if a poet's house were violated. Rather like the Press today, he enjoyed immunity by reason of a general fear of his enormous list of correspondents. In a letter he wrote to describe the crime to the Duchess of Urbino he says 'every man considers that the Duke of Valentinois brought this about', and although he does not say so, we can assume that it was Albanese who told him so, and he was a first-class witness.

Some ambassadors were more outspoken than others, but all were equally certain. Francesco Capello says cautiously: 'It has been spread through Rome that these things happened among themselves (the Borgias), for in that palace there are so many hatreds, old and new, and so much envy and jealousy in *State and other matters* that such scandals must needs occur often.' Sanudo writes: 'It is not known who committed the assassination, but it is said to have been perpetrated by the hand that murdered the Duke of Gandia.' The Neapolitan observer, Notar Giacomo, reports the news on July 15 and adds that 'Valentinois brought it about through envy'. Cattanei, wittily reticent, speaks the plainest of all: 'The originator (of the crime) is without doubt a man more powerful than him (Alfonso), although he (Alfonso) is a Lord, the nephew of a living King, the son of a dead King, and the son-in-law of the Pope.' The pointer is unmistakable.

Meanwhile Alfonso of Bisceglie had been carried to the Borgia tower and laid in the first room of the apartment frescoed by Pinturicchio. The Pope, who 'suffered grave distress on account of Don Alfonso's wounds', made haste to summon the ambassador of the King of Naples to be present when the wounds were tended. Lucrezia, pale but resolute, had taken charge with Sancha's help. The two women slept on improvised beds a few feet away from the wounded man. They assisted him in all things, and prepared his food with their own hands on a field stove so that 'it should not be poisoned'. The guard outside the room consisted of sixteen Papal soldiers and trusted servitors of the Bisceglie household including a little hunchback of whom Alfonso was very fond. Lucrezia and Sancha were shortly joined by two famous Neapolitan doctors sent by King Federico – Messer Galeano da Anna, a surgeon, and Messer Clemente Gactula, a physician. Another arrival at this time, if he was not already there, was Giovanni Maria Gazullo, the brother of Madonna Tuscia and the Duke's uncle. It was unfortunate for him that he came to Rome for he was destined for a tragic end.

Life in the Vatican during that summer was a nightmare. For though Alfonso was soon saved by the doctors and with the help of his robust young constitution, no one in Rome had any illusions about the fate in store for him. 'The wounds are not fatal if they are not added to,' wrote Calmeta. Cesare called on his brother-in-law and it was said that he had muttered something to the effect that things that failed at lunch would be successful at supper. Even if he did not say this in fact it can be attributed to him accurately enough, especially after the Pope had abandoned Alfonso. About this latter point the Venetian ambassador culled some information when in conversation with Alexander VI. After the Pope had held forth at length about Cesare's innocence, the ambassador managed to corner him by conclusive arguments until he changed his ground and said that if Cesare had struck the blow then Alfonso must have deserved it. No one knows what dastardly plots the Pope intended to father on Alfonso by those words. But alone and away from his own country Alfonso could hardly be expected to do otherwise than show the Aragonese feelings natural to him, especially as he was a daily witness of an active policy leading to the ruin of his family. Anyway, the Pope certainly made it plain that he accepted Cesare's guilty quibbles as justification, and was growing to look on the whole Alfonso affair as tiresome, a problem which he cared less to solve than to be free of. Lucrezia, in the fastness of the Borgia tower, seems to have had forebodings of the silent tide of danger, for she arranged with King Federico for Alfonso's departure to Naples as soon as he was fit to travel and possibly thought either of accompanying him or rejoining him later. Alfonso was now much improved and could walk about the room as far as the windows which opened on to the cool Vatican gardens, and he must have been intent on planning a life of his own in Naples and on his estates in Apulia, and perhaps he recalled the panorama of Bisceglie. With convalescence his spirits revived and so did his love for Lucrezia who was now his sole defence. But, and he can hardly be blamed for it, his hatred of his persecutor grew with the return of strength. There is a story, probably invented by Cesare, that one day when Alfonso saw his brother-in-law making his way through the gardens, he shot his crossbow at him. But the rancour of the little group of Aragonese must have found vent in words if not in deeds. What attitude Lucrezia and Sancha adopted when they found they had to condemn the man who was brother to one and lover of the other, is a problem of feminine psychology we could dismiss had it not influenced them in making a mistake. Their mistake was to leave Alfonso alone on August 18, 1500.

The Florentine ambassador reports that on that day 'the wife and sister (of Alfonso) were not in the room because, as they saw him much improved and recovered, they had gone a little earlier to visit some of their women'. The Venetian ambassador's account is quite different. According to him it was Valentinois in person who came to Alfonso's room and forced the two women to leave so as to be alone with his brother-in-law. Of the two versions the second seems at first sight the more likely because it is not easy to suppose that Lucrezia and Sancha would be so careless as to abandon Alfonso merely so as to visit their women. But the Venetian version is not very satisfactory either. For one thing Cesare was not the active protagonist in the drama; he used Don Micheletto Corella for that purpose. Moreover if Cesare wanted to use force, why in the world did he await Alfonso's recovery before getting rid of him – for everything would have been easier in the confused days immediately after the first attack. If Cesare bided his time it was so as to persuade his father that he should be wholeheartedly against Alfonso and the House of Aragon for political reasons and thus win his neutrality in whatever was to happen; and also so that Lucrezia should regain confidence and keep a less strict watch. Yet there is something in common between the Florentine and Venetian versions, corroborated yet further in the account of a man who was well-informed and meticulous.

This was the famous blind preacher and humanist from Florence, Raffaele Brandolini who, as we have already seen, had been Alfonso of Bisceglie's tutor. Now Brandolini had not only enjoyed a position of trust and authority with the young Duke, but he also had connections with the Aragonese party and thus was in the know. His story, which is contained in a letter written from Rome to Florence, is in substantial agreement with the others and completes and explains them.

On the afternoon of August 18, when the Duke of Bisceglie was in his room with his little hunchback and several other

companions, Cesare Borgia sent a squad of armed men, headed
by Don Micheletto Corella, with orders to arrest everybody in
Alfonso's company; they were to answer for an anti-Borgia plot
hatched, according to the accusation, with the Colonnas. All the
Duke's followers were seized and thrown into prison, including
Messer Clemente the physician and Messer Galeano the
surgeon. The coup was so sudden and so unwarranted that
Lucrezia and Sancha, who rushed to the scene of action, were
left breathless. As soon as they recovered their composure they
insisted on an explanation of the outrage: 'muliebriter objur-
gant,' says Brandolini, and his fine Latin gives a good description
of their excited indignation. They were astonished to find that
Don Micheletto gave them a straight answer saying that he had
no detailed knowledge of the business but had merely done what
he had been commanded to do. His apologetic and uncertain
tone encouraged the girls to think they could dominate the
situation and so they continued with their protests. On seeing
their persistence Don Micheletto hesitated still more. Finally he
appeared to make up his mind to give them some advice. Why
did they not go to the Pope who was only two doors away and
beg him to free the captives before they were taken to prison?

This suggestion seemed reasonable in the circumstances and
was made too much on the spur of the moment to arouse any
suspicions of a trap. And yet how could Sancha and Lucrezia,
who knew Cesare and were on their guard, come to act on it?
How did they come to overlook the fact that one of them was
essential to Alfonso's safety at all times?

We must remember that by this time the two women had
ceased to live in a state of nightmare and had regained some
feeling of security based on the Pope's assurances and the
hypocritical behaviour of Cesare. By natural inclination Lucrezia
thought well of her brother in spite of everything. She loved him
and even though she knew that men were subject to hatreds that
cry for blood, she may have thought that as she with her own
hand had restored what Cesare had sought to destroy the game
could be considered over – the more so as Alfonso's intended

departure for Naples amounted to an admission that the House of Aragon had abandoned all thought of carrying on the struggle through him and that the Bisceglie couple wished to live henceforward as private people. Cesare could have the Vatican, so ran the supposed tacit agreement, and Alfonso could have his life. And arguments that were good enough for Lucrezia were good enough for Sancha, the more so as Sancha was totally unperceptive and when she trusted or distrusted, did or left undone, she was always prompted by the impulse of the moment. In a word she was a creature of passion and a natural troublemaker. But to return to our story. The two women (here there is no contradiction either with the Florentine account which says they left the room voluntarily, or with the Venetian version which says they were forced to leave) found Don Micheletto's advice reasonable and fled to the Pope saying that they would only be gone a moment. But as soon as the door was closed Don Micheletto advanced with ferocious calm towards the alcove where Alfonso was lying. The Florentine account records that Alfonso, who was still weak, rose to his feet and it seems to suggest that his sudden gesture was an agonized attempt to protest against the inhuman death in store for him. He fell with his hand upraised, asking for mercy. It was all quickly over in the silent Borgia tower.

When Lucrezia and Sancha returned from the Pope's apartment they found the door barred by men-at-arms, and realized at once that Alfonso was dead. Don Micheletto embarked on an explanation of how an accidental fall had brought on death by haemorrhage, but the two women knew better and felt at the mercy of a general betrayal. Piteously they called on Alfonso's name and filled the palace with their wailing. But though they wept distractedly, we are not sure that they were granted leave to see the murdered man's body, and they were certainly not allowed to follow the modest funeral hurriedly arranged on the evening of August 18. By the light of twenty flares and with a small company of friars murmuring the prayers for the dead, the Duke of Bisceglie, accompanied by the

Archbishop of Cosenza, Francesco Borgia, was borne to his obscure burial place in Santa Maria delle Febbri, a little church near St Peter's that occupied the site of the sacristy of the present basilica. All worldly pomp was now vain, but the words of religion brought pity, hope and the promise of justice.

'The Pope is out of humour because, by the very nature of the case, the King of Naples and his own daughter are in despair,' wrote Cattanei, and his account is corroborated by all the other observers within reach of the echoes of Lucrezia's grief. She had to endure derision as well as sorrow. Two days after Alfonso's death Valentinois called on her with a company of halberdiers a hundred strong to make it clear to everyone that he needed protection against plots hatched within the walls of the House of Bisceglie. His supporters spread rumours substantiating these supposed plots, but they were quickly exploded. Alfonso's household was still detained in the Castel Sant' Angelo and Valentinois announced his intention of holding an enquiry and sending a résumé to all the courts of Italy – and first and foremost the Signory of Venice – so that everyone should be put wise to the nature of the enemy he was up against. But the news fell flat and the résumé 'never arrived', as Sanudo says, leaving it to be understood that it never could have been made.

Lucrezia was left alone with her despair and with Sancha for company. Her tears soon got on the Pope's nerves, for he was congenitally incapable of understanding why anybody who was only twenty years old and had all her future before her should be so upset. One of our best informants for this period is Polo Capello, the Venetian ambassador. 'Earlier on Madonna Lucrezia, the Pope's daughter, who has wisdom and breadth of character, was in the Pope's good graces, but now he does not love her so much.' But she mourned her young husband obstinately, for she felt not only a sense of loss but also, probably, of remorse for having played the part of an evil genius in his life. What the Pope failed to understand was that it was the very intensity of her genuine sorrow that saved Lucrezia in her own esteem and prevented her from feeling that she had lost all dignity. Her tears were a form of revolt carried through at the cost of losing Papal favour, even losing it deliberately. She did not want to be consoled. The time came when she could no longer endure the sight of her rooms in the Vatican or of the stone that lay over Alfonso's grave. She longed to be far away. She asked and obtained permission to retire to her estate at Nepi and left on August 30 with a company of six hundred horse. She crossed the Roman campagna along the via Cassia and the via Amerina and on August 31 arrived within sight of the ancient walls of the Etruscan city.

Nepi is a place that lends itself to weeping though, for little Rodrigo's sake, Lucrezia tried to smile through her tears. It seemed to her that her life was over, that all doors to the future were barred. But in Rome they were already scheming to marry her off once more.

After he had reconquered the Duchy of Milan and routed the Sforzas, the King of France remembered his agreement with Valentinois and dispatched a strong detachment of French troops to Romagna; while in Rome Valentinois, with the Vatican at his beck and call and no one left to undermine his influence, was making preparations to join up with the French regiments. He had a well-paid, well-equipped army of 10,000 men who were treated with a liberality the Pope viewed as sheer waste. First-class commanders from noble Italian houses, such as the Orsini and Savelli from Rome and the Baglioni from Perugia, were on the pay-roll, the level of which had been augmented by the money paid by the new Cardinals of September 1500. Directly after their nomination Cesare had invited them to a big dinner held in the rooms above the Borgia apartment – i.e. where Raphael painted his Dispute and the School of Athens a few years later. To have so many Cardinals at his table strengthened his prestige and it was increased still more before he left Rome, for envoys arrived from Cesena begging the Pope to make over their city as a fief to Valentinois who, they said, was so outstandingly liberal and wise and one of the most distinguished soldiers in the world – all of which Cattanei describes as 'tripe' or 'bread and milk'. Cesena having been thus annexed without cost, Cesare's soldiers and allies advanced on Pesaro where Lucrezia's first husband was kept in a chronic state of nerves between one alarm and the next.

The fate of Alfonso of Bisceglie had given Giovanni Sforza a certain bitter satisfaction at being out of the running for such dangers, but he had few other reasons for complacency. He had not found it easy to console himself for his unlucky adventure with Lucrezia and as late as 1499 a Venetian informant wrote that 'The Lord of Pesaro can ill endure being separated from his wife.' His powerful cousins in Milan whom he had always looked on as invincible had been defeated, and he was terrified when it became apparent that his own doom was at hand. When Valentinois' advance began, Giovanni sent protests and appeals to all the powers, but it was a mere waste of time, and all he could do when his enemies were approaching was to seek refuge with his first wife's brother, Francesco Gonzaga, at Mantua. There he found a little group of distinguished émigrés amongst whom was Lucrezia Crivelli, the beautiful ex-mistress of Ludovico the Moor, who travelled round with the diploma the Duke had given her in recognition of her services as a mistress: 'Ex jucunda illius consuetudine ingentem saepe voluptatem sensimus.' There were also exiles from the Papal States such as Guglielmo Caetani, Lord of Sermoneta, whom the Borgias had dispossessed of his estates. Giovanni Sforza was an appropriate addition to their number, and the witty and literary court at Mantua, whose presiding genius was the Marchesa Isabella d'Este Gonzaga, indulged in poisonous criticism of the Borgias, as we can well imagine.

In Mantua as elsewhere the march of Valentinois' army was followed eagerly and people sought to guess its ultimate direction. The conqueror, helped by the King of France and backed by the Pope, was observed to be smashing up ancient Signories that had come to be viewed as immovable dynasties, and there was every reason to fear that Florence, Bologna, Siena or even Ferrara or Mantua might be his next prey. It was rumoured that the Pope was gaily repeating a prophecy made him by a gypsy, that he would have a son who would be King of Italy. So we can understand how welcome the news was that Valentinois had met his match under the walls of Faenza. Faenza was defended by Astorre Manfredi, a comely boy of eighteen who had the courtesy and loyalty of an angel. Buoyed up by the faith and love of his subjects, and by the – alas platonic – admiration of the whole of Italy, he held out for month after month. Finally he saved his city from devastation by making a treaty with Valentinois and giving himself over, with a cousin, as hostage. Little did he know that the horrors he spared his citizens were to be inflicted on himself and would include prison, dishonour and death.

After Valentinois had taken Faenza it looked as though he was going to advance on Bologna. It was rumoured that the King of France had asked the Pope to subdue that area and give it in fief to Valentinois. But the Bentivoglio family, who were Lords of the city, managed to circumvent the danger for the time being by offering Cesare Castel Bolognese together with a substantial annual revenue and five hundred men to assist him in his war. Florence followed Bologna's example and was thus left in peace, and the conquering army advanced on a broad front towards Piombino, seizing cities and castles and territories with a lightning speed that recalled the wars of Julius Caesar.

The army had everything it wanted and combined a picturesque variety of costumes with firm discipline. The soldiers were followed by a mass of civilians including merchants, priests, musicians, men of letters, and women who took it on themselves to provide recreation for weary warriors for but little reward. Towering above all the others stood the figure of the Renaissance genius, the boldest adventurer in the realms of the intelligence that the world has ever seen – Leonardo da Vinci. As Valentinois wrote: 'May there be no let or hindrance to our most outstanding and beloved servant, the general architect and engineer.' And so the general engineer could study the flow of the waters in the conquered cities, could invent new engines of war, and could sketch in his notebook the shape of a hut or the way in which the vines were bound together in garlands in Romagna: he could listen to the sound of a fountain in Rimini or resolve the problem of the navigable canal at Portocesenatico which still exists today.

Meanwhile Cesare never forgot his French wife, Charlotte d'Albret (whom the Pope had already started summoning to Italy), and he made it his business to cut a splendid figure in her eyes. He personally selected the gifts that he sent her, such as the precious objects that he acquired in Venice in December 1501. They included the purest moulded wax, white sweetmeats, fine sugars, syrups, nine barrels of Malvoisie, oriental spices, oranges and lemons and cloth of every kind. True, Cesare did not feel that he was bound to her by the duty of fidelity, but this surprised nobody. While in Milan he fell in love with a young noblewoman, Bianca Lucia Stanga, and in July 1501 it even looked as if he wanted to have her in Romagna; and there was also the mystery of the beautiful Dorotea.

While waiting for Faenza to surrender, Cesare had visited the court of Urbino for the carnival of 1501 as the (perhaps unwanted) guest of the ducal family of Montefeltro. His reputation had now become so bad that no sooner had he set foot in the city than a rumour spread that he had tried to poison his hosts – a thing difficult to suppose in view of the circumstances. He enjoyed the elegant pastimes of the court where the intelligence was highly valued, and among the women finishing their education under the Duchess Elizabeth he made the acquaintance of a beautiful Lombard girl, Dorotea, who came from a noble Mantuan family and was engaged to be married to Gian Battista Carracciolo, then serving as a captain in the Venetian army. Cesare fell in love with her but seems to have failed to achieve the kind of thing he was after owing to the careful chaperoning of the girls, especially when suspect visitors were around. Moreover the girl was virtuous, and this was a further titillation for a man who liked each love affair to be a battle.

When carnival was over Cesare went back to his camp. On February 10 Dorotea and her suite set out from Urbino to join her betrothed, passing by way of Cervia which was part of the Venetian republic. They were crossing the countryside gaily and cheerfully, thinking about the forthcoming wedding, when, on the Cervia road, they were attacked by a group of cavalry under the command of a man who, though wearing a bandage over one eye, was easily recognizable as the Duke of Valentinois. The story, told by someone who escaped, goes on to describe how the whole company was overmastered and Dorotea, dishevelled and weeping, was carried off on horseback to an unknown destination. As an act of courtesy to show their regard for Dorotea's noble rank, the kidnappers also carried off one of the girls-in-waiting. Both girls disappeared, but we can well imagine their fate. This rape caused an immediate scandal and aroused general indignation. The King of France sent Louis de Villeneuve and Yves d'Allègre to Cesare's camp to protest. Ambassadors were sent from Venice bent on obtaining satisfaction for Carracciolo who had raised an outcry and said he wanted to leave the Republic's service to set out and search for Dorotea. His departure would have been a heavy blow to Venice, for at this time the Venetian troops were marshalled in Friuli to forestall a possible invasion by the Emperor Maximilian and they were under Carracciolo's command. Ambassadors were also sent to the Vatican. The Pope deplored what had happened and denied that his son was involved in the affair. Cesare, with an air of calm assurance, finally admitted that he knew something of the business but the person involved was the captain Don Diego Ramirez to whom, incidentally, the girl had given a present of some embroidered shirts. Speaking for himself, Cesare failed to understand why they kept on accusing him for it was common knowledge that he had no shortage of women. His explanations were so well worked out and fitted in so well with the general picture that the French and the Venetians accepted his excuses even though they were not entirely convinced. But Carracciolo refused to accept them and in formal council in Venice he protested vociferously and threatened a fantastic revenge. However, the girl's whereabouts were never discovered and she must have resigned herself to her fate after shedding many tears. In the long run she was to end up much better than her kidnapper.

As for Lucrezia, she couldn't escape from Cesare; she had to put him up for a night at Nepi. He went there with the leading personalities of his army and forced her to listen to talk about life and death, war and military exploits, interspersed with lively allusions to a forthcoming marriage. And yet perhaps this brief visit from clever and lively people lifted her out of herself a little and left her with feelings of vague unrest.

> Per pianto la mia carne si distilla
> *My flesh melts away with weeping.*

Perhaps this is the finest line written by the Neapolitan and pro-Aragonese poet, Jacopo Sannazzaro, and it would be a good description of Lucrezia's state at that time, while her grief was daily recalled to her by her solitude, her widow's weeds, and the sight of her fatherless little Rodrigo. But after the departure of Cesare's army, with its fanfares and trumpets, perhaps a faint hint of looking forward was mixed with the constant looking back.

The time for making plans was soon to come. The Pope, for whom match-making was a favourite form of politics, was all too eager to listen to the embassies of the potentates who asked for Lucrezia's hand, only a month after her husband's murder. Among the reckless suitors was Louis de Ligny, a cousin and favourite of the King of France, whose claim had Cesare's support. Ligny would have gladly married the Pope's daughter – 'these Frenchmen would do anything for money and for a (Cardinal's) hat', as Cattanei put it – on condition that he was given a fabulous dowry and that the Petrucci, the reigning tyrants, should be banished from Siena and himself put in their place. But Lucrezia herself put an end to negotiations with Louis de Ligny by declaring that she would never under any circumstances go to France.

The next suitor to appear on the scene was a man who had already made an offer in 1498. This was Francesco Orsini, Duke of Gravina. In the middle of October 1500 he set out from his domain in the South with high hopes and reached Trani on the 26th, where a young mistress of his had already arrived with a great cavalcade on her way to the convent of Santa Chiara to become a nun. The public break-up of their relationship was obviously intended to be noticed and talked about. The Duke of Gravina reached Rome on December 6, where he was courteously received by the Pope who began haggling with him though without reaching a decision – as he had done already with Ottaviano Colonna. Gravina had every reason to suppose that he had a clear field for in the second half of November people in Vatican circles considered the marriage as settled. As the future husband was a widower with two sons, the agreement would include a clause providing that the children should enter the ecclesiastical career and be given fat benefices – provided partly by Cardinal Orsini, who was extremely rich, and partly by the Pope. This arrangement would secure that the offspring of the new marriage should inherit the titles and duchy.

As the autumn drew in Lucrezia returned to Rome and to life in the Palace of Santa Maria in Portico which she must have found repugnant. When the Pope summoned her to the Vatican to tell her Gravina had asked for her hand, she calmly refused it. 'Why?' asked the Pope who was less surprised than curious to know what she would answer. But instead of the reply he expected, namely that she did not want to remarry but to devote her life to her son, Lucrezia answered in a loud voice, 'Because my husbands have been very unlucky.' Sanudo adds that she went out in a rage. When he heard of her refusal, the Duke of Gravina was furious in his turn for he suspected that the Pope was playing with him, for surely he could impose his will on a mere woman; and indeed he was right, for if the Pope had been really keen on the Orsini marriage he would not have exposed their candidate to a refusal which, knowing Lucrezia, he must have foreseen. But it suited the Pope to have his daughter surrounded by suitors for they increased the value of her consent and left him freer to manoeuvre according to his own well-tried system. He could now produce once more the hoary idea of a Spanish marriage and in February he dispatched a bishop with the task of arranging it. The Spanish suitor was a 'certain Count' and he must have been a first-class match, for the Cardinal's hat was promised as a reward to the negotiator: however, we do not know how this project ended. The traffic round Lucrezia grew heavier, making it amply plain that people were not afraid of marrying the Pope's daughter. Meanwhile, the King of France, whom Valentinois considered as his most loyal ally, was making fun of the Borgias' matrimonial mania. He told the ambassador of Ferrara that he had heard that the Pope wanted to give his daughter to the Marquis of Monferrato and had promised to give him the admirably fortified city of Alessandria on the Tanaro which commanded the whole of the upper valley of the Po. King Louis thought it absurd to promise to hand over possessions so hard to come by, and this trait in the Borgias was a sign of the superhuman self-confidence that was an integral part of their psychological make-up. By now Lucrezia had refused the Count of Ligny, Ottaviano Colonna and Francesco di Gravina, yet at each refusal her resolution diminished. Her meditation and self-searchings were leading her by stages to yet another capitulation.

Though she was only twenty she had no illusions left and now she lacked even self-confidence. She had only one way, she realized, of overcoming her melancholy, disgust and cold exhaustion, and that was by acquiring an inner strength that could rise above life's pitfalls and lead to the patience of spirituality. This required solitude – which Lucrezia loved – but a solitude broken up by events that provide the mind with rich memories. With this end in view Lucrezia decided that she needed a modicum of physical security, so that each dawn would not bring some possible threat, and to achieve that she realized that she must get away from Rome and be with a man at least as strong as her father and whose future was independent of Cesare's. The only possible solution lay in becoming the wife of a sovereign in a reigning court. So, without the least thought of judging her family and condemning it, she now for the first time consciously abandoned it and looked elsewhere. This was necessary indeed but none the less a betrayal.

6

THE THIRD MARRIAGE

While Lucrezia was still mourning at Nepi, the Vatican had been pondering a possible marriage for her with Alfonso d'Este, the eldest son of the Duke of Ferrara and a cousin, through his mother, of Lucrezia's assassinated husband. His name seems to have been mentioned casually, like many others, but there seems to have been a general feeling that Alfonso of Este wanted to aim higher, and that for the proud family of Ferrara – one of the oldest and most powerful in Italy – it would seem to lack decorum to stoop to a woman of Lucrezia's reputation and a member of a mere 'private House', as Guicciardini later called it, by which he meant an insignificant dynasty. But after the capture of Faenza and the consolidation of Cesare's power, all the ruling families and especially those who, like the Estes, were feudatories of the Pope, had good reason for fearing Borgia expansion and for seeking guarantees of peace through alliances with the Pope. So that when in February 1501 Gianbattista Ferrari, the Cardinal of Modena, wrote to Duke Ercole of Este suggesting a marriage between his son Alfonso and Lucrezia, no one was surprised that the proposal led to negotiations which proceeded with every likelihood of success, although it was not easy for Lucrezia to enter a family that up to now had always contrived to make good marriages. The reigning Duke Ercole was a widower – the Duchess Eleanora of Aragon, the daughter of King Ferrante of Naples, having died. Alfonso, his heir, was a widower too; his first wife had been Anna Sforza, the sister of Gian Galeazzo, Duke of Milan, whom he had married at a moment when the ruling House of Milan was at the peak of its fortunes. Both the late princesses had been virtuous and had had no love affairs outside marriage. In Ferrara and also in the neighbouring State where Alfonso's sister, Isabella, was wife to the reigning Marquis Francesco Gonzaga, the Borgia story was common knowledge and was repeated in the cruellest of versions. It will be recalled that Giovanni Sforza's accusation about the Pope's unnatural sexual relationship is contained in a letter sent to Duke Ercole of Este by his ambassador in Milan, and that our information about the birth of Lucrezia's mysterious child in March 1498 is derived from the correspondence of the House of Mantua. So the whole Este family shuddered on hearing that the Pope was delighted with the marriage and Lucrezia herself not averse to it. Duke Ercole was a wily man and stood on his guard; he began suggesting defensive phrases to his ambassadors and closed the ranks of the spies whose duty it was to inform him about Vatican manoeuvres.

It was true that Lucrezia had not shown hostility to this last proposal. She had succumbed at last to her longing for calm and to her conviction that the walls of Ferrara would guarantee a happy ending to her life. Everything about the Este family was solid. They were of ancient and noble lineage. The State of Ferrara occupied a dominating position between central and northern Italy and the wide river Po brought fertility to the soil. Justice and administration were orderly. The university – known as the Studium – was famous throughout Europe. The city was beautiful and the court decorative and a home of all the arts. The Pope, in a Consistory held on May 8, 1501, expatiated on the subject of Ferrara as though it were his own personal domain. Indeed, all the Borgias were in agreement about Ferrara. Even Cesare thought that an alliance with the House of Este would help him in his conquest of Romagna and he immediately began exchanging gifts and courtesies with Ercole's children, especially with Cardinal Ippolito, as was widely noted at the time.

It was a highly successful *coup* when Louis XII succeeded in establishing a Franco-Spanish alliance for the conquest of the

Kingdom of Naples. It meant that Ferdinand the Catholic abandoned his cousins, the Neapolitan Aragonese, and agreed on a partition of southern Italy. The agreement which provided that Naples, Terra di Lavoro and the Abruzzi should go to France, and Apulia and Calabria to Spain, was a shabby and impolitic affair. The two armies, with the Pope's approval, were now on the point of arriving, one commanded by Marshal d'Aubigny from the Alps, the other coming by sea from Spanish ports in sister-ships to Columbus' *Pinta* and *Santa Maria*.

Cesare, in accordance with the agreements, had to interrupt his personal enterprises to follow d'Aubigny; but in his new Duchy of Romagna he left first-class garrisons and a good administration. The end of June 1501 saw him in Rome – so much against his will that he did not even bother to arrange any kind of victory parade. As Cattanei wrote: 'He is displeased and uncertain because his affairs are held in the air. If the French win they will not take him into account; if they lose and others defeat the French, he will be in a bad way.' Cesare's discontent was increased by news from Germany that the Emperor Maximilian was furious at the Franco-Spanish agreement and the Pope's part in it, and was threatening to descend into Italy himself so as to prick the State of Romagna like a bubble and punish the Borgias for their ambition. Moreover Cesare felt that the French were forever watching him and noting the stages of his campaign and criticizing his 'restrained progress' – and that must have been insufferable. Perhaps he himself felt doubts about his conquests and their lack of historical meaning. However the fury that devoured him found an outlet with the capture of Capua, an extremely bloody feat of arms followed by a murderous sacking.

As the French forces approached, King Federico made an agreement with Louis XII whereby he went into exile in France. He was received with all honours and died several years later. Naples was French once more and there were singing and brilliant gatherings. Cesare seemed to have recovered his spirits and enjoyed his triumph with women at masked parties. Finally he fell ill and, sensing the hatred of the Neapolitans (perhaps Alfonso of Bisceglie's mother was still alive), he sent for two doctors from Rome, carefully specifying their names. Under their treatment, and guarded by people who were loyal to him because of what they got from him, he managed to recover his health and his spirits.

Meanwhile Lucrezia, in Rome, was pondering over a portrait of Alfonso of Este. His look of powerful virility must have reassured her and convinced her that if she fulfilled her duties as a wife he would let her live her own life. She was more than willing to fulfil these duties, rather like a schoolgirl who wants to be good. Since she had been born, and until now lived, as an outlaw, the discipline involved in her new social position seemed to her highly enviable. To uproot herself, change her country and suffer separations, like other young noblewomen, and conform to a set of rules that were common to all – these things seemed to her very desirable. The more she thought about it the more Ferrara seemed a paradise, and she pressed her father to clear up all the tangles of the marriage agreement as soon as possible.

All the Pope's love for her returned when he saw her changed frame of mind. He wanted to make the Este family appreciate the value of the woman they were to take to their hearts and, to this end – as well as to give Lucrezia a proof of his own devotion – he handed over to her the government of the Vatican while he made a tour of the States of the Church. He gave her permission to open all correspondence not concerned directly with ecclesiastical affairs, and Lucrezia duly installed herself in the Papal apartments and, bending her scented and jewelled head over parchments, she concentrated her thoughts on the grave affairs of State. The Cardinals on their side showed a thorough grasp of the situation and entered into the spirit of the game without being shocked. Cardinal Giorgio Costa led the way. A magnificent old man of eighty-five who, in Polo Capello's words, was 'much esteemed at court and talks openly with the Pope, and the Pope laughs and does not mind', Costa had been one of the favourite candidates at the Conclave of 1492, and for Lucrezia he appears to have felt a mixture of ironical esteem and benevolence that was almost paternal. In September 1501, in full Consistory, he declared that he felt disposed to favour the Este family out of regard for Lucrezia. The Pope knew what he was doing, then, when he advised his daughter to take counsel with the old Cardinal whenever she felt uncertain about any decision. In fact we know that on one occasion she did have a problem and did expound it to the Cardinal. After listening to her, the old prelate's eyes twinkled for he saw at once that she had come across an equivocation and he enjoyed her serious and intent expression. The matter, he explained, had to be taken into consideration. Now, whenever the Pope proposed a matter for consideration in Consistory there was always someone present – either the Vice-Chancellor or one of the Cardinals – who wrote down what had been said and made a note of the voting. Full of enthusiasm Lucrezia proposed herself for this task. Whereupon 'interrogavit Lisbonensis (the Cardinal of Lisbon, i.e. Costa) "Ubi est penna vestra?"' At this outspoken allusion to her limitations as a woman, Lucrezia joined in the Cardinal's laughter and the noise they made re-echoed through the apostolic palace. (This incident is told us by Burchard and quoted by Gregorovius who didn't, apparently, see the point.)

The Pope was satisfied with his journey and with Lucrezia's conduct of his affairs, and he prepared to comply with her wishes. He listened attentively to Duke Ercole's conditions and finally agreed to them. Lucrezia's dowry was to consist of 100,000 ducats and the castles of Cento and Pieve which were worth about as much again and were unlawfully detached from the diocese of Bologna. She was to have jewels, clothes, silverware, carpets, brocades, tapestries and other precious objects to the value of another 75,000 ducats. The annual tribute paid by Ferrara to the Pope would be reduced from 4,000 ducats to a hundred. The male heirs of the marriage would inherit the Duchy of Ferrara. Cardinal Ippolito of Este, the Duke's second son, was to be made arch-priest of St Peter's and to receive further minor benefices. It was a big mouthful but his daughter's happy face enabled the Pope to overcome his bitterness about such plundering of his wealth. And so while Lucrezia was stripping Rome of brocades and velvets, as the Duke of Gandia had done for his Spanish marriage and the Duke of Valentinois for his French marriage, the contract was drawn up and signed in the Vatican on August 16, 1501. Remolino rode hell for leather to Ferrara to hand it to Duke Ercole in one of his favourite country residences, Belfiore. And within those walls decorated by the paintings of Ercole di Roberti the contract was finally signed by the Duke.

A weary messenger, bringing news that the agreement had been signed, arrived in Rome on the evening of September 4, and fireworks were let off at the Castel Sant' Angelo so that the people could take part in the new family triumph; as an informant tells us there were 'gunshots and fireworks as for the Pope's election'. Lucrezia felt she wanted to offer her husband as much pomp and ceremony as possible and, when the celebrations began on November 5, she ordered a cortège of five hundred knights and ladies and, in the company of bishops and with the French and Spanish ambassadors on either side of her, she set out for Santa Maria del Popolo, the Borgias' favourite church. At the steps she dismounted, entered through the Renaissance doorway and advanced to the high altar where the great marble tabernacle presented to the church by Alexander VI shone with all its splendour. There she said her prayers and thanked God for helping her. We have no means of knowing details of what names she mentioned or with what emphasis; we do not know whether she remembered the Duke of Bisceglie or in what context she breathed his name. Her return to the palace in the Roman twilight was even more triumphant, and the crowds cried 'Long live Pope Alexander! Long live the illustrious Duchess of Ferrara!' – for although she was not officially Duchess as long as Duke Ercole lived, the fact that Duke Ercole had no wife allowed the latitude of calling the young bride by the title for which the Borgias hungered.

The King of France seemed satisfied by the marriage, but the Venetians were highly discontented, for they were antagonistic to Ferrara and foresaw that it would bring the Este-Borgia alliance to their door. The Emperor Maximilian's attitude was even more hostile; he was furious at the thought of a kinship between the Este family (who in Reggio and Modena were vassals of the Empire) and those he held responsible for the ruin of the Sforzas. Secret intrigues began, and were aggravated by general comment. Lucrezia had been put on her guard by rumours of difficulties, and she waited with obvious impatience for the arrival of the envoys dispatched by Duke Ercole, at the end of the first week of September, with the task of settling the final details connected with the dowry.

The envoys, Gerardo Saraceni and Ettore Bellingeri, were expert jurists and diplomats. On arriving in Rome on December 15 they descended at Santa Maria in Portico where Lucrezia received them 'with sweet and wise words'. But, compliments over, they turned to business. The dowry had to be settled, and so had the Bull investing the future progeny of the marriage; the annual tribute had to be reduced and above all Cento and Pieve di Cento had to be handed over. These two properties could not be subtracted from the diocese of Bologna without the consent of the archbishop, Giuliano della Rovere. The archbishop, though it went against the grain, had given his consent but was now travelling somewhere between Milan and France and rather inaccessible. Like other questions, the one of procedure became embogged in details.

Each day the envoys from Ferrara watched Lucrezia pay her visit to the Pontiff, accompanied by a brilliant escort of ladies, bishops, cardinals and ambassadors, and take her seat a step below his throne for the presentation of the marriage contracts. They also saw her privately in Santa Maria in Portico and she struck them as being preoccupied but gentle and kind. She was always harping on the same question: when could the Ferrarese come and take her away?

The envoys explained that everything depended on the quick implementation of the Pope's promises, and gave her to understand that it was in her own interest to have everything settled before she reached Ferrara so as to avoid unpleasant surprises. When it came to making demands, Duke Ercole was shameless and knew no limits, and he thought he had done enough in return in calling Lucrezia his 'woman advocate'. When confronted with the exaggerated claims of the House of Este the Pope sometimes drew back and treated Duke Ercole as a 'merchant', yet in the end he always climbed down and gave way. The Pope enjoyed questioning the envoys about Alfonso: was he taller than the Duke of Valentinois, was he handsome and well made, was he fond of arms? Decency and dignity forbade Lucrezia to ask questions about her fiancé but despite the commonly-held view which Gregorovius shares, she did keep up a direct correspondence with him, as Saraceni tells us in so many words. Admittedly the exchange was one of official messages, not love letters; but the fact that the correspondence existed means that Lucrezia had one less humiliation to undergo.

Alfonso of Este meanwhile amused himself in making preparations for the wedding on which the officials of the ducal house were already 'cheerfully spending'. There was much talk about the costumes ordered by the women and above all about the bride's dress. Those who had met her described her as one of the most seductive of women, as well as wealthy and generous. 'Pray heaven this be true,' said the courtiers. Women exchanged information on the new Duchess's fashions. It was known that she did not do her hair in curls but let it fall over her shoulders, hardly plaiting it at all, or else she wore it in the style of a young girl as we see in Pinturicchio's fresco at the Vatican and on the medal struck at Ferrara called the Amorino Bendato. Her bearing was elegant and dignified, and as someone wrote, 'she carries herself so gracefully that when she walks she hardly seems to move'.

The itinerary of Lucrezia's journey had been studied and the lists of names for her suite had been prepared. These included some twenty young women and girls, some noblewomen amongst whom was Adriana Mila, servants (mostly Spaniards), a majordomo, a secretary, two chaplains, a *maître-d'hotel*, a keeper of the wardrobe, tailors, cooks, a smith, a saddlemaker, an intendent, a reader, ten grooms, ten pages, and fifty muleteers. There were also members of the nobility, of the Houses of Colonna, del Bufalo, Paluzzi, Massimi and Frangipane. The list was completed by three bishops and one Cardinal, Francesco Borgia. To these Cesare Borgia added over two hundred gentlemen who were to go to Ferrara to await his wife's expected arrival in Italy. A light touch was provided by twenty trumpeters, and four Spanish clowns.

The delegation from Ferrara was also planned on a large and noble scale, and Saraceni and Bellingeri forecast the names that were expected to figure on the list. But though the Emperor Maximilian's intervention had been a mere bluff, still not a soul stirred from Ferrara, and there was no hope of getting there by Christmas. Lucrezia tried to penetrate the secret reasons for the delay hidden in the Ferrarese envoys' eyes, and meanwhile adopted the only sensible attitude possible, and masked her ever-increasing desire to get away from Rome under a cloak of docility. One day she said to Saraceni in the presence of Monsignor Sabino that if she did not marry Alfonso of Este she would listen to no more talk about marriages, but change her way of life altogether and go into a convent. She called on the Monsignor to bear witness to her intentions.

Meanwhile she was worried about what was to become of her little son Rodrigo of Bisceglie, for it had been made plain that he would not be welcome at Ferrara. A story is told of how she contrived to bring about a meeting between Saraceni and the child in her apartment so that the burning question could be raised. And in the end she announced in a firm voice to the envoy that the child would remain in Rome, that he would enjoy a revenue of 15,000 ducats a year, and that he would be in the charge of her uncle Francesco Borgia. In a Bull dated September 17, 1501, the Pope confirmed that Lucrezia handed Sermoneta over to him and all the land and castles in the neighbourhood. The same Bull made over Lucrezia's other possessions around Civita Castellana and in the Roman Castelli to another Borgia baby, the famous Infante of Rome.

This child has presented great problems for historians, beginning with the coincidence of his date of birth. On September 1, 1501, when Lucrezia's marriage agreement was being signed at Belfiore, the Pope signed two Bulls. In the first he announced the legitimization of the child Giovanni Borgia, who had been born three years earlier to the Duke of Valentinois and a woman out of wedlock. In the second, following the procedure he had employed when Cesare was made a Cardinal, he claimed the paternity of the child for himself, though the mother remained the same woman, and he said that his object was to remove impediments to the eventual inheritance of properties that by rights belonged to the child. These subterfuges are all quite incomprehensible unless there was something that had to be covered up. 'Canon law,' writes Gregorovius, 'forbade the Pope to recognize a son.' But Pastor, who went to the sources and consulted the canonists at the Vatican, contests this view and says no such law existed. What then was the motive? Was it to safeguard the Pope's dignity, at least formally? The second Bull was kept secret, for at least until 1508 the Infante was assumed to be Cesare's son. Later, certainly by 1517, he was officially known as the Pope's son and Lucrezia's younger brother.

What was Lucrezia's attitude to all this, and had she any reason to know who the child's mother was? Burchard refers to the mother as 'a certain Roman woman' and this reference has caused even Giulia Farnese's name to be brought up, in spite of the inconsistences thereby involved. Giulia was regularly married to a long-suffering husband and she would have had no reason to conceal a son, especially as she readily referred to Laura Orsini's Borgia father although the little girl may not have had a drop of the Pope's blood in her body. Moreover there is nothing to show that Giulia ever at any time looked after the Infante, though she could easily have done so, especially when she became a widow.

Now the person who did look after the Infante and take on herself the responsibility of his education was Lucrezia. Borgia history is so tangled that as soon as we begin suspecting anything we immediately suspect something serious, and unless we restrict ourselves to the documents our imagination may well run away with us. The documents prove one point beyond all doubt, namely the concordance between the date of the Papal Bull legitimizing the Infante and that of the dispatch announcing that Lucrezia had had an illegitimate child. Is there a connection between the two births? Were they one and the same birth? Are we to attach significance to the fact that the legitimization was established in September 1501, at the time when Lucrezia's marriage agreement was being drawn up, and may have been intended to remove doubts about the bride? A further point has been noted. On her departure for Ferrara, Lucrezia left orders for her remaining possessions to be divided up between Rodrigo of Bisceglie and little Giovanni Borgia. And, as we learn from hitherto neglected documents in the Este archives, when catastrophe finally overtook the Borgias, Lucrezia was so worried about the Infante that she had him brought to Ferrara so as to keep him near her and supervise his education. The question we would like to answer is whether her love for the child was that of a sister, an aunt or a mother. At this point we should recall Lucrezia's tragic love affair with Perotto whom Cesare murdered. It would not be unreasonable to suppose that the Pope may have included her baby in the list of his own children so as to clear his daughter for the future while enabling her to look after it and attaching it to the House of Borgia. The fact that the Este family later reluctantly allowed Lucrezia to keep the child at Ferrara shows that, though they had grounds for feeling some antipathy towards him, these grounds were not of an unmentionable kind. I use the word 'unmentionable' deliberately, for we have to face the suspicion that the Infante may have been the son of the Pope and a Roman woman who was none other than Lucrezia.

Suspicions of this kind are not only repulsive in themselves but they are also difficult to discuss for there are no documents to go on. And as for inductive arguments, this is precisely the time to be on our guard against them. If Perotto did not give Lucrezia the child, why was he killed? The only possible reason could be that he knew too much. The mystery is insoluble, but the fact remains that by September 1501 the whole world knew of the existence of little Giovanni Borgia.

From the moral point of view it would have been better for Lucrezia if the events of the end of that year had never occurred. There are too many witnesses for us to doubt that the supper party with fifty prostitutes took place. Burchard relates it word for word in his diary; there is an allusion to it in the famous anti-Borgia pamphlet written in the form of a letter to Silvio Savelli; it is recounted, in less detail, in a report written at the time by the Florentine envoy, Francesco Pepi; and it is also told though confusedly by the Umbrian historian known as Francesco Mattarrazzo. And we can be almost certain that these witnesses did not hear of it from each other. The Florentine envoy and the pamphleteer speak only of a very loose supper party which took place in Cesare's apartments and at which the Pope was present. 'The Pope,' wrote Pepi on November 4, 'has not come to St Peter's or the chapel on these days of All Saints and All Souls owing to catarrh; however he was not prevented on Sunday night, the eve of All Saints, from staying up till midnight with the Duke who had summoned courtesans and prostitutes to the palace for the purpose of dancing and pleasure.' In Pepi's account Lucrezia is not mentioned; but Mattarrazzo and, which is more convincing because he lived at the Vatican, Burchard refer to her explicitly as having witnessed scenes of collective orgy that cannot possibly be described in terms of decency. We cannot appreciate the kind of enjoyment the spectators must have derived from what they saw unless we bear in mind the sensuous blood of the Spaniards which gave them a predisposition to all forms of sexual excess. According to Burchard,

Lucrezia sat between her father and brother and presided at the festivity and herself selected the prizes.

It is very difficult for us to reconcile this Lucrezia with the one who wanted above all things to make a good impression on the Ferrarese envoys, who wanted to be thought perfect, and who was mobilizing all her friends to write about her to Duke Ercole emphasizing always the word 'virtue'. And it is out of the question that the envoys shouldn't have heard of the party. And yet not one of the daily accounts written by Saraceni or Bellingeri contains even the vaguest allusion to this event. What, then, are we to suppose? That it never happened; that it was a legend that began in the Vatican ante-cameras and was spread by the eager enemies of the Borgias? Or that it did happen but involved only Valentinois' followers who, like all soldiers between campaigns, seized on any and every opportunity of having a good time? Possibly Cesare invited Lucrezia to the first part of the evening and only proceeded with the second part of his programme after she had left. We would have better grounds for accusing Burchard of inaccuracy were it not that a few days later his diary tells of a similar episode also known to Mattarrazzo and the pamphleteer. Two woodcutters were leading their loaded mares towards Porta Viridaria when, as they passed near the Vatican, they were surrounded by Papal servants who freed the two mares and put them in the first courtyard of the Apostolic Palace. Then four stallions were released from the pontifical stables and the Pope and Lucrezia watched the ensuing spectacle from a window over the palace gate, 'cum magno risu et delectione'. It is hard to deny this story. However malicious Burchard may have been, we cannot overlook that, as master of ceremonies, he prided himself on being exact. And he could so easily have maligned the Borgias in other ways, whereas in practice he barely mentions Giulia Farnese or Vannozza, and never once refers to the Giovanni Sforza divorce. Moreover in the case of this incident, and the supper party, he does not even admit – as he often does – that he was not present, which suggests that he witnessed both scenes either through the slit of a half-closed door or from the embrasure of a window. However, he does speak of these two scenes as of two isolated events: had they been more frequent he would not have failed to record them. And finally we must remember that they occurred during the last period of Lucrezia's engagement when she was waiting from day to day to be escorted to Ferrara, so they may have had to do with the Pope's fanatical desire that his daughter's marriage should bear fruit; for even Ercole of Este, despite his rigid and narrow religious feelings, included a 'very filthy' comedy as part of the marriage festivities at Ferrara.

There is no indication that anything was ever known at Ferrara about these two episodes, and yet, as the year drew to a close, instead of sending for the bride, Ercole of Este asked for ecclesiastical benefices for his very handsome bastard, Don Giulio, and the Cardinal's hat for his councillor, Gian Luca Castellini da Pontremoli. When the delay became noticeable gossip spread all over Italy. The Pope knew this and minded it very much, and finally Duke Ercole had to send some sort of explanation to his ambassador in Florence. The delay, he said, was merely due to the fact that the gentlemen needed to change their clothing from 'cloth for the intermediate seasons' to winter cloth. But the resistance of the Estes had now reached its last stage. In November Ercole had written confidentially to the Emperor Maximilian that, as the season was advanced and the roads unsafe, he felt certain that he had got out of the Borgia marriage until the spring; but now he wrote declaring that he could not possibly postpone the marriage without a public breach with the Pope. So he gave final orders and wrote to Lucrezia begging for the fulfilment of the marriage agreement, for 'every delay involves danger'. Putting aside all ceremony he charged his envoys to see that the Pope fulfilled his part of the bargain. On December 8, 1501, the advance guard of the cavalcade composed of intendants and seneschals set out from Ferrara. The following day Duke Ercole rode with his eldest son to the Certosa Palace, residence of Cardinal Ippolito, his second

son, to give him the task of leading the nuptial company to
Rome, supported by his two young brothers, Don Ferrante and
Don Sigismondo of Este. The bridegroom would remain at
Ferrara.

Included in the nuptial company was one man in whom Duke
Ercole placed entire confidence: his councillor, the sharp-eyed
Gian Luca Castellini da Pontremoli, who knew all about the
marriage – from the Este family's cautious hesitations to the legal
details of the negotiations which he had discussed with the Pope's
ministers in the Duke's name. The Duke also had a high opinion
of Niccolò da Correggio, a gentleman who combined the
qualities of warrior, political adviser, poet and humanist; and he
also trusted Count Ugoccione dei Contrari, the first baron of the
Duchy and husband of Alfonso's cousin, Diana of Este. Ercole
had less confidence in his own sons who were young (the
Cardinal, who was the eldest of the three included in the
cavalcade, was still only twenty-five) and difficult for him to
understand. And yet he knew that, as they were members of the
House of Este and had good advisers, they would inevitably
bring affairs to a satisfactory conclusion. Apart from his own sons
there were three other representatives of the family in the
company – Niccolò Maria, Bishop of Adria, Meliaduse, Bishop
of Comacchio, and one of Alfonso's cousins, also called Ercole.
The hereditary jewels of the Este family which Eleanora of
Aragon and Anna Sforza had worn were taken out of their
coffers and remounted for the new bride.

As soon as he heard the news of their departure from Ferrara,
the Pope dashed off two briefs, both dated December 8, to
express his satisfaction: one was to Ercole and the other to
Cardinal Ippolito. Then he summoned Saraceni and Bellingeri
and expressed his pleasure with an outburst of affability. He
recalled (for now his recollections of affairs with Ferrara were
untarnished) 'when he was a young man and the things he did in
Ferrara in the days of Duke Borso', and then he went on to
review Ercole's achievements. He asked who was the taller,
himself or Duke Ercole? Saraceni answered that he could not

judge them apart but he knew that his master the Duke was taller than he was. At that the Pope got up so as to measure his height against Saraceni's, and 'it was found that his Holiness was the taller'. The Pope was delighted. He went on to say he would love to see the beloved Duke once more and hinted not for the first time that he would shortly like to go to Ferrara himself – this, doubtless, to soften the separation with Lucrezia. He loved Ferrara, he did indeed, and as for Alfonso he loved him like a son and considered him unique in the whole world. Words were not enough to express his satisfaction.

The Ferrarese cavalcade reached Florence in the middle of December, Poggibonsi on the 17th, Lake Bolsena and pontifical territory on the 20th. Lucrezia hastened her preparations. Her trousseau was ready and had that impersonal perfect look of things never yet worn: her two hundred blouses, some of which were sewn with gold and pearls, took away the breath of the women who were allowed to admire them. Her clothes became a fable. There were velvet dresses, brocades, satins, materials with filigrees of gold and silver, there were hems of beaten gold and sleeves sewn with pearls, and embroideries of flowers. The poorest women enjoyed a vicarious magnificence in the greyness of their daily round when they told the tale of a dress that cost 20,000 ducats, of a puff that cost 15,000, and a hat 10,000.

At eight in the morning of December 23 the Ferrarese cortège numbering 500 had gathered at Ponte Molle to wait for the Pope's masters of ceremony. These were two hours late, so it was at ten o'clock that the cavalcade again set out. It was led by the household of the Cardinal of Este and of his brothers, and the households of the gentlemen who had brought fine suits of clothes: those without proper clothes were relegated to the rear with the grooms. Then came the Cardinal himself, between Don Ferrante and Don Sigismondo, the two Este bishops, Meliaduse and Niccolò Maria, the new Ferrarese ambassador to Rome, Monsignor Beltrando Costabili, the Duke's councillor Gian Luca Castellini da Pontremoli, and finally other noblemen and the servants and grooms.

Across Ponte Molle they were met by people representing Giovanni Borgia, Cardinal of Monreale, Cardinal Costa and Cardinal Santangelo, who apologized that their masters had been prevented from coming by old age or illness. From that moment onwards there were constant meetings: with the governor of Rome, the senator, the conservator, the chief of the Chancellery, and various Papal secretaries and scribes – in a word with the whole Papal household. Finally, near the Piazza del Popolo, they espied the cavalcade of the Duke of Valentinois: 'and here we saw many fine coursers which were carefully shown off to us and made to go forwards and backwards and sideways', as Gian Luca da Pontremoli noted, putting his emphasis on Cesare's vanity. Cesare was escorted by eighty halberdiers wearing the Pope's colours of yellow and black. He was superbly dressed – 'all one could see was gold and jewels' – astride a horse 'that seemed to have wings', and followed by 4,000 horse and foot. Cesare embraced the guests ceremoniously. He then placed himself beside Ippolito of Este, while the other Este brothers fell behind with the French and Spanish ambassadors. Monsignor di Adria took his place next to the governor of Rome, the Bishop of Comacchio next to the pontifical secretary, Adriano Castelli – who was also representing the King of England – and Castellini next to the Venetian ambassador who made his usual pointed conversation, deliberately paying innumerable compliments so as to confuse the Duke's councillor.

At the Porta del Popolo they were greeted by the College of Cardinals which had turned out nineteen strong. There were more speeches and bowings and then 'we came to the Apostolic palace by the most handsome (road) in Rome to the sound of trumpets, fifes and horns'. As soon as the first horse set foot on the bridge of Castel Sant' Angelo, the mortars began thundering and the horses shied, putting their riders' skill to the test, and thus they arrived in the Piazza San Pietro where the ambassadors and some of the Cardinals took their leave, and the others went in to visit the Pope. Their entry was disordered but dramatic. After Cardinal Ippolito had kissed the Pope's foot and hand, the Pope took him in his arms and kissed him cordially, and he did the same with Don Ferrante and Don Sigismondo, his brothers. Then all the gentlemen were allowed to touch his slipper, and so enthusiastic were they that Castellini couldn't get there and the Pope's secretary had to clear the way for him. The Pope meanwhile was radiant. He talked and laughed in his most fascinating way and won everyone's heart. Finally he gave the blessing and ordered dozens of flares to be lit as night had fallen, and sent the company to visit the bride.

The most distinguished guests were led by Valentinois to the Palace of Santa Maria in Portico. Although they were sophistic-ated men of the world they were dazzled by the sight of Lucrezia as she appeared on the great stairway, in a dress of her favourite brocade (very dark, shot with violet), her shoulders covered with a mantle of gold lined with sable, her hair caught up in a small green and bejewelled silk net, and great strings of pearls and rubies round her neck. Lucrezia had decided to make her appearance not alone but on the arm of a gentleman dressed entirely in black and with austere white hair (no one knows who he was). The greetings over, she addressed herself to the redoubtable Duke's councillors, and whenever Ercole and Alfonso were mentioned she adopted a submissive air. In talking with Ippolito and his brothers she allowed herself to be freer and gayer – in a word, she adapted herself to everyone. Even the most critical of her guests admitted that she was 'a sweet and graceful Madonna'. The evening closed with gifts of cups and silver plates that Lucrezia offered to recommend herself to her future subjects.

The account we have followed in describing the Ferrarese escort's entry into Rome is an unpublished one, but it is more amusing than Sanudo's, with which, save for one or two details, it is in agreement. The letter written by Gian Luca Castellini to Duke Ercole on the evening of December 23, though quoted by Gregorovius and very well-known, is too important to be omitted. The bride, he wrote, 'is of an incontestable beauty and her manners add to her charm. In a word, she seems so gifted that we cannot and should not suspect her of unseemly behaviour but presume, believe and hope that she will always behave well ... Your Highness and Lord Don Alfonso will be well satisfied because, quite apart from her perfect grace in all things, her modesty, affability and propriety, she is a Catholic and shows that she fears God.'

This tribute must have been of supreme value to the Estes. They based their future conduct on it and, had it been unfavourable, they would have found some pretext for breaking the agreement. Castellini plainly indicates that the 'unseemly' things that had caused apprehension could not be attributed to Lucrezia. If we consult the substantial correspondence in the Modena archives we notice something else – that there are two letters from Castellini to the Duke bearing the date September 23. The one containing the long account of the ceremonial entry into Rome is in double copy and written in chancery script and only signed and occasionally corrected by Castellini. The other, containing the description of Lucrezia, is written in Castellini's own hand and is plainly a secret letter intended to answer questions the Duke and Alfonso were urgently asking.

The Estes and their suite were lodged in different places – some in the palace of Santa Maria in Portico, some in the Vatican and some in the Belvedere where Caterina Sforza had been a prisoner the previous year, before being sent to the Castel Sant' Angelo and finally set free. Other members of the suite lodged with the households of the Cardinals, who were so unco-operative about it all that some of the guests had to move out to inns. But all the visiting noblemen got a fine welcome from the Pope who felt deep pride at the thought of his daughter reigning over such handsome and cultivated men. He announced that he would say a solemn Mass in St Peter's in honour of the Ferrarese and give the blessing with a plenary indulgence and, to cap all, he would exhibit the relics of the Holy Spear and the Veil of Veronica. The religious programme was accompanied by a worldly programme with all kinds of dances and plays, and by special edict the Pope made Carnival earlier so as to enable the common people to participate in the rejoicings of his fatherly heart. Each one of the Borgias had his part to play. The Pope received and conversed with the members of the House of Este, he made them sit near him and insisted on their keeping their caps on, and he appeared at solemn functions with such an apparatus of imposing majesty as to impress even the most critical. Valentinois made friends with the Cardinal of Este and initiated him into the pleasures of the major Roman prostitutes. They went out together wearing masks. Lucrezia was busy preparing for her departure and so was not often to be seen.

They passed a holy Christmas and on December 26 Lucrezia gave a reception at Santa Maria in Portico surrounded by her court and fifty Roman gentlewomen who wore 'draperies on their heads according to the fashion' – which must have corresponded approximately to Raphael's picture of *La Velata*, painted a few years later. But the gaze of the visitors was fixed primarily on Lucrezia's young attendants who were to return with her to Ferrara: they discussed their charms and tried to ingratiate themselves with them. Flutes and viols played light music and Lucrezia danced with Don Ferrante, looking lovely in a black and gold satin dress. Some of the guests noticed the outstanding beauty of the Duchess's cousin, the fifteen-year-old Angela Borgia who was engaged to Francesco Maria della Rovere. The restraint and decorum of this reception had a wonderful effect on Castellini who wrote off fresh assurances about the Duchess to his master. He said that she had promised never to make her father blush for her, and this could well be believed in view of 'her great goodness, honesty and discretion' – virtues that every day became more apparent. The letter ended by saying admiringly that at home her life was 'more than Christian, it was religious'.

Apart from Castellini's letters, other accounts were sent daily to Ferrara. Ippolito wrote and so did Don Ferrante and Don Sigismondo. The Este brothers wrote not only to their father but to their sister, Isabella d'Este Gonzaga, who trembled at the mere thought of the rivalry her beautiful and wealthy sister-in-law would provoke. She needed more precise and detailed reports than her brothers could provide and started looking around for a man of her own to send. She found him in the household of Niccolò da Correggio; he was a man who combined the rôles of fool, secretary and confidant for his master and had the additional advantage of being intelligent and able to undertake the job without compromising himself. He must have had a name, but he was known only by the nickname of 'el prete' or 'the priest' which was the way he signed his letters. 'I will follow the most excellent lady Lucrezia as a shadow follows a body,' wrote 'the priest', 'and where the eyes fail to reach I shall go with my nose.' His letters have not been preserved in large numbers but such as exist show that he was faithful to his promise and well deserved Isabella's thanks. She called him her 'good hound'. It was 'the priest' who sent her the private details about Lucrezia's 'great pomp and dresses of gold', and whose curiosity even took him to the Roman dressmakers for a description of a dress 'all laden with sewn-on goldwork, beaten and enamelled'. The bride-to-be, he said, wore 'a coffer-full of gold'.

On December 20 Bellingeri left Rome to take possession of the estates that the Pope had given as guarantee that he would fulfil the marriage contract, and Saraceni and the Duke's councillor were left to keep an eye on the final negotiations. They were so cautious and scrupulous that on the evening of December 28 they had an argument with the notary, Camillo Benimbene, about the form of the dowry contract. This was a matter for lawyers and the Pope had immediately decided it by giving an order that everything was to be carried out as the Ferrarese wanted, thereby 'showing with open heart that he had no fear of any unfavourable dealings' – in other words that he feared no trap. Now everything was ready for the marriage by proxy and this took place on December 30.

Lucrezia arrived in a dress of crimson velvet with gold brocade lined with ermine, escorted by Don Ferrante and Don Sigismondo of Este and followed by her court and the fifty Roman gentlewomen. Her arrival was announced by a flourish of trumpets. First the marriage rite was read and then followed the appropriate sermon which the Pope cut short with a gesture of his hand. Then Don Ferrante handed her the wedding ring in the name of his brother, Alfonso, and she answered in a clear voice that she accepted him. As soon as the deed had been registered, Cardinal Ippolito came forward looking very dapper in special fancy purple, his long hair kept smooth and orderly with little ivory combs provided by his sister. He made a short speech and opened the coffer, and he and Don Ferrante passed round the jewels: 'they caused a full appreciation of the great and precious presents made to the Holiness of Our Lord, to the Cardinals and to the aforesaid lady Lucrezia ... the illustrious Ferrante was much busied in showing off the perfection and excellence of the jewels.' When the onlookers had valued the jewels in terms of ducats (70,000 was the figure given by the Cardinal of Santa Prassede) Lucrezia's little voice was heard giving her judgment, admiring the jewels, but above all 'the ornaments and workmanship surrounding the jewels' – the labour of art.

There followed festivities in the Piazza San Pietro, after which the Pope gave himself the pleasure of seeing his daughter dance with Valentinois in his own apartment, an extraordinary performance done entirely for his sake. Subsequently Lucrezia's girls joined in the dance two by two, performing choreographic figures and causing the Pope much amusement. Then came a comedy which the Pope stopped with one word – 'boring' – and then an eclogue probably written by some member of the Roman academy though not by Accolti or Calmeta. Finally the guests were given leave to retire and the Este and Borgia families held a party among themselves.

The following day – it was the last day of 1501 – Castellini returned to the Vatican for further discussions with the Pope. With all his practised ingenuity he endeavoured at one and the same time, and without one aim conflicting with the other, to further his own desire to be a Cardinal and bring the agreements about the dowry to a successful conclusion. He had seen the Bull remitting the dues paid by the State of Ferrara and had verified the signatures of the Cardinals. He had also seen the other Bulls which had been duly drawn up and were to be entrusted to Lucrezia to take to her new relations. But he still had something to say to the Pope, with Ercole's undoubted connivance, and he did not feel very happy about it. However, on the evening of December 31, after the Pope had announced that the next day they would begin counting out the 100,000 gold ducats on account, he managed to say what had to be said, namely that the ducats must be 'large' and not 'chamber' ones – for between these two kinds there was a difference in weight. Alexander VI denied that he was obliged to make out his accounts in this way, and when Castellini insisted he said that he would hand the matter over to a lawyer. 'I think that he will speak no more about it,' concludes Castellini in his letter to Ercole of Este, 'and that he will not pay in large ducats.' And he went on to say that the Pope had complained at length to Cardinal Ferrari about these excessive demands, and recalled to mind that over and above the whole of the dowry they had asked for, he had conceded to them advantages worth 25,000 ducats.

On January 1 the piles of golden ducats began to be spread out on the counting table in the presence of the treasurers and witnesses, while outside in the Piazza San Pietro the merry-making went on. There was an exhibition of triumphal cars with figures of Scipio, Paulus Emilius and Julius Caesar – all of course allusions to Valentinois. In the evening there was dancing and a performance of two eclogues, one – considered 'very cold' – devised by the Cardinal of Sanseverino, and the other – which had a magnificent background of 'woods, fountains, hills and mountains' – by Cesare. There was a banquet of allegories. Cesare made the shepherds say that Alcides (Ercole) would no longer need to fear either lions or wolves because the 'shepherd of shepherds would free him from all monsters; and then they went on to say that this was to be the work of a young man living on this side of the river Po in collaboration with another living on the far side, thereby wishing to signify the Lord Duke of

Romagna and the illustrious Don Alfonso'. This eclogue, adds Saraceni, was 'most elegantly recited and easily understood'.

The year 1502 was heralded in with the ringing of bells and the hoisting of banners. On that day representatives of the thirteen Roman districts, wearing caps of the ancient fashion and carrying white rods, appeared in Piazza San Pietro at the head of a procession of two thousand foot-soldiers who looked ready for battle, and thirteen triumphal cars each of which symbolized a district. Castor and Pollux represented the Quirinale; there was Marcus Aurelius on horseback which then stood in the Piazza of St John Lateran, there was the Hercules of the Campidoglio, the allegory of the drawing of the furrow and other conceits inspired by the pomp of ancient Rome. When they had finished watching the spectacle from the windows, the court gathered in the hall of the Papagallo to see a comedy. The Pope was seated on his throne, with Lucrezia on a cushion at his feet. This time the eclogue recited had been composed specially in Lucrezia's honour. Thence they moved into the hall of the Popes where symbolical dances of the 'Moorish' type were enacted. The most graceful of these represented a genie who stood on the top of a tree and had the dancers bound to him with coloured ribbons; he seemed to be guiding their evolutions for no ribbon became entangled with another. Cesare came on to the stage, masked, but easily recognizable by the extreme elegance of his clothes. Finally Lucrezia danced with a girl from Valencia, in a costume of rich dark velvet trimmed with gold and embroidered with jewels. On her hair she wore the finest network of jewels that had been sent from Ferrara and round her neck cascades of precious stones. That evening everyone commented on the appearance of Lucrezia's ten girls-in-waiting who were dressed in crimson velvet and gold brocade, and wore coloured cloaks of gold-embroidered silk.

On January 2 there was a bull-fight in Piazza San Pietro with Cesare playing the principal part on horseback, on foot, alone, or assisted. His exhibition with the banderillas was 'truly very graceful' and his suit of gold braid showed off his good looks.

That evening there was another play – the self-same *Menaechmi* of Plautus that had been acted at Lucrezia's marriage to the Count of Pesaro. This time the *Menaechmi* was preceded by an allegory in which Cesare and Hercules conquered fortune, and Juno promised to favour their houses with a marriage. Rome on a triumphal car, and Ferrara on foot, struggled for the possession of Lucrezia until Mercury ordered peace and harmony. Rome and Ferrara ended in a joint triumph.

The days went by with Lucrezia waiting for the date of departure to be fixed, unaware that Ercole had given precise instructions that the arrival in Ferrara was to occur on January 28, with a solemn entry the next day, followed by ten days' carnival lasting until Ash Wednesday.

Shut up in a room in the Vatican, the representatives of Ferrara and the Pope were meanwhile counting out the dowry into neat piles. By January 2 they had counted up to 25,000 ducats. Confusion and suspicion arose on finding some 'worn' and even false coins, and thereafter the counting proceeded more slowly and never after nightfall by torchlight. By January 5 Don Ferrante agreed that the account was settled and the Pope made affectionate promises about the magnificent plans for Ferrara he had in mind. 'If his promises are fulfilled,' wrote Castellini, 'our affairs will be very well concluded.' The Pope gave Lucrezia endless presents – money for her personal expenses, for her suite and for her horses. He also gave her a magnificent litter and everything else she asked of him. The coffers were so full that they would not shut, and Papal Bulls with their heavy red wax seals were piled up on one another before the ink was dry.

The weather had been mild but on the morning of January 6 a cold spell started: the north wind blew and snow began to fall, but so slightly that no one thought of postponing the departure. From early morning horsemen trotted through the city streets making final arrangements. Lucrezia took her last breakfast at Santa Maria in Portico and said good-bye to little Rodrigo and the Roman Infante. She left the palace where she had lived for ten years – and what years – and went to visit her father. There everything was as usual. The Pope was on his throne and her cushion was still on the step. She knelt down in silence and all present went out, leaving them alone.

There is no means of knowing what passed in that conversation between father and daughter. It was a memorable good-bye for both of them. After an hour the Pope summoned Valentinois, and conversation between the three of them was resumed in Valencian dialect, their secret jargon that cut them off from everyone else in the conspiracy of their lives. They reviewed the political situation and the attitude Lucrezia should adopt in Ferrara. They spoke of little Rodrigo of Bisceglie and of the Roman Infante. They must also have discussed Alexander VI's intended journey to Ferrara within the coming year. When all had been said, the attendants were dispatched once more and returned with Cardinal Ippolito, Don Ferrante, Don Sigismondo and the other main guests from Ferrara.

This was the final good-bye. The Estes knelt down and kissed the Pope's slipper, and Alexander VI said he granted Lucrezia in advance everything she could think of asking, and gave orders that Cesare and Cardinal Ippolito should accompany her on her journey as far as they could. As she stood between them ready to depart she hesitated for a moment, and then her glance returned to her father's face and she felt a renewal of that deep warmth which had so often resolved her confusions and anguish in the past and restored her love of earthly things. Everything was all right, said Alexander VI. If she needed anything she should write to him, for now that she was going to be absent he would do much more for her than he had done when she was present. He said these words in a loud voice in Italian so that everyone present could hear them. They were the last words that she was ever to hear from his lips and they were intended to protect her as far as Ferrara. Now at last she passed over the threshold and went through the hall and down into the piazza. Her eyes saw the great cavalcade spread out before her, the horses snorting steam from their nostrils. She mounted a mule that was caparisoned with dark velvet and bore a travelling chair. On one side was Ippolito of Este, on the other Valentinois. She was followed by Don Ferrante and Don Sigismondo, the Cardinal Legate Francesco Borgia, ambassadors, bishops, her court of ladies-in-waiting and girls, noblemen, knights, soldiers, grooms and a hundred and fifty coaches covered with cloth and velvet in her colours, yellow and dark brown.

Burchard describes the snowy weather and adds that this prevented Lucrezia from wearing a ceremonial dress. But the Ferrarese ambassador, Monsignor Beltranto Costabili, refers to a dress of gold and crimson brocade and a golden mantle lined with ermine, and says that the Duchess was 'very elegantly dressed'. We have no reason to suppose that Burchard, normally so meticulous, made a mistake, yet we cannot question Costabili's account for he accompanied Lucrezia many miles out of Rome and paid his personal respects before he turned back. We may therefore suppose that Lucrezia had put on a simple woollen dress in the morning and later changed on her father's and brother's suggestion: she may have slipped back into Santa Maria in Portico by the private entrance to do so. Or alternatively she may have dressed herself with pomp and ceremony for her official visit to her father and then set out on her journey in something of a more practical kind. Given the fact that Burchard saw Lucrezia in the Vatican and Costabili when she had already set out on her journey, the first hypothesis seems the more likely.

There were few people about and the streets had that hollow silence that makes things seem distant and as though they do not belong to the surrounding world. Lucrezia's treasure was guarded by Cesare's soldiers: as an observer ironically put it, with this treasure the Pope had tried to 'fulfil the commandment of the Church to marry women and virgins'. Next came the litter, 'a room built of wood and lined with gold and the richest upholstery'. Then the bride's horse and mule, the first caparisoned with golden brocade, the second with crimson; then

Lucrezia herself. This was the last time that she was to ride on horseback through the streets of Rome. The Pope moved from one window of the Vatican to another to watch the cortège with the anguish of the first shock of separation.

The company followed the Tiber banks towards Ponte Milvio, passing through the Piazza del Popolo in front of the Church where the Duke of Gandia was buried. So the years had passed and with them that turgid life of passions and quarrels in the midst of gold, Cardinals' purple, merry-making and terror. Lucrezia, child of the South, was abandoning the ripe gold of the Roman sun for the grey sky of Ferrara. Voices were muffled in the snowy silence and it seemed pointless to try to raise them in triumph. The city, peaceful and tumultuous, rich and poverty-stricken, was silent. It did not turn out to greet her; it deprived her of the picturesque scene familiar to her; it turned its back on her questions and her gaze with the hostile reticence of things abandoned. The woman who was leaving Rome was no longer the Pope's daughter but the new-born Duchess of Ferrara who was a foreigner, no longer to be taken into the city's confidence. Rome and Lucrezia were strangers to each other.

PART TWO

7

AT THE ESTE COURT

The duchy of the Estes lay in the great plain of the Po to the south of Venice and Lombardy and north of the Emilian Apennines. It was green with rivers and marshes and cultivated by tough fanners whose land was so fertile that they were stimulated to make large-scale experiments. The heart of the courtly civilization of the country, Ferrara, rose out of the flat mirror of the landscape. Ferrara has no mountains or even hills; it lies open to the winds from the north sweeping across the nearby Po.

The climate of Ferrara is bracing. Fresh gusts of wind blow through the city under the wide sky, across the principal piazza, round the old Cathedral with its Romanesque sculptures – already four hundred years old when Lucrezia first saw it – over churches, convents, palaces, houses and gardens, from the shadowy medieval streets to the cheerful open spaces of the quarter constructed at the end of the fifteenth century, and finally against the four towers of the Este castle.

The citizens of Ferrara were ready to give or accept battle, energetic in their sacrifices, their hatreds and their pleasures, violent, obstinate and at times turbulent (there was a saying that no one was too poor to own an inch or two of knife-blade). But all were united in loyalty to the reigning House, and noblemen and common people alike derived a thrill of patriotism from the Eagle of the House of Este, it being commonly agreed that the glorious history of Ferrara was one and the same as that of the House of Este.

The Este family, as we have already seen, was one of the most ancient in Italy. Its earliest roots are to be found in the

Longobards and it was associated with the names of King Beringer and Otto the Great. The Este family had ruled the city since the twelfth century. Ferrara belonged to the Guelph party and had formed part of the donation of Countess Matilda; at one period of parenthesis in the wars between Pope and Emperor it had given itself a republican government. The overlordship of the Este family was forever in dispute until 1329 when the Pope made them Vicars of the Church in exchange for an annual tribute. Later the Emperor made them Vicars of the Empire in Modena and Reggio, which were the two most important cities in the province after Ferrara. The Este lords were masters, therefore, both by imperial and Papal investiture, and in any case their own strength prevented them from being removed. They were ready to affirm their rights with arms, and for generation after generation the family produced outstanding personalities: Obizzi, Folco, Aldobrandino and Azzo – all men of politics and war, inspired by a passion for the State, and so hardy and lordly that poets quoted them as examples as early as 1100.

The family fortunes were established by Aldobrandino, increased by Niccolò II and consolidated by Alberto whose investiture was renewed by Pope Boniface IX. Alberto is portrayed in an austere statue in the wall near the Cathedral entrance wearing a suit of armour and bearing the Papal Bull in his hand. His son Niccolò who ascended to power in 1402 was one of the most distinguished members of the family. He had a ferocious character but also the ability to bring things to a successful conclusion. He was brave in war and inspired by lordly visions, and his reputation as a lover of women was so great that he is said to have deserved the title of 'Pater Patriae' on the grounds that all the inhabitants of the banks of the Po were his children. It is in fact known that he had twenty-seven children who were all – bastards and legitimate alike – brought up at court without any distinctions being made between them. During his reign the Este castle was the scene of the passionate affair between Parisina Malatesta, Niccolò's second wife, and his bastard son, Ugo, and the tragic adultery which ended up with the beheading of both unlucky delinquents. After he had delivered sentence, Niccolò gave orders that all women who committed adultery should be beheaded without appeal – a strange command, that bore witness to his savage fury and was also an example of the kind of legislative spirit that raises a personal affair into a common ruling so as to get the backing of all the trappings of the law.

Yet Niccolò had some discernment for, before he died, he appointed as his successor Leonello – a bastard son born to him by Stella del Assassino, a beautiful Sienese, who also gave him other offspring including the unfortunate Ugo. Leonello was the kind of prince whose authority and prestige does not need to be bolstered up by fear, and he was passionately loved by the common people. Pisanello has left us a penetrating portrait of this humanist lord. He was a subtle politician who, like Lorenzo dei Medici, tried to establish a peaceful balance of power throughout Italy; he protected and inspired learning and science, corresponded with the great men of the epoch, founded libraries and hospitals and re-organized the University of Ferrara.

Leonello died in 1450 at the age of forty-seven (they said that he sacrificed too often to Venus), and he was succeeded by another son of Stella del Assassino, Borso.

We see Borso in the Schifanoia frescoes. He had a wide, fleshy and intelligent face which expressed longings for greatness, princely virtue and dignity. His court was at once splendid and simple for the exaggerated respect and subservience that came with Spanish etiquette had not yet struck roots at Ferrara. Under Borso's rule, courtesy was improvised but magnificent. Like his father Niccolò and his brother Leonello, Borso aimed at extending the State. He built villas, he opened up roads; he had certainly studied early projects for reclaiming the fertile soil of the Ferrara marshland. He lacked Leonello's cleverness but had wide vision, and the ideal of the State became so much part of his nature that he never married or even had love affairs of any significance, not wanting the direct line of succession to be upset by the claims of bastards. Thirty years later, when old courtiers wanted to prove that they were men of honour and patriots, they referred to themselves as 'the peasants and henchmen of Duke Borso'. Borso was a protector of learning, but as by nature he was a man of imagination and pomp, his greatest passion was for the figurative arts and he had maps, pictures and frescoes painted by the masters of the vigorous school at Ferrara, which reached the height of its perfection with Ercole de Roberti, Cosimo Tura and Francesco Cossa.

The famous scenes of courtly life on the walls of Schifanoia which we owe to these three painters show the healthy joy that colours and shapes gave to Borso's eye. Another revealing example is the famous Bible, illustrated with miniatures by Taddeo Crivelli and his assistants, which later enriched the palace of Maffia Corvino. Before his death in 1471 Borso had raised the Este estate from a marquisate to a duchy. He was succeeded by his brother, Ercole, the eldest of the legitimate children of Niccolò III and Ricciarda da Saluzzo.

When he took over in 1471 Ercole was thirty. He too had a fine head for politics, but whereas Leonello had been subtle and sensitive and Borso magnificent in the most colourful sense of the word, Ercole was a man of measure, cautious even in his pleasures, by nature inclined to avarice, and religious not in the Renaissance manner but in the severe spirit of the Middle Ages. He had profound convictions about the necessity of a reform of the Church, and these bound him in friendship with Savonarola – who of course originated from Ferrara himself – though when later he saw Savonarola's political mistakes he drew back. He had great respect for friars and nuns, and would invite the cleverest and most learned friars and theologians to debate in his presence, carefully following the syllogistic deductions that made their talk seem like the music of pure intelligence.

The land reclamation which had been begun by Borso was carried on by Ercole who managed to drain a large area just outside the city. It was during his reign, and with the co-operation of the great architect Biagio Rossetti, that Ferrara took on the elegant and decorative appearance of Lombard Renaissance art. Even the map of the city was changed by the addition of the wide straight streets known as the Addizione Erculea. Ercole promoted letters and the arts. He loved music, but his great passion was the theatre, and for this purpose he forgot even his avarice, and never wearied of ordering translations of classical comedies and new compositions from the humanists of Ferrara. Actors from all over Italy played in the great hall of the Palazzo della Ragione or else gave private shows. From time to time members of the Este family themselves joined in the plays.

In 1473, shortly after he succeeded to power, Ercole made a political marriage with Eleanora of Aragon, a daughter of King Ferrante of Naples who was then at the height of his power. His wife had that kind of royal beauty that is beyond criticism. There was a stupendous series of festivities to welcome her arrival at Ferrara and she aroused her subjects' admiration, confidence and respect. She bore six children to the House of Este: Isabella, Beatrice, Alfonso, Ippolito, Ferrante and Sigismondo.

When Eleanora died in 1493 the event was a national misfortune, for she was the only person who had been able to persuade her daughter Beatrice to temper the disastrous ambitions of Ludovico the Moor. But in 1497 Beatrice died prematurely in her turn and the political situation deteriorated. Alfonso, the eldest son, had grown up in a closed world without much contact with his father. He seemed to hold himself apart from government and political affairs, as from the society of men of his own rank and the refinements suited to a fifteenth-century prince. He had been born in 1476 and thus had passed his childhood and early adolescence in the midst of anxieties caused by the war against Venice and the bitterness that followed. In that disastrous enterprise the Ferrarese lost the valuable lands of the Rovigo Polesine, and this experience had convinced Alfonso of the necessity of military strength and he became a man of war. The recent discovery of artillery seemed to him of the utmost moment, and he himself directed a foundry and had such respect for the artisans who worked there – today we should call them technicians – that he caused quite a scandal in court by his habit of chatting with them. In his amusements Alfonso displayed a spirit which was at once simple and vicious; he indulged in a coarse venting of his instincts that recalled Niccolò III. His father, who was such an aristocrat and man of reason, a politician in the purest sense, inevitably looked on Alfonso as almost a monster. There was a clash of temperaments between father and son. There is a story that when Alfonso was twenty-one he had gone out in broad daylight into the streets of Ferrara, naked and with a drawn sword in his hand, possibly as an act of bravado or to win a bet.

When Duke Ercole saw his son passing from one prostitute to the next he felt that all refinement was lacking. Ercole himself was not chaste – that, in a man of the Renaissance, would have been synonymous with impotence – but he displayed a certain continence; he only had two love affairs, one with Ludovica Condulmiere, a young noblewoman who bore him a daughter, Lucrezia, and the other with Isabella Arduino, a Neapolitan and one of his wife's ladies-in-waiting. Isabella Arduino had a son, Don Giulio, famous for his beautiful eyes, who was brought up with his half-sister, Lucrezia, at court and under Duchess Eleanora's motherly eye. Alfonso's tastes were of quite a different kind. He liked large, sexy women who shared his sensuality, and he preferred women of easy virtue who dispensed with preliminaries; as a result of frequenting such women he had caught syphilis and his hands were threatened with gangrene. With his first wife, Anna Sforza, who was a woman of capricious moods, he had lived on terms of formal agreement, and he had not spared her tears. She had consoled herself at nights, when her twenty-year-old husband forgot to visit her, by sleeping with a charming little black slave girl. Poor Anna died in childbirth, a fate very common at that time. There was nothing unusual about the sadness of her marriage, either.

It has often been said that Alfonso was not popular. The truth is that he was not loved at court – the distinction is important – that is to say, by courtiers and noblemen, who felt they had little ground for trusting him and even wondered whether Cardinal Ippolito were not more worthy of their esteem. The Cardinal would have been better suited to a life of arms than to the purple, and between him and Alfonso there were frequent disagreements, and members of the two households beat one another up regularly. The younger sons made the atmosphere even more turbulent. Sigismondo was not responsible for this – he was unambitious and pious and content with a life of prayer. The trouble-makers were the handsome and gay Don Ferrante and the popular bastard, Don Giulio. Ercole tried to find a niche for Don Giulio in the Church, but was quite incapable of getting him to adopt that career. Don Giulio was too handsome and too successful with women to agree to bearing any kind of yoke.

Such was the family Lucrezia was to enter with the help of the Pope's authority and for a price in gold. Duke Ercole and Alfonso had yet to come to terms with her and each was to do so with his characteristic roughness. The member of the family who was already prepared to do battle with her was Alfonso's sister, Isabella d'Este Gonzaga, Marchesa of Mantua. Isabella was a famous woman. She was a true member of her House, as was obvious at first sight. She had a mind capable of governing and of conceiving and carrying out bold deeds in the name of the State; she was intelligent, ambitious, and her whole character was built on a grand scale – a dominating personality who had no intention of letting herself be thwarted by her womanhood. As the government of the Marquisate of Mantua was in her husband's hands and she could only advise him when he agreed to listen, which was not often, she tried to become an absolute monarch in the realm of intellectual, artistic and courtly life. She did not mind not being a man so long as no one disputed her position as 'the first woman of her age'. She liked to have exotic clothes which she often designed herself, and her innovations were frenziedly imitated. She dressed herself with the subtlest attention to detail, the materials she chose were perfect, the furs she used were unrivalled, and all the colours, designs and embroideries were original.

Her court was kept perennially fresh by pretty and witty girls and it was the most brilliant in Italy. Her castle on the Mincio was an ideal setting for a woman of letters and was crammed with classical statuary, paintings, books and objects found in excavations. Isabella knew Latin, had studied Greek and kept up a famous correspondence with all the poets, artists and men of letters whom she had been able to get to know. She answered their complimentary letters in the style in which they were written. Her renown increased with the years and her title to be the most representative woman of the Italian Renaissance will never be disputed. Yet, contrary to the common belief, though she had an educated taste in art and followed the fashion, she lacked an artistic intuition of the first order; she had more information than illumination and was capable of praising men like Calmeta, Accolti or Trissino in terms considerably warmer than those she used for Ariosto. Whereas as soon as she could turn her mind to matters of government she seemed to set herself free, she brightened up, showed originality of thought and was almost diabolically clever at turning events to her favour.

As was to be expected, her efforts to make her way in the external world left little time for the woman's world of tenderness and intimacy. The only thing tender about her was a fleeting sweetness in her expression that was not so much native to her as a remote inheritance from her gentle Aragonese mother. She was not as attractive as her courtiers made out, for she tended to be stocky, yet she held herself so well that she gave the impression of majesty. She was a real Lombard and her conversation was rich and spicy.

Lucrezia's imminent arrival brought clouds for the first time into Isabella's solid world. She did not know what to expect of her new sister-in-law from Rome, and from a court which no other could hope to rival. By this time everyone was telling her about Lucrezia's beauty and virtue, but she herself had heard straight from the mouth of Lucrezia's divorced husband (whose first marriage had been with the Marquis of Mantua's sister) a libellous version of Lucrezia's scandalous past. The obligation to consider such a woman as her equal, and to pay her reverence as mistress of Ferrara, was nothing compared with the thought of the part Lucrezia might play on the frontier of her own domain, in her native city and amongst people who called her Isabella, 'the first woman of the world', and even 'goddess'. Every time she heard tell of her rival's wealth and fascination, Isabella's pride was hurt.

The slow winter months between October and January were very busy ones at the Court of Mantua. Isabella regimented her maids of honour, spent whole hours studying new fashions in clothes, comparing colours and matching velvets and furs to find original blends. The mere luxuries of gold and brocade did not satisfy her, and she sought out new ideas for embroidery in illuminated manuscripts. She practised her singing, accompanying herself on the lute. She knew that Lucrezia's favourite art was dancing, and made up her mind not to be outdone even in this. She practised with her girls the French and Italian dances then in fashion, and on observing her lack of aptitude she acquired a dancing-master.

On November 14, 1501, while Lucrezia was still going through tortures of doubt in Rome, Duke Ercole had sent Isabella the official invitation to the wedding. The original text has only recently come to light and it helps to explain an obscure point which has puzzled historians. Why did Isabella go to Ferrara alone for the Borgia-Este marriage? Why was she not accompanied by her husband? Luzio, the most reliable historian of the Renaissance courts of Mantua and Ferrara, interprets Gonzaga's remaining at home in terms of his distrust of Valentinois' manoeuvres which at that moment were the nightmare of all the lords of Italy. Luzio quotes a letter from a certain Matteo Martino da Busseto written to the Marquis of Mantua from Bolzano, saying that the Pope had made a secret alliance with the French and the Venetians, and had arranged for Valentinois' armies to fall on Ferrara during the wedding celebrations and capture a whole netful of heads of States whose dominions he would then invade. The hypothesis seems so absurd that we feel it must have been hatched at the court of the Emperor Maximilian whose mind was unhinged. Busseto strongly advised the Marquis of Mantua not to leave his domains but to keep a close watch on his frontiers. This letter was written on December 9, 1501, and, as we now know, had nothing to do with Francesco Gonzaga's decision to absent himself from the wedding. It was Duke Ercole himself who prevented Gonzaga from going, and for reasons that he explains in his letter.

The official document began with the invitation to the Marchesa of Mantua for the wedding, 'as it is only fitting that your Ladyship should be present, being our daughter'. And it went on to say: 'Yet for motives worthy of respect it seems to us preferable that his Lordship Francesco Gonzaga should not come in view of present conditions to which his Lordship, as I believe, has had the prudence to give full consideration and of which he is fully aware.' This is more than advice, it is an order. 'And this,' the Duke ended, 'your Ladyship can make him understand . . .' thereby showing that he had more confidence in his daughter's understanding than in his son-in-law's. Thus if Gonzaga was afraid, it was with good reason, and the Duke of Ferrara, who was not a man to be frightened by fantasies, was the first to support him. Valentinois' hunger for conquest was known to everyone, and Ercole knew that the Pope had complained of Gonzaga to Saraceni and Bellingeri in Rome, saying that he was 'too free of speech' and above all was guilty of giving refuge to his – the Pope's – enemies including, even, Giovanni Sforza. So Isabella set out without her husband. She was accompanied by the Marchesa of Cotrone and, at Ferrara, was met by her sister-in-law Elisabetta Gonzaga, Duchess of Urbino, and her intimate friend Emilia Pio di Montefeltro – one of the wittiest women of her time. Isabella knew that they shared her views and would lend her their support in everything.

*

At Ferrara the Borgia marriage had set a huge machine in motion and had even untied the Duke's close purse, though he kept a detailed account of what he spent, for which his daughter-in-law would have to pay. The casket-makers, Giacomo and Maestro Niccolò, were given orders for caskets. The court jeweller reset new jewels and old. The Venetian engraver Bernardino, with Giorgio dalle Cordelle and Francesco Spagnolo, was working at the new harness for the bridegroom's horse with lavish plates of beaten gold. The painters, Fino and Bartolomeo da Brescia, were drawing and painting and gilding the carriages that were to bear the women of the court. Stands were put up in the streets, one in Castel Tedaldo, another at Saraceno and San Domenico. They were built of wood, paper and painted cloth and were intended for garlanded actors who would welcome the bride. But the largest number of workers, a veritable army, was employed in the preparations for the theatrical shows which were under the Duke's own direction. There were to be comedies, interval pieces and choreographic dances of the so-called Moorish type. The producers, Ercole Panizzato and Fillipo Pizzabeccari, had racked their brains to produce effects worthy of the audience and of the occasion. And at court in the great hall of the Palazzo della Ragione painters and decorators, under the artist Jacopo Mainardi, decorated the steps that were to hold 5,000 spectators, with white, red and green materials. They draped cloth of gold for the Duke's canopy, festooned green plants and painted huge Este and Borgia coats of arms and also the arms of Ferrara's great protector, the King of France. While a hundred actors and musicians and dancers were rehearsing their parts, loads of theatrical properties were being brought in – a fantastic list of objects including plumes of ostrich feathers for Giovanni Massariato, forty pounds of special tow prepared to safeguard the mouths of the fire-swallowers, bells, tambourines and coloured balls for Maestro Beltrame, twenty-four mirrors for Maestro Giorgio, sixteen red silken awnings for Messer Luca, embroidered gloves for Marino, striped coloured hose for

Salvatore Baioni, thirty-nine rings to deck the ears of the 'sham Moors', spurs, gorgets and masks by the Ferrarese specialist Gerolamo della Viola, a mysterious 'ball to make music', false heads, furs, candelabras, belts, swords, bells, trumpets, down to the strangest trousseaus of clothes, shirts, jackets, doublets, cloaks, boots and shoes.

Lucrezia and her company travelled to Ferrara by stages. They passed through Spoleto where she had once been Governor. At Gubbio, in the territory of Urbino, they were welcomed by the famous Elisabetta Gonzaga, Duchess of Urbino, who was the sister of the Marquis of Mantua. They passed through Pesaro and as they advanced further north the company was upset by rumours – which turned out to be unfounded – that Gian Battista Carracciolo – the betrothed of the beautiful Dorotea whom Valentinois had raped – intended to attack them. On January 28 they reached Bologna where they were entertained by the Bentivoglio family, the tyrants of that city. Outside Bologna at one of the loveliest country houses of the Bentivoglio, Lucrezia was visited by Alfonso of Este, and the bride and bridegroom spent some time 'in diverse and pleasant discussion in the presence of us all', after which Alfonso departed. The last part of the journey was made by barge along the riverways. Isabella of Este Gonzaga, and her brother Don Giulio, set out to meet Lucrezia on the last stage of her journey on the morning of February 1, 1502.

The next dreaded meeting was with Ercole of Este at Torre della Fossa where he awaited his daughter-in-law with a group of his court dignitaries. As soon as the barge touched the banks Lucrezia, passed rapidly over the little bridge, and bowed to kiss his hand at the water's edge. He in turn lifted her up, embraced her, pronounced the expected words of welcome, took her by the hand and led her and the most important members of her court to his great golden Bucentaur or ceremonial galley. Here the ambassadors waited their turn to pay their respects to the bride, and, this done, all present entered a kind of pavilion where Lucrezia was given the place of honour between the French and Venetian ambassadors. Isabella of Este was given second place, between the Venetian and the Florentine ambassadors, and the Duchess of Urbino came third, between the Florentine ambassador and the ambassador from Lucca. In the subsequent conversation the gallant French ambassador, de la Roche Martin, behaved as if he were the chivalry and courtesy of France personified. Outside they could hear echoes of the fooleries of Lucrezia's clowns who were on the galley deck diverting Ercole of Este and Alfonso amidst the roaring laughter of the lords and courtiers. As the galley drew near Ferrara, they heard the joyful rumbling of Alfonso's cannon mingled with the blasts from the trumpeters riding along the banks with Alfonso's crossbowmen, keeping abreast with the boat. And thus, towards four o'clock and with repeated salvoes of artillery, they reached the villa of Alberto of Este just outside Ferrara, where Lucrezia was to remain until the morrow. Here the bride was received by Lucrezia d'Este Bentivoglio, Ercole of Este's eldest illegitimate daughter, and a crowd of Ferrarese and Bolognese gentlewomen. Teodora Angelini was presented by Alfonso's seneschal, with her team of twelve girls-in-waiting selected by Duke Ercole, timorous and laughing in red satin and black velvet. Lucrezia smiled continually, acknowledging compliments, smiling at the women, the girls, the five carriages presented by Ercole, one decorated in gold with white horses, one in brown satin with brown horses, and so on. When these presentations were over it was time for leave-taking and the great Este company returned to Ferrara.

When Lucrezia mounted to her apartment and was alone, she could at last remove the smile that had been fixed on her lips since daybreak and think her own thoughts. She could not yet claim to have won through, but she had arrived, and she had glimpsed the towery rectangular mass of the Este castle in the distant plain. The climax and the completion of the marriage would be on the morrow. She must have trembled at the thought of this new intimacy. She was tired and her ideas and feelings were confused. But before she lost consciousness she perhaps saw two plumes in her mind's eye, one white and one red, both clear and free in the unclouded sky.

Her wedding dress was of satin and curling gold, with wide, French-style sleeves lined with ermine; and her cloak was of gold woven upon a golden background in an ample sixteenth-century design, and ermine-lined throughout. The gold and ermine against a background of dark satin showed off the famous Este jewels to perfection – gorgeous rubies and diamonds hung round her neck and sparkled in the golden net that loosely held up her long hair, leaving her forehead free. As soon as her women had finished preparing her, Lucrezia mounted a great grey stallion caparisoned with crimson velvet – a present from the Duke – and set out for the city in the company of the French ambassador and part of her suite. At the gates stood the doctors of Ferrara University, the flower of the city's intelligentsia, ready to carry the canopy of crimson satin beneath which the bride rode alone. The French ambassador kept beside her, but outside the canopy, so one informant tells us, and another that he followed behind in the company of the Venetian ambassador. The procession formed and moved off. It was led by Duke Ercole's mounted crossbowmen to the blare of eighty trumpets and twenty-four fifes and trombones. Immediately after them came the nobles of Ferrara with their rich golden chains and lively glances as they were recognized and applauded by the populace. Then came the Duchess of Urbino's noblewomen dressed by her command in black velvet or satin; then Don Alfonso on a horse adorned with great pieces of gold worked in relief by Messer Bernardino, the Venetian. Whether by personal taste or by chance Alfonso himself was wearing quiet colours against which the gold gleamed – a beige doublet, a black cap with a white feather, and beige hose touched with pink. Beside him rode his brother-in-law, Annibale Bentivoglio, surrounded by his friends, Gerolamo dal Forno from Modena, Alessandro Faruffino, Andrea Pontegino and Bigo dei Banchi.

Next came the Roman and Spanish noblemen, who filled popular feeling with curiosity and distrust. They looked foreign (and perhaps they genuinely felt so) and too arrogant for their lack of ornamentation, though some of the Spaniards whose delicate faces were frozen in an expressive pallor and whose dress was either gold brocade or plain black velvet, aroused admiration for their sombre nobility. And then came five bishops, as was to be expected in the suite of a Pope's daughter, and the ambassadors, two by two, from Lucca, Siena, Venice and Florence, and four from Rome in long coats of gold brocade. Then came six drummers and two clowns. The clowns heralded Lucrezia who advanced slowly under the flaming canopy. She was so full of the moments she was living through that even when her horse reared and shied at the fireworks she continued to smile. She slipped from her stallion's back and mounted one of her mules which the grooms brought up, while the stallion was given to a page who rode ahead of Lucrezia's canopy with great theatrical effect. There followed the solemn entry into the city. Duke Ercole drew up beside her and they advanced between the houses and across the piazzas of Ferrara, with the Duchess of Urbino in a new sophisticated dress of black velvet sewn with golden astrological symbols. Behind came the three Orsini women, Orsina Orsini Colonna, Jeronima Borgia Orsini and Adriana Mila, followed by twelve court carriages bearing local and foreign beauties who were much admired and discussed. Then came Lucrezia's personal cavalcade and the baggage train of mules, caparisoned in their uniform of yellow and brown satin or cloth.

Despite the fact that she was entering a foreign city, Lucrezia was composed and assured. She was free at last and enjoying a triumph which for once owed less to her power than to her grace. She had smiles and greetings for everyone – noblemen and common people, artisans and soldiers, and they all felt like knights engaged in the defence of a frail woman. She may just at first have disappointed some of the onlookers by her small irregular features and slight figure. But as soon as the first feelings of disillusionment were over their hearts were won by her sweet expression and the way she moved her eyes, as if begging for life. Lucrezia reached the Piazza del Duomo amid fanfares, cheers and songs. Everything passed off without a hitch. Homage descended on Lucrezia from the sky itself, in the form of two acrobats who slid down from the Rigobello towers and the Palazzo of the Podesta to her feet. By this time the leaders of the procession had entered the courtyard and were taking up positions along the arcade on the far side and along the flanks under the windows decorated in the flowery style of the Lombard Renaissance, with Borso's Este symbols, basilisks, eagles, crosses and roses. They left the space at the foot of the great marble stairway free.

There Isabella of Este Gonzaga had taken up her position, resolutely dominating the noblewomen from Ferrara and Bologna and wearing her famous dress embroidered with 'pauses in music', which formed a remarkable contrast with the astrological gown of the Duchess of Urbino. Lucrezia dismounted at the bottom of the main staircase for the ritual embraces and the customary ceremonial. Alfonso's and Ercole's archers struggled for her canopy and mule while she ascended the stairs for the last phase of her triumph.

The doorway of the reception hall was flanked by two gigantic statues in gilded wood bearing clubs. Under their symbolical guard she passed into the hall – 'amongst the loveliest in Italy' – decorated for the occasion with gold and silver tapestries and silken hangings. Here she was welcomed by an aged man whose face betrayed his life of study – the humanist Pellegrino Prisciano who recited an official speech in solemn, boring and over-ornate Latin. His point of departure was not even Adam and Eve, but the marriage of the elements, earth and water, and after references to the Chaldeans, Egyptians and Greeks, and quotations from Homer and Aristotle, he came at last to the praise of Lucrezia. In a few sentences he extolled the Borgia family, especially Callixtus III, and became ecstatic about the person and achievements of Alexander VI to whom he dedicated an extraordinary period that was the corner-stone of his enormous oration. He compared the Pontiff with St Peter and added: *Habuit Petrus Petronillam filiam pulcherrimam; habet Alexander Lucretiam decore et virtutibus undique resplendentem. O immensa Dei omnipotens mysteria, O beatissimi homines . . .* [1]

Valentinois was also given a place in the family tree of the spiritual life, his military achievements providing good material for eloquence. With the Borgias disposed of, the orator tackled his principal argument, the glory of the Este family, which he traced from its beginnings and developed at great length.

We have found no evidence of other speeches made that day nor of verses recited by any of the poets. The gentlefolk of the court were presented, and later Lucrezia, accompanied by Isabella of Este, the Duchess of Urbino and a procession of ambassadors, retired to the nuptial apartment and with a final blast of trumpets the doors were shut against the curiosity of the courtiers. No one thought of indulging in the customary quips made by relations round the marriage bed, as had happened at Alfonso of Este's first marriage when they sang aubades to the couple until Alfonso threatened them with a stick. Lucrezia was too nervous and modest for such acts of coarse hilarity and she had many reasons for wishing to draw the curtain over her adventures in love and marriage.

Directed by Adriana Mila, the girls removed Lucrezia's golden dress and with swift and skilful hands they did her hair and laid her nightdress ready. Probably she had no time to go back over the story of her life up to this point before Alfonso entered the room. It was a warm night.

[1] Peter had a very beautiful daughter Petronilla; Alexander has Lucrezia radiant with all grace and virtue. O unfathomable, almighty mystery of God, O men most blest . . .

8

ANXIOUS DAYS

At a late hour on the morning of February 3, 1502, Lucrezia awoke to her new circumstances in the ducal bed.

She found herself alone. Alfonso had made his appearance and behaved as a gallant and chivalrous husband. He had been handicapped in demonstrating his ardour (though the well-informed assure us that he did so thrice) by the presence of all the informants, women, Spanish prelates and the Pope's kinsmen or intimates who had been sent specially to Ferrara to watch over the nocturnal behaviour of the married couple. We do not know whether Alexander VI was satisfied. Lucrezia was lazy and voluptuous. She postponed dressing and ordered a light breakfast; conversed in Spanish with Adriana Mila and Angela and doubtless received some trusted member of her suite, such as the Bishop of Venosa. Now that she had found another stable home she resumed the pleasant leisurely habits she had once shared with Alfonso of Bisceglie. Even when guests were already in the palace and ambassadors were marshalled in order, when Isabella of Este or the Duchess of Urbino or Emilia Pio and many others were waiting impatiently for celebrations to begin, Lucrezia took her time: they could wait.

Duke Ercole was busy writing a letter to his ambassador in Rome which he intended the Pope to see. It was full of honeyed compliments about his daughter-in-law who 'surpassed all accounts of her'. 'Last night,' he added, 'our son the illustrious Don Alfonso and she kept company, and we are convinced that both parties were thoroughly satisfied.'

Lucrezia appeared towards midday. She was judged very beautiful by all the company of curious and libertine visitors who sought for traces of the 'battle with the husband' on her face. She wore a French-style dress decked with gold and a cloak of dark satin bordered with little stripes of beaten gold with pearls and other gems embroidered on it, and she had pearls and rubies at her neck and on her head. The French ambassador came forward, for it fell to him to offer the new Duchess his arm for the duration of the festivities. And then the procession descended solemnly into the great hall. Lucrezia, the ambassadors and the most important ladies took their seats under a golden canopy, and there were the usual ceremonial bows and applause. Music struck up and there was dancing, but the crowd was so great that several women fainted.

As night began to fall a hundred and ten actors appeared on the stage dressed in the classical manner with togas and tunics. They were to play, on five consecutive days, five comedies by Plautus chosen by Duke Ercole and translated by the court humanists. They were the *Epidicus*, the *Bacchides*, the *Miles Gloriosus*, the *Asinaria* and the *Casina*. To watch the performance the company moved to the great hall of the Palazzo della Ragione which held 5,000 spectators. Members of the ducal family sat under a canopy on seats of gold brocade. Lucrezia gazed over the vast hall with 'eager and happy' eyes, as the chronicler Zambotto put it. If she raised her head she could see the great coats of arms on the ceiling, the Papal tiara recalling the feudal origins of the duchy, the lilies of the King of France, and the Borgia bull set beside the black and white eagles of the House of Este. The vast audience was assembled; on the right and left were the retainers of the Houses of Este, Gonzaga and Bentivoglio who wore so much 'brocade and so much gold embroidery as to look like a goldmine'. The hall was resplendent with colour, warmth and luxury, and even Duke Ercole's face became less icy when he gazed on the scene. But it was time for the comedy to begin. The stage sprang to life and the *Epidicus* was played in the light of 'so many chandeliers and candlesticks that everything was seen in the fullest detail; the recitation took place in great silence and no one was sorry to go late to dinner'.

Isabella, the Marchesa of Mantua, disagreed with this commentator. She found fault with the verses and the actors' voices jarred on her. But even she had to admit that the allegorical and fantastic dances performed during the intervals 'were well presented and with much gallantry'.

The following morning, February 4, Lucrezia allowed no one into her bedchamber which she herself did not vacate before midday. Isabella of Este was on the watch and noticed that she took a very long time to dress, whereas she herself was always up bright and early and ready to receive her brothers and various women, who were prevented by a barred door from paying court to Lucrezia. As February 4 was a Friday and commemorated Christ's passion, Lucrezia's ladies-in-waiting dressed in the plain black proper to a court that was Catholic in the Spanish style. There was no dancing. The comedy of the day, the *Bacchides*, began at once, and Isabella, we are told, found it very long and tedious. There were only two 'Moresche' or symbolic ballets, one of men made up as nudes with silvery wigs who bore cornocopias burning bengal fire, and the second of madmen in strait-jackets with stockings on their heads. These ballets were not a success and the audience yawned and complained. The best moment of the evening came when the guests left the Ducal Palace to sup in small groups in noblemen's houses, for there they could gossip at length about what had happened and criticize the details. In view of the antipathy felt by members of the House of Este and especially by Duke Ercole and Isabella for the people in Lucrezia's suite, they had a good laugh about the young Romans and Spaniards who were vainly haunting the houses of the beauties of Ferrara. It was Isabella who had started the fashion of laughing at them, though taking care to show a partiality for one or two so as to be sure of having supporters at the Vatican in case of need. And she allowed only those in her immediate entourage to hear her comments about Lucrezia's elusiveness and unfriendly attitude to her Ferrarese attendants, and the fact that on Saturday, the third day of the festivities, she had given out that she would remain in her apartment so as to wash her hair and write letters.

But Lucrezia's non-appearance on Saturday enabled Isabella to take stock of her position. She put on a costly dress of silver and white and laid plans to ensnare the most important person at court – Philippe de la Roche Martin, the French Ambassador. This was not mere pique, for Isabella had enough political sense to realize that the King of France suspected her for her obstinate friendship with Ludovico the Moor. Now, unfortunately for Italy, the power of the King of France was waxing and Isabella realized that she was in need of friends at the French court.

Isabella found out how the French Ambassador organized his day and learnt that on returning from Mass in the Cathedral he had invited a few Ferrarese gentlemen to his lodging. Next he had to present the French King's gifts – for Ercole a gold medal enamelled with a figure of Saint Francis, for Lucrezia a golden rosary with hollow beads filled with scented musk, and for Alfonso a medallion with an enamelled figure of Mary Magdalen, an astonishing choice but not a chance one, for Cagnolo informs us that Louis XII meant it as a reference to the new bride who was a 'madonna of valour and gentle manners like a Magdalen'. In view of the donor the comparison had to be put up with; but Alfonso must have much preferred the King's other gift – a recipe for founding cannon.

After seeing to these presentations the Ambassador mounted his horse and paid a series of feminine calls, ending up, as if by chance, with the Marchesa of Mantua – Isabella – who invited him to supper. Philippe de la Roche Martin asked for nothing better than to spend his time with such an agreeable and well-informed woman who was surrounded by witty girls, free and gay and very ready to please. The supper party was cultivated and rather priggish. The Ambassador, who sat between Isabella and the Duchess of Urbino, played up to the conversation in all its moods. A lute was brought out and the Marchesa herself sang fifteenth-century arias in a slight but pleasing voice, letting the song die out as if overcome with emotion, her eyes shining.

Finally, accompanied by two waiting-girls, Isabella introduced de la Roche Martin into her own private room, and, with an air of gallant complicity, she peeled her scented gloves from her lovely dimpled hands and presented them to the knight with 'sweet and honourable' glances and words. Intoxicated with emotion he answered that he accepted the gloves with reverence and love and promised to keep them in 'a consecrated place, *usque ad consummationem saeculi*'.

On Sunday there was a solemn Mass in the Cathedral in the presence of the people of Ferrara and of various dignitaries – though de la Roche Martin was the only ambassador – and Don Alfonso was invested with the sword of honour and the blessed cap, presents that Lucrezia had brought from the Pope. The company returned to court early in the afternoon. On being asked to dance, Lucrezia descended from the ducal tier followed by one of her girls, and to the music of lutes and violas she danced eagerly and well – 'very gallantly', as Isabella herself had to admit. The company danced for over two hours in the ducal hall and then made its way to the Palazzo della Ragione for the comedy. But for some undiscovered reason, possibly owing to the excitement of the dancing, the attention of the audience was distracted as soon as the *Miles Gloriosus* began. There was reason enough, for the lines were involved and badly translated and the acting was poor. The spectators in the front rows began whispering and soon the rustling became general, so that the actors had to yell their parts to be heard above the din. What with the howling on the stage and the chattering in the auditorium the show would have petered out entirely had not the situation been saved in the nick of time by the happy idea of dancing.

But it was almost certainly during this disorderly occurrence that the scene described by witnesses between Isabella of Este and 'a great foreign personality' took place. Isabella had been the ringleader in hostile criticism of the play, and at one point she turned away from the stage and began bantering with her neighbour, concentrating her attention on him and laughing in little gusts at everything that was said. She even ordered sweetmeats to be brought and shared them with her companion who was highly flattered and joined in the game whole-heartedly. She was so carried away that she entirely forgot that the celebrations were in honour of her sister-in-law and that she was under an obligation to keep up some show of decency.

What was Lucrezia's reaction? She had no experience of the ways of this court, with its atmosphere of levity so unlike the Roman one, and there was no one to help her. Alfonso performed his marital duties at night and treated her respectfully in public, but apart from this there was no intimacy nor confidence between them and he left her very much to herself. Duke Ercole was taken up reckoning in cash the cost of Lucrezia's habits and those of her court and was already devising a plan to cut down her expenses. The Este family and the Ferrarese, under Isabella's influence, were obsequiously hostile to the new Duchess. But Lucrezia was not really downcast. By way of reprisal she shut herself up with her own women and refused even to interview the ladies-in-waiting Ercole had chosen.

Monday began with a tourney in the Piazza del Duomo between Aldrovandino Piatese da Bologna and Vicino da Imola – the latter was a pupil in arms of the Marquis of Mantua. After an hour of insignificant passes of attack and defence the combat ended in a victory on points for Aldrovandino. There followed the *Asinaria*. The actors had learnt their lesson, and the play was cut down to essentials; it was a success even with Isabella. During the intervals there was other entertainment – a concert given by the famous coloratura singer Tromboncino, a pantomime of dancers with tinkling bells, and another 'Moresca' representing farm work, seed-sowing, harvest and so on.

On February 8, the last day of Carnival, the ambassadors took their gifts to Lucrezia. There was cloth of gold from the Florentines, silverware from Siena and Lucca, while the Vene-tians sent two great cloaks of the finest Venetian velvet lined with ermine. That day the company saw their last Plautus play, the

Casina – a 'filthy' story of whores and pimps that gave Isabella an opportunity to display virtue and modesty, for she forbade her ladies-in-waiting to be among the audience. (These had little enough virtue for they are said to have implored their mistress to be so good as to marry them off to porters – anything to end the control over their exuberant virginity.) Isabella herself attended the play but pursed her lips with a melancholy and affronted look. But Ercole knew all about his daughter's malicious ways and it seemed obvious that Isabella, who, following the customs of the age, tolerated extremely indecent addresses made even to herself, was making this great show of virtue for Lucrezia's benefit. Anyhow, Lucrezia failed to understand her intentions, or pretended to. She herself enjoyed the comedy which was performed 'with lovely and new acts of love', and she listened with the delight that a courtier once defined as 'most sweet and impure'. The dances during the intervals were superb. A globe fell upon the stage and the virtues emerged from it singing the praises of the bride. Don Alfonso and Don Giulio exhibited their fine legs and their gymnastic abilities in a war dance. Then Alfonso returned to the stage and played in a concert for six violas. Tromboncino sang, and the evening ended with a ball which was full of light and movement. At supper that evening people began talking of their departure.

The good-byes began on Ash Wednesday. The ambassadors called on the Duchess in her apartment. Lucrezia had agreed at last to open her doors, and Isabella of Este and Elisabetta Gonzaga made their way in and had a good look everywhere for clues to Lucrezia. The Venetians made a fine speech, and Isabella answered them in an eloquent and ornate discourse about the splendour of the House of Gonzaga, the high military abilities of the Marquis of Mantua and the traditional friendship between Mantua and Venice. Elisabetta then spoke briefly, and finally Lucrezia uttered a few modest words which, according to an informant, added little to what the others had said but showed her good breeding and sense.

The guests began to leave Ferrara, but on February 14, five days after the end of Carnival, there were still four hundred and fifty people and three hundred and fifty horses to be housed and fed. As Isabella wrote to her husband: 'Your Lordship can imagine how pleasing this is to the Lord Duke.' Ercole of Este read over the expenses sheet with silent indignation and began looking for an immediate way out. It was easy to find a pretext for dismissing the gentlemen of the Duke of Valentinois, and he sent them away on the grounds that their sojourn at Ferrara was doing little honour to His Holiness or to the Duke of Romagna. In a letter to Beltrando Costabili in Rome he pointed out furthermore that the women who were staying in Ferrara had so many cavaliers and grooms and servants that the burden of providing hospitality was very heavy.

Isabella of Este also delayed her departure from Ferrara. She was becoming aware that her sister-in-law's affairs were not in such good order as they had seemed at first, and the evident chinks in her armour made it worth staying on. When she talked with Teodora Angelini, a Ferrarese lady-in-waiting to Lucrezia, she found it easy to turn the conversation in a pessimistic direction and, thus encouraged, the girl admitted that the time was fast approaching when the Duchess would sack all the Ferrarese from her court and keep on only the Romans and Spaniards. Isabella felt agreeably certain that this alarm – which she immediately spread – would provoke a reaction amongst the courtiers and still more in the Este family. She had now had her revenge and, on February 16, when she felt sure that she had done enough, she departed with Emilia Pio, the Marchesa of Cotrone, and Elisabetta Gonzaga and all their following. Lucrezia and her court said a ceremonious good-bye followed by sighs of relief. Isabella and Lucrezia exchanged icy and courteous little letters and there, for the time being, their relationship remained.

The result of Isabella's hints became immediately apparent. By the end of February, on the Duke's orders, the majority of Lucrezia's Spaniards and some of her ladies-in-waiting had to depart. This, said the courtiers, was only the first instalment. Lucrezia found the blow especially hard to bear because it was unforeseen. But she raised no protest and had she done so it would have served no purpose. As she had come to realize, she had no authority and was obliged to harmonize her life, at least outwardly, with that of her new family.

On the day the Spaniards left, Ercole of Este arranged an elegant hunting party for Lucrezia in the well-stocked park of Belfiore, when trained falcons were sent after herons, hares were hunted with the help of leopards, and foxes with the Duke's magnificent pack of hounds. In the nipping March air and thin sunshine, Lucrezia watched knights and ladies galloping on their fine horses through the wintry woods which were just wakening with the promise of early violets. Lucrezia enjoyed herself, yes, though she certainly felt a pang at the thought of the people she loved on their way South. But the thought of those who had left was less pressing than her need to defend those who had stayed behind, and perhaps Lucrezia had already made a plan by the time she got back to the castle that evening.

She did not rebel. Instead she pretended to give way on all points, accepted the list of servants and ladies-in-waiting that Ercole had drawn up, and feigned ignorance of her father-in-law's plan to dismiss Adriana Mila, Madonna Ceccarella and others, before Easter. She took to summoning the Ferrarese girls and even invited Teodora Angelini to her table, an honour much coveted in Lent. Teodora could hardly believe it and wrote off to Isabella in high praise of the Duchess who had now become normal and 'sweet and human' and 'full of patience for those in waiting'. In addition someone must have explained to Lucrezia that her cold treatment of Isabella had been a serious diplomatic mistake to say the least, for in talking with Teodora she turned the subject to her sister-in-law and listened to her praises with assent. One of the Spaniards, a man whom Isabella had won over to herself, pointed out to Lucrezia that the Ferrarese had noticed her coldness towards the House of Este. Lucrezia assumed a desolate expression and made the excuse that she 'was new' to the country and she bitterly regretted that she had not made use of such excellent opportunities – all of which, of course, was intended to reach Isabella's ears.

In making up his accounts the avaricious old Duke had allotted 8,000 ducats a year for the maintenance of his daughter-in-law and with this she was expected to provide her court with clothes, food, horses and carriages, quite apart from the alms-giving and entertaining expected of her rank. The decision must have offended Lucrezia when she heard of it, for it was her habit to spend as lavishly as a queen and as carelessly as a courtesan, and she knew full well that her dowry gave her a claim to at least 12,000 ducats a year. This was what she now asked for. Ercole's miserliness came into play and he asked Isabella how much she spent. Isabella answered promptly that she found 8,000 ducats adequate, whereupon Ercole split the difference and offered Lucrezia 10,000. Lucrezia gave out that she had no skill for bargaining and left the adjective 'mercenary', which Alexander VI had already used, to be understood. Alfonso of Este observed the altercation with a lack of interest that might seem surprising though it was really no more than a further demonstration of his conception of balanced hierarchy. The conflict was exclusively between father-in-law and daughter-in-law. It grew and became embittered and did not always preserve the forms of courtesy. Soon Lucrezia had an additional argument on her side: in March it became apparent that she was expecting an heir and it remained to be seen whether Duke Ercole would be moved by this.

He does not seem to have been very much moved, though he kept up the comedy of fatherly courtesy and accompanied his daughter-in-law on visits to convents and churches and even went in her coach on Palm Sunday to see a daughter of Sigismondo of Este, Ginevra, take the veil in the ancient convent of Sant' Antonio near the Porta Romana, a favourite family place for religious ceremonies. The cold glances between father-in-law and daughter-in-law were more expressive than words, but Ercole remained as hard as the diamond on his seal and it was Lucrezia who had to give way. Discomfiture and bitterness led her to seek the consolation of the cloister.

It was Wednesday in Holy Week. The cloister she chose was not Ercole's favourite Dominican convent, naturally, but that of Corpus Domini belonging to the Poor Clares which had been founded by Eleanora of Aragon for the children of noble houses. It still exists today.

As Lucrezia's silk-lined carriage proceeded between the homely walls she could count the March buds on the little trees. She descended at the truncated façade of the church and entered under the little arched doorway with its unobtrusive decoration. Abbess and nuns were awaiting her, amongst them Sister Laura Boiardo, cousin of the poet. Lucrezia imagined she was back at San Sisto as she heard with delight the rustling of the nuns' habits. She saw once more those quiet little smiles that nuns put on their faces as part of modesty's make-up, smelt the odour of incense, and heard the summons of a bell and the singing of gentle voices. Lucrezia slept deeply on her first night in her little cell in its lake of silence. The future seemed full of promise and she no longer felt strangled by the need to hurry, or upset by the struggle with hostile forces.

From the Vatican Alexander VI had been following the details of his daughter's daily life. Besides the official letters sent by Ercole of Este to his ambassador Costabili and to himself, he got news about nuptial developments through a secret *cameriere*. He was delighted to hear of the splendid festivities and of Lucrezia's triumph, and one day in an outburst of good feeling he told the Ferrarese ambassador that he made no distinction in his affections between Don Alfonso and Valentinois. He added: 'Remember that the Duchess will be pregnant before Easter is upon us and when she is pregnant I wish Don Alfonso to come here.'

But the Pope's great affection for the House of Este was tempered with wariness. There were constant appeals for special ecclesiastical privileges from Ferrara. Cardinal Ippolito had to be made to feel at home in Rome and invited to hunts and junketings and, during Carnival, to the receptions, balls and plays held in the Pope's apartments. These receptions had a special interest owing to their participants. The dark profile of Cesare Borgia, on his way from one conquest to another, was to be seen. There was Sancha of Aragon, who had been forced into retirement during the period of Lucrezia's marriage, but was now back again, bolder and more restless than ever. There would be some favourite prelate, a henchman of the Borgias, or an occasional Spaniard. The Pope made the girls dance and was never tired of commanding plays to be put on. The warm licentious atmosphere helped to start up a love affair between Sancha and Cardinal Ippolito. The two were cousins, for King Alfonso, Sancha's father, was a brother of Ippolito's mother, Eleanora of Aragon. Sancha was in no way held back by the thought of Cesare's suspicion or jealousy; indeed this merely fanned her desire. For his part Cardinal Ippolito characteristically viewed his whims as dictated by fate. Both lovers were excited by the risks of their intrigue.

The end of February and the first days of March saw the return to Rome of the Spaniards and Romans from Ferrara. The first to arrive were Cesare's chevaliers and we can easily imagine the rumours they spread around Rome. 'I hear on all sides that the Spaniards returned from Ferrara are giving an unfavourable account and saying they were driven away, and that all in the service of the most illustrious Duchess have been dismissed,' the Ambassador of Ferrara duly reported. Costabili sought to put a stop to the gossip and was to be seen with his soutane in the palaces of the most influential Cardinals trying to sound the impressions of the Roman court and of the Pope. But the Pope was coy. All he did was to pester Costabili for Lucrezia's letters, which came to Rome in the Este diplomatic bag. That Lucrezia sometimes delayed writing can be gathered from his requests: 'What, the Duchess has not answered (my) enclosure of Wednesday?' he asked on February 15, and when Costabili spoke of Lucrezia's nuptial activities 'the Pope began to laugh and to talk with the Lord Duke (Cesare)'. When letters at last arrived there was a great to-do. Alexander VI summoned Costabili and told him that he had had disagreeable news from Ferrara; it appeared that Lucrezia had no money to spend and had even been obliged to pawn her jewellery so as to buy presents for her Spanish friends on their departure. What had the ambassador to say to that? Costabili waxed eloquent and explained how everybody loved the Duchess very much in her new family. He recalled the gifts she had recently received from the Duke and enumerated all the public and private functions organized in her honour. Why, the Duke himself called on her almost every day to take her out. As for Alfonso, as the Pope was well aware, he was warm and active as a husband, and beyond all reproach. Moreover, as the Pope knew, the outcome of his attentions would shortly take a concrete form. When he heard this Alexander VI's good humour returned and he gave a great laugh and turned to another subject. Did the ambassador still remember what he (the Pope) had prophesied a month ago? Costabili replied that he remembered perfectly and that His Holiness was an excellent prophet. No, there were no grounds for fear on this score for Alfonso went every night to his wife's bed. The fact that during the day he solaced himself with other women had no significance – on the contrary. 'As he is young, that is as it should be,' exclaimed the Pope, perhaps with a faint sigh of regret. The situation was put in a nutshell by the Cardinal of Modena who, when people came back from Ferrara with tendentious stories, answered: 'If the couple make love, that is enough.'

In her solitude Lucrezia made fast the links of a chain which, for all its apparent fragility, was sufficiently compact and strong to be unbreakable even by Ercole of Este.

Her apartments were in something like a state of siege. She had now left the showy rooms in the ducal palace and lived in the great square castle built by Niccolò III which is surrounded by a moat of green water that scarcely ripples even in the gustiest wind. Her rooms opened on to a hanging garden that gave an illusion of open spaces and perhaps even a nostalgia for them. One was furnished all in blue with a blue bed and canopy and tables and carpets. Lucrezia's private room was decorated in golden satin, and a third in green velvet with a long bench on which the ladies-in-waiting and visitors usually sat. The decorations had been made before Lucrezia arrived and she thought that the colours and shapes failed to harmonize. She planned to effect a complete change as soon as she could.

As Duke Ercole refused to budge an inch in the matter of money and would not add a single ducat to the 10,000 he had offered, Lucrezia withdrew all the bridges she had thrown across to the men and women of Ferrara. The effects of her ill-humour were soon apparent, for four gentlemen 'of the best quality' announced that they were shortly to be dismissed from her service as 'only Spaniards find favour' with the new Duchess. Teodora Angelini was obliged to go back on all the laudatory and optimistic forecasts she had made in the month of March, and confess that the Duchess kept her and all her Ferrarese ladies-in-waiting at a distance and had made it plain that she did not wish to see their lovely faces 'till the Day of Judgment'. She also helped to spread the view that the Duchess only liked the women she had brought from Rome, and as for them, they were making themselves at home and, in their feminine way, were being very successful.

Like all people who are inclined to the spirit of withdrawal and feel the need to keep their personality intact, Lucrezia needed only very limited companionship, but it had to be the kind that suited her mood and on which she could count. She could not endure suspicion and when she became aware that she was being spied upon she experienced acute discomfort. She felt no obligation to be popular, but wanted to be loved as a person by a few people – appreciating to the full the glances or silences of those around her. Those in her confidence constituted a family group in her eyes and, as they were necessary, they were also privileged – though less for their particular qualities than for the common quality of being members of her clan. The girls-in-waiting imitated their mistress and pretended to be withdrawn even when they let themselves be tempted. And the few remaining Spaniards went to and fro between Lucrezia's apartments and their offices with a determined and pathetic conspiratorial look which was enough to freeze the blood of even the best-disposed among the Ferrarese. The mood of the Duchess's household can be imagined if we remember the comments about Duke Ercole's avarice that were made by her majordomo in Rome. All her clan was united in the spirit of resistance, for she had instructed them to fight not for her but for the standing of her court. Yet for all this the Ferrarese were quite wrong in supposing that the inhabitants of Lucrezia's isle of Hispanidad mortified themselves over their pleasures.

Meanwhile Angela Borgia was making a pleasing impression on Ferrara. Though rather brainless, she could laugh and enjoyed laughing, and she was fun in every sense of the word. She found a niche in the Este family in the heart of Don Giulio, Ercole's bastard son. And Don Ferrante, not to be outdone, also found a mistress among Lucrezia's women – the Sienese Nicola. These two were said to be 'going strong' together though 'without committing sin'. The Duke made it his business to put a brake on their passions before sins had time to mature. He forbade Don Ferrante to visit Lucrezia's quarters more than twice a week.

And so Lucrezia's voluntary exile was under the sign of Eros. She rose late in the morning, dressed at leisure, and went to Mass in her little chapel. She lunched. She received the few people who were allowed into her presence, chatted with her women and read religious stories or love poetry to them. She planned new dresses with her robe-makers. Or she would send for one of the strong boxes that contained innumerable appeals and secret Vatican documents, and would read old letters, turning her thoughts to the past in the belief that she could cut herself away from it by tearing up a few sheets of paper. In these crises of melancholy she needed help. Nicola had a good grasp of the finer points of passion and would propose or agree to spend the afternoon discussing tender and intimate feelings. With a festive air Lucrezia would prepare powders and braziers and golden nets and Moorish shirts and a great receptacle of warm, aromatic water, and then, when alone with her favourite, would take off her own brocades and undress her girl-in-waiting and together they would get into the bath which the little maid, Lucia, kept supplied with hot water. The two young women would play and laugh and bask through the aromatic hours. Later, wearing only their shifts, their hair held up in a mesh of gold, they would stretch out on cushions and burn sweet-scented incense in the braziers. These details were made known to the courtiers at Ferrara and Mantua through the indiscretion of 'the priest', Isabella of Este's 'good watch-dog'. With caresses and bon-bons he won over little Lucia and so got his stories straight from the source. In any case Lucrezia's pleasant hours of feminine idleness were discussed in the courts of Ferrara and Mantua with no trace of severity or disapproval.

By this time Ercole Strozzi had already appeared and found a place in Lucrezia's life. We find his name mentioned for the first time in documents concerned with preparations for Lucrezia's solemn entry into Ferrara. 'This evening we go to supper with M. Hercule Strozo', wrote Isabella of Este to her husband on January 29, 1501. Strozzi, like other courtiers, must have been presented to the new Duchess in the days that followed, though we do not know with what effect. A little later, in March, it became known that the poet of Ferrara aspired to be made a Cardinal and had made an offer of 5,000 ducats for the hat and that Alfonso of Este himself had written to his brother, Cardinal Ippolito, in Rome, to back his appeal. Probably Lucrezia added a word of her own. But by the end of March no more was heard either of the red hat or of Strozzi's departure from Ferrara. Something must have happened to make him change his plans: he had made an appropriate answer or given a penetrating piece of advice or showed his understanding by a significant silence –

something that had made Lucrezia find a bond with him. From that day onwards Strozzi enjoyed Lucrezia's protection, had free access into her apartments and was well on the way to becoming her favourite. He was an elegant poet and an impeccable courtier and would have done honour to any great lady. But despite his many solid qualities, he was somehow morally lacking.

What was this hint of evil about him? Ercole Strozzi came of the Ferrarese branch of the famous Florentine family that had migrated to Ferrara in the early fifteenth century with Nanni Strozzi. He inherited a noble name, wealth, high rank and standing from his ancestors, and in particular from his father, Tito Vespasiano Strozzi, who was one of the most admired old men of the duchy and a famous writer of Latin verses. Ercole Strozzi inherited his father's good taste in poetry and letters and developed it with study to such a fine point that, by the time he was only thirty, he had already surpassed his father and was held by all to be one of the most elegant Latinists in Ferrara and the whole of Italy. But he was born lame and always walked with a crutch and, as often happens with cripples, his physical defect caused him much suffering of spirit. His critical intelligence goaded him on to cynicism and pessimism and an icy corruption that affected his ideas. But his velvety grace, elegant phrases and bright eyes won him the friendship and love of women, especially of women who had suffered and saw their own sufferings corroborated by the male authority of his. As was to be expected he was often disliked by his own sex, but his crisp intelligence was appreciated by the old Duke who gave him protection at court as a humanist, a poet, a translator of plays for his theatre and an adviser. Alfonso of Este, however, loathed him, disapproving among other things of the harsh way in which he carried out his public offices. But as he was honest with himself, Alfonso did not consider that his feelings of repugnance gave him the right to censure Strozzi and he did nothing to prevent him having access to Lucrezia's apartment. Perhaps he saw that there

was no one better equipped than Strozzi to endow Lucrezia's
court with wit and culture.

Strozzi was clever at urging women to vanities and caprices
that he could then satisfy, and he set to work to give Lucrezia
some advice about her clothes. He told her about the great
Venetian stores that were then the wonder of Western Europe,
and suggested that she could glut herself with whatever she
wanted there. As a result the 'cripple of a Strozzi' set out for
Venice with his crutch, his fine romantic air, and a shopping list.
In Venice he visited his friend, Pietro Bembo, then the shining
light of Italian humanism, and he also saw a moody and
sensuous Venetian gentlewoman with whom he was winding up
a long love affair. Finally he bought precious materials on the
Duchess's behalf, making merchants bring out cloths of royal
quality, brocades of crimson and gold, marvellous light velvets of
every rare and delicate colour. In the Fondaco of Venice, which
was cool even in July, the rolls of material were spread out so
that the poet could judge to the satisfaction of his exquisite taste
their colour and texture. The results of his selection were
forthwith dispatched to Ferrara and exhibited to the women who
all sang his praises. Lucrezia's wardrobe swelled – and all on
credit. For rather than endure the restrictions that Ercole's
avarice had imposed on her, she had started – perhaps on
Strozzi's advice – to spend beyond her means. It was on credit
that she had her Venetian stuffs made into dresses and
embroidered, and on credit that she dressed all her girls-in-
waiting in coloured camlet. And finally it was on credit that she
ordered from Messer Bernardino, the Venetian engraver, a
cradle for the baby she was expecting. She said publicly that she
had spent 10,000 ducats on this birth – a whole year's expenses;
and at a supper party to which she invited all the members of the
House of Este, including her father-in-law, she made a special
display of silverware.

This supper party was a challenge, and those who saw the
arms engraved on the objects noted a deliberate irony. Numerous pieces from the 'credenza' set given her by Cardinal Ascanio

Sforza for her marriage with the Count of Pesaro displayed the
armorial bearing of the Sforzas. And reminders of her Aragonese
episode were not lacking either – flasks great and small, a box
with leaves in relief, and a salt-cellar of delicate workmanship.
Her adventures with the Orsini family were recalled by objects
flaunting the Orsini bear, and there were the arms of Francesco
Gacet, the Canon of Toledo, who had played such an intimate
part in the love affair between Alexander VI and Giulia Farnese.
But the Borgia arms dominated all the rest – conjoined with the
Duke of Gandia's crown and flame, or with Francesco Borgia's
hat, or, finally, with the Papal tiara. On the lid of a great cup, in
the midst of intricate golden leafage, stood a massive gilded bull
looking like the golden calf of the Bible. Smaller bulls were
engraved or stood in relief on cups, glasses, caskets, vases,
inkstands, water jugs; and on a great font of silver gilt was the
Pontiff's name in all its massive solemnity:

ALEXANDER SEXTUS PONTIFEX MAXIMUS

There were cold rays from Lucrezia's eyes as she presided at
the supper, and she referred to her father at every turn. The old
Duke replied with courteous glances that at most expressed
indifference, and if she were to suggest to him that, after all, she
did not lack resources, he had his answer ready – that, speaking
for himself, he had supposed as much for some while.

It cannot be said that the Pontiff counted for very much at the
court of the Estes. Ercole of Este was already beginning to feel
that the quality and quantity of the advantages that came from
Rome were falling short of what had been promised. And when
Lucrezia received a brief from her father supporting her claims
for her allowance, and passed it on to one of Ercole's gentlemen
for Ercole to read, he answered icily that he would not give way
'even if God came to see us'. Lucrezia's fury increased. It
reached such a pitch that one day, when the Duke was paying
her a customary call, she could not endure the irony of small talk
any longer and burst out saying that it would have been better if
the Duke had stayed at home to 'settle his accounts'. Ercole dealt
with Lucrezia's outburst by pretending not to notice it and,

despite the bad weather, set out with a packet of books on French chivalry to watch Lazzaro Grimaldi painting the adventures of Filocolo and Biancofiore in his villa at Belfiore.

By June Lucrezia was beginning to suffer from her pregnancy, and she asked Duke Ercole's permission to take her court to the cool air at Belfiore. Ercole refused on the grounds that too many painters and workmen were engaged there. After some bickering Lucrezia moved to Belriguardo, the loveliest of the Este summer palaces, where she lived so retired a life that she refused to see even Niccolò da Correggio who was sent by the Duke to talk with her. Nor did she stop there. On the day she returned to Ferrara, knowing of her father-in-law's intention to meet her, she lingered longer than was necessary over lunch at the villa of some friends and enjoyed keeping the old Duke waiting by the roadside. A few days later a religious procession was held in Ferrara, and once again Lucrezia kept the gentlemen and friars waiting and only made her appearance when the procession was over. And her polished ironical smile caused the courtiers to exclaim: 'So we've reached this point already!'

Cesare Borgia fell unexpectedly on Urbino on June 24, 1502, and his attack – which the Montefeltro family had hoped to avert by the hospitality they had given Lucrezia during her wedding journey – was yet another proof of his unscrupulousness. On the night of the 23rd, however, the Duke, having been warned just in time, effected a miraculous escape and fled on horseback with two companions, wearing only his doublet. He sought refuge at Castelnuovo in Venetian territory, but the Governor of the fortress refused to take him in. He therefore pressed on to Mantua where his wife, Elisabetta Gonzaga, was staying as a guest of her brother and sister-in-law, Isabella.

As soon as Cesare entered the ducal palace at Urbino, the famous seat of Italian culture and humanism, he ordered statues, books and pictures to be packed and carpets and hangings to be rolled up – treating them as his booty. But Lucrezia wilted under this new Borgia conquest. She observed the courtiers eyeing her reproachfully and had to admit that their blame of Cesare was justified. Her old fear of Cesare returned, and her household related how she said that she would willingly give 25,000 ducats never to have known Elisabetta Gonzaga, so as not to have to blush now.

So suspicious was the Este family of the Borgias that Lucrezia's genuine distress at what had occurred was doubted until several Spaniards had been questioned and had given the same assurances. In a letter to Isabella of Este, Prosperi said that there were some things deserving of pity even in the devil's house; while Isabella herself remained cool enough to remember that the little Venus from an excavation, and the famous Sleeping Cupid by Michelangelo ('among new things it has no peer', said the Marchesa) – both in the palace at Urbino – would do very well for her own collection, and she wrote to her brother Ippolito in Rome to appeal to the Pope and Cesare for these pieces of sculpture. When she at last gained possession of the Cupid and the Venus she accepted them with tears of joy, and of course there was no question of their ever being returned to their original owners.

All the tyrants of Italy were in a state of consternation. Though Ferrara had Lucrezia as a guarantee and enjoyed the protection of the King of France, feeling there was by no means tranquil. As for the other states they already saw themselves, in the Marquis of Mantua's words, as being 'hanged one after another and unable to do anything about it'. One urgent point that everyone wanted to be cleared up was the attitude of the French to Valentinois. It was common knowledge that without support from his great ally, Cesare would not be able to extend his Duchy any further. The ablest informants whispered that the King of France really aimed at using the Borgias for his own ends, to further his unalterable intention of conquering Naples, and that he had not the slightest desire to support a Spanish dynasty, above all in Italy. So the little courts waited in hope while, in July 1502, Louis XII entered the reconquered Duchy of Milan.

The King of France took up residence in the castle at Pavia and Italian lords and ambassadors went there one after another. Ercole of Este represented Ferrara, Francesco Gonzaga, Mantua. But when lords and ambassadors and informants reached Pavia it was only to witness the King's affectionate welcome to Cesare Borgia and the festivities in his honour. The King made Cesare reside in rooms near his own, gave him clothes to wear, kept him company at supper and ordered rare foods and dishes for him. Those around were amazed and exclaimed that 'never was greater favour shown'. Cesare, alone, showed no surprise. He dominated the situation and adopted a tone of indifference towards everyone, never even returning the calls paid him by older men such as Duke Ercole. One day when he was playing at soldiers with a French jester known as Monsignor Galerin he was nearly stabbed to death by Galerin's dagger, but he escaped, laughing, with barely a scratch.

The marriage that had been under negotiation for some time between the only daughter of Cesare and Charlotte d'Albret, Luisa, and Federico, heir to the Marquisate of Mantua, was now confirmed. It was to take place at some later date, the girl being three years old and the boy not yet two. They were extreme contrasts. The Borgia baby was ugly with a 'hideous' nose and a face that expressed only intelligence. The Gonzaga baby was beautiful and already prefigured the lovely child who was painted and admired by Pope Julius II. But these considerations were unimportant in comparison with political considerations. Cesare Borgia was so keen on the marriage that the Gonzagas were in no position to refuse: he needed only some small pretext to extend his dominions into upper Italy.

It was Isabella of Este who finally took charge of the marriage arrangements and kept a close watch over them. It would take too long to describe all her manoeuvres, the feigned enthusiasm with which she sent envoys to Valentinois and received those he dispatched in return, how she overwhelmed them with grace and courtesy and fascinated them, and the art with which she contrived to cause continual delays without making them apparent. The instructions she gave her envoys were enough to deceive even Valentinois, who in sharp dealing was second to none. One of her envoys to the King of France was advised in confidence by Louis XII to be very careful before making an official pact with the Borgias because 'between now and then (the day of the marriage) who knows what may have happened'. The King of France had advised the House of Este in the same sense at the time of the Este-Borgia marriage negotiations, and it is not difficult to imagine the pleasure the Gonzagas felt at hearing his words, nor their eagerness to follow them. The Marchesa used them as cards in her bold game of holding her adversary at bay.

Halfway through July an epidemic of the kind that frequently devastated Italy and Europe reached Ferrara and struck the ducal court. It was not one of the worst, but it infected everyone. Lucrezia, who had a delicate constitution and was rendered still more vulnerable by her pregnancy, was one of the first to fall a victim. Doctors were immediately summoned to Ferrara from all over Italy. Gaspare Torella, Bishop of Santa Giusta, came from Urbino, and Niccolo Marini from Cesena – both mobilized by Valentinois. From Rome Alexander VI sent Berardo Bongio-vanni, Bishop of Venosa, a doctor whom the Borgias trusted implicitly. The Pope let Costabili see his anxiety, and he took the opportunity of insinuating that the Duchess's illness obviously arose from her exasperated condition of melancholy because of the 10,000 ducats. Of course, continued the Pope, he would never write to the Duke of Ferrara himself because he did not want to be thought to be laying down the law in someone else's house, but he felt he must insist on his daughter being allowed 12,000 ducats – which would please her so much that she would soon recover and live a contented life. Duke Ercole seemed to have forgotten that his daughter-in-law was in his house. He ought to look to what he was doing because Lucrezia's death would not suit the Borgias at all. But – and here the Pope emphasized his words – *he did not know how it would suit the Este family.*

In Ferrara they were very uneasy. The girl who was burning with fever in her bed became an object of value even to those who were the bitterest enemies of her name. Amongst the latter, those who were honest expressed themselves as follows: 'God preserve her, for it would not be suitable if she died *for the time being.*' Borgia messengers followed thick and fast – there was Troche, there was Michele Remolino, suspicious, able, sniffing the air of the apartments and ante-chambers of the Duke. Finally, on August 12, there was the secret and unexpected arrival of Valentinois. Lucrezia's condition had improved, she was sitting up in bed and when she heard the well-known footstep and saw her brother, she seemed to take on a new lease of life. The Pope's two children spent the whole night together conversing in the incomprehensible dialect of Valencia, and it may well be that Cesare promised his sister then that his new conquest should go to the Roman Infante. The hours passed quickly. Valentinois left at dawn and Lucrezia, exhausted by long discussion and emotional strain, had a relapse. There were reports of delirious nights, setbacks and new systems of cure in the packed bulletins given out by the doctors. But by August 13, when the court was laid low by the epidemic, she was somewhat improved. By that time Angela Borgia was in bed, and Lisabetta da Siena and Madonna Ceccarella, whose attack was so severe that she died. Then four of the doctors caught the sickness and the oldest, Carri, died. Finally Teodora Angelini fell a victim and went off to her own house taking her daughter with her and making it plain that she would never again return to the office that had caused her so much humiliation.

In Lucrezia's case the most accurate diagnosis turned out to be the one made by Francesco Castello, the Duke's doctor, whom Ercole had expressly sent to tend his daughter-in-law. Castello wrote to the Duke telling him that Lucrezia would be freed from her illness only when the child was born. Violent crises attacked her almost daily, with alternating heat and chill, and these were to be ascribed to her bile and could not be cured owing to her delicate condition and to the fact that she was a woman (which seems rather mysterious). The Bishop of Venosa took the opposite view and spoke of 'mental disturbances' and phenomena of hysteria – and in that vein he wrote to Rome.

On September 3 and 4 Lucrezia was so ill that Castello put everything into the hands of God. On the evening of the 5th she was suddenly struck with a spasm in the back and gave a groan. She was immediately surrounded and assisted and that night gave birth to a still-born child of seven months. She now developed puerperal fever which caused anxiety, and all the doctors were in attendance. Two days later Ferrara resounded with the rapid clatter of horses' hooves, the castle gates were opened, and a group of weary and dusty travellers from the court of the King of France were admitted and given sleeping accommodation in the castle. It was Valentinois with his brother-in-law, Cardinal d'Albret, and thirteen gentlemen. The following morning Valentinois visited his sister whom he found in a very grave condition. As her temperature had gone up the doctors decided that she must be bled, and Valentinois himself held his sister's leg and tried to distract her from the little operation by telling her funny stories. That night, between seven and eight, she had a relapse and at eight o'clock the next morning she was given Communion. People around her were saying that she would not recover, but the doctors seem to have taken a more optimistic view for that very evening Valentinois left Ferrara as suddenly and unexpectedly as he had arrived.

If there was an improvement it did not last. On September 13 she seemed again in mortal danger and her condition was a subject of discussion all over Italy. 'May God put His hand on her head and set her free,' wrote Bartolomeo Cartari, a Ferrarese envoy to Venice, 'also so as to put an end to the tittle-tattle here.' The subject of the tittle-tattle in question is not hard to guess in view of the ease with which suspicions of poison were aroused. On that day Ercole of Este received two medical reports from the castle. In the morning Lucrezia had felt her pulse when she awoke, had noticed that it was irregular, and a sigh had escaped her, 'oh good, I am dead'. She had expressed a wish to make a will and, dismissing all the Ferrarese, she summoned her secretary and eight friars. Duke Ercole's men tried to spy out the ground for their master and find out about the will, and they succeeded in discovering that the question at issue was a codicil concerning Rodrigo of Bisceglie, which Lucrezia wanted to add to the will she had brought with her when she arrived from Rome.

The Ferrarese were thoroughly disgruntled by her fluctuations between life and death, by the comings and goings, and the sudden appearances of Valentinois. The more perceptive courtiers had already noticed Duke Ercole's feelings about Cesare and shared them – the feelings of hostility experienced by the head of a State against a probable enemy, the repugnance of a pure aristocrat for an adventurer, and the aversion of a man of ideas towards a man who talked of war and achieved his conquests with a formidable army and boundless good luck. Valentinois intuited this attitude towards him, for he told an envoy from Ferrara jokingly that Ercole's blood did not suit his own because that of 'His Excellency is become tepid whereas mine is boiling'. He said he would find it easier to reach an agreement with Alfonso 'because the aforesaid lord is young, and I am not old'.

That Cesare's blood was boiling with dark unrest was obvious to everyone. One day he would be at Genoa with the King of France (whose favour towards the Borgias was still a matter for astonishment); the next he would be at Ferrara; the next he would be seen in Urbino surrounded by his Spaniards, wearing a mask and hunting with leopards. One day he disappeared. The whisper went round that he was preparing an attack against Florence, and the Florentines, who had failed to get into the good graces of the French King, were in a state of panic. For eight or ten days nobody knew Valentinois' whereabouts, and the Ferrarese and Mantuan envoys, who had been posted to Romagna ostensibly on missions from their masters but really so as to spy, refused to believe his henchmen who said he was ill. In reality it emerged that Cesare was in Rome. We do not know what he was doing there nor what new enterprise he was discussing with the Pope. Though Cesare wished to consider himself independent, Rome was still his centre and the Vatican the reason and basis of his power.

Amongst the subjects discussed by father and son at their secret meetings, one of the most urgent must have been Lucrezia. The Pope expressed his satisfaction that Valentinois had been with Lucrezia in the worst moments of her illness. He must also have referred to the fact that her still-born child had not been a son and heir but a girl, for the Pope had gone through days of anguish on that score and had rebelled against the injustice shown him by fate. Yet he was consoled by the fact that Alfonso of Este had made his wife a solemn promise on her sick-bed that he would give her another child, and that a son, within the next few months. But the Pope was not completely satisfied until, round about September 20, he received news from Ferrara that Lucrezia was out of danger and convalescing. Even when serious anxiety was over the Bishop of Venosa was still chivvied and told not to discontinue sending news, for the old Pope never received enough information and details. He was always talking about his daughter who was 'so sweet and dear', and the Ferrarese ambassador had to be armed with answers to every kind of question, even advancing the theory once that after a serious illness a slow recovery is better than a quick one. When the Pope reverted to the subject of the allowance and asked why Duke Ercole failed to give Lucrezia 12,000 ducats, the ambassador hinted that the difference of 2,000 ducats could be made good from some other source. It could not be said of the Pope that he was mean. He had just handed over Cento and La Pieve to the Este family for good, with all the seals exempted from Chancellery costs; of his own free will he had granted Cardinal Ippolito an annual revenue of 3,000 ducats to meet his living expenses in Rome incurred in keeping up his position; and finally he had provided Costabili himself with comfortable quarters in the Borgo palace for which he had had to turn out some of

Valentinois' Spaniards. It may well be that Valentinois had mentioned the subject of Lucrezia's allowance to Alfonso on one of his visits to Ferrara, but Ercole still held out.

Lucrezia and Alfonso were by now worn out mentally and physically by the long months of wrangling and illness and anxiety, and they agreed to separate for a while. Alfonso declared that during his wife's illness he had made a vow to go on a pilgrimage to Our Lady of Loreto. His original vow had been to go on foot, but on his father's insistence and with a Papal dispensation, he was now going on horseback instead. Lucrezia wanted fresh air and had decided to retire to the convent of Corpus Domini. She set out on the morning of October 9 in a litter borne by two splendid white horses, 'in very good cheer' and accompanied by Don Alfonso and his brothers. The populace applauded, feeling that her restoration to health had in some way strengthened the safety of the State. Alfonso set out for Loreto on the same day, delighted at the opportunity of making a reconnaissance along the coast of the Adriatic, a subject possibly more interesting than the sanctuary of the Madonna. Under the standard of religion each of them had chosen solitude and the kind of life they best preferred.

9

HER GREATEST LOVE

In the village of Ostellato there was a large melancholy villa that Ercole of Este had given to the Strozzi family as a gesture of benevolence. The Strozzis used it as a centre for hunting and merry-making and entertaining their friends. There Pietro Bembo arrived from Venice on October 15, 1502. He had crossed the blue lagoon of Comacchio in a big boat crammed with Greek and Latin books.

Pietro Bembo, at thirty-two, was recognized by everyone as the prince of humanists in Italy. He had been the pupil of Leoniceno the philologist, philosopher, mathematician and doctor of the University of Ferrara; Aristotle and Plato had guided him towards the Christian conception of God; and Petrarch was his poet. However, Bembo was capable of coming down from the heights of poetry and philosophy to join in the conversation of courts with wit and charm: and of course the courts adored him.

Ercole of Este had first made his acquaintance when he came to Ferrara in 1497 in the company of his father, Bernardo Bembo, who was a nobleman and Vice-Domino of the Republic of Venice and himself an ardent humanist. We can be sure that the Duke of Ferrara had many reservations to make about the extremely pro-Venetian policy of the father, which to the Ferrarese bristled with thorns, but he undoubtedly appreciated the vast culture and measured taste of the son. He invited Pietro Bembo to court and listened to him with quiet esteem, which is the greatest compliment cold temperaments can make; and at court Bembo, having talked, could work.

Bembo had numbers of friends and learned companions in

Ferrara. They included Sadoleto the Ciceronian, Ludovico Ariosto, Celio Calcagnini and Antonio Tebaldeo as well, of course, as the two Strozzis, father and son – in a word the whole élite of the humanists of Ferrara who were loyal to him and, oddly enough, remained so. But he loved Ercole Strozzi more than all the rest because they understood each other and had the same taste in literature. Bembo admired Strozzi as an elegant Latinist and sent him his Latin elegies to revise. They talked together of women and love, and wrote letters of allusions that each borrowed from the other. Indeed it was because Bembo advised Italian poets to write in the vulgar tongue so that their verses could be read by women, that Strozzi began using the Italian language, not very successfully.

Bembo loved women – not only because he was a Petrarchan and thought it obligatory to be always yearning after a Laura, but because he had an amorous temperament and derived a pleasure from women that was neither entirely pure nor entirely sensual. He had fallen headlong in love, for instance, with the Venetian woman known as Helena, who inspired the most outspoken letters he ever wrote. 'Love me, love me, love me a thousand times over', 'Love me if you can', 'May it please you to love me a little more than you do' – there are a thousand appeals of this kind. These two lovers made a story worth retelling, with the restless demands of their minds which failed ever really to understand each other.

Ercole Strozzi, from Ferrara, kept an anxious eye on his friend's well-being at Ostellato. 'Were I a Satrap,' wrote Bembo reassuringly, 'I could not be served more diligently.' He had no inkling of the surprise in store for him. By now Strozzi had won first place in Lucrezia's esteem and had become indispensable to her, and knowing her mind to be restless and curious he had probably told her all about the poet from Venice. So one day Bembo's meditation at Ostellato was interrupted by the arrival of Lucrezia. She was now twenty-three, remember, and was wearing her cloth of gold and emeralds and pearls; her hair was fine and fair, and she was accompanied by her suite of women, girls-in-waiting, clowns and drummers. The happy company stayed for a short while only, and it was Bembo's task to do the honours of the Strozzi villa. It was good-bye to Aristotle. Bembo spoke in a free and flowing style and Lucrezia's answers were clear and to the point. The conversation took more or less the usual society tone but it was obvious that it was being conducted by a master. An understanding was established between knight and lady on a field that was half-literary and half-chivalrous, and dominated by Petrarch.

Bembo was frequently invited to court. At this time music was the rage at Ferrara because all the members of the Este family were musicians. Concert followed concert, in which Alfonso was alternately listener and player. When January came round bringing the festive season Ercole Strozzi gave a magnificent ball in his palace in Ferrara. And Bembo, who had written to his brother a few days earlier that he was grateful to the Duchess for the honours and courtesies she had shown him, must have been present on this occasion. All the young members of the Este family including Alfonso, Ferrante and even the pious Sigismondo, went to the ball with Lucrezia. Duke Ercole alone was absent. Ignoring Carnival, he set out by boat on a solitary and melancholy journey to Belriguardo with the great State ledger of accounts under his arm.

It was at this time that Lucrezia finally won a major victory over her father-in-law who conceded her her famous 12,000 ducats a year. But actually it was a false victory. After long meditation Duke Ercole had pretended to yield and had proposed an arrangment that would satisfy both his daughter-in-law's demands and his own parsimony: that is to say, he proposed to pay her allowance half in ready cash and half in provisions for maintaining her court. As is plain, it was easy for him to save on the provisions by juggling with their quality. Indeed we know that his courtiers, including Ariosto, whose services were paid in the same way, sometimes complained bitterly about the distributions by the court providers. But Lucrezia was in a mood of optimism and wanted to be happy, especially as now there was no more talk of dismissing the few Spaniards she had managed to keep, namely Sancho, Navarico and several others, and above all her ladies-in-waiting.

But for all her beauty and her gold and velvet she was a prisoner in the castle. Those walls were a perpetual obsession and Lucrezia could not help slipping away on any reasonable pretext. She would go off to visit the churches and monasteries such as San Lazzaro, Santo Spirito, Sant' Antonio, the church of the Poor Clares at Corpus Domini, of the Dominican nuns at Santa Caterina, or the church of the Olivetans at San Giorgio. At other times she would set out on little journeys through the lands of the Duchy to 'enjoy the country'. The court carriages were always out despite the snow, rain and fog of the long winter days. In the evenings torches and fires were lit, and there was dancing at the castle or in the palaces of the nobility. Ercole Strozzi's ball – he being Lucrezia's favourite – was countered by a dazzling ball organized by Bernardino Riccio, Alfonso's favourite. There followed another in the house of Diana d'Este dei Contrari, and then Ercole Strozzi gave a second in grand style in which he tried to out-vie all the others. In February the Duke came back from Belriguardo and began organizing performances of the *Menaechmi* and *Cimusco*. Everything seemed to be one round of excitement. But the general gaiety concealed dark threats.

In the middle of February Cardinal Ippolito of Este turned up unexpectedly in Ferrara with a very small suite and scarcely any baggage. He was not in flight, he said, but had come because 'he could no longer afford' to live in Rome (this was the official reason). But Burchard informs us that the Cardinal was really putting an end to his love affair with Sancha of Aragon who was still a prisoner in the Castel Sant' Angelo. The Cardinal of Este was no fool and must have realized that the air of Rome was becoming unhealthy for him, and thus he took action before there was anything worse than pointers to his peril. Valentinois' 'jealousy' was a threat that might get worse, especially as by now the Borgia friendship for the Estes was slowly but surely on the decline.

The Cardinal had been at pains to avoid giving his departure the appearance of flight and had therefore thought of adequate reasons for obtaining the Pope's permission to leave for Ferrara. Once home, he set about paying court to his sister-in-law with such assiduity that, in the ambassador's words, she could be said to belong 'at nights to the Lord Don Alfonso, but by day to the Cardinal'. And he added that they were 'three bodies in one soul'. But in this the ambassador was mistaken. Lucrezia readily accepted the attentions of such a distinguished Eminence who, as a woman of Ferrara put it, had 'all the grace of his young sister' – that is Isabella of Este – but her trip to Ostellato and the winter encounters had put other ideas into her head.

Ercole Strozzi was always with the Duchess, either bringing her beautiful cloths and 'delicate things' or giving her information and advice, and they constantly talked of the Venetian poet who was watching the buds of spring in his solitary garden on the lagoon. One day, when April could just be divined through the scented mistiness of the air, Strozzi showed Lucrezia a letter he had just written to Bembo in which he told the poet that he was always a lively topic of conversation between the Duchess and himself. Lucrezia read the letter and was delighted by the flowing courtly style, but on folding it again she noticed that it had not been addressed. So, on the impulse of the moment, she indulged in the innocent flirtation of writing Bembo's name on it herself. Her ladies-in-waiting watched her, gladly joining in the fun of a small act of insubordination. The letter was dispatched and reached Ostellato. When Bembo saw the writing he gave a start, but on opening the letter he understood and felt a wave of satisfaction at the thought that the Duchess had him in mind. The idea of her made him happy for she was so beautiful and elegant and free-minded, 'she is not superstitious about any-thing', as he had already written: he had entered into the climate of love as if it were his natural element without any of the preliminary artifices and gambits. Now he had something to write about, and he wrote. The year was forging ahead and June had already begun. Alfonso of Este set out on one of those annual journeys that were so much criticized by the older generation at court, though they enabled him to gain, in his slow and solid way, that knowledge of politics and geography and military science which were to stand him in such good stead in the wars to come.

Winter had been cold and spring a little treacherous – as it is in Northern Italy – but the early summer was beautiful and clumps of roses blossomed in the ducal gardens. The sun brought Lucrezia back to life and yet made her languid. She wrote little notes in Spanish to Bembo. She opened her books of Spanish songs, read love poems and even copied out some couplets by Lopez de Estuñiga:

> Yo pienso si me muriese
> y con mis males finase
> > desear
> Tan grande amor fenesciese
> que todo el mundo quedase
> > sin amar
> Mas esto considerando
> mi tarde morir es luego
> > tanto bueno
> Que deuo razon usando
> gloria sentir en el fuego
> > donde peno.[1]

---

[1] I think that should I die
And should desire end with my other ills

Such great love would come to an end
That the whole world would be bereft of love

But when I consider this
My tardy death becomes a thing so good

That I should by reasoning
Feel glory in the fire in which I suffer.

'I think that if I died the whole world would be bereft of love.'
Lucrezia's heart overflowed. She began re-writing 'Yo pi ...',
crossed out this new beginning and then again wrote 'Yo pienso
si me muriese.' Here the writing breaks off. Did someone come
into the room, or was Bembo himself there and did he steal the
sheet of paper so as to keep it? Bembo was prompted by the lines
to write a little lyric himself which owes its inspiration either to a
Spanish poem which he unearthed from his memory or – if we
follow Rajna's interpretation – to an Italian lyric since lost.

> Tan biuo es mi padesçer
> I tan muerto mi sperar
> Que ni lo un puede prender
> Ni lo otro quiere dexar.[1]

This he sent to the Duchess together with a little homily on
aesthetics in which he warned her that 'the melting sweetnesses
of the Spanish have no place in the grave purity of Tuscan, and
if they are introduced strike a false note and seem foreign'. After
this literary parenthesis the letter took on a freer tone. The poet
confessed that the Ostellato countryside no longer pleased him as
it had done before and he wondered what this meant? Supposing
Lucrezia were to search her books for an answer ... As he
wrote he was seated by a little window watching the bright green
leaves that fluttered in the sea-breeze, and for every leaf he sent
her a thought. During those days he often went to Ferrara. His
quiet straightforward manners caused no irritation; even the
Duke protected him as the Duchess's official poet and an
ornament of her court. 'Ad Bembum de Lucretia' as Tito
Vespasiano Strozzi dedicated a Latin epigram, and on his own
account (for at the age of eighty all the ardours of literature are

---

[1] So lively is my suffering
and so dead my hope
that the one cannot seize
nor the other seek to hold.

permissible) he had already written verses of burning admiration for the Duchess.

Lucrezia had a medal coined with the design of a flame. It was planned and engraved under her eye by Maestro Ercole or Maestro Alfonso, the goldsmiths. She had got so far when she realized that she had no motto to illustrate the meaning of the flame. Immediately she wrote off a note to Bembo at Ostellato: he must quickly think of some suitable words to be engraved. The poet answered that only one place could be symbolized by fire – the spirit – and suggested the platonic phrase 'Est animum'. Then he sent the messenger back saying that he had not detained him as 'too many things could have been thought on that theme'. This is the first intimation we have that Bembo's and Lucrezia's intimacy was such that a hint at prudence was advisable. She should be cautious and not send him too many messages. But he himself was already her prisoner.

Avess'io almen di un bel cristallo il core

he exclaims in one of his best-known sonnets (which later inspired Ronsard's *Eusse' je au moins une poitrine faicte – Ou de crystal ou de verre luisant*) and sent it to her with a passionate letter. Supposing she tried to read in her own crystal? Or perhaps she would evade the question . . . Lucrezia hesitated for several days before replying. Bembo's verse sang in her head. Then she sat down to write in her fine Borgia hand – 'Messer Pietro mio', and that 'mio' after his name took on almost the authority of love. The note was short and unsigned and seemed like the hurried conclusion of an inner conflict. Yes, she too had searched the crystal of her heart and found deep community with the poet – a community 'never at any time equalled'. Let Messer Pietro know it and let it be a perpetual testament. Then she suggested a screen for their love. He should not write to her directly and, when he did write, he should always call her FF. 'This,' she ended up, 'is to be my name.'

Bembo answered immediately. He proposed to do great things in the name of their love; he felt strong and courageous. The names of Aeneas and Dido, Tristan and Iseult, Lancelot and Guinevere, passed before his mind as in one of Petrarch's *Trionfi*. His love, as we see, was both literary and warm, it was not so much a love of the senses as of the mind and the blood, an ardent outpouring of every vital faculty. 'I feel that I am burning and on fire', he wrote several days later, feigning a reference to the great heat of June. And he asked Lucrezia whether she felt the heat in the same way.

During July Lucrezia spent a few days in the country on her doctor's orders, but she was back in Ferrara on August 1 and she made no sign of leaving again for the time being save for an occasional supper in the open air – at Belfiore, for instance. Bembo was also in Ferrara now, but either owing to the heat or to fatigue he contracted a high fever and had to go to bed. We can imagine what was the effect on Lucrezia when this news was brought her – by Strozzi or Tebaldeo her secretary – and imparted in secret. Was the handsome cavalier ill? He was immediately sent messages and comforts. Supposing Lucrezia herself were to go and see him? After all, several months ago she had gone to visit Ludovico Gualengo, a gentleman attached to her court, when he had fallen ill. (Indeed the older courtiers had wondered at that time 'whence came such great humanity' and why 'she had moved for so slight a thing'.) It was a sign of official benevolence that was not permissible for an ordinary woman but perfectly permissible for a princess.

So Lucrezia gathered together her intimates and on August 11, in the full heat of the flat and silent streets, the ducal carriage made its way. The women's eyes shone brightly from quiet composed faces amid the satin upholstery. They arrived at Bembo's house, mounted the stairs, entered the room and reached the sick-bed. Lucrezia sat near him and asked him about his symptoms. Like every educated woman of the Renaissance she knew something about practical medicine and talked of cures, listened and gave advice. The conversation became less formal. Under the tender eyes of so many beautiful women the young man began to surrender to the delights of fever. '*Beato in sogno e di languir contento*' he could have said with Petrarch ('Happy in sleep and well content to languish'). Lucrezia was radiant with joy and comforted him with simple words; but her smile and her glance said more. Time passed and the visit was prolonged. No one would ever be able to take from her the experience of this hour. She had seen how her beloved lay in repose, how his young powerful head rose from his loose shirt, and she had an impression of him that she would never forget. After this, the fact of being spied on meant nothing to her. She faced her enemies with Spanish and Borgia pride. For if her action in visiting him had been lawful, how could anyone put her on trial for her intentions?

Certainly Lucrezia's visit required courage, for the plague had been brought to Ferrara by a boy from Pesaro, and many people were falling victim to it: indeed there was no longer any justification for lingering in town. Duke Ercole had already gone to Belriguardo taking the reluctant Don Ferrante with him. Don Giulio had stayed to keep Lucrezia company, and that fiery bastard, who had made huge boasts of libertinism during Carnival, was delighted at the prospect of escorting so many women and girls, especially as Angela Borgia was among them. They were all happy to leave, including Lucrezia who had a plan of visiting Modena and Reggio and of staying meanwhile in a villa at Medelana not far from Ostellato. There she took her waiting-women dressed in gaily-coloured Tripoli silks, her clowns and her musicians. She felt a desire for amusement now that she was on holiday from marriage with Don Alfonso, removed from Duke Ercole's eagle eye, and away from Cardinal Ippolito's icy gallantries. She felt the keen delight of being on her own, of loving and being loved in secret and without guilt. Bembo had left Ferrara before Lucrezia and set out for Ostellato. 'I am leaving, O my most sweet life', he wrote to her to say good-bye. It may well be that this time Lucrezia dared to be happy.

The enemies of the Borgia family felt deeply resentful when they thought of Alexander VI sitting on the Papal throne as if for all eternity, never examining his own motives and always busy drawing up new plans. Every morning the old Pontiff started his day by thinking of his children. He thought of Lucrezia, was impatient for her to have a new pregnancy and spoke about it with the Ferrarese ambassador. Was it not strange that a little Este baby was not yet on the way? So as to satisfy the Pope, Ercole of Este had questioned his daughter-in-law outright and had been told that there were no signs of any such thing. However the Pope was pleased that she was now in fine health and gay and passing the happiest Carnival in the world with festivity after festivity – and the ambassador gave a list of balls and parties. As we have seen it was not quite correct to say that she was consistently happy in herself, and the courtiers of Ferrara had seen her with a long face more than once. Troche was aware of this and one day in the Vatican he smiled on hearing Costabili's brilliant descriptions of amusements and revelry and said it was not as continuous as all that. The Pope may have had direct information from the Spaniards as well as from his daughter (Lucrezia, even after receiving her allowance, had asked her father for substantial sums of money saying that she had had to pawn her jewellery so as to buy new clothes for entertaining the Marchesa of Mantua), for he did not seem quite convinced by Costabili and was considering going to visit her, and when he considered doing something he immediately made concrete plans. Cattanei says, though we do not know how accurate this is, that the marriage agreement between Lucrezia and Alfonso contained a secret clause allowing for a visit from the Pope to Ferrara. Already in April 1502 Alexander VI had made it plain in consistory that he intended to go to Ferrara in June, '*cum tota curia*', and that any Cardinal who did not accompany him would lose his hat. This made the Venetians say that the Pope's affections were serving as a cover for political ends and that the journey would include a meeting between the Pope and the King of France. They may have been right. But in the meantime other matters had intervened, including Lucrezia's illness and the urgent need to keep an eye on the Spaniards in the Kingdom of Naples, and so Alexander VI had not stirred from Rome save for brief visits in the neighbourhood. And now, a year later, the plan was brought out once more though in a modified form. The meeting of father and daughter was not to happen at Ferrara – for the split between the Borgias and Estes was beginning to be noticeable – but at Loreto, a place of holy pilgrimage that deserved a visit from the head of the Church. The Pope's intention was to set out in September when the summer heat was on the wane, and take the opportunity of visiting and blessing Cesare's new State, Romagna, on the way.

Apart from the Pope's affection or weakness for Lucrezia, Cesare was by now master of the Vatican, for he had taken over all his father's forces and held Rome in a state of suspicion and terror. Since the Senegalian murders there seemed no longer any limit to his crimes. This was the epoch of the famous Borgia poison which was for centuries to be synonymous with the family name, and with which even Lucrezia's name was to be associated – the dark imagination of the Romantics, and especially Victor Hugo, turning her into a poisoner and evil genius. There have been interminable discussions as to whether the famous 'canterella' was really a very clever discovery, a masterpiece of wickedness, able to deal out death after a calculated lapse of time. Modern chemists and toxicologists take the view that this long-term poison forms part of the Borgia legend. As for what the 'canterella' or 'aqua tofana' was made of, Flandin, in his *Traité des Poisons*, and Lewin and others, suppose it to have been an arsenic acid capable of producing intermittent fevers manifested in two forms; one, and the commonest, a gastric fever, the other a cerebro-spinal fever which was rarer. Whether it was made of arsenic or something else, it was a poison that was carefully prepared. But more terrifying than the poison itself was the state of mind of those who used it. The wealthy Venetian Cardinal, Michiel, was killed by a Borgia murderer, Asquinio Colloredo, who later confessed that he was paid 1,000 ducats for pouring out the deadly phial. Michiel's enormous fortune went to the Pope and hence to Valentinois and his wars. Meanwhile, to raise money for those same wars the Pope created new Cardinals in 1503 and made a profit of 150,000 ducats. Cardinal Gian Battista Orsini was imprisoned at Castel Sant' Angelo for having wished to poison the Sovereign Pontiff, and the fact that they made such a grave accusation as this was a sign of the Borgias' intention to get rid of him. He was rich and powerful and courageous, and was not afraid to appear in the Vatican after nightfall with an escort when summoned by the Pope, despite the supplications of his beautiful mistress who asked him not to go because she had dreamed of wine changed into blood and foretold some misfortune. It was rumoured that the Cardinal had been subjected to torture and that he had attempted to throw himself from the battlements of the Castel Sant' Angelo. Every morning, when members of the Orsini family looked at the round castellated walls of the great fortress, they wondered whether he was dead or alive. But they did not waste their time in vain sighs. The Cardinal's mother sent a message to the Pope offering him a large sum of money. His beautiful mistress attempted something more romantic. She disguised herself as a man and in her male clothes succeeded in reaching the presence of the Pontiff and offered him a wonderful pearl that Orsini had given her – it was a famous jewel that was known to the Borgias and coveted by them. At this price a corpse was handed over.

The Cardinal was the third member of the House of Orsini, counting the Duke of Gravina and Paolo Orsini, to be assassinated within the space of a few months. The struggle between this powerful Roman family and the Borgias was of long standing and destined to continue. On this point Cesare's plans of conquest were in harmony with the policy that Alexander VI had been pursuing for the last ten years – that of ridding the Papal States of the aggressive power of the Roman barons. Just as once the Duke of Gandia had been sent against Bracciano, so now Jofre was dispatched to lay siege to Ceri. The Orsini begged for mercy and sent the chief of their family, Giulio Orsini, Lord of Monterotondo, to Rome and in exchange took Jofre as hostage. But they felt so insecure about this arrangement that they were all terrified when the news came that Giulio had been put into the Castel Sant' Angelo. This was probably done as an act of mental cruelty so as to frighten the head of the Orsini family, for when peace had been signed again Giulio returned to his estate safe and sound. In Rome rumour had it that when his mother saw him still alive she dropped dead with joy. King Louis XII from France thundered that no one must touch his friends, the Orsini. But Alexander VI stuck to his guns and claimed that he had the right to govern his State in his own way just as he had left the King of France all freedom in dealing with his own barons. These were matters of home policy.

As regards foreign policy and relations abroad the Borgias were at that moment shilly-shallying. They were trying to probe a dilemma – which of the two nations disputing dominion over Italy, namely France and Spain, would be successful in achieving it? They were uneasy about Spanish manoeuvres in the Kingdom of Naples and the regular and continuous landing of the Catholic King's troops under Mount Vesuvius. Louis XII was also worried about Spanish movements and began preparing a new expedition against his rivals in Italy, and was even heard to speak of Valentinois as though he were almost an enemy. When Bartolomeo Cartari, the Ferrarese ambassador, asked him whether it were true that Borgia intended to attack Pisa, the King of France answered that he did not believe that the Pope and his son would go against his will – at this time Tuscany was under French protection – and moreover that he was in a position to make Valentinois lose everything that he had allowed him to conquer within a matter of four days. Cesare seemed to be alluding directly to this when he told some Frenchmen in Rome that he had never had any designs on Tuscany and that the troops encamped between Todi and Perugia were his own personal guard. One should always have a good personal guard, he said.

And so while Lucrezia was weaving her delicate web with

Bembo at Medelana, and the Pope and Valentinois were at the crossroads between France and Spain, the August of 1503 came upon them. At the beginning of the month Cardinal Giovanni Borgia of Monreale died. He was the miser of the Borgia family, and though he had held 'a single ducat' in high esteem he had left much more than that behind him, 'unable to take it with him' – money, jewellery, silverware, splendid horses and many other possessions. Cesare had postponed his departure from Rome on the grounds that he wished to celebrate the eleventh anniversary of his father's election to the Papacy with him, but his real intention was 'to wait and see what the Spaniards would do'. On August 10, the feast of St Laurence, the Pope's former secretary Adriano Castelli da Corneto, who was by now a new and very wealthy Cardinal, offered the Pontiff and his son a sumptuous luncheon with a few intimate friends in a vineyard just outside the city. So began the downfall of the Borgias.

It is not quite clear what exactly happened at this luncheon. There is an anonymous story inserted in Sanudo's *Diaries* which relates that Cardinal Adriano Castelli, having heard that Alexander VI had cast eyes on his wealth and planned to have him killed that day by means of poisoned jam, persuaded the hired murderer to offer the Pope and Valentinois the poisoned jar instead. This is one of the numberless Borgia mysteries which has been a subject of heated argument for centuries. The old historians – Guicciardini, Giovio and Pietro Martire – all believed that the Borgias were poisoned. But modern writers such as Pastor, Luzio, and Woodward reject this theory on the evidence of the contemporary witnesses, Burchard, Costabili, Cattanei and Giustinian, who speak of tertian fever. On the following day, August 11, Adriano Castelli had to retire to bed. If the story of the poison is true we would have to explain this either in terms of the Cardinal being terrified of what he had done, or because he did, after all, taste a little of the jam himself. On the 12th the Pope fell ill, and on the 13th, Valentinois. Many others fell ill too and it was said that a cook and a carver had died. There is some support for the theory that the affection was general. Monsignor Beltrando Costabili wrote on August 14: 'It is not surprising that His Holiness and His Excellency (i.e. Valentinois) should be ill because every single outstanding man in this court is either ill or else sickening, and especially those of the (Apostolic) Palace, owing to the bad condition of the air.' As for Cattanei, he had written as early as August 5: 'Many are unwell though there is no actual plague – only fever *by which they are soon finished.*' But apart from these informants the whole of Italy began talking about poison – perhaps because it seemed logical that a Borgia should die in that way. Even Valentinois' followers were convinced of it, though this may have been pretence. One of them told Cattanei in confidence that the poison had been put in the Trebbia wine which the Pope had drunk neat and Valentinois had diluted with a good deal of water. In view of this even Cattanei began to reconsider the poison hypothesis – though he came to no definite conclusion.

The truth, whatever it was, has never been discovered. On the morning of August 13 the Pope had the Bishop of Venosa (who was ill himself) and another doctor summoned to the Vatican. When it grew late and neither of them was seen leaving, things were presumed to be serious. On the same day the story spread that Valentinois had been attacked by vomiting and a high fever and that his condition was worse than his father's. The news reached the Borgias' enemies like the peal of a bell. They lifted their heads once more for the hour of vengeance was at hand. Cesare's intimates were well aware of what was afoot and agreed to pass the order round to present a united front of calm. If the Duke was said to be ill they would dismiss the idea as groundless alarm. With a valiant effort Cesare had the first visitor to the Apostolic Palace brought into his room, and he assumed an air of confidence and good cheer despite the pain it caused him. But his pretence did not escape the visitor who was far too clever not to know that the interview had been granted him so that he could report that he had seen Valentinois alive and in good health. It was plain that the Duke's appearance had been touched up.

On the following day the Pope was bled for his fever. He recovered sufficiently to play cards with members of the household, but on the 16th he had a relapse. On the 17th he was slightly better but on the morning of the 18th, after he had heard Mass and received Communion, he was heard to say that he was feeling very ill indeed. In the evening he was given Extreme Unction. And as night began to fall, in silence, as though yielding to a heavy torpor, the Pope died. His heart had not been strong enough to resist the fever and he had had apoplexy.

There were only a few people near him. The silence was broken by a murmur of muffled voices – still distant, but obviously threatening. Suddenly the doors were flung wide open and a group of men-at-arms under the command of Don Micheletto Corella entered, closed the doors behind them, and stood on guard. The Cardinal Treasurer was offered a choice: either he must hand over the keys of the Pope's treasure or else he would be thrown out of the window. When he felt Don Micheletto's dagger at his heart the Cardinal handed over the keys to the coffers of silverware and golden ducats. In their hurry Cesare's men had a lapse of memory that they were to regret bitterly later. They overlooked Alexander VI's casket of marvellous jewels. As soon as they had seized their booty they made off.

By now Cesare had a high fever. He was watched over by Don Micheletto and the little Prince of Squillace who made a display of arrogance and courage. At the head of a posse of mounted men-at-arms Jofre Borgia issued boldly from the Vatican and rode through Rome as if on a tour of inspection in his own territory. In Piazza Minerva he espied people putting up barricades. 'What is the meaning of this?' he asked. 'To avoid scandals,' was the answer. 'Very well, we will take the other side and you can take this,' he said referring to the Tiber, and as soon as he returned to the Castel Sant' Angelo he fired a bombard in the direction of the via dei Banchi as a warning. Don Micheletto showed more wisdom and caution; his vigilance was unrelaxed and he gave his orders with a combination of prudence and energy.

Meanwhile the Borgia apartments in the Vatican were being ransacked by a crowd of servants who made off even with the pontifical throne. In the denuded room, and upon Burchard's orders, the Pope's body was washed and laid on a catafalque decorated with crimson satin and a beautiful carpet; he was dressed in white clothes with a golden chasuble and velvet slippers. These final attentions were bestowed on Alexander VI not out of love but as a result of the cold and punctilious precision of a master of ceremonies from Strasbourg. In this garb the body was removed from the squalor of the sacked apartments and taken to the Sala of the Papagallo where it was visited by some members of the family – certainly by Jofre and perhaps by Vannozza Cattanei. Towards evening it was borne into St Peter's to be exposed, as was the custom, to the people. But as the hours passed the Pope's body began to undergo a monstrous decomposition which was helped by the heat. It became twisted and black and swollen and turned into an unseemly wreck of its former pontifical and even human quality. Legends of pacts with the devil, of monstrous visions and of evil spirits seemed to be justified by this corruption. In the end people believed anything and those who filed through St Peter's spread hair-raising stories of what they had seen with the usual popular relish. Finally out of feelings of humanity and decency the decomposed body was covered up. Late at night by the light of a few flares the funeral was held. The Pontiff's body was accompanied by the Bishop of Carinola and a few other prelates to the little chapel of Santa Maria della Febbri, where the body of the murdered Duke of Bisceglie had been taken just three years earlier to the day, with expressions of greater honour and sorrow. Here the scene was nightmarish. The Pope's body had by now swollen beyond all measure and there was no way of fitting it into the coffin. It had to be forced in with blows and tugs by the two powerful gravediggers. The flares shed an uneasy light on those brutes until at last the Pope's body was crammed into the coffin and buried under a stone – which was merely provisional, they said. And the little company of gravediggers and prelates turned away and departed, silently and without lights, in a hurry to be off.

Cesare, confined to his bed, realized his ruin in a flash. As his rooms were above the Papal apartment he may have heard the cadences of the funeral prayers. He failed to get better and yet he was bound to leave the Vatican free for the new conclave, and his anxiety grew as he realized that the enemies of the Borgia family would be rushing in to take their revenge. The Borgia women were assembled in the Castel Sant' Angelo. There were to be found Sancha of Aragon, Dorotea da Crema who had been kidnapped on the road between Cervia and Ravenna (the meeting of these two women, united in their loathing of the man who had loved them, had been dramatic), all the Borgia children, Lucrezia's little Duke, the Roman Infante, the offspring of collateral branches of the family and, possibly, the latest fruit of Alexander VI's life of lechery – Rodrigo Borgia – who was born between 1502 and 1503. Shortly afterwards the whole harem including Vannozza Cattanei was sent off to the fortress of Civita Castellana. And Cesare himself, having been asked by the Cardinals not to put obstacles in the way of the conclave by his presence, set out for Nepi with a large military escort and some prostitutes. His litter of crimson satin, with drawn curtains, was borne by eight grooms, and in front of him on horseback was a bound and masked prisoner whose name is unknown – he was perhaps an Orsini hostage. Cesare was seriously ill, having been laid low by the remedies he had taken to get better. His feet were swollen, his body shrunken and he had violent headaches. His brain, normally so acute, had begun wandering. Prospero Colonna had sent a message offering him the protection of the Spaniards on condition that he would use his influence in the interests of Spain at the forthcoming conclave. Cesare had accepted, and at the same time he had also accepted French protection and promised to use his influence in French interests at the conclave. His double game became known immediately; it alienated the Spaniards and prepared the way for the distrust of the French.

In point of fact Cesare was placing all his hopes on the election of a French Pope, namely the ambitious Cardinal d'Amboise. But now that they had seen the harm done to the Papacy by Spaniards, the Italians felt chary of electing another foreigner – though the French, logically enough, could not see why a bad Spanish Pope should jeopardize the chance of a French Pope. It was at this time that Ascanio Sforza reappeared in Rome. He had been freed from the dungeons of Bourges, was on excellent terms with the King of France and his period in prison had increased his ambition and determination. He arrived on September 10 in the company of Cardinal d'Amboise, and was met at Porta del Popolo by the Cardinals of Bologna and Volterra, Cardinal d'Albret and Cardinal Sanseverino. He was welcomed by a tumult of popular applause and even by fireworks. Women leant out of their windows and shouted 'Ascanio, Ascanio, Sforza, Sforza' almost as though they were in love. No one had expected this outburst of enthusiasm and it was a little disconcerting to the French Cardinal who looked on Ascanio as a vassal. It was said that Sforza had been set free so as to work for d'Amboise, but it was also said that he was busy on his own behalf. When the conclave met, however, and he found himself face to face with his old enemy of the year 1492, Giuliano della Rovere, he set himself first and foremost to shipwreck the latter's chances. In the midst of discord, confusion and dissension, the conclave elected an upright man of good morals, intelligence and doctrine, but ill to the point of being moribund. This was Francesco Todeschini Piccolomini who took the name of Pius III. He was to be a transitional Pope.

The French were marching on Naples with the intention of fighting the Spaniards. They passed through Nepi and continued on their way leaving Valentinois alone and weak. When Valentinois was told that Bartolomeo d'Alviano was on his way to Nepi with the intention of avenging the Orsini, he fell into something like panic. He sent envoys to Rome begging the new

Pope to grant him refuge in that city. He could not conceal his helpless condition, thereby giving his enemies great delight, but the good Pope Pius III had pity on him and let him return to Rome and take up lodgings in the palace of Ippolito of Este near the Vatican.

Soon after this large numbers of troops were to be seen in the streets of Rome. They were those of Alviano, of the Baglioni and of the Orsini who were preparing to have their revenge and, while waiting, were killing and torturing Spaniards and violating women. One of their victims was the Roman, Pietro Matuzzi, who had married one of Alexander VI's daughters, Isabella Borgia, even before he had been elected Pope. The Orsinis broke into Pietro Matuzzi's palace and carried off his wife and daughter to their dwellings as reprisal for the outrages to which their own women had been submitted. Cesare began to feel that no amount of guards could make the Este palace safe. He could hear the mob in the streets and the voices of his enemies shouting out 'Kill that dog of a Jew, sack him before the others do.' He was well aware of the efficacy of such incitements on mercenary soldiers – for all his own soldiers were mercenaries. Moreover his Spaniards, finding themselves distrusted by the King of Spain for taking service with Cesare, who was looked on as a traitor owing to his intrigues with France, disaffected in large numbers, leaving only German mercenaries and a few Italians and French. When he saw his shrunken guard, Cesare thought of retiring to the Castel Sant' Angelo whose commander was under his thumb, but even this commander had now turned his coat and was obsequious only to the Pontiff, who could make or unmake him. It was said in Rome with a laugh that it was a miracle to see Valentinois proposing of his own accord to put himself in prison, and meanwhile young Jofre was showing grim courage by leading the German mercenaries in a number of sorties against the Orsini.

On August 19 certain news of Alexander VI's death reached Ferrara. Immediately on hearing it, Cardinal Ippolito rode through the dried-up countryside to take the news to Lucrezia at Medelana.

Lucrezia went almost mad with grief for she was too much of a Borgia not to feel deep bonds with her father. She dressed in black and decorated her room in black; she went without light or food and, as she said later, 'thought she was dying'. Life on earth seemed fundamentally hopeless and vain. Don Alfonso paid her a short visit and left again because tears and melancholy irritated him. Ercole of Este does not seem to have bothered to express strong feelings of condolence and this was much noticed in Ferrara. For some time now the old Duke had been at loggerheads with the Pope, especially since his favourite, Gian Luca Castellini, had been excluded from the list of new Cardinals. Ercole's feelings were made amply clear a few days after the Pope's death in a famous letter he wrote to Gian Giorgio Seregni, an envoy of Ferrara in Milan. In his letter he explained that the court of Ferrara was not mourning the Pope's death: on the contrary, 'for the honour of our Lord God and for the universal benefit of Christendom, we have on more than one occasion wished that divine goodness and providence should make us provision of a good and exemplary pastor and that this great scandal should be removed from his Church.' On this occasion Ercole spoke as a follower of Savonarola, and he said that he had almost desired the death of the Pontiff. It is not difficult for us to imagine his feelings for the daughter of this 'scandal', or for Cesare who was now moving headlong towards disaster.

Thus Lucrezia was lonely, but proud, in her sorrow. True, a few of her courtiers dressed in mourning, but she was fully aware of the import of their dark clothing and knew what she would have to give out in favour and protection as a result. Her consolation lay in her women, in Strozzi and Tebaldeo, but most of all in Pietro Bembo who, when the news was announced, arrived at Medelana even before Alfonso of Este. Bembo's mind was full of comforting words. But when he entered the room and saw the shining lady of his imagination sitting on the floor and moaning, he did not dare to speak. All his eloquence was turned to compassion and, afraid of what he might do, he fled in silence back to Ostellato. From there he wrote her an affectionate letter containing strong and bracing words of wisdom. He showed a grasp of problems, for he advised her to see to it that no one should suspect her of weeping for her 'fallen fortunes' – so he must have known that her fortunes were in the balance, and perhaps had heard what was being said on the King's authority in France.

It was now plain that Louis XII had left Cesare Borgia to his own devices, showing 'how fickle is the favour of those from beyond the Alps'. The King also spoke quite openly of Lucrezia, even going so far as to say that she was not really the effective wife of Alfonso of Este. We do not know whether this was meant as a pretext for repudiating her, or as a promise of help should the Este family repudiate her. We have no information that there was ever any intention in Ferrara of attempting to get a divorce. Her enormous dowry would have had to be given back, and Cesare Borgia was still powerful in Romagna. Lucrezia grasped at once that Romagna was a guarantee of her brother's life and, though she was distracted by sorrow, she tried to find ways and means of helping him. She did not have much money for she was extravagant and spent her allowance in advance. But she managed to enrol 1,000 infantrymen and a hundred and fifty crossbowmen under the command of the Spaniard Pedro Ramirez, and these were given the task of going to the help of Cesena and Imola, now threatened by the Venetians, and Pesaro, now besieged by her divorced husband Giovanni Sforza. But the troops of ex-husband and ex-wife never actually came to grips, for it was already written that the Borgia star should undergo total eclipse and that even Giovanni Sforza should be victorious over the family. Sforza succeeded in getting back to his little city and there he exercised his petty tyranny by putting to death Pandolfo Collenuccio, the most illustrious humanist, poet and citizen of Renaissance Pesaro.

Rimini also fell, but the fortresses of Cesena and Forlì

remained firmly in the hands of Valentinois. Their loyalty was remarkable. It inspired, for instance, the Governor of the castle of Forlì to hang a Papal messenger who came with instructions that he should hand over the fortress. It appears that Lucrezia had given this castle Governor a substantial sum of money to help him hold out. Duke Ercole's position was ambiguous: he knew what Lucrezia was up to, and was accused on all sides of wanting to 'keep Valentinois going'. In a letter to his ambassador in Rome he admitted that he would prefer Romagna to belong to the Borgia rather than to the Venetian Republic whose armed forces were already waiting on the frontier: yet when the Venetians complained about the small bands of soldiery setting out from Ferrara, the Duke assured them that he was ignorant of what his daughter-in-law was doing and had not given a penny to the enterprise – and that at least was certainly true. Thus even Lucrezia's love for her brother served the purposes of others, while she remained where she was and her deeds had no echo and no importance.

In the countryside round Medelana and Ostellato the last threads of the love story between Lucrezia and Bembo were woven.

Bembo wrote to Lucrezia and she answered, impelled by courtesy, gratitude, or a stronger motive that she must have confessed to him in early October, for he wrote to her: 'There is no treasure I could value more than what I heard you say to me yesterday, which you might properly have let me know sooner.' And he added: 'My savage misfortune has not such power over me as to prevent, while my life lasts, the fire in which FF and my destiny have placed me, from being the highest and purest flame ever felt in the heart of a lover. The nature of the place in which the fire burns will make it burn strong, and the flame itself will light it up so that it will be a witness to the whole world.' These are the words of a platonic lover, yes, but a lover ardent enough to hope that Lucrezia, far from wanting to put out her own flame, might be caught up in the same frenzy of love as himself – to quote a Spanish proverb found among her papers.

There can be no doubt that at the end of this autumn there was much tender interchange between the afflicted Lucrezia and her consoler Bembo. With him in view the Duchess had some black taffeta sent from her wardrobe in Ferrara with which to make a gown that would soften the Spanish austerity of her mourning. This stiff material, with its great folds, gave her slim figure and fair complexion a delicate and sacrificial air calculated to please – too much – a man like Bembo. We can imagine her thus dressed, with no jewels on her head, greeting him from the window when he arrived or departed; or, protected from the chill of evening, going out with him on to the balcony to see the moon. On this balcony, which he was to recall later with longing, Bembo would linger and talk of love, while in the shadows Lucrezia's girls-in-waiting and friends would wait in discreet complicity.

He wrote: 'I kiss that sweetest hand that has caused my death', and 'I kiss that hand for a sweeter was never kissed by man.' It is possible that there were too many kisses and Alfonso of Este, whose spies kept him well informed, got to know about them. For he set out in the company of his court and arrived at Ostellato on October 7. We do not know whether he was prompted by his passion for hunting or by his desire to show Bembo and Strozzi that, though silent, he was vigilant. If we look at the dates we see that on October 10 Bembo returned to Venice and thence went to visit friends in the Veneto. This may have been sheer coincidence. But it is worth noting that Ercole Strozzi, who was deeply involved in this love story of Lucrezia's – as in another one later – was far too clever not to understand such warnings and take steps to forestall suspicion. Bembo may have had to leave but, in any case, his separation from Lucrezia caused him such pain that by the end of October he was back at Ostellato. But the life of the lovers was no longer easy and they soon became aware of the fact. On November 2 Bembo wrote to Lucrezia from Ferrara telling her that he had left Ostellato because, as the court of Don Alfonso was there, there was nothing left for him to eat. It seems impossible to suppose that where more than fifty people were being dined it was really impossible to find a place for Pietro Bembo. This lack of hospitality seems to me the first indisputable sign of Alfonso's lack of sympathy for a man held too dear by his wife.

The country sojourn at Medelana was a long one that year owing to plague in the cities. At one time Lucrezia had a plan of going to Carpi to stay with Alberto Pio who was a close friend of Bembo and Strozzi, and the barges were ready and waiting when thirty-four members of her court fell ill. The contagion spread and the cases increased to fifty-four, so there was no more talk of making a move. Lucrezia returned to Ferrara in late December. Alfonso went to meet her, and he himself conducted her to the castle which was a courteous way of shutting her up in prison.

And now began another season of festivity, but Lucrezia's mourning and the old Duke's weak health were an obstacle to balls and parties. Lucrezia renewed her conversations with Bembo who promised to spend the winter in Ferrara, but at the end of December he was summoned to Venice by his relatives and had to leave in a hurry. The good-bye was a melancholy one. Bembo opened Lucrezia's Bible in her room and read out some words to celebrate their parting. The words chanced to be about death – '*Obdormivit cum patribus suis et sepelierunt eum in civitate David*[1] – and they both felt the burden of this prophecy upon them as they said good-bye. But before Bembo finally left Lucrezia sent him a little note that must have been a cry from the heart because it contained no involved words or 'studied fictions'. This was Bembo's viaticum. When he reached Venice he found that his brother, the lovable young Carlo, had been dead for several days. The poet mourned him; while far away, shut up in the red masonry of the castle at Ferrara, Lucrezia

---

[1] 'He fell asleep with his fathers and they buried him in the city of David.'

wept with him and her tears comforted him; once more they were united in the fellowship of grief.

There is a letter written in March 1504 that proves how real this comfort was. The poet had been told that she was becoming more beautiful every day (Strozzi must have been his informant on this for he was a constant traveller between Ferrara and Venice in search of precious wares for the Duchess) and he trembled for his heart. He implored her to write to him in her own hand. 'Messer Pietro mio', she answered, and went on to say that he must excuse FF who for many good reasons had been unable to write as she would have wished and she, the Duchess, was writing instead to intercede on behalf of the guilty creature of fiction. Bembo should excuse her and should remember that FF had no other desire but to please him.

Her words were brief and guarded, and we can see how difficult and dangerous it was to write them. But the poet was satisfied. He was happy, he exclaimed, to be able to think of her every hour of the day and night. In August 1504 the *Asolani*, considerations on, and poems about, love, left Bembo's hands and reached Lucrezia, to whom the work was dedicated.

The epistle dedicatory of the *Asolani* is famous. Despite the rhetoric, Bembo's praises of the Duchess have here and there gleams of psychological insight. For though we may see nothing but virtuosity in his play of concepts – where he says that as Lucrezia was superior to all other women in physical beauty, she should surpass herself in spiritual beauty – his affirmation that she loves 'much more to please herself within than to please others without' seems genuine and exact. Lucrezia's spirit had a self-containedness that Bembo alone perceived. While she listened to people discussing and commenting on the various chapters of his work, or to Strozzi dissecting them with minute and brilliant analysis, she must have heard Bembo's Venetian accents tapping at her heart, and perhaps she sighed with longing.

The twenty-six days of his pontificate were too much for Pope Pius III. He endured them bravely and finally died of them on

October 18, 1503, thereby reopening the struggle over the succession to the Papacy. However on October 31, 1503, Giuliano della Rovere was elected, took the name of Julius II, and became the Pope of Michelangelo.

Had Cesare's mind been as clear as in the days of his prime, he would have grasped that his authority had by now fallen so low that not even a Pope could do anything about it. He had now been abandoned by the King of France and the King of Spain, and had neither soldiers nor friends nor credit among the powerful. Julius II could do one thing only, and that was to let him go as far away as possible, but not before handing over the fortresses in Romagna that were still occupied by his troops and decisively threatened by the Venetians. Cesare had already reached Ostia and was preparing to embark for Leghorn on his way to Romagna when he announced that he refused to give the order to surrender. He was therefore seized and imprisoned in the della Rovere fortress at Ostia, where he spent his time on the high towers trying to deceive himself that he was still strong by firing great salvoes of artillery in the direction of the sea. Soon he was taken to Rome. When he learnt that he really was a prisoner he collapsed and wept. He suddenly gave way to the emotions he had held at bay throughout his life, despair and grief. Everything was undone; the superman was finished. The man, however, was not, as his gaolers observed. They saw him accept his imprisonment honourably, sleeping peacefully with his drawn sword by his pillow, watched over by three of his servants, given good food ordered by himself, receiving those who went to visit him to gloat over the sight of a powerful man brought low. He liked playing games with the guards – the Pope's men – and they were amazed at the zest with which he entered into them (and which perhaps he put on for their benefit). When one of them showed his surprise at Cesare's apparent indifference to his fate, Cesare said, 'I am thinking of the many others that I have caused to be like this.' The Pope was infuriated by his prisoner's resilience.

At that time there took place the great battle between the French and the Spaniards on the Garigliano, the outcome of which was to leave Spain absolutely predominant in Southern Italy, to chase the French from the country, and to add new laurels to the already distinguished reputation of Consalvo de Cordoba. When Cesare heard of this he remembered the personal friendship that had existed between Consalvo and his family, and he thought that his salvation might lie there. So he handed over the fortresses of Romagna in exchange for freedom and a safe-conduct to Naples. Informants of the time tell us that as soon as he found himself in the open air he ordered a horse and began charging and rearing furiously. 'Lord Duke, you were always a man of spirit', they said and he answered proudly: 'the more things go against me, the more my spirits thrive'. The fact that a man who had fallen so low could adopt the tone and language of Plutarch may have been due to the humanistic atmosphere of the Renaissance. However this may be, Valentinois set sail from Ostia to Naples towards the end of 1504.

His choice of Naples was his final and most serious mistake. For there were assembled all the women of the House of Aragon, the dynasty that had been sacrificed by the Borgias, including the old Queen Giovanna, widow of Alfonso II, the young Queen Giovanna, widow of King Ferrandino, the ex-Queen of Hungary, Beatrice, against whom Alexander VI had pronounced a divorce in favour of King Ladislaus, and Isabella d'Aragona Sforza, the former Duchess of Milan. Apart from belonging to the House of Aragon, each with his or her personal reason for hating the Borgias, they were all aunts or cousins of the murdered Duke of Bisceglie. There were also in Naples relatives of the Duke of Gravina, Francesco Orsini, and many members of the Orsini following, and the relatives of Jeronimo Mancioni who had had his tongue and hand cut off by Cesare for writing a literary composition 'pleasing but dishonourable' on events during the capture of Faenza. Finally there was Sancha – seen mostly in the company of Consalvo de Cordoba – and probably little Rodrigo of Bisceglie in charge of his cousins, aunts and great-aunts and particularly of Isabella of Aragon, ex-Duchess of Milan.

So Valentinois did not hold out for long. It was said that he was busy plotting the reconquest of Romagna, but he was no longer the man he had been and he felt hatred all around him. Moreover important things were happening in Spain. Giustinian and Cattanei, though we cannot confirm their story, state that the black and silent figure of the Duchess of Gandia had made an appearance at the court of Ferdinand the Catholic and asked that justice should at last be done for the murder of her husband. The King and Queen of Spain had always hated Alexander VI for his pro-French policy, which they termed downright treachery, and they had always felt that Valentinois was behind it. So they did not need much persuading. They ordered Consalvo de Cordoba to arrest Cesare and ship him to Spain. When he received this order Consalvo was put in a very difficult position, for he had given his word of honour that Valentinois should have his freedom. Years later when the Great Captain recalled his long life of adventure, he said that in the whole of it he had been obliged to break his word three times, and each time had caused him pain. This was one of the occasions. But he had to obey his King. After nightfall he sent a message to Cesare exhorting him to come immediately to the Castel del Ovo because there were powerful bands on the prowl, headed by the relatives of the man whose tongue had been cut out. Valentinois had been saved by this kind of warning on previous occasions, and he trusted Consalvo's word. Once again he handed himself over to imprisonment, and this time it was the end.

In August 1504 the man who might have been King of Italy was put aboard a Spanish ship that bore him to the country of his forebears, and to prison. With him was Prospero Colonna, who overcame the embarrassment of the situation by nobly pretending to treat Valentinois as his equal and a free man. Cesare was immured in the fortress of Cincilla, and it was said that the King intended to give him a public trial and execute him, or that if he let him live it was only to scare Julius II. As soon as Valentinois was far away and locked up, people began to forget about him, including his wife. The only person who concerned herself about him was Lucrezia, and this she did with tireless energy and persistence. On a number of occasions during the early months of Julius II's pontificate there had been talk of setting Valentinois up at Ferrara. The Pope had discussed it with Costabili who said, without mincing matters, that he did not think that Duke Ercole would be disposed to take on such a burden – which was probably the reply Julius II expected. Still anxious to clarify Cesare's position, Julius II had also written to the King of France asking him whether he would allow him to live in his dominions. Louis XII answered with a courteous letter of agreement saying that he was willing to welcome him principally to satisfy the very strong appeals of the Duchess of Ferrara. But the purpose of this letter was to deceive Valentinois by whom it was intended to be read; for at the same time the King sent a second private letter with the curt declaration that never, under any circumstances in the world, would he consent to Borgia taking up residence in France. And he had even written to the Duke of Ferrara warning him not to concern himself with that priest's bastard, either. There is no doubt but that his advice was welcome to the Duke. These letters are not only a proof of Louis XII's duplicity, but the first shows how lively and urgent was Lucrezia's concern for the fallen Valentinois. It was part of her destiny to be deluded.

Alfonso of Este was a frequent traveller. When he journeyed his reflections were restricted to practical here-and-now aspects of knowledge, such as the form of cities and landscapes, and the architecture of fortresses and ports. His principles made him consider a number of problems – such as the dynasty, which was of course legitimate and hereditary, such as fair play and friendship between brothers, and also the relationship between husband and wife. But he had not the faintest interest in playing the part of the heir to the throne in politics, though this did not mean that he lacked political convictions of his own; indeed his predilection for Venice was common knowledge, and made people suppose that the future would see a policy of alliance with the *Serenissima*. But in the meanwhile Alfonso bided his time and only busied himself with his foundry, with his beloved cannons, with his spicy love adventures, with his lathe at which he worked for hours, and with making majolica vases which enabled him to enjoy the pleasures of artisanship. The courtiers despised Alfonso's inclinations towards the people, and Ercole disapproved of them too. But it was much worse when the Duke's thoughts turned to his second child.

Cardinal Ippolito was not to be swayed by anyone, least of all by his father. His ecclesiastical and humanist education, against a background of warlike pride, had given him an appearance that combined finery with frigidity. He had a smile that immediately undermined trust and inspired fear. Ercole longed to warn him, in his austere way, to use his arms less and his breviary more. Ippolito would take off his soutane, don a leather jerkin and go forth with his quarrelsome courtiers as if impelled by a fury for destruction: he would kill all the wild game that he could possibly find, and if this was short he would kill the farmers' geese and hens. He answered his father's letters with unction or wrath, but always with insolence. The general turmoil and discord in Ippolito's entourage boded ill for the future. The moderate party at court murmured that when 'that poor old man' – meaning the Duke – was no longer there, who could tell what would happen?

The other two brothers, Don Ferrante and Don Giulio (for no one even referred to the youngest, Don Sigismondo), were a problem too, for they were intolerant and self-willed, but as they were less able than the Cardinal, and showed no signs of wanting to remake the world, they were viewed with less apprehension. Don Giulio, the bastard of Isabella Arduino, was handsome and charming and passionately fond of good clothes and good living. He knew the power of his eyes, the brown eyes of his Neapolitan mother that were always moistened by desire. 'All the women were putting on airs to try to lure me to deign to dance with them'; 'The Lady Duchess (Lucrezia) did not dance at all except at the end when I made her dance the torch dance . . .' I am beautiful, I am irresistible, I am unique – that was Don Giulio's tone. Was he really monstrously vain or were his words the sort of playful boasting that is an integral part of conversation among brothers? In a letter to Ippolito, Don Giulio refers to himself as the son and brother of clowns, and this is a good example of the Estes' family banter. Don Ferrante rivalled his brother and paid court to all the women. From the political point of view both brothers were nonentities. Don Giulio had taken up a defensive position against the will of his father who wanted him to enter the Church, and Don Ferrante nominally exercised the art of war and was always looking round for good 'cushy' jobs and pay. Both of course were extremely discontented.

At the end of 1504 Duke Ercole fell seriously ill and it was realized that the end of his life had come. Envoys were immediately posted after Don Alfonso who was travelling in England, and members of the Este family and the principal dignitaries of the Duchy all went immediately to put themselves under Lucrezia's orders 'in case the Duke should die'. Ercole of Este took his farewell of existence soothed and consoled by music and the sound of the harpsichord. He dwelt on the values of the notes and the rests and listened to the melody of fourteenth-century compositions, beating time with his aristocratic hand. His end was peaceful. He spoke of his daughter Isabella (at Ferrara it had been generally noticed that the Marchesa of Mantua had made substantial excuses to justify her failure to visit her father's bedside). He glanced at his heir, Alfonso, who had arrived in time and stood nearby, and at the vigorous group of members of the family who were there to continue his line and who seemed to be at peace with each other. And then he died.

The bells of Ferrara sounded to summon the Council of the Savi – the Wise – for the election of the new Duke. Reasons of State insisted that even before mourning the dead the succession of a young living lord should be established. And so Alfonso left his father's body to the prayers of monks and friars and went to his quarters to give the necessary orders. He was wearing a mantle of white damask lined with squirrel, and a white cap in the French style, when he received the Savi and many other people in the great hall. There was the presentation of the sword and the golden rod, followed by a speech and acclamations. Then the new Duke with his brother the Cardinal and the Vice-domino of Venice, followed by Don Ferrante and Don Giulio in brown velvet, descended to receive the acclamation of the populace. The weather was extremely cold. There was deep snow in the streets and a nordic frost, but when Alfonso set out on horseback through the city, he found that the snow had been shovelled away and the streets were crowded and gay, and all his subjects were ready to warm the air with their enthusiasm. Alfonso rode on with his set clear-cut face, receiving the shouts of applause with serene silence and looking his subjects straight in the face. He entered the cathedral and as soon as High Mass was over Tito Vespasiano Strozzi, to whom venerable old age had given a great solemnity, crowned him Duke. And in the early hours of the afternoon, now consecrated by the approval of the people and by divine sanction, he went forth from the cathedral and appeared under the flowery Romanesque doorway between the two lions that hold up the columns of the arch, and showed himself to the crowd.

Lucrezia had watched the cavalcade from the palace balcony facing the cathedral. The ceremony had been solemn for her too. From early morning she had received visits from the principal ladies of Ferrara, led by a great lady still in her youth, Ginevra Rangoni da Correggio. The speeches, good wishes and acts of obeisance were numerous and warm. Then, surrounded by a group of noblewomen and beside Niccolò Maria d'Este, Bishop of Adria – for Lucrezia never forgot to support herself by the dignity of religion – she watched the triumph of the new Duke from the balcony, and then went down to the door of the ducal palace. There she met her husband and bent down to kiss his hand in sign of submission, but he lifted her up and kissed her on the cheek, and, taking her hand, he went with her to hold the reception by the great fire. There followed twenty-four hours of festivity with amnesties, a reception and a supper. And then the day after they reverted to mourning and turned their thoughts to

the funeral of the old Duke, which was carried out with great
solemnity.

The experience of being in power made no difference to
Lucrezia's emotional problems. She had received Bembo's good
wishes and congratulations. But meanwhile what had happened?

Throughout the whole of 1504 Bembo had been kept in
Venice by family cares, by the 'accursed chains' of business, by
political negotiations and also, perhaps, by reasons of simple
prudence. But he corresponded with Lucrezia. She had had a
plan of going to Venice before Lent and then for the Ascension,
but she does not seem to have managed to leave Ferrara. It was
in March that she first awakened the love of Francesco Gonzaga,
the husband of Isabella of Este. Possibly Bembo had an inkling
that something was afoot. Their correspondence was not over
frequent but it had a tender and melting quality. Most of their
letters have been lost or destroyed and only one of this period
has come down to us. It is not addressed to Lucrezia but to
'Madonna N.' who must have been Nicola, wife of Trotti, an
obvious go-between who could pass letters on to the Duchess
without comment. It is the most expressive of Bembo's letters
and has fewest mannerisms. 'Remember that I think of, admire
and honour only you, and if when I were dead my spirit could
hover around you, I would no longer wish to live.' The ills and
buffets of misfortune, he went on to say, would no longer matter
to him if he knew that he was really loved by her who was his
'sweetest harbour and repose'. He sent her an Agnus Dei that he
had worn for a long time at his breast. She should wear it at
night so that 'the dear hospice of your precious heart may be
touched by the pendant that has touched the hospice of mine'.
This was not the innocent gift it seemed, but a subtle and oblique
form of sensuality. And what follows in the letter was not
innocent either though for different reasons. Bembo urged
Lucrezia not to let anyone see what she did or even know her
thoughts lest 'the roads that lead to our love should be even
more restricted than they are already'. She should trust no one

'until I come to you which in any case will be before Easter (or after Easter?) if I am still in life. The bearer of this, in whom I have utter trust, is passing by Carpi and will return later to know whether you may wish to command me in anything. You will deign by this means to make an answer and give it to him most secretly and it will be well delivered. Indeed I beg you regarding this, for as we can speak but little together by words, you should write at length and give me an account of all your doings and all your thoughts, tell me whom you trust, what things torment you, and what solace you; and take care you are not seen writing because I know that you are much watched'. 'After Easter I shall come to Ferrara as I told you and I shall then go to Rome for a month or more', Bembo repeated at the end of the letter. And so this became a rendez-vous, a goal for their desires and a stage in the course of their mutual uneasiness.

There has been a great deal of discussion about this letter. Its date, as included in the Collection of Bembo's letters read almost religiously throughout the sixteenth century and after, is very curious. It is February 10, 1503. Morsolin, who was the first person to make a careful study of the letters, has rightly pointed out that in 1503 Lucrezia's friendship with Bembo had barely begun and any communication between them at that time was through Strozzi. It was not until June 1503 that the poet confessed to the first pangs of his love-sickness. The sixteenth-century copyist, bowed down by the weight of words transcribed, probably read a 5 for a 3, a mistake it is easy to make when dealing with certain handwritings. Morsolin's theory is confirmed today by a few lines hitherto unpublished in a document in the Gonzaga archives at Mantua.

Bembo's visit therefore was promised for after Easter. But it was not known for certain if he ever really went to Ferrara. The question remained so undecided that Morsolin thought it possible that the lovers didn't see one another then or indeed ever again. But evidence has now come to light which proves the contrary, for on April 9, 1505, Benedetto Capilupi, a most scrupulous informant, sending from Ferrara an account of political and other events in that city, says that 'Messer Pietro, son of the magnifico Messer Bernardo Bembo, says that tomorrow the ambassadors should set out from Venice taking the road to Rimini and Urbino, where it is his intention to go and await them'.

Capilupi was referring to a Venetian embassy sent to Rome to discuss the cities of Romagna which, on Cesare's fall, had become the property of the Venetian Republic but which Julius II was claiming as a feud of the Church. Young Bembo, who was a member of the diplomatic party, must have gone ahead a few days earlier to see his Duchess. He then rejoined the others at Urbino and thence seems to have gone on to Rome exactly in accord with the programme he made in February in the letter to Lucrezia. This evidence cannot be invalidated by a letter from Bembo to Isabella of Este dated April 8 and written from Venice, for it is perfectly possible that Bembo wrote to Isabella immediately before setting out and that he started his journey to Ferrara on April 8 itself. If he did so he could have arrived at his destination before nightfall as the journey between Ferrara and Venice could be made fairly comfortably in five hours' good riding. So there is nothing to contradict Capilupi's valuable item of information. On April 9 Bembo was in Ferrara and must certainly have seen Lucrezia and indeed gone there for her sake. We do not know whether the lovers had an opportunity of seeing one another privately for any length of time, whether the coming and going and confusion caused by the foreign guests (there was a French embassy in Ferrara at the time) gave cover for, or prevented, the calm discussions needed by their love. As Bembo travelled along the road to Urbino to rejoin the Venetian embassy and then undertook the long journey to Rome, he must have carried in his heart the anguish of a question which his clear head could only answer in a logical and cruel way – for it was obvious that their relationship could have no future.

However, Bembo seems to have stopped at Ferrara on his way back from Rome, for in the middle of June Emilio Pio wrote from Gubbio to Isabella of Este that Bembo had left Gubbio to

stay for five days in Ferrara and then go on to Mantua. The
accuracy of this information can be checked in a letter written
five days later from Ferrara by Antonio Tebaldeo to Isabella. It
is dated June 20 and it announces the arrival of his two friends
Pietro Bembo and Paolo del Canale – 'two luminaries in all
three languages' – who were on their way to Mantua. Bembo
himself carried this letter to Isabella – 'the bearer of this will be
Messer Pietro Bembo', wrote Tebaldeo – and this shows that he
followed his programme down to the last detail. He left Gubbio
on the 15th, Ferrara on the 20th, and between the 20th and the
27th he finally went to Mantua where the Marchesa believed she
could avenge herself on her sister-in-law by deploying all her
fascination for the benefit of the Venetian poet.

What did the lovers say to each other in their last conversation, for it is obvious that between April and June 1505 the fate of
their love was decided? From then onwards there were no more
passionate letters and no more was heard of FF. True, Bembo
sent congratulations, good wishes or messages of condolence in
accord with the events of Lucrezia's subsequent life, but the
upheavals had given way to calm. It may well be that Alfonso of
Este had made his suspicions and ill-humour felt in some
threatening way. He does not seem to have had any sympathy
for any member of his wife's circle of intimates. During that self-
same summer of 1505 Tebaldeo complained that 'the Duke holds
me in loathing and I do not know why'. And as for Ercole
Strozzi the rumours of the disfavour in which he was held were
continuous. Moreover Bembo must have understood that his
love might be very dangerous to Lucrezia's position and that
there was no possibility of making up for this. It may well have
been that in the course of their discussions together they decided
to sacrifice their love for reasons or even necessities of state.
When Lucrezia had been engaged in struggling against her
father-in-law, in facing the agony of her father's death and the
blank of the future, she had felt a deep need of her lover, but
now that she was a crowned Duchess and vested with recognized

powers, a prisoner behind the golden bars of her dignity, she drew away from him.

We can conjure up the sensitive profile of the poet as it appears on a medal made when he was young, and imagine him bending over the lock of fair hair that Lucrezia cut for him and which, though a little discoloured by time, still preserves its bright texture in a transparent casket in the *Ambrosiana* in Milan. Three centuries later this same lock of hair touched the heart of Lord Byron and he could boast that he had taken one hair from it.

Bembo recovered of course. In later life he was the immensely influential secretary of Leo X and finally (though Lucrezia did not live to see this) a Cardinal, and a magnificent one. He loved a woman of the name of Aurora or Topazio, and in the end he loved the Genoese woman Morosina by whom he had three children. And Lucrezia, too, though this may be displeasing to relate, was faithless to his memory and lent her ear to the consolation of another love.

Whether Bembo's and Lucrezia's love went beyond the limits of platonic feeling must be answered by each reader for himself. It would be difficult to base a calculation on circumstances, for though Lucrezia was very closely watched she was surrounded by people who would be ready to act as accomplices, and we know how easy it is for those who are set on it to isolate themselves during sojourns in the country. Yet it should be borne in mind that sensitive lovers such as Lucrezia and Bembo need not only physical opportunity but, so to speak, spiritual opportunity – and that is provided much less often than is generally thought, and rarely coincides with the safety of time and place. Finally, the answer to our question is of no great moment. The nature of their love, with its urgency and restrictions, would not be altered if we had more explicit documents and letters. It would always remain Lucrezia Borgia's greatest love affair.

10

CONSPIRACIES AND INTRIGUES
AT COURT

On June 4, 1505, Bernardino de Prosperi wrote to Isabella of Este as follows: 'It seems that the will of the Lord (Duke Alfonso) is that Madonna Elisabetta and all the other foreigners, both male and female, who are in the household of his most illustrious Lady and Consort, should depart ... Hence everyone is in a state, as your ladyship can imagine.' This letter and others on the same subject, written on the 10th and the 23rd of the month, reveal the smug nationalism of the Ferrarese courtiers as they reiterated: 'All Spaniards have to go away.' Moreover they marvelled when Lucrezia showed her 'distress', as though the honour of being a reigning Duchess should make up for such deprivations.

Meanwhile Alfonso had had built an inner passage by which he could go from his own apartments to his wife's whenever he wanted. This might be supposed to have been prompted by an outburst of affection, had any intimacy been possible between Lucrezia and her husband. As things stood, it was almost certainly just another means of keeping her under his eye. When the guard around her became tighter Lucrezia understood, or else Strozzi told her, that the best method of defending herself and her household would be to revert to her original plan of making friends with the Ferrarese and abandoning the retirement among her own people that the Este family and courtiers found so irritating. As soon as she adopted a policy of cordiality their aversion to Spanish and 'foreign' manners would automatically die down.

So Lucrezia agreed to act as Chairman over the Commission for the examination of citizens' petitions – and here the experience she had had in Rome and Spoleto came in useful – and she performed this work with such good grace that even her enemies had to admit it, though reluctantly. She received people frequently, especially now that ambassadors were arriving thick and fast to offer their congratulations to the new Duke, and she was to be seen with Angela Borgia taking the Venetian ambassadors through the city. She gave receptions, balls and concerts. And she acted as godmother – the reasons were political – to the little nephew of the Vice-domino of Venice (Cardinal Ippolito was the other god-parent) and the whole of Ferrara was set talking about the shawl trimmed with gold, 'more than lovely, superb', that she presented to the baby. She wore strict mourning in memory of Duke Ercole but her dresses were always of fine black cloth that showed off her figure. The women-in-waiting were ordered to dress in brown and, like their mistress, they wore Bologna veils on their heads that they drew over their faces when they went out. These veils were light and beautiful and they enhanced the seductiveness of their owners' glances and smiles.

It is not easy to say exactly when things began to go wrong in the spirit or mind of Don Giulio. Riccardo Bacchelli, who has studied the Este conspiracy of 1506 with great care, is perfectly right when he says that Don Giulio's head was too weak to stand up to the passions that were seething within him. He was highly undisciplined, and even his refusal to commit himself to the ecclesiastical life came less from an honest conviction that he had no vocation than from a fretful inability to put up with limitations. He must have noticed the questionable esteem in which Ercole of Este held his eldest son and even the Cardinal during the last period of his life, and as a result he let his own respect for his elder brothers' authority wane; he felt he had a right to criticize them and didn't see why he shouldn't. It may well be that subconsciously Don Giulio had expected some kind of rising, or at least party strife, at the time of Ercole's death which would somehow have put the younger brothers in a stronger position. Instead what really happened was a mysterious agreement between Alfonso and Ippolito – mysterious because there had been so much tension between them in the past. Obviously when the senior members of the House of Este got together in this way the juniors felt left out and it was almost inevitable that they too should band together.

But disappointment and disgruntlement do not usually give place to actual hatred, and in the early days of Alfonso's reign things seem to have been fairly quiet. The correspondence of the period speaks of the gratitude of the younger brothers towards the Duke, who had given Don Giulio a palace of his own to live in and had increased the allowance of both of them, thereby lifting them out of the state of semi-poverty in which Duke Ercole had left them – not without reason. And possibly Don Giulio would never have gone to such extremes had it not been for the provocations and suggestions of Cardinal Ippolito. The first open act of strife between these two was when Don Giulio released a chaplain whom the Cardinal had imprisoned.

Alfonso was going through a difficult period. Over and above the grave preoccupations of the plague, the food shortage and the bad behaviour of the hoarders, there was now added the situation between his brothers. For when the Cardinal heard that the chaplain had been set free he began raging in a way that cannot be described. The deed appeared to him as a defiance of his authority both as man and Cardinal. He asked Alfonso to impose an exemplary punishment and at the same time made it plain that if need be he would do the punishing himself. Alfonso was afraid of family turmoil and wished to nip it in the bud. He decided on a line of conduct which he set down in writing and sent, not to his younger brother, but to Lucrezia, telling her to communicate it to Don Giulio. The gist of his words was: that Don Giulio should leave the Duchess's court, go into banishment on the estate of Brescello, remain within a two-mile radius of the estate, and report every day to the Este commissioner on the spot. Let everyone bear well in mind, added Alfonso, that were he not obeyed immediately and entirely he would take the very gravest measures. Lucrezia had already been concerned in the affair, for she had received a visit from the humanist, Alberto Pio da Carpi, and together they had agreed that the best thing to be done was to try to persuade Don Giulio and his ally Don Ferrante to put the liberated chaplain back into his prison. The two brothers, 'more hardened than ever', answered jointly that this they would never do – and it was at this point that the Duke's letter arrived. Don Giulio was furious – but none the less set out for his banishment, while Pio returned to Carpi and persuaded the cause of all the trouble, the chaplain Don Rainaldo, to go back to the castle of Gesso in Monte with a solemn guarantee that his life would be spared.

Towards the middle of August Lucrezia arrived at Reggio. She had been ill with a difficult pregnancy but was now feeling better. In letters to her husband she gave bulletins of her health – dry, precise and clinical. The most affectionate phrase that she managed to pen was the formula 'I commend myself to you'.

On September 19, 1505, an heir to the House of Este was born in Reggio. The subjects of the Duchy expressed what little joy they felt in view of the fact that they were 'all under tribulation' with plague, famine and want. He was given his grandfather's name, Alexander, and an amnesty was published that included Don Giulio with the others. Alfonso was only too glad to pardon his brother, and he was pleased to have found a formula whereby all the family should be restored to peace. Ippolito, so he thought, would now have put the affair from his mind, especially as the chaplain had gone meekly back to prison. What he failed to understand, or purposely shut his eyes to, was the fact that the Cardinal's anger had deeper grounds than the immediate pretext of Don Rainaldo: Don Giulio's act of rebellion had not been redeemed by a few weeks' comfortable banishment.

Unfortunately Lucrezia's baby lived for twenty-five days only, but her distress was partially alleviated by a new friendship, that of her brother-in-law Francesco Gonzaga, Marquis of Mantua and husband of Isabella of Este. Lucrezia had first met him, it will be recalled, almost ten years earlier in 1496, when he had come to Rome in the splendour of his military glory as the victor of Fornovo, to receive from the hands of Alexander VI the golden rose and the Papal blessing.

It will be recalled too that the Marquis of Mantua had had his reasons for not being present at Lucrezia's wedding. But he had gone to Ferrara in the spring of 1504 and had made the acquaintance of his sister-in-law. Quickly and gaily he appraised and then understood her – her suffering, her boredom, her confinement. He promised her things far beyond his power to perform – such as the liberation of Cesare Borgia. But to Lucrezia, surrounded by the Este family's hostility towards her brother, Gonzaga's attitude opened up new and unexpected horizons. She let herself be captivated. Having lost Bembo she yielded to the restorative properties of another emotion. And so though Bembo had scarcely gone out of her life (and she still suffered when she thought of him) his image was little by little replaced by that of the Marquis of Mantua.

Francesco Gonzaga belonged to the race of those dark men who are still to be seen in the Po valley (their most distant and noble forebear is Virgil), tall, thin, with a delicate apparatus of nerves and a solid apparatus of muscles, men who carry their bodies as though they were a piece of architecture, from the architrave of the shoulders and flat wall of the back down to the long and shapely columns of the legs. Their eyes are deepset, half-closed and brilliant. Their lips are full and soft with hungry sensuality. Their hands are supple. Whether they liked it or not, those who saw Francesco Gonzaga's face could never forget it, any more than we can forget it when we see it in the portrait attributed to Bonsignori or in the profile by Mantegna at the Louvre. Gonzaga was discursive and warm-blooded; he loved wine and he loved women, as is shown by his many illegitimate sons scattered throughout the country round Mantua, and also by the documents of the time. To complete our picture of Gonzaga we must remember his wonderful ability for keeping the saddle when riding the superb horses of the Gonzaga stables, his good military discipline, his almost romantic kindness which endeared the weaknesses and misfortunes of women to him, his love of art, and his religious feeling – at times superstitious, at times generous. About his qualities as a prince and as a head of state there is only one thing to say: that they seemed non-existent beside those of his wife, Isabella of Este, and this must have wounded his pride. He loved and admired his wife, yet her cold superior political sense made him set up his own defences and surround himself with ministers whom Isabella hated. Even so he was not entirely successful. And precisely because he felt that she guessed what he was up to, he sought relief in other women who not only provided the comforts of sensual love but were quite ready to be dominated by his mind. His happy surprise at discovering Lucrezia's warm faith in him, when he rashly involved himself in undertaking the liberation of Valentinois, led him to be moved by her fairness and fragility, and soon he was entirely conquered by her.

It did not take long for them to reach an understanding. As soon as Gonzaga had left Ferrara, Lucrezia's women-in-waiting wrote to him to say that they were only half alive now that they were deprived of the 'divine virtues and exalted and angelic manners of your Lordship'. They all adored him, especially Madonna Angela and Madonna Polissena – the two who had been Bembo's favourites. No one enjoyed the parties any more. The garlands of flowers, the high spirits of the courtiers, the beautiful women in all their finery could not compensate for their loss. 'Every pleasure was but little pleasing to the most excellent Lady (Lucrezia) and to me who serve her,' wrote Polissena when sending him an account of a reception, 'because your most illustrious Lordship was not present.'

Francesco Gonzaga had promised to send some sonnets (whether his own or not we do not know) and then excused himself because he was ill. He was ill, he said, because he was deprived of the air of Ferrara which suited his constitution so well. But even between Mantua and Ferrara exchanges of gallantry were complicated by political friction. The fact that Francesco Gonzaga and the Este family were related did not help to make their relationship a brotherly one except in appearance.

When Gonzaga heard that Lucrezia's baby was dead and that she was alone and melancholy at Reggio, it occurred to him that this was his moment, and he invited her to meet him at Borgoforte on the banks of the Po in Mantuan territory. Lucrezia accepted his invitation, and at the end of October planned an itinerary back to Belriguardo almost entirely by water so as to land her near Borgoforte: nor did she inform Alfonso of her intention of visiting her brother-in-law until it was too late for him to prevent it.

When the Marquis of Mantua heard of her intended arrival he was delighted. He would have her in his house and would be able to minister to her in the presence of none but complacent witnesses; she on her side would see him as absolute lord of his subjects. Borgoforte was a military stronghold, but none the less he intended to do everything to make the Duchess and her suite comfortable during their stay. We can imagine the town bustling with workers and decorators and carpet-layers, bringing linen, beds, furniture and every kind of comfort for the Duchess, who was to stay not at the military residence known as the Rochetta but at the little fourteenth-century palace of Gerolamo Stanga. Isabella had been left out of the party and made no effort to join in, wisely content to watch from a distance. Lucrezia set out from Reggio on October 26, 1505.

The day of October 28 dawned at Borgoforte. The air was soft and autumnal over the river landscape and the meadows. Now that everything was ready, Francesco Gonzaga had a moment to wonder if Lucrezia's visit was really possible and if it really would take place. But she was approaching. On the milky water of the great river her low boat was to be seen through the mist, moving forward between the two wide banks bordered with feathery birches. The colour of the women's dresses could be discerned, and the brilliance of their jewels and their hair. The brightest light of all was Lucrezia and it lay in her smile. Gonzaga approached her, offered her his hand, helped her as she walked, and protected her in his courteous soldierly way. They began talking, first in small groups, then more freely in general conversation. There was an air of holiday-making such as comes with a unique occasion and a feeling of freedom. Of course Lucrezia and Francesco spoke of Valentinois' imprisonment, and he promised that he personally would send an envoy to the court of Spain to ask for Valentinois to be set free (and this he really did, and Lucrezia thanked him warmly for it on November 6). Their conversations set the tone of their future affectionate relationship: there was no going back now. Words and gestures were fixed in their two happy minds to be remembered later when they were alone.

The days of the 28th and the 29th were passed in the vagueness and obliviousness that accompany the beginning of love. Then Gonzaga had an idea. Why should Lucrezia not come to Mantua to visit Isabella? Surely she could not refuse such a conventional invitation? Lucrezia wrote off to Alfonso of Este explaining how her brother-in-law had urged her and persuaded her 'with such vehemence and determination that I should go tomorrow to visit the most illustrious Marchesa, that though I have used considerable resistance, I have been obliged to obey'. Alfonso answered civilly expressing his gratitude for the honour paid to the Duchess of Ferrara.

The city of Mantua had a beauty calculated to appeal to Lucrezia. Isabella was awaiting her in the tall castle overlooking the lakes that are formed by the waters of Virgil's river, and led her through her halls to see her art collection, her books, her paintings and her rare objects. She tried to dominate her by the force of her intellect but she was too acute not to see how far all this was from Lucrezia's mind. When these two parted they were colder than ever towards each other. After two stolen days of holiday Lucrezia set out again on the morning of October 31, exchanging her little boat for Francesco's heavy barge in which the journey would be quicker and more comfortable. On the evening of the 31st Lucrezia reached La Stellata and stayed there for the night. On November 1 she left the course of the Po and followed its tributaries and so arrived in sight of the painted towers of Belriguardo. There, before she had time to rest, she was plunged into the atmosphere of tragedy.

Meanwhile Angela Borgia had been reaping the fruits of her love affairs. It was not supposed to be known, but in fact it was common knowledge, that this hot-blooded young woman was shortly going to have a baby, and the family was trying to keep the scandal quiet. This explains why Lucrezia's court stayed away from Ferrara for so long that year, right until December. The secret of the baby's father was so well kept by the Estes that we who live centuries later are hard put to it to discover who he was. But the most likely hypothesis seems to be the one that attributes eighteen-year-old Angela's pregnancy to Don Giulio. The love affair between Don Giulio and Angela must have begun a good deal earlier. The first clue to it that we can trace is among the documents of the Gonzaga archives. On June 9, 1502, Bernardino de Prosperi wrote to Isabella Este that when old Duke Ercole had set out for the country he had taken Don Giulio with him 'who would have been only too willing to stay behind'; and two days earlier, on June 7, he had written an account of the departure of Lucrezia for Belriguardo mentioning that Angela had stayed behind because she was ill and did not leave Ferrara until June 11. Bearing in mind de Prosperi's extreme discretion and understatement, especially in affairs of this kind – the Marchesa of Mantua reproved him for his reticence – it is not difficult for us to see why Don Giulio was reluctant to go away with his father. And with temperaments like theirs the relationship would not have been one of mere companionship. But Cardinal Ippolito, too, had begun paying court to Angela who had been reckless enough to tell him – as Guicciardini informs us – that she preferred Don Giulio to him because of his beautiful eyes. Tradition holds that Angela had added that the eyes of Don Giulio were worth the Cardinal's whole body. This may or may not be true. But in any case, to see his young brother preferred to himself would certainly have touched the Cardinal's pride and self-love on the raw. Probably Angela's pregnancy had aggravated the brothers' mutual dislike and jealousy, for it was proof positive that one of them had been successful with her. The events that followed showed the extent of the ill-feeling and bitterness.

On November 1, 1505, just after midday, Cardinal Ippolito was outside Ferrara with his court when he met Don Giulio coming alone on horseback from Belriguardo. When he saw him approaching, looking dashing and pleased with himself, the Cardinal could not contain his rage. 'Kill that man, gouge out his eyes,' he ordered (remembering, perhaps, Angela's words of praise). His grooms, with the terrifying alacrity of men accustomed to cruel commands, fell upon Don Giulio, unhorsed him and stabbed him in the eyes with their daggers. Even Ippolito must have realized that this deed was both cruel and pointless when he had recovered from his fury and saw his brother's blood. Leaving Don Giulio lying on the grass in a frightful condition, but still alive, he rode rapidly towards the borders of the State of Ferrara.

How long Don Giulio lay in the meadows of Belriguardo we do not know. But when he was found he was taken back to Belriguardo and there nursed. We have no document to inform us of Lucrezia's horror nor of Angela's tears. But we can easily imagine them. There were words of execration heard in all the three hundred rooms of Belriguardo, while doctors and surgeons who had been sent from Ferrara tried to save what they could of Don Giulio's eyes.

When Duke Alfonso heard the macabre story he was stunned. And since the circumstances made it impossible for him to take council with the Cardinal, he made a political mistake. Forgetting that the head of a State should deal with such dangerous matters by himself, he wrote a letter to his sister Isabella and his brother-in-law Francesco Gonzaga. It consisted of two parts –

one containing the official account of the incident in which Ippolito's two grooms were accused of the crime, and the other telling the true story of what had happened. The young Duke was torn in two. He knew that it was his duty to impose a punishment and his sense of right urged him to administer justice. But on the other hand, his admiration for Ippolito's abilities, his respect for the Cardinal's robe and the difficulties and scandals inherent in punishing a prince of the Church – not to mention his own need of Ippolito – gave him pause. So that when the Gonzagas wrote to him urging the greatest severity and expressing their horror at such an unheard-of deed – Isabella had a weakness for her fascinating bastard brother, and Gonzaga saw that if the Cardinal were punished the House of Este would be weakened – Alfonso answered that this was not a matter that could be rushed. Only a short time afterwards he was allowing the Cardinal to come and go through the Duchy at will, and after a month he got his cousin Alberto of Este to write to Ippolito to tell him that he could return to Ferrara, because otherwise he would provide propaganda for the enemies of the State.

Don Giulio had been so well attended by the doctors of Ferrara and of Mantua – sent by Isabella – that little by little it was hoped that partial sight might be restored to both eyes. On November 6 he was transferred by the Duke's orders from Belriguardo to the city, where he was lodged in the castle and treated with affectionate care. But he was a ghastly sight, for his left eye was monstrously swollen and his right had no lid. He was too human not to seek comfort in thoughts of revenge, though by now Alfonso was pressing for conciliation and pardon.

Alfonso felt that a policy of appeasement was urgent – to put an end to the incitements he repeatedly received from Mantua, and to silence all those operating against the Este family even in Rome, where Julius II was now throwing doubt on the official version of the facts and wanted further clarifications. So Don Giulio was promised many things and in the end the poor fellow perforce agreed to keep quiet. On December 23 he was introduced into the presence of Alfonso and the Cardinal in his pitiful condition. It was evening. His pale disfigured face in the light of the flares brought tears to Alfonso's eyes, but the Cardinal seemed totally unmoved – his voice was perfectly calm when it was his turn to speak. He said that he was displeased at what had occurred and intended henceforward to be a good brother. Don Giulio appealed to the Duke, showed him his wounds and pointed out how cruelly he had been treated. There was a pause. For a long time Don Giulio could not bring himself to utter the words of forgiveness. When he did, Alfonso could breathe again, and he exhorted the brothers to live in harmony and enjoy his reign with him. What he said was wise, prudent, but perfectly useless. Then came the very unwelcome moment in which aggressor and aggressed had to embrace.

So the metaphorical wounds were patched up and the optimistic Alfonso trusted that the brothers' verbal reconciliation would be made good by a moral one. Meanwhile he ordered the care surrounding Don Giulio to be doubled. Then, what with the ills of the past months – the death of his father, the death of his baby son, plague, famine and the mutilated eyes of Don Giulio – Alfonso felt an understandable reaction. He restored all the permits for dressing-up that Duke Ercole had withdrawn in his later years, and he invented new amusements for the populace such as fights between men and maddened pigs, and games and theatricals and jousts. This was the first Carnival he had held as Duke, and he wanted to make it memorable. Every day there were masquerades and every evening in the halls of the palaces there were balls and theatricals, after which the guests went in groups to finish the evening in the Duchess's apartments. The elder courtiers thought of Don Giulio and shook their heads, uttering phrases of censure for such unbridled cheer. The censure increased when they saw that the affairs of State were being neglected and even the suppliants' court, as Prosperi said, was 'dozing'.

The first topic of the season was the betrothal of Angela Borgia. This, of course, was not with Don Giulio for whom the order and discipline of ecclesiastical life now seemed more than ever necessary – so much so that Lucrezia wrote in her own hand at this time to the Prior of the Gerosolimitani at Venice asking for a post and benefices for her brother-in-law in the Order of Malta. The Este family must have been at one in wanting to see the hot-headed Angela tied up, so as not to have any more domestic surprises nor dispatches such as Prosperi's important one on January 18, 1506: 'I gather that the lady Angela gave birth to a child when coming here by ship' – (from Belriguardo). A man was quickly found who was prepared to overlook Angela's unvirginal past in view of the great advantages that she would bring – with her close relationship to the reigning house. This man was Alessandro Pio, the Lord of Sassuolo.

Naturally Carnival aroused the melancholy and fury of Don Giulio who was forgotten by his selfish brothers and the inconstant Angela.

When he heard from his darkened room the echo of the revelry at court, he brooded on the injustice of his plight and railed against fate. Don Ferrante, fascinated by his brother's strong language, spent a lot of time with him using even stronger words himself, and little by little they laid plans for revenge. The Cardinal's guilt now became the Duke's guilt who had been loath to impose lawful punishment. The thought of taking action against them, killing them both and receiving the Duchy as reward, seemed a splendid and justified one, and they discussed it at length until what was at first no more than a consoling fantasy became with its own momentum a plot. Others, inspired by resentment, joined up with them, including old Albertino Boschetti whose domain of San Cesario had been contested by Alfonso of Este, his son-in-law Gherardo de Roberti, a captain of the Duke's guard, and Gian Cantore di Guascogna, a priest who had been over-favoured by Ercole and Alfonso for his beautiful voice. There is no difficulty in understanding why the first two joined the plot, but considerable difficulty about the third. Gian Cantore had everything to lose and it might well be little to gain once Don Ferrante and Don Giulio were in power. But whether because he had high hopes or because he had personal reasons to hate Duke Alfonso, this fair fat Gascon priest joined the conspiracy. The plotters now began holding meetings that showed their ineptitude even for crime. They tried out poisons without ever deciding the way they should be administered. They had every opportunity, for Alfonso was very trusting and during a day of coarse amusements even let the Gascon bind him to a prostitute's bed. But Gian Cantore did not dare to draw his dagger and in the end it was he himself who set the Duke free, who was bursting with laughter at the novelty of the game. On another occasion the conspirators took up positions with arms at a crossroad and waited, but Alfonso passed some other way.

In April 1506 Alfonso went on a journey leaving the government of the city in the hands of his wife and the Cardinal. It must have been at this time that the Cardinal finished gathering together the net he had been weaving round Don Giulio's hare-brained scheme. The Cardinal played his hand brilliantly. He pinned down the delinquents and recalled his elder brother.

On receiving the message Alfonso set out from Bari where he had been visiting castles and fortresses with his cousin Isabella of Aragon (and where he must certainly have seen Lucrezia's son, Rodrigo). On July 2 he reached Lugo where he found Ippolito who had come secretly to meet him on the pretext of going to Vigogna. When he reached Ferrara on July 3 everyone noticed Alfonso's pallor and bewilderment. Don Giulio had intuited that something was afoot and had gone to Mantua to be with his sister Isabella. But the Cardinal's trap was sprung without warning and hide-outs were of no avail. Boschetti, Roberti and Don Ferrante were arrested, and Don Giulio was handed over under orders against a formal promise that his life would be spared and his prison be a healthy one. Gian Cantore, who had managed to get to Rome and win the goodwill of a Cardinal's mistress for his arts as an actor, was seized at a later date. When the conspirators had confessed, the trial proceeded inexorably and ended with condemnation. Boschetti and Roberti were beheaded and quartered in the square in the presence of Don Giulio and Don Ferrante who had been sentenced to the same fate. It was only when the Este brothers were about to mount the scaffold in their turn that they heard the announcement that the Duke, in his magnanimity, spared them their lives which they were to pass in perpetual imprisonment. The prison was prepared in one of the towers of the castle, in two rooms above each other whose walls had been whitewashed and whose doors had been walled up. Food and the infrequent visitors who came for the duties of their office were let down by a little ingress high up in the walls near the ceiling. Later the two prisoners were allowed to communicate with each other and a third room was put at their disposal, bright and airy, from which they could see the street as far as the hospital of Sant' Anna and comment on passers-by. But the most astonishing thing of all is that they lived in this confinement through two generations of Este Dukes. Don Ferrante died after forty-three years and Don Giulio was liberated after fifty-three years by Alfonso II, Lucrezia's nephew (the Duke we know through Tasso's life).

'Evil reaps its own reward,' said Niccolò da Correggio, summing up the general feeling. There was a gay riot of bell-ringing and salvoes of cannon and Te Deums. Don Giulio's and Don Ferrante's belongings were distributed to Alfonso's friends, to the courtiers, and to Andrea Pontegino, known for his courtly gesture of spitting in Don Giulio's face as he was brought in chains from Mantua. Lucrezia managed to save one of Don Giulio's followers, namely the chaplain Don Rainaldo who had been the original cause of the ill-feeling. In Lucrezia's wardrobe register for the year 1508 he is named as receiving a stipend from the Duchess for his services as chaplain.

Meanwhile the world of politics was in a state of ferment. As we have already seen the warlike Pontiff Julius II, though he hated the very name of Borgia, carried on and strengthened the policy of Alexander VI and Valentinois: he wanted the domains of the Church, for centuries in the hands of unruly feudal lords, to be restored directly to Church control. Venice had been forced to give back a few of the domains she had seized in Romagna at the time of Valentinois' fall – and so had Florence. Nepi, Sermoneta and Camarino, the ephemeral duchies of the baby Borgias, had gone back to the Pope who restored them to the Roman barons dispossessed by Alexander VI, so as to win their friendship and protect his flanks. And so as to consolidate his alliance with the Orsini he thought out a plan for a double marriage. The first was that of his daughter, the beautiful and intelligent Felice della Rovere, with Gian Giordano Orsini, and the second that of his nephew, Niccolò della Rovere, with an Orsini whom we know already, namely Laura, daughter of Orsino Orsini and Giulia Farnese who had formerly been thought to be a daughter of Alexander VI. In 1508 Giulia Farnese, now a little over thirty, had the satisfaction of returning to the Vatican where she was reported to be the loveliest and most fascinating of all the women there including her own daughter. Julius II probably shared the view that Orsini was Laura's father – otherwise he would never have arranged a marriage between her and a member of his house. Laura was later to have a restless life and pass from one man to another – which in itself is one of the dullest things in the world. Thus she let down the tradition of true love set by her forebears.

Having fixed these marriages and restored the Orsinis, Gaetanis, Colonnas and Savellis to their domains, Julius II felt safely established at home and prepared to go forward with his programme against the feudal lords of the Church. The first to realize their peril were the Baglioni of Perugia and the Bentivoglio of Bologna. Against these admittedly corrupt families Julius II began war in earnest, making alliances with Ferrara, Urbino, Florence and Siena, and managing to circumvent the danger of French intervention in favour of the Bentivoglio. Italy, though accustomed to picturesque armies, had never seen one like this, led by a Pope who seemed the very personification of

Dante's Santa Gesta, followed by the whole court of Cardinals, ready to camp under canvas, lead the advance, and endure all hardships. The Baglioni, beset by popular hatred at home, submitted without a struggle and allowed the Pope free entry into the city on September 13. In the eight days that he stayed in Perugia Julius II restored Church sovereignty, re-organized the magistrature and banished everyone guilty of civic crimes. He then marched on Bologna.

In spite of all their affection for the Bentivoglio, the Este family had not been able to avoid joining the Papal League because they, too, owed allegiance to the Pope. The Cardinal of Este went to meet the head of the Church at Imola, preceded by a gift of provisions that included a hundred capons and a hundred sacks of flour. The provisions were more welcome than Ippolito and when he met Julius II, whose prejudice against him had been aggravated by the events of the previous year, he came up against the Pope's plain forthright character. Through a prelate in the Papal court he was given a violent ticking-off which touched on points affecting his vanity – such as his 'mop' of long lustrous wavy hair, his gallant manner, his 'nymph-like' behaviour with his little airs and graces, and his famous hands whose beauty filled literary women with enthusiasm, including the poetess Veronica Gambera. Alfonso was more welcome than his brother when he arrived in his turn to pay homage to his ally. But the Pope did not indulge in amiable exchanges with the Este family. After the tragedy of Don Giulio and Don Ferrante it had been said in Rome that the State of Ferrara would not survive very long, the more so as the Este family was suspected of secretly supporting the Bentivoglio.

On November 10 the Pope made a triumphal entry into Bologna under the pontifical canopy surrounded by Cardinals, prelates, officers and masters of ceremony, and he wore superb vestments sewn with gems. When the Pope passed through the great city of Emilia the people shouted '*vivas*' of enthusiasm. In Ferrara the echo of this applause caused something like terror.

*

Towards the end of 1506 Cesare Borgia finally managed to escape from his prison at Medina in Spain and sought refuge with his in-laws in Navarre. Once he had reached their barely hospitable shelter, he sent a Spaniard to Lucrezia to let her know of his escape so that, if she could, she should help him. Lucrezia trembled with joy. Who could she express it to if not Francesco Gonzaga? She wrote to him and as she wrote she felt her delight increasing. Then, inspired by her longing to help her brother, she wrote to the court of France and to the ambassador of Ferrara in Paris, Manfredo Manfredi, charging him to send her daily news of what was being done for Valentinois. Manfredi answered that an envoy of the Duke of Romagna, Monsignor Requesens, had arrived in Blois to ask in the name of his master for permission to come and take possession of the Duchy of Valentinois. But now that Pope Alexander was no longer there to help him in his Italian enterprise, Louis XII felt it not only risky but absurd to hand over one of his provinces to Cesare. Louis' excuse was well thought out and depended on the mutual respect between kings: how could he possibly welcome and set up someone who had escaped from the prisons of Ferdinand the Catholic?

Lucrezia read these depressing reports, but with her father's obstinate optimism was not discouraged: she suggested answers, invented arguments and appealed with prayers. At the mere thought that her brother was free she foresaw the resurrection of the Borgia bull. Cesare was now thirty and if only he could play a part once more in the political game in Europe he would soon find a way of regaining power. Gossip already said that the Venetians wanted to summon him to Venice to make use of him to counterbalance the conquests of Julius II. It was only a matter of time ...

Between her hopes for her brother and her secret feelings of love, Lucrezia found even the walls of the Este castle bearable. During that Carnival Francesco Gonzaga was a visitor at Ferrara. Julius II had named him Captain-General of the Church and he bore his title like an additional ornament to his charm. The Duchess descended to the great hall to greet him wearing cloth of gold and velvet and brocade and embroidery. She danced with her beloved Gonzaga and, alone together in the intricacy of their steps, she made him see the exotic grace of her movements and the lightness of her tread as she bent to the persuasive music of the violas. There is no detailed account of their conversation, but the whole of Ferrara noticed the 'great cheer and affection' with which Lucrezia honoured her brother-in-law. She danced so tirelessly that the third Este offspring was lost. As Prosperi put it: 'The Lady miscarried yesterday, which was Friday, and the Lord (Alfonso) was very displeased, more displeased, according to what I hear, (than) when the one who was born died, because this time she is weakened in the spine.' Alfonso had not the delicacy to conceal his ill-humour and let his wife know that he held her responsible for what had happened because of her excessive dancing. Alfonso enjoyed rude health, was strong and even coarse as is shown by his taste in prostitutes, and he found Lucrezia's fragility, which so moved Francesco Gonzaga, very irritating. But Lucrezia was not to be put out by married nagging, and a few days later was up and about again to help entertain a group of young and pleasure-loving Cardinals, who had come from the suite of Julius II in Bologna to enjoy themselves at the Court of Ferrara as guests of Ippolito. When she saw the young ecclesiastics around her she was in a seventh heaven of delight for even though they lacked their purple – they had all come incognito and disguised – they reminded her of her distant past, of this or that consistory that had marked the stages in her power. She felt in her element and showed it; so much so that she cast aside her aloof reserve and it was said that the Duchess really deserved 'praise and commendation' for her excellent and courtly manners.

This fresh excitement harmed Lucrezia and she had a relapse. But she recovered in time to give a supper and dance for Camillo Costabili and his wife on February 26. The whole of Ferrara joined in the Duchess's sociable mood. There were festivities on all sides. Besides the great gatherings in the ducal palace there were lesser private ones in which women shone even more in the informal atmosphere. Bighino Trotti and his wife started the fashion of giving very select parties composed of a few people who knew each other well. His parties became famous for their exclusiveness, snobbery and the quality of the guests who frequented them. Amongst the brilliant women were Nicola, Trotti's wife, with her wild yet controlled moods, Barbara Torelli with her eloquence and humanist culture which was intellectual without being pedantic, Giovanna da Rimini and Angela Borgia – all four beautiful and celebrated for their love affairs. We have no idea who the men were (our informant is silent as to their names) but they must have been worthy of the women.

The merry-making ended when Carnival ended but the women were still as busy as ever. That year Lucrezia had summoned Friar Raffaele da Varese who, according to his lovely penitents, was 'a man truly most useful to the soul'. When he saw so many beautiful faces around him, intent though painted, the eager friar thought of launching a little reform, and thus attacked the luxury of the women's dresses, the extravagance of their ornaments and the vanity of rouge and cosmetics. There lay the way to hell, etc. – the age-old anathemas.

At that time women used to put a pomatum on their faces called *liscio* containing a sublimate which made a white compact foundation on top of which majolica pink was painted on the cheeks. However Lucrezia was convinced by the sermons that she should effect a severe reform, and she commanded all the women at court to forgo the pomatum if they wished to retain her favour. A little rouge, she said conciliatingly, would just pass. And she herself ordered her alchemist, possibly Maestro Fabrizio delli Mucchi who had long provided her with Cyprus powder, to prepare distilled waters and the juices of aromatic herbs for washing and smoothing her face, which would surely be less ostentatious and more hygienic than the pomatum. At the sermon on Good Friday the women and girls exhibited their changed faces to the people of Ferrara who had come to enjoy watching them file in. They all seemed very beautiful and it was noted that 'rouge had been abundant, beginning with the wise

Chief', which is almost certainly a reference to Lucrezia. Inspired by the suggestions of the Friar, Lucrezia began planning further reforms. The women of Ferrara raised a cry of alarm. 'They are going to stop us wearing *décolleté* dresses,' they exclaimed, foreseeing a time in the near future when they would have to cover themselves up as far as their throats. There was also talk of additional reforms such as making Jews wear yellow caps by which they could be distinguished from afar, and severe rules were made against blaspheming with a fine imposed on a sliding scale – two ducats for blasphemies against God and the Madonna and one ducat for blasphemies against the saints, thereby preserving the hierarchy of heaven.

But the women of Ferrara were not of a mind to let themselves be bullied. When they saw themselves threatened in all that was most important to them as women they organized a great rebellion and, with the backing of their menfolk, sent a protest to Court. It seemed to them, they said, that everyone had the right to spend their money in their own way and that it would be more fruitful to attend to 'things of greater moment wherein there is offence against God and one's neighbour with more harm to the soul and greater detriment to temporal goods', than to concentrate on these external reforms. Lucrezia was well able to appreciate the wisdom of such arguments and there was no more talk of measuring *décolletés* and the length of trains. There was no shortage of worthy subjects for Friar Raffaele's sermons and so he could easily turn his attention elsewhere.

On April 20, 1507, Lucrezia was engaged in conversation in her court apartments with some members of her household and relatives among whom was Ercole of Este, Alfonso's cousin. The Duke had gone off on one of his journeys and had left the government of the Duchy in the hands of his wife – to the great irritation of Isabella of Este who could not tolerate that another woman, above all her rival, should be thought capable of managing a state. But even the most cautious of her informers was obliged to confirm this news. Prosperi wrote to her that he 'almost' believed in Lucrezia's capability because 'one hears no talk of the Cardinal'. Lucrezia presided alone and tirelessly at the examination of appeals and as regards the other affairs of the Duchy. And though the Cardinal may have advised her and directed her in private, he did not appear officially.

Suddenly a Spaniard, dusty and with deadly news written on his face, entered the palace courtyard, dismounted and made the simple announcement to the servants that Cesare Borgia was dead. The news spread round the castle like wildfire. It was Friar Raffaele who broke the news to Lucrezia. She remained motionless under the watching eyes of her household and kinsmen, and the first words she spoke were ones of revolt against God: 'The more I try to do God's will, the more He cold-shoulders me.' A little later she added: 'I thank God I am resigned to His will.'

The Spaniard was summoned. He was one of Valentinois' pages and he was asked to relate the circumstances of his master's death. Cesare had been fighting at Viana together with his in-laws against the Count of Lerin in a provincial guerrilla war. He had led a hundred horse in a sortie and routed the enemy: he had then pursued the enemy with such impetuosity that he outstripped his escort and fell into the enemy's hands. He had been assaulted by a strong squad, wounded, killed, stripped of his arms and clothes, and left naked on the wintry ground until his soldiers arrived to look for him. He had died a warrior's death, they said, and asked for military honours. But perhaps Lucrezia realized that this death had been almost a suicide. Valentinois always knew what he was doing, as he had shown yet again in his escape from Spain, and he was not a man to let himself be carried away by the fever of battle or by sheer love of a feat of arms. If he rode so recklessly after the enemy it was surely because he was haunted by the agonizing feeling that the world no longer had a place for him. Only a few days earlier Requesens had come from Blois bearing a sentence of banishment, and Cesare had probably felt that his d'Albret in-laws, while finding him useful for their war, at heart looked on him as a poor relation and might at any moment sacrifice him to the will of the King of France. Charlotte, his wife, as far as we know, did not take any steps to help him, and Lucrezia's little voice, lost in a swamp of indifference, only served to bring home to him how poor she too was and how humbled by the great collapse of the Borgias. Perhaps the thought of himself as a fugitive living the life of a beggar spurred him on in his mad pursuit of the enemy.

Lucrezia listened to the Spaniard's story in silence. Everyone around her paid tribute to her admirable behaviour and 'staunch spirit'. She walled in her sorrow and then returned to her life as Duchess in charge and went on with the examination of appeals. But when night came and she was left alone she called out for her brother and the women-in-waiting in the neighbouring rooms listened and held their breath as she repeated his name a thousand times over and lived again with the loved but awesome figure of her girlhood. True, there was the murder of the Duke of Gandia, of Perotto and of Alfonso of Bisceglie. But had she not, on her side, connived at these crimes by accepting them – after the first moment of horror – and, worse, by forgetting them? A bond beyond human laws, based on instinct itself, bound her to him and the Spanish and Valencian words that came to her lips when she called for him that night may, in some bitter sweet way, have been words of love.

While the churches in Ferrara were re-echoing with prayers and requiems, and the Duchess was weeping in the monastery of Corpus Domini, in Italy and beyond people were feeling that the news of Cesare's death had freed them from some poisonous hornet. They breathed again. First and foremost among these was the King of France and, second, Julius II who had pictured Cesare fighting against him under the Venetian flag. Then the members of the Este family who were relieved of the necessity of steering between their own interests and those of Lucrezia's emotions. And there were many private people in addition who could relax – eased of the burden of settling difficult accounts.

Cesare Borgia, ch'era dalla gente
per armi e per virtu tenuto un sole
mancar dovendo, andò dove andar suole
Febo, verso la sera, all' Occidente.

Cesare Borgia who was held by all
to be a sun in courage and in arms
obliged to depart, went whither Phoebus goes
as evening falls, towards the West.

Such was the epitaph of the indifferent. Cesare was mourned by his mother Vannozza, by Jofre, now established in the principality of Squillace with his second wife, Maria de Mila (Sancha had died in 1504 when she was only just twenty-seven. Her last adorer, Consalvo de Cordoba, paid homage to her at her funeral), and also doubtless by various captains and soldiers who admired his outstanding mastery of their craft. But it was Lucrezia who gathered together the remnants of her brother's life and gave refuge not only to the page who had brought the news but also to the Spanish priest who had helped Cesare in his flight from Medina and was now homeless. She summoned an illegitimate daughter of Valentinois' from Rome – also called Lucrezia – confided her to Angela Borgia, and clothed her in satin, velvet and fur.

As for Lucrezia's private life at this time, a prominent figure in it was Ercole Strozzi. As if to counterbalance Alfonso's disapproval of him, Lucrezia had attached him even more closely to her court and to her person. Apart from her secretary Tebaldeo, Strozzi was the only person to be received in her private rooms – granting of course that the Duke was absent. Often, if she was ill or convalescing, she received him in bed and he would take into her room some fresh thought, some verdant image, happiness for today and hope for tomorrow – recreating her world in a poetic way as Bembo had done in the past. Lucrezia's attachment to her poet was well-known, and everyone became aware of the extent of it when Strozzi needed her help in his very much opposed love affair with Barbara Torelli which was to become famous in Italian literature.

Barbara, a fugitive and a rebel, had all the fascination of people who struggle courageously on when the odds are against them. At twenty-seven she had been disastrously involved in a marriage with Ercole Bentivoglio of Bologna who had given her two daughters and then made her live a life of humiliation, sordid and inhumane in the extreme, involving every kind of moral and sensual brutality. He eventually went so far as to sell her for 1,000 ducats to a bishop and when she refused to play her part in the transaction he threatened to accuse her of being a poisoner. This was more than any woman could endure, even at a period when much had to be endured for the miserable right to have a home, and Barbara fled. She was related to the Gonzagas on her mother's side and so, with affectionate recommendations from the Duchess of Urbino, she went and took refuge in a monastery in Mantua. Thence she moved on to Ferrara to stay with the nuns of San Rocco, as is proved by an unpublished document of April 1502, to be found in the Gonzaga archives: Francesco Castello, doctor and gentleman-in-waiting to Ercole I and a good judge of character, who frequently passed between the Este court and the convent on business, used to talk about Barbara Torelli with enthusiasm, saying she was 'very beautiful and clever'. On obtaining the protection of the Duke of Ferrara who was a close friend and relative of the Bentivoglio, Barbara felt she was in a safe enough position to claim her rights. All she asked was permission to lead a simple life in which she would not be humiliated and threatened, and that her dowry should be restored, or at least enough of it to allow her to live 'in a lowly way and as a humble person'. But like all brutes when they see their victim slipping through their fingers, her husband answered that he would not grant her so much as a ducat, and his intransigence and avarice coupled with her innocence and beauty caused Barbara's story to become one of the favourite romantic tales in the chronicles of Ferrara. Public opinion and private sympathy were on her side; she became the fashion, and was much sought after. But well before she triumphed in this way, she had got to know Ercole Strozzi and had centred her life on him. What had made the poet fall in love with her? Was it her intellectual qualities or her beauty, or was it those things added to the fact that she was a victim involved in a struggle fraught with pitfalls and dangers? To win Barbara Torelli and defy the anger of the Bentivoglio family were only too tempting for someone of Strozzi's temperament, especially in view of the material wealth that victory would yield. On her part Barbara found herself in the company of a man of great distinction and intelligence whose lameness gave him such obvious weakness as to be a delight to her, after the bullying depravity to which she had been used. It must have given her a new lease of life to be wooed in the cultured manner that was in keeping with her own education and tastes. She accepted the wonder of this love with the zest and gratitude of an upright and passionate nature, and it was a happy duty to let herself be guided by the poet – a way of showing that she recognized his powers and accepted them totally.

Meanwhile the feelings of sympathy between Lucrezia and her brother-in-law had increased with the passage of time, and there is no need to explain what increasing sympathy meant in a man and woman of their temperament. Strozzi was a personal friend of the Marquis of Mantua and had grasped at once where things might end, but instead of being alarmed he had taken on himself the task of being an intermediary between the two lovers. The letters that Luzio discovered in the Gonzaga archives in Mantua and which I compared (quite unnecessarily) with original letters of Strozzi's, leave no room for doubt on this point. The man who signed himself by the pseudonym of 'Zilio' and made it his task to act as go-between for the lovers was none other than Ercole Strozzi himself.

We can only reconstruct the intrigue in part, for the letters are few in number, and cryptic. The intrigue started at the beginning of the summer of 1507 (the understanding was perhaps reached during the Carnival of that year when the Marquis of Mantua passed twice through Ferrara) and evolved within an extremely cautious and secretive correspondence which had the additional safeguard of accommodation names, addresses and signatures. The procedure was as follows: Strozzi would write on Lucrezia's behalf to Gonzaga (sometimes she also wrote in her own hand) and addressed the letters to Guido Strozzi, one of his brothers who lived in Mantua. Guido Strozzi then either took the letters to court himself to pass them on to the Marquis, or conveyed them there through his brother-in-law, Uberto Uberti, or through someone known mysteriously as J. A. The answers were sent by the same method in reverse. In the letters Gonzaga was called 'Guido' – to bear out the address – Lucrezia was called 'Barbara', Alfonso of Este 'Camillo', Ippolito 'Tigrino' and Isabella 'Lena'. Strozzi, as we have said, was 'Zilio'. All we can say of these assumed names is that they were not of great significance and were only intended to serve as a last line of defence, for the correspondents were quite sure that they would never be discovered. The comparisons of handwriting which we can make today could have been made much more easily then, and it would not have taken long to perceive that the 'Barbara' mentioned by 'Zilio' concealed some trickery, for in one and the same letter he would refer to two Barbaras, 'my Barbara' – meaning Barbara Torelli – and 'your Barbara' – Lucrezia.

Lucrezia could no longer justify her letters by saying that she was enrolling Gonzaga's help on Valentinois' behalf. Why did she acquiesce in this dangerous tangle of secrets? Was it because, being still so young, she could not bear to relinquish love so soon? She was certainly risking a great deal, and the risk was even greater for her accomplice, Strozzi, who wrote to the Marquis that he was risking his life for him 'a thousand times every hour'. Lucrezia could persuade herself that if she kept her relationship within the limits of affectionate friendship she could not be accused of sin, and in any case the game was worth the candle: but what did Strozzi hope to get from his intervention? A large reward, yes, but he already had villas, palaces, glory, wealth and love. True he spent so much that he was always short of money and Lucrezia had to make him substantial loans on numbers of occasions. But that is not an adequate reason, for he was neither so poor nor so miserly as to take on this rôle out of self-interest. Strozzi's friendship for Gonzaga, Alberto Pio and Bembo – all of whom were hated by Alfonso of Este for one reason or another – coupled with his position as evil genius with Lucrezia, suggests that he had a secret hatred for the Este family and especially for Alfonso. It is known for certain that the Duke did not love him, for he had deprived him of his public offices and aimed at taking back some of the lands given to his father by Ercole I. Strozzi's grudges may have pushed him to the exquisite revenge of encouraging Lucrezia's restless longings. And so the wheels of this intrigue were set in motion and secret messengers passed backwards and forwards across the Po. It is not known whether, after the Carnival meetings of 1507, the in-laws were able to be together again during the summer in one of the holiday places of Ferrara. What we do know was that in December Lucrezia was once more pregnant, and this time had hope of giving birth successfully because she felt well and in good spirits.

It was probably during Carnival of 1505, and quite certainly some time between 1504 and 1510, that Lucrezia's portrait was painted – lost, alas, in the original but copies of which are to be found in the Nîmes museum and the Nessi collection at Como. The Nessi copy comes from the well-known collection of portraits of famous people that the sixteenth-century historian, Paolo Giovio, put together, and this is a strong argument in favour of its being a true likeness. The copies do not give us a clue as to the painter of the original. It has been said that the full-face pose and the treatment of the face suggest the name of Bartolomeo Veneto, who was working at the redecoration of Lucrezia's apartments at the time and is mentioned a number of times in her wardrobe register for the year 1506. He was a first-class portrait-painter and would very likely have undertaken this task – but we have no document to confirm the hypothesis.

On the other hand in the National Gallery in London there is a fine, delicate portrait of Lucrezia frankly attributed to Bartolomeo Veneto. No one has recognized it as being of the Duchess of Ferrara until just recently. She is elegantly dressed in a garment of black velvet cut away against a yellow background, with wide sleeves decorated with sinuous black embroidery in palm-leaf gold. From her neck there hangs a necklace with beads of enamelled gold on which are depicted symbols of the Passion and letters that probably form a Latin phrase. The white voile tucker is ornamented in white and pink. Round her head is a delicate floral crown of pearls and rubies. The face is young but not dazzling, though the painter has treated it cleverly. The neck and throat are rounded, the nose sharply drawn, the hair fair and fine and the chin receding (recalling the portrait of Alexander VI). These characteristics show very exact similarities with portraits known to be of Lucrezia, medallions, the copy at Nîmes, and even Pinturicchio's fresco.

At this time some ancient 'columns with their capitals' were brought to the castle, possibly from Rome, to decorate the Duchess's apartments and hanging garden, and Strozzi must surely have been with her to advise on the best places to put them. Fine books also arrived, sent by the bookseller Giovanni Marocco, the pages and smooth bindings of which must have been fondled by Strozzi's sensitive hands. And for his delight Lucrezia turned herself into a picture, sitting beneath her sky-painted ceiling surrounded by her girls and busy with her goldsmith, Ercole da Sesso, choosing the design for an ornament, or a chain, or a lead for a little bitch. Above her chair, in a cage of golden filigree, a gaudy parrot swung.

Now that the Este baby's birth was approaching there was no end to the discussions – about the cradle, for instance, many designs for which were submitted by the engraver Bernardino Veneziano. The final choice was very complicated and had something of a temple and something of an altar about it. The baby's place was carved out in gilded wood to look like rock, and at its four corners there were delicate pillars holding up a classical architrave. The roof of the cradle was scattered with leafy and flowery branches of beaten gold to form a shining pergola over the baby. There were white satin curtains, and the coverings and little pillows were of fine linen bordered with gold. For further elegance and also as a safeguard against draughts, the cradle was placed under a satin awning of striped white and crimson; and other protective measures were taken to keep the baby warm in his corner of the great room – a stove was installed and precious Este arrases draped around. The court embroiderer, a Greek woman, wore her eyes out embroidering the baby's trousseau and Lucrezia's sheets. The Keepers of the Wardrobe brought out luxurious treasures of the House of Este, carpets, tapestries, lace, and satin curtains that had belonged to Eleanora of Aragon. But Lucrezia insisted on having everything re-made, and in one of her little withdrawing rooms she had prepared a bed with a canopy of silver linen edged with coloured silk. She insisted on having her own colours on the walls – brown and gold – which were touched up by a thread of red, both heraldic and princely; and to protect herself from the cold she had another little room lined with wood and gilded and provided with a stove where she could take her daily bath, a habit that in those days was considered almost vicious, and that she probably owed to her Arabic-Spanish upbringing. The midwife, Frassina, was the most renowned in Ferrara. She adopted an attitude of royal sedateness as she went to and fro in the castle, scattering optimistic assurances about the expected arrival. On her advice a wet nurse had been chosen already, a young married woman of striking beauty who was brought from one of the Duke's farms.

No traces of Lucrezia's deepest emotions as her confinement drew near are to be found. But when we read Strozzi's letters from 'Zilio' to Gonzaga we get the curious impression that, far from feeling absorbed by the life in her womb, she was developing an increased sense of personal independence. She spoke at length about the Marquis of Mantua with Strozzi, and as the Este and Gonzaga families were in almost open quarrel about the usual question of servants who had fled from one domain and were sheltered in the other, she worked out plans for effecting a reconciliation so that she would be able to visit her brother-in-law and be with him. 'We talk about you at length every day', 'Zilio' reported when he described Lucrezia's anxieties to Gonzaga. She had heard that he was ill and was distressed, and anxious to hear more – for 'she is not as little loving as you are' – she made Strozzi say with the teasing crossness of lovers. That was April 2. On the 3rd Lucrezia was confined and Sanudo informs us that Duke Alfonso 'left Ferrara without saying anything, and his wife was in labour'. Alfonso had political reasons for going to Venice, but his departure on that very day was due to the fact that he could not face witnessing another misfortune; it would be too humiliating. But on the following day an heir was born. The future Ercole II was a little creature with a narrow nose, and he was put to lie in his allegorical and humanistic cradle.

Lucrezia recovered immediately, and Alfonso showed his satisfaction by an immediate return to Ferrara. He did not find the baby beautiful, as he had been told, but thought it looked healthy and normal and showed a will to live. At last he could indulge his pride, when the ambassadors came with congratulations, by showing them his heir naked so that they could see 'he was healthy and well-provided with all things'. To the merrymaking and baptism and visits of congratulation was added an amnesty, though there was not even a thought of letting it include Don Giulio and Don Ferrante. And five days later the Duke set out for France.

Lucrezia spoke of Gonzaga as soon as she was able to speak of anyone. She was indignant with Alfonso because the Este family had officially informed only Isabella of the birth of the baby, and had deliberately ignored the Marquis so as to offend him. She condemned 'the error and perfidy of Camillo (Alfonso) and Tigrino (Ippolito)'. Why shouldn't Gonzaga make a public protest so that Lucrezia could send him an official apology and confound Camillo and Tigrino? And why shouldn't Gonzaga find a way of visiting Ferrara, where Lucrezia would see him most willingly, the more so as Alfonso was away. 'Camillo is leaving tomorrow to post to France,' explained Strozzi, and pressed for a quick answer because a visit was what the Duchess held most dear.

While anxiously awaiting an answer, Strozzi whiled away the time by means of the enchantment of poetry. He read the Duchess the first verses of his latest little poem, the *Genethliacon*, that he had composed for the birth of the baby. The land and sky of April is all laughter:

> Rideat omnis ager, tibi rideat omnis Olympus,
> et patris et matris gaudia magna, puer . . .

and all graces and pleasures had come to the garden:

> Hic Venus, hic Charites, hic est moderata voluptas
> hic amor arcitenens . . .

The poet repeated the words 'moderata voluptas' slowing his voice and letting it dwell on the syllables, savouring the rare sweetness of this measured pleasure. Everything around them – the gold, silver, velvet, the case of luxury and wealth, the spring sun and Latin verses – seemed to forecast happy things. Francesco Gonzaga had not written but perhaps he would come unexpectedly. Lucrezia told herself over and over again that before Alfonso left he had said that he saw no objection to a reconciliation with his brother-in-law, indeed he would like to be at peace with him. But Francesco did not write. What was the explanation, and what should she do? As Lucrezia became stronger she became more impatient and Gonzaga's failure to reply baffled her. She decided to send Strozzi to him, but then suddenly changed her mind for she had not the courage to do without him herself. And so 'Zilio' wrote again to Gonzaga, using all the pressure and appeal of a skilful intermediary and painting a picture of Lucrezia's emotional state. The Marquis would see to what point the beautiful Duchess of Ferrara and wife of Alfonso of Este was reduced. 'I am sure that you have no better servant in the world than I, nor one who would do more for you.' It was alas too true.

'If you come,' wrote 'Zilio', 'it would mean more to her than 25,000 ducats. I cannot express the fever she is in – both because she longs to see you and because you have not answered and have set her wondering about the cause . . . If you had followed my advice on a number of occasions, you would have understood that I advise you as the true servant I am . . . I guarantee that she (Lucrezia) loves you. She does not like your coolness, but commends your discretion – this, over and above the other thousand parts she praises in you. I wish you had come . . . I have a thousand times supposed you to have gout . . . I see such a good disposition in Madonna Barbara (Lucrezia) who loves you . . .' 'She (Lucrezia) loves you exceedingly, far more than you believe, because if you really believed that she loved you as much as I have told you, you would be warmer than you are when you write, and would try to come where she is . . . I give you my word that she loves you, and if you continue as I have told you, you will certainly achieve what you desire. If not, blame me – I give you leave to do so. Show that you love her warmly for she wishes for nothing else. When you answer me do not refer to this, because I do not wish her to think that you need to be pressed to love her; I know that this would seem to her lack of love on your part. Show every diligence in hastening to come where she is and then you will understand if I tell you even less than what is true. She has made me delay the messenger because she wanted to write to you with her own hand, but her eyes still ache owing to her weakness (of childbirth). She recommends herself to you exceedingly and says that Camillo (Alfonso) said before he left that he hoped to be reconciled with you, and you should try to do this so that you can come immediately where she is. She would like me to come to you but she cannot do

without me. Write to her in any case so that it should not appear
that you are cold. I am writing you another letter of my own that
you can show . . . '

These appeals and promises and assurances leave us in no
doubt. The woman here is Lucrezia. Yet it seems that at that
moment Gonzaga was experiencing certain misgivings about his
amorous projects. Strozzi could provide the tonic to infuse fresh
life into the projects when he promised Gonzaga that he would
'achieve what he desired' – that is, love's final aim. 'I am writing
another letter that you can show', he had said, and sure enough
in the Gonzaga archives we find another letter addressed to the
Marquis of Mantua and signed in Strozzi's own name and dated
April 25, the same day – dealing with business matters. This
would confirm, if confirmation were needed, the identity of
'Zilio' and his accomplices. But were they as successful as they
thought in deceiving everyone, including Ippolito and Isabella?
Lucrezia and Strozzi knew quite well that they were surrounded
by spies – this they had known since Bembo's time. They were so
keenly on the watch that they could recognize a spy at first
glance and indeed they spotted immediately an *agent provocateur*
sent by their enemies to trap them – as we gather from another
'Zilio' letter dated March 1508. A certain 'M.' had presented
himself to Lucrezia and talked at length about the wisdom and
fruitfulness of a reconciliation between the Houses of Este and
Gonzaga, declaring that he was prepared to go to Mantua
himself to help with the patching up of a peace, and to persuade
the Marquis to go to Ferrara. Lucrezia had replied agreeably,
but without undue enthusiasm. This 'M.' had then repaired to
Mantua and presented himself to the Marquis, giving him
to understand by allusions that he had been sent by Lucrezia to
invite him to join her secretly in Ferrara. Gonzaga's suspicions
were at once aroused by the style of the embassy and by the
spokesman himself, so he answered vaguely, side-tracked the
discussion, and pretended not to understand. So 'M.' also
changed the subject and talked about other things, and then
quite unexpectedly offered Gonzaga a little miniature of

Lucrezia. Gonzaga's temper rose. Did they imagine he was a man to be taken in by such an elementary ruse? He refused the portrait, dismissed the man and wrote off to 'Zilio' telling him the whole story.

Lucrezia and Strozzi had seen at once that the mysterious 'M.' was acting on behalf of a third party, and who could that be if not the Este family? And who was 'M.'? As he was someone who had easy access to both courts he must have been a courtier, and a favoured one. If we could identify him as Masino del Forno called the 'Modenese' and therefore doubly M. – who was a sinister figure in Este crimes – we would have found a thread that would help to guide us through the dark events that followed. Masino del Forno was an intimate member of Cardinal Ippolito's household.

Possibly Ippolito and Isabella loomed larger in these events than Alfonso. Why should Isabella suggest offering the miniature except to have proof of the affection binding the in-laws? But why suggest the visit to Ferrara at the very time when the two reigning houses were at enmity? And once Gonzaga was in Ferrara – what then? Or was the suggestion made merely to see whether he would bite? He did not bite – possibly out of fear of the Estes, for Strozzi had kept him well primed. Strozzi on his side was as cunning as his opponents, and he always remained calm and cool. He had thought of everything. The lovers' letters could never be discovered, any more than his own, because they were carried by loyal and trustworthy people who went by various routes and always had official motives for crossing the Po. The letters were guarded most secretly and when there were two or three of them they were returned to the senders who burnt them. As 'Zilio' wrote to the Marquis of Mantua: 'I have received yours (your letter) with all mine and the one from Madame Barbara, and they are perfectly safe. I have given hers to her and the others to the fire . . . If you wish it your own will always be returned to you.' Thus as the intrigue developed the evidence of it was destroyed, and this explains why, out of the whole correspondence, only a few letters survive, ones that

Gonzaga did not return in time. Nor were these secret fires the only ones lit in the houses of Dukes and Marquises. There was unquestionably a secret correspondence between Isabella and her brother Alfonso as we can see from a revealing note. Strozzi's intrigues with her husband had not escaped Isabella, nor had Gonzaga's close friendship with Strozzi's in-law, Uberto Uberti, for halfway through 1507 she wrote to her brother:

Messer Hercule (Strozzi) is related by marriage to Uberto degli Uberti, the greatest rebel of the land and my enemy. He has offended me and his only concern is to offend me, as I will tell your lordship by word of mouth when I can speak to you. He often goes to Ferrara and has been there recently, after Messer Hercule was here. I make no doubt that he came to spy, because that is manifestly his office. I have told him what I had to tell him. I pray you *that my letters may be burnt as I burn yours*, for the sake of my honour and benefit.

So we see that the letters of Ercole Strozzi, Lucrezia, Francesco Gonzaga, Isabella and Alfonso were all burnt. If those of Ippolito were not burnt, it was because he was the cleverest of all and never wrote any. In this tangle of suspicion and uneasiness where husbands, though bound to their wives, were their enemies, and each person had some plot or lie to hide, only Lucrezia had a genuine reason and desire for love of a kind that can claim rights in the world. 'Show that you love her,' 'Zilio' had said, 'she wants nothing else from you.'

First came the tragic prologue and then unexpectedly the drama. It will be remembered that when Valentinois died, Lucrezia took in a young Spanish priest who had accompanied him on his fight from Medina. She had quartered him at the Convent of San Paolo and frequently invited him to court and to her own table. On the evening of June 4, 1508, he was on his way back from the castle as usual, going by the direct road – now called Corso Porta Reno – that leads from the main square to the convent. This street is darker and narrower than the Gorgadello, a street of drunkards whom you seem to hear singing to the moon and emerging in groups from the underground cellars beneath the little windows of the cannonry, as dark as the medieval via delle Volte with its façade of Gothic shadows. Beneath the ancient porticoes the unterraced houses form black corners and juts – excellent hiding places for bats and assassins. The eyes of the Spanish priest were never again to see the convent of San Paolo with its graceful fifteenth-century cloister. Its porticoes spelt his doom and gave cover to his nocturnal assailants. They saw him fall 'with his throat cut', as an informant puts it. He made no sound and no one was able to guess by whom or why the attack was made. Are we to suppose that during his few months in Ferrara the priest had made such bitter enemies as to cause his death? And if this was not the case, what then? Further questioning would bring us to the Este family. Might they not have decided that this was an opportune moment to have a purge of all the germs of rebellion and treachery in the entourage of the Duchess? This murder – as far as motives are concerned – should be seen in conjunction with another that occurred shortly afterwards.

Ercole Strozzi, who had recently had a baby girl by Barbara Torelli, was busy writing an elegy that the whole of intellectual Ferrara was eagerly awaiting. It was either in Latin or Italian. It has been lost, but someone who knew a few lines of it said that the idea of death recurred throughout the poem like a dire presentiment. Possibly he had his poem in mind on the night of June 5 when he was limping through Ferrara on his crutch – though we do not know whether he had come from the Duchess's quarters or Barbara's. He was never to see either again.

The dawn of June 6, 1508, rose on one of the most famous homicides in the history of Italian literature. The body of Ercole Strozzi was discovered at the corner of via Praisolo and via Savonarola near the fourteenth-century wall of casa Romei. It had been pierced by twenty-two dagger thrusts, but its elegance and expression of haughty disdain were not affected. By his side was his crutch and he had spurs on his feet. The tufts of long smooth hair that had been wrenched off during the struggle had been replaced round his head, showing that, though unaware of it, even the murderers had entered the poet's aesthetic world as a final irony.

The city immediately buzzed with excitement. Strozzi was not popular, indeed the people had hated his harshness when fulfilling his post as judge. But he was a very powerful man, one of the foremost in Ferrara for his social position, his fame as a poet, his place at court, and his wealth. And now all the transitory things of his life which had aroused envy, admiration or hate were at an end. Who was responsible for the crime? When Prosperi sent the news to Isabella of Este he said there were conflicting views as to the perpetrators, and no one was over-keen on talking 'so as not to have their heads on a wall'. Was he referring to the wall of the Este castle? It was observed that Tebaldeo panicked and asked permission to go away, preferably as far as Rome – but actually he had to remain until the storm abated. The secret was immediately locked away; people said nothing, pretending they suspected nothing and deeming it safer not to probe. A pall of fear settled on Ferrara and concealed the close web of hypotheses and suspicions. Legends sprang up and side-tracked the solution of the mystery. Meanwhile there was the pomp and splendour of the funeral that derived an added glamour from the circumstances. There was not a single Ferrarese nobleman or intellectual absent when, under the arcades of the cathedral, the great philologist and humanist, Celio Calcagnini, rose and began the rounded periods of his oration, *presente cadavere*.

'*Magna me cruciat miseratio, torquet iactura, magnitudo vexat indignitas rei . . .*'[1] His voice resounded in a composed and eloquent expression of sorrow. 'Where was the work of so many years,

---

[1] 'The great pity of it torments me, the sacrifice wracks me, the greatness and indignity of the crime . . .'

where was the great light of spirit and endeavour? In a day, in an hour, all had disappeared . . . where were the brilliant mind, the subtle acumen, the love of letters, the suave poetry?' The wave of praise gathered momentum. 'If the biting iambic couplet, the grave heroic verse or the gentle elegy tempted him, he achieved it with such spirit and felicity, bursting into song so sweetly and smoothly, that he was the envy of everyone . . .' And he went on to say: 'Is it surprising, therefore, that he was so appreciated by Lucrezia Borgia, the wife of the prince, to whom he always showed a most religious devotion?' If anyone in the great assembly trembled on hearing these words he didn't let it show, for everyone knew the value of discretion. Discretion governed Bembo, too, who was staying at the time in Urbino, for he must have heard the news of his friend's death with anguish. But the only voice raised openly in despair was that of Barbara Torelli.

Barbara was still in bed with her baby of thirteen days beside her when Strozzi was murdered. Though all her hopes fell to the ground she did not lose her oustanding qualities as a woman. She immediately gathered Strozzi's children together in her house – the two that were hers and the other four illegitimates – and though she was weak she set herself to defend the fatherless nest. Ercole Strozzi's brothers, Lorenzo and Guido, wrote a letter to the Marquis of Mantua expressing the hope that he would have revenge on 'the murderer of such a faithful servant', and Francesco Gonzaga responded by offering a reward of five hundred ducats and a guarantee of impunity for anyone who would reveal the name of the assassin, and he wrote to comfort the widow. Furthermore he acted as godfather by proxy at the baptism of the baby who was called Giulia. But the days passed and no one came forward to claim the handsome reward, and justice in Ferrara seemed asleep. The general belief that the crime had its origin in high quarters was strengthened.

This view has always been shared by historians, though until a few years ago they were divided about who was responsible. In telling the story they have adopted one or other of the two traditional versions. The first version was that Lucrezia had fallen in love with Strozzi and had had him killed out of jealousy of Barbara Torelli. This account makes much play of Lucrezia's Borgia ancestry. The second version is that Duke Alfonso had fallen in love with Barbara Torelli and wished to remove her husband so as to have easier access to her. No support whatsoever can be found for this latter version, either in the documents or in the testimony of the period. More recently Luzio and Catalano, who both knew of the 'Zilio' letters, have worked on the basis of an Este vendetta against the Duchess's daring go-between: though they do not seem to have been convinced that this was the cause of Strozzi's death. They preferred to look for the most ferocious enemies of Barbara Torelli and Strozzi, and came to the conclusion that the murder had been ordered by Barbara's relatives, namely the Bentivoglio, who viewed Strozzi as the sly and inexorable claimant to Barbara's patrimony and rights. The most convincing proof for this lies in a letter of Barbara's to the Marquis of Mantua, imploring his help in her difficult situation as a widow with six children to bring up and educate, and cruelly crushed by the Bentivoglio and Galeazzo Sforza. 'He who has taken my husband from me,' she wrote, 'is causing his (patrimony) to be reft from his children and is endeavouring to do me harm in life and make me lose my dowry.' Clearly this is not a reference to the Este family who could have had no thought of appropriating her dowry, for they had backed her up in her struggles against her greedy relations, but rather to her eternal enemies the Bentivoglio and Galeazzo Sforza, who had removed her husband swiftly and surely so as to reduce her to penury. A further pointer to the tenability of this thesis is contained in a letter to Cardinal Ippolito from one of his informants in Bologna – where, according to the letter, it was taken for granted that Strozzi's murder had been ordered by Alessandro Pio, the husband of Angela Borgia and the son of Eleanora Bentivoglio, on behalf of the Bentivoglio family, and that the man who actually did the deed was Masino del Forno (il 'Modenese').

Having reached this point we must think some more. It is important to remember that Pio was whole-heartedly dedicated as a servant to the Estes, and that he sought the favour of the ducal house so as to keep his dominion over the little feudal territory of Sassuolo. How in the world could he have ordered the killing of a courtier who was the Duchess's favourite unless he knew that his deed would go unpunished, and unless he had at least the tacit approval of the Estes? In the same way Masino del Forno, though an expert in killing and bloody deeds, and certainly capable of using his dagger in the service of the Bentivoglio, would never have involved himself in the crime unless he had a pretty shrewd idea that it would be pleasing to his masters, and above all to Cardinal Ippolito.

A few years later Giovio said that the magistrate never wanted to get to the bottom of the mystery. As Ferrara was a city renowned for its well-trained police force, the lack of inquiries and arrests is a very important datum, especially as it was common practice at that time to put suspects to the torture for much lesser offences. It has been said that we cannot rightly assume neglect of justice in view of the fact that the books dealing with the trials of those years have been burnt. But it is pretty certain that had arrests or public inquiries taken place our informants would have let us know of them, whereas in fact they seem to avoid the subject. The neutrality of the Este family points to their complicity. Popular legend laid the blame at the door of the House of Este – and this is corroborated by the panic of Tebaldeo, and the rhyme of Gerolamo Casio:

> Ercole Strozzi cui fu dato morte
> per aver di Lucrezia Borgia scritto

> Ercole Strozzi to whom death was dealt
> for having written about Lucrezia Borgia.

Until recently this couplet has seemed nonsense to the historians, because it was common knowledge that Strozzi always wrote in respectful praise of the Duchess; but it takes on a startling significance in the light of the 'Zilio' correspondence.

Lucrezia's reactions are a problem. All our informants knew of her close bond with Strozzi but none of them even mentioned her name in accounts of the crime. We do not even know whether she assisted Barbara Torelli who doubtless had recourse to her as her natural protectress. And as we lack documents it is better not to embark on too many conjectures. We find it easier to think that Lucrezia protected Strozzi's widow than that she abandoned her, at least if the members of the Este family did not find some way of preventing her. In any case the matter was extremely involved, and Barbara Torelli may have left Ferrara and gone to Venice on Lucrezia's recommendation precisely because she was unable to guarantee her life.

In the Este castle Lucrezia seemed to have lost all contact with Gonzaga. She must have felt deep remorse for the dangerous tasks Strozzi had undertaken on her behalf. And when she scrutinized the Este faces around her and saw them pretending to be in the same doubt and suspended judgment as herself, she was unable to decide whether or not they had been responsible for the crime. The Bentivoglio hatred for Barbara may have suggested that there lay the root of the matter, and in the end perhaps Lucrezia became convinced of that explanation. But, though quite capable of mourning her friend for the rest of her days without uttering his name or complaining, she was now in unbroken solitude. Lucrezia, possibly in an attempt to flee from herself like a frightened bird, struck up a close friendship with Isabella of Aragon, the last Queen of Naples, who, after the death in France of her husband King Federico, had come to Ferrara where she was well received and honoured by Duke Alfonso. Hardly a week after Strozzi's death the Duchess complained that she felt the weather to be unseasonably hot and began talking about leaving for the country: apparently she gave the impression of being almost possessed. On the feast of Corpus Christi, on the pretext that she wanted to have a close view of the solemn procession, she got the Queen of Naples to invite her to her windows which overlooked the route, and she arrived early at Palazzo Pareschi, the Queen's residence. This low long palace (completely altered in the eighteenth century) lies in the via Savonarola opposite casa Romei, and from the first-floor windows the site of Strozzi's assassination could be seen. Lucrezia must have looked at it, and that, coupled with the tragic face of the widowed Queen, and the pathos of the procession, led her to weep in a heartfelt and piteous way that could not be shared with anyone.

How could she recover and regain possession of herself except with the help of Gonzaga? She was already on the look-out for a new intermediary. The one she found was the last we would expect – namely Ercole's brother, Count Lorenzo Strozzi. We know little about this man's relationship with the Este family, but we do know that in June, 1508, the very month of the crime, he was at the Este castle with Lucrezia and ready to take up the task of go-between for the Duchess and the Marquis of Mantua. It is almost with stupefaction that we read the words of introduction written by Lucrezia in her own hand to Francesco Gonzaga on June 30: 'Herewith comes the Count Lorenzo Strozzi, a devoted servant to your Lordship, no less than was Messer Ercole his brother . . .' She added that he could trust him as herself.

In this way Lucrezia felt that she had regained her grip on life, and to make sure of it she planned a holiday at Modena and Reggio. The citizens, mindful of the depredations committed by cooks, pages and grooms in 1505 (they had even carried away sheets and candlesticks), watched the arrival of the court of the two great ladies with some apprehension. The Duchess and the Queen enjoyed the calm landscape round Reggio. The Queen left again after a few days but Lucrezia stayed on in a restless mood, not attempting to hide the fact that she had come with the tortured hope that Gonzaga would remember how easy the road was from Borgoforte to Reggio and would turn up unexpectedly. When she realized that Francesco would not make up his mind, she trembled with impatience and ordered Count Lorenzo to write an appeal to the Marquis. He should come soon and not miss the opportunity, for at the end of August she would be obliged to return to Ferrara. 'If it were possible for you it would not be far to come', wrote the new intermediary who was a pale imitation of his brother. The Duchess had been told that Francesco was ill, but she had commanded the monasteries in Reggio and Ferrara to say so many prayers for him that he would surely be better by now. Let him hurry up and come, or anyway answer immediately.

The answer was written on August 25, and was in the hand of Tolomeo Spagnuoli, the Marquis's favourite secretary. It was affectionate yet guarded and implied a refusal. The Marquis was indeed anxious to see his very 'cordial sister' but what could he do in view of his illness? Lucrezia could no longer contain her impatience, and even before receiving this letter had made up her mind, if Gonzaga were ill, to visit his bedside in Mantua. Now that she had found the perfect excuse she made her preparations for departure and would have set out had not the arrival of Duke Alfonso prevented her. Lucrezia was now pinned down. 'The Lady Duchess, who had thought of visiting you, has stayed here and here she still is', as one of the court jesters wrote to Gonzaga; and he went on to tell the Marquis that the Este family did not believe that he was really ill, for sorcerers had enabled them to see his image and they were astonished to note that 'the illness did not seem excessive'. Now that Ercole Strozzi was no longer there, the Duke and the Cardinal could afford to look on the Marquis's unsuccessful flirtations with a smile.

Lucrezia had no choice but to resign herself, and this she did with the help of poetry. On her arrival in Reggio she had found Bernardo Accolti, the *unico Aretino*, already installed there. To meet him at a moment when he was disengaged, and ready to brush up his rhymes and dedicate them to her, was a gift from the gods. Though her literary tastes were not selective, Lucrezia could not live without poetry – she needed it for the harmonious development of her reflections and even for her physical well-being. So she adopted Accolti and kept him at her court; she overwhelmed him with favours and gifts and enjoyed the clever histrionics with which he courted her. He lacked Bembo's delicate magnificence and Strozzi's metaphysical subtleties, but she was quite satisfied to be able to discuss with him the old subjects that had absorbed her in the past – the problems of literature and the life of princes.

WAR OVER FERRARA

In September Lucrezia returned to Ferrara without having seen Gonzaga. The baby Ercole, now bigger and better looking, lay in his cradle under the golden pergola sleeping the protracted sleep of early infancy. He had retained – it was to last for ever – his narrow nose and light eyes – his mother's famous 'fair' eyes – but, as an old courtier put it, he was 'lovely and soft and white like a little reed'. Lucrezia needed help for she was once again, and even more than before, lamenting the void that the death of Ercole Strozzi had left in her life. She came to realize that as a companion Strozzi was without peer and no one could take his place – though perhaps she did not realize that her need for him was linked with a concealed desire to sin. The courtiers were rightly astonished when they saw her appear in public with an absent air and as if she were 'quite lost'. As happens when people are dissatisfied with things as they are, and yet are powerless to change them as they want to, Lucrezia spread a feeling of restless discontent, upsetting everyone around her, doing impulsive uncalled-for things. Without any warning, though courteously, she dismissed Madonna Beatrice dei Contrari who had come a few months before to look after the Este baby. She received no one, and was unwilling to hold court. The only person who came to her rescue in her desolation was the poet Bernardo Accolti who had followed her from Reggio and was treated like a prince. But we can find no reference to him after September, which is a sign that he had left Ferrara, though we do not know whether the Este family had sent him away or whether he sensed an unfriendly atmosphere and went away of his own accord. The courtiers noted that Alfonso kept his wife's company more assiduously than usual though he failed to cheer her up. He went to supper with her almost every evening, possibly because he realized that he had abandoned her too often and was in her debt. Possibly, though not probably, his vague feeling of husbandly remorse was animated with an idea of finding some deep fellow-feeling with her. In any case it was now too late. Lucrezia listened to his talk about the affairs of State and gave him loyal and patient advice or, more often, merely approved of what he said: but she kept all her affectionate thoughts for Gonzaga. She had invited him to Ferrara and once more had been disappointed, so she now dispatched Count Lorenzo with verbal messages that were too important, she thought, to be written. She had established a whole code of symbols with Francesco which included words such as 'hawk' meaning a letter, or perhaps a kiss or even love, and 'a falconer' meaning herself, but she no longer felt the magic of keeping dark secrets as in the days of Ercole Strozzi. Now that she had lost the stimulus of Strozzi's dynamic energy, her feelings became dissipated, and she was slow and listless. She felt that this was a fresh enemy and became almost hysterical. She summoned Count Lorenzo, for it hardly seemed possible that no message had come from Mantua. But no message had come, said her mortified go-between; and he had to endure the Duchess's scoldings and recriminations for it seemed to her that her letters were now taking a very tortuous route. Either she really suspected something, or else merely chanced to make use of an expression that may well have been all too accurate. Count Lorenzo immediately informed Gonzaga of his restless lady's complaints and advised him for pity's sake to write. But Gonzaga had been put on his guard – possibly, which would be in keeping with his extreme wariness, by insinuations emanating directly from Isabella – and though he was most distressed, he kept well out of reach of Ferrara and hardly wrote at all. So Lucrezia had to fall back on herself; she became more dejected and more ungovernable. She even ordered a field tent to be erected in the cathedral in which she and her girls-in-waiting could be withdrawn from the public eye when it took her fancy to go and hear a sermon. But during the whole of Lent she only went once or twice. It never occurred to her that she would be given fresh life by the very thing she held most in horror – war.

It was now obvious that the armies would take the field in the spring of 1509. Future developments were heralded by the League of Cambrai which was formed on December 10, 1508, against the over-bearing pride of the Venetian Republic, by the King of France, the King of England and the Emperor Maximilian. In Italy Julius II's efforts to persuade Venice to restore to the Church the territories and fortresses in Romagna that had been conquered by Cesare Borgia and subsequently seized by the Venetians were in vain. They gave back very little. Moreover, intoxicated with pride, the Venetian envoys – each of whom had the typical conviction of the lagoon-inhabitants that he had the whole force of the Republic behind him – began to assume a tone of insufferable arrogance when refusing to surrender territories and strongholds. In March, 1509, the Pope joined the League taking Alfonso of Este with him who could hardly believe in his good luck, for his efforts to reach a peaceful agreement with the Venetians had failed, and he badly wanted to reconquer the Polesine of Rovigo. Francesco Gonzaga also went with the Pope, for he had always wanted to have his revenge on the *Serenissima* for having been dismissed from the post of Captain-General of the Venetian army after Fornovo in 1497. The Duke of Ferrara was appointed standard-bearer of the Church and began preparing his artillery and making necessary decisions on questions of government. When Alfonso took the field, Lucrezia was to govern at the head of a Council of ten of the most important citizens – with Cardinal Ippolito by her side. But she would in practice be in sole charge herself, for the warlike Cardinal had already got out his breastplate and sword and was only too anxiously waiting for the opportunity to wear them.

The League's first act of war came with the Pope's solemn excommunication of Venice. The Venetians responded with an icy smile. Talk in the lagoon city was optimistic, with an optimism based on solid and accurate reasoning. The Venetian politicians were kept minutely informed about everything by their ambassadors; they were told of the disposition and strength of the forces of the League, and they worked out their chances with that exact and subtle logic of the great tradition of Venetian diplomacy, coming to the conclusion that all would work out to their advantage. They calculated rightly that the King of Spain had joined the League against his will, and that the Emperor Maximilian's words would be bigger than his deeds, for he had no money and no army. They considered that the Pope's mercenaries gave no guarantee of trustworthiness and his officers even less, and finally that the allies were divided amongst themselves by an unconquerable distrust of one another. But when they spoke of the possible disloyalty of the Pontifical troops they forgot to offset the faithlessness of their own mercenaries; and they overlooked the existence of one powerful bond between the confederates in the League – namely their hatred of the wealth and splendour and pride of the Republic of St Mark.

The Venetian army was a powerful one judged by the standards of the age. It consisted of 50,000 men who were well-paid, well-armed and well-clothed, and they set out to the Risorgimento cry of *Italia Liberta* on an April morning, with the sun shining on their banners embroidered with the motto *Defensio Italiae*. But the Republic was to be punished for the pride that led it to take on the whole of Europe without allies. On May 14 a great four-day battle at Agnadello near Cremona ended with the triumph of the League, and heralded the decline of Venetian supremacy on land. The Pontifical army, under the Pope's nephew, Francesco Maria della Rovere, the youthful Duke of Urbino (the gentle Guidobaldo had died the year before) now began a victorious advance through Romagna. The Venetians at last realized their mistake and hastened to send a mission to the Pope to beg for peace and to offer the fortresses of Romagna to the Church, and the coastal cities of Apulia to the King of Spain. 'The hand that has struck should heal', they said, borrowing from the New Testament. But the Pope's conditions were so stiff that, as the ambassadors put it, Venice would rather call in the Turks than accept them. In the meantime a new situation had developed.

Francesco Gonzaga, in one of his fits of impetuosity, had pushed blindly forward into Venetian territory with very few followers. He had been surprised by his enemies at night, surrounded and captured together with his baggage, horses, tents and silver. His attempts to hide and flee had been in vain. When the Pope heard the news he threw his pontifical cap on the ground and gave a shout of rage, a literal roar. For now that the Venetians had an important prisoner they could change their tone for they were in a better position to negotiate. Francesco Gonzaga was not only an illustrious prisoner and the head of one of the confederate states whom the Pontiff – who was not Alexander VI – was obliged to protect; but he was a man who had previously been allied with Venice, and it was far from unthinkable that in his straitened circumstances, and subject to the clever politicians on the lagoon, he might change his alliance and join up once more with the Republic.

The capture of Gonzaga cheered the citizens of Venice considerably, and they gathered together in the piazza of St Mark to see his disembarkation. 'Rat in a cage! Turk' – this was Gonzaga's own warcry – 'captured! Hang the traitor!' – the shouts rose up on all sides, savage, unrestrained, almost joyful, the typical expression of uneasiness in wartime. When he felt the people's hatred at such close quarters, and heard the word 'traitor' that harked back to old scores of the time of Fornova, Gonzaga's emotions can easily be imagined. Yet he was master of a kind of lordly and dynastic dignity. When an onlooker shouted sarcastically: 'Welcome, Marquis of Mantua,' he paused, looked him full in the face and said: 'I do not know who you are talking about. The man before you is Francesco Gonzaga and not the Marquis of Mantua, who is in Mantua.' His implication was that the Gonzaga line would continue in the person of his son, Federico, regardless of what happened to himself.

He was thrown into a prison which, though not too vile and filthy, was nevertheless prison, with all its psychological ills. The sadder and more desperate his letters, the greater the speed with which they were sent off to their destinations. He remembered everyone. Not only his wife and children but his favourite singer, Marchetto, his painter Lorenzo Costa, his friends, his horses, his hawks, his dogs and all his companions in the sweet days of liberty. First and foremost he recommended himself to the prayers of friars and nuns for spiritual help. His disjointed letters reveal his hasty, affectionate, impulsive character, and they made a great impression when they arrived at Mantua – on everyone except Isabella.

For Isabella had at last reached her short hour of glory. When she first heard the news of the capture of her husband she had taken a deep breath, urgently summoned a council of citizens and used the occasion to exercise her eloquence, managing to find words to inflame people's hearts while appealing to their minds. She sent her little son to ride with a cortège through Mantua – the people adored Federico and he was much acclaimed. She summoned her councillors over and over again and persuaded them to suggest what she herself really thought, and then set to work to save the State, herself and her husband. We cannot accept the accusation made by Venetians that she was prepared to let her husband rot in prison so as to satisfy her passion for government, though this accusation was later repeated by Julius II. There is no doubt, however, that when she found herself in command she experienced more than mere intoxication: she must have felt that her genuine qualities were being given full scope at last. At such a moment as this she had no time to bother about Lucrezia's court.

The King of France, the Emperor Maximilian and the Pope were at one in their distrust of Francesco Gonzaga. They negotiated so as to free him, yes, but they wished to hold his heir, Federico, as a hostage to his loyalty. Federico should be sent to France and then they would find a way of liberating his father. Isabella was anxious not to be separated from her child and above all not to pledge the State too far, and so she adopted a strategy of passive resistance: she cavilled on minor points, followed little by-paths of sophistry and played for time day after day, giving ample proof of her hard head and limited affections. She knew that her husband lay in prison, that he had had a recurrence of his illness and was uncared-for. When he wrote to her he advised her to send the child as a hostage, and thereby gave a guarantee of his own loyalty while freeing her from future responsibility. A gentler, more compassionate woman would have found it intolerable to be free to move about in elegant salons, and to sleep under the painted ceilings of their nuptial room, while thinking of the discomfort of the prisoner. But when Isabella had State affairs in mind it was of very small moment to her that her husband was languishing in captivity and realizing how easily one is lost to friends and family if unseen. She did not know – or if she did know she smiled contemptuously – that Lucrezia was attempting to alleviate Gonzaga's sufferings.

As soon as she heard that Gonzaga was a prisoner, Lucrezia felt not only acute sorrow but also a keen revival of her love. This was the first occasion, since Ercole Strozzi had worked on her feelings with allusions and suggestions, that her love really blossomed, and night and day were spent in delicious restlessness. She was unable to understand the controlled affections and cold calculations that made Isabella of Este so obviously her father's child and a great stateswoman – and yet the fact that she was like that was a joy to Lucrezia, for it left her a clear field as consoler of the Marquis. She could see that the Este family were not bothering about their brother-in-law's fate, for they sometimes even laughed at him with their dry military humour for having been captured in such an inglorious way. However, such considerations only increased Lucrezia's sympathy and turned Gonzaga into a kind of hero who had been betrayed by circumstances. She immediately curtailed the supper parties in the Este villa, summoned Angela Borgia, her trusted confidante in the affairs of the heart, and began to look for ways and means of helping Gonzaga.

She soon found them. We do not know the means by which she managed to send letters, messengers and possibly even medicaments to the prisoner. None of the Ferrarese – and this gives us an idea of Lucrezia's secrecy – ever refers to her activities and we would never have known about them had not Francesco Gonzaga himself mentioned them some time later. She wrote to Gonzaga, and ordered prayers to be said in the monasteries. She went herself to pray in the monastery of Corpus Domini although she felt so ill (she was pregnant again) that there was fear for her health. She recovered immediately saying it was nothing, and that she could not allow herself to retire from active life especially at this moment, when the Marquis needed her help and the Este family had entrusted her with the affairs of the State. Her quiet good sense won her such esteem that Cardinal Ippolito, trembling with military impatience now that the enemy was at hand, donned his arms and set off against the Venetians leaving her alone.

With a favourable wind a squadron of the Venetian fleet had penetrated the river Po and sailed up the delta towards Adria. As it proceeded, moving inland and already threatening the territory of Ferrara, it met the left wing of the Ferrarese army commanded by Cardinal Ippolito. The two sides joined battle. The Cardinal had a chance to rid himself of all the humours in his quarrelsome blood in a lawful way, and he made the most of it. He threw himself into the fray like a true general, taking absolute command, directing assaults and ambushes in accord with a strategic plan that he unfolded as events developed. The battle lasted the whole day. Between one charge and another Ippolito sent off news to Mantua and Ferrara. Isabella received a little note written on the field that told of the final phase and ended up 'before evening the Venetian squadron will be utterly smashed, with the help of Our Lord'. The word 'smashed' reflects the impetuous character of the Cardinal to the full. That night there was news of a great victory – the capture of eighteen galleys, five smaller ships, twenty-eight pieces of heavy artillery, a hundred and forty of light, and a rich haul of prisoners, arms, flags and trophies. The Cardinal offered it all to his brother for the ducal triumph.

The captured ships were brought up the Po and filed under the walls of Ferrara, bright with cannon and standards, furrowing the surface of the water in a slow and measured movement. On the flagship stood the Duke with eighty guards of honour in gilded helmets that caught the rays of the autumn sun. The insignia of the standard-bearer of the Church, the eagles of the House of Este, the colours of the victorious captains and the flags taken from the enemy, filled the scene with colour. The walls of Ferrara were crowded with onlookers. Trumpets, fifes, mortars and cannons answered one another making a huge festive noise, and Alfonso, on the *Marcella*, was magnificently dressed and bejewelled, and acknowledged the greetings of his subjects with cordial calm, while behind him the Cardinal, arrayed in mere purple again, was bursting with pride.

Lucrezia, dressed in cloth of gold, had the feminine pleasure of playing a rightful part in her husband's triumph. She went out to meet him at the head of a veritable army of gentlewomen crammed into twenty luxurious coaches – all rejoicing in their youth and beauty and in the possibility of participating in the exuberant acts of licence in which the returning warriors would indulge. Alfonso disembarked from the ship and made all the customary reverences to his wife, exchanging compliments with her and her women. Then he rode on horseback through the streets to the castle, followed by his court and surrounded by popular acclamation.

In Rome Julius II was thinking things over. He knew about the ambitions of the King of France and realized that to bring such a formidable enemy in, and let him establish French supremacy over Northern Italy, would be a huge mistake and would enslave the whole peninsula including the Church States. A bulwark against this danger was required, and what power could serve the purpose better than Venice? So the Pope decided in favour of peace with the *Serenissima*, which promptly handed over the

Romagna fortresses, allowed freedom for shipping in the Adriatic and exempted the Venetian clergy from taxation. On February 24, 1510, Venetian envoys went to Rome to be absolved from the excommunication in St Peter's. This done the Pope declared the war over, and ordered all the members of the League of Cambrai to lay down their arms.

It was at this point that Ferrara became the scene of a *coup de théâtre*. Duke Alfonso, intoxicated by his success in arms and wishing at all costs to retain his conquest of the domains lost by his father in 1484 and – more important – backed up by the French, refused to end the war and made it known that he intended to proceed against the Venetians whatever the Pope's orders. Such a decision on the part of a man who had just been bearer of the Pope's colours amounted to a revolt. Was this the way a standard-bearer of the Church and a Papal feudatory should behave? However, Julius II at last had an opportunity of airing his personal hostility to the Este family and the various resentments he had been nursing against them. Was not this rebel the self-same Duke of Ferrara who had had his brothers buried alive in a tower; the man who exploited the saltbeds of the Comacchio and said they were his by imperial investiture, whereas the Church had reasons for claiming them for herself; the man who dared to judge ecclesiastical affairs without taking the court of Rome into account? Alfonso's stand made the Pope indignant, but it probably did not displease him, for it gave him a pretext for waging the war against Ferrara that had long been foreseen in Vatican circles. The Este family, like the Baglioni and the Bentivoglio, would lose their agelong dominion. Once he had driven them from Ferrara, Julius II would be able to establish the great temporal domain of the Church.

So a new excommunication in the most solemn form crossed Italy and fell on the rebellious city. Immediately afterwards the Pope, now allied with the Venetians, gathered an army and artillery; he knew what he was up against, what with Alfonso's courage, the warlike spirit of the Ferrarese nobility and the loyalty of the people – and the French, who had come out as

Ferrara's allies, would do their best to make a hard war harder. Both Julius II and the Venetians realized that the French were behind the Duke's rebellion, and that the rebellion was in fact Louis XII's answer to the anti-French motives underlying the Pope's peace with Venice. 'These French have taken away my desire to eat and sleep,' said the Pope to his household, 'but I hope with the help of God to drive them completely out of the country.'

The Pope's words were the same as those used by the Doge of Venice on setting Francesco Gonzaga free: 'We must destroy all these Frenchmen and repeat the deed of the Sicilian Vespers: we shall call it the Mantuan Compline.' Now that the Pope and Venice had become allies the question of the imprisonment of the Marquis of Mantua was automatically solved, and he left his prison not only at peace with his warders but destined to become both captain of the Venetian army and standard-bearer of the Church. But before leaving for Mantua he had to hand over his son Federico as a pledge of his loyalty. So sure was Francesco Gonzaga about his plans that he ordered his wife to send the little boy to Venice. But Isabella refused on various pretexts, relying largely on all that the statement 'I am a mother' implies. So Julius II stepped in and offered to have the boy in Rome at the Vatican, in charge of people chosen by his mother and directly under the surveillance of the young Duke and Duchess of Urbino – Francesco Maria della Rovere and Eleanora Gonzaga, the boy's elder sister. But Isabella still held out, declaring herself to be in anguish and thinking up endless excuses – so much so that the Pope exclaimed one day to the Mantuan ambassador that 'that whore of a Marchesa' was prolonging her husband's imprisonment so as to satisfy her desire to go on running the State, and that the Marquis had every reason to be furious for he was no longer a prisoner of the Venetian signory but of 'that wretch'. Francesco, for his part, wrote to his wife that if she did not send Federico to Rome immediately he would strangle her with his own hands. His threat left Isabella cold for she was too familiar with her husband's wild rages. Finally, when she had temporized as long as she possibly could and upset half Italy, Isabella dispatched her son to the Pope, though not without public demonstrations of a broken heart.

Lucrezia was sad and weary. The ban of the Papal excommunication made her uneasy and deprived her of the consolation that at least she was all right regarding religion. She made no open judgment on the Este family but in her inner thoughts she must have considered their enterprise rash, for it destroyed the peace of her scrupulously Catholic conscience as well as the peace of Ferrara. Fortunately, though on the enemy side, the Marquis of Mantua was better disposed to her than ever, for he did not forget the help and consolation she had given him. Immediately after his liberation she sent him a warm letter of welcome, and sent Count Lorenzo once more on his journeys to and fro across the Po. The response of the Marquis must have been affectionate and encouraging for she never wearied of hearing it repeated by the Count. 'Lorenzo,' she said, 'were it not for the hope that I have in the Lord Marquis that he will help me and protect me in my need, I would break my heart with sorrow.' This admission showed her disgust at the Este policy and her lack of confidence in Alfonso's ability and artillery, as well as in the Cardinal's posturing. Yet Alfonso must have been at pains to reassure and convince her that she was well defended, for when the Pontifical troops began their advance into the territory of Modena her dismay was such that she thought of flight. She began packing hurriedly, with the intention of escaping northwards to Parma or Milan which were under French protection. But when the citizens of Ferrara heard of the preparations under way at Court, they sent a message saying that if the Duke's wife and children left, every citizen would feel free to do what best suited him. So Lucrezia reopened the trunks and unrolled the carpets and hung up the parrot, and entrusted herself to God and the Marquis of Mantua.

Ippolito of Este had been obliged to leave to avoid ecclesiastical censure, but before setting out he had made a speech to an
assembly of nobles and citizens in which his natural eloquence
was given substance by his passion for the State, and he struck
exactly the right note of strength and forbearance. Not a single
word of the many that he spoke regarding the salvation of the
State sounded like an attack on the head of the Church, for he
viewed the war as a fatal necessity rather than a conflict of wills
between the two leaders. In the fervour of their admiration, the
Ferrarese swore that they would prefer to be buried under their
houses than give way and witness the downfall of the Este
dynasty. 'The Cardinal is worth the whole world', they said as
they went away from the meeting, and their praise included
Alfonso who was busy studying plans for defence, strengthening
walls and bastions and improving his artillery.

It was a blow to him to hear that Francesco Gonzaga had
accepted the posts of standard-bearer of the Church and
Captain-General of the Venetian army, for this made Gonzaga
the leader of Ferrara's enemies. Possibly Alfonso had been over-
confident in his sister's ability to keep Mantua in some kind of
neutrality. But how could Gonzaga have said 'no' to his allies
and liberators, who, moreover, held his eldest son as hostage?
The affection between the Gonzagas and the Estes had never
been of the kind to induce Francesco to sacrifice the honour and
glory of his new nomination. And there were other reasons for
his acceptance which, unfortunately for historians, are rather
obscure. In the autumn of 1511 the Pontifical forces had captured
Masino del Forno, known as 'il Modenese', and as he was, in the
Pope's words, 'an accomplice and perpetrator of the treacheries
and assassinations of the Cardinal of Ferrara', a detailed case
had been produced against him. The fact that 'il Modenese' had
been present at the blinding of Don Giulio proves that he had
been, once at least, an accomplice. But when was he a
perpetrator? Would it be going too far to accuse him of having
murdered Ercole Strozzi? And at some point the Marquis of
Mantua was involved – for the Archdeacon of Gabbioneta, who

was in the Pope's and the Gonzagas' confidence, wrote at this time to the Marquis asking him to go immediately to Bologna where Julius II would like to talk to him about facts affecting him, abominable deeds that had been revealed during the trial of Masino del Forno. The Archdeacon could not possibly explain himself in writing because the Pope had forbidden him to do so under pain of excommunication, but he should warn him of 'unspeakable things' hatched by Alfonso and Ippolito of Este against himself. This is the moment, perhaps, to call to mind the mysterious courtier, 'M.', who in 1508 had acted as an *agent provocateur*, visiting both Lucrezia and the Marquis and trying to induce the latter to visit Ferrara. Was 'M.' Masino del Forno? And was the visit a trap that the Este family had prepared against their brother-in-law? – or did it concern a subsequent act of violence in which Lucrezia all unknowing was involved? All we know for certain is that as soon as Gonzaga received this letter, which was dated September 26, he went to Bologna, and on September 30 he took over the command of the Venetian and Papal army.

But the allies had one adversary who yielded to no man's will: Isabella of Este. She was anything but enthusiastic at the idea of her brother's ruin which would also weaken the State of Mantua; but as she knew that her husband had no option but to follow the path on which he had embarked, she quickly took her bearings, made calculations and came to a decision. On her side of the Po she would support the Pontifical and Venetian army, but on the other side she would inform her brothers of the movements of the allies and try to put as many spokes in her husband's wheel as possible. She began her campaign by allowing the French, coming from Milan to assist the Ferrarese, to pass through Mantuan territory, and she instructed her envoys to pretend that she had had to yield to force in this, while asking the French themselves to do as little harm as possible to local agriculture. Messengers crossed the river daily and by means of a relay of post horses, organized with minute precision, the journey between Ferrara and Mantua could be made in a few hours. The

Venetians soon got wind of Isabella's complicity and denounced it to the Pope. The Pope grumbled to the people around him, but these included men who were secretly devoted to the Marchesa of Mantua, such as the Archdeacon of Gabbionetta, and they did everything they could to allay his suspicions. So Isabella remained in communication with her brothers and enabled men and arms to be sent to them. She even took the liberty of pawning some of Lucrezia's finest jewellery, including a bright emerald that had moved Bembo's heart. She managed to persuade her husband that he was still too ill to proceed against Ferrara, thereby causing the allies to mark time and giving the French an opportunity to get to Ferrara and strengthen its defences. The Venetians thundered. The Pope, delighted at his own cunning, gave an order to one of his doctors to go to Mantua and check up on his standard-bearer's health: it never crossed his mind that if Isabella's treasurer gave him ten ducats, the doctor would write out a certificate of ill-health.

By the middle of December the Pope was so impatient that he decided to set out himself at the head of his army, despite his sixty-seven years, his gout and the wintry snow. He reviewed his troops in the company of Cardinals and bishops, taking with him his friend, the architect Bramante of Urbino, with whom, in the evenings, when he had finished studying and discussing his plan of campaign, he could read and comment on the *Divina Commedia*. Dante suited the heroic stature of Julius II. When he accompanied the poet on his harsh pilgrimage through Hell and the arduous journeys through Purgatory and Paradise, he was lifted up into the world in which he belonged, liberated from the narrow confines of earth and transported to the austere and glorious kingdom where even the damned are great. Julius II did not like war for its own sake; he viewed it as a necessary condition for the re-establishment of a civil society based on the iron laws of justice. The vaster the proposals and plans, the more they pleased him; such, for instance, as the project suggested by James IV of Scotland for a great crusade launched by the whole of Europe for the liberation of the Orient – made at the very moment in which he was enmeshed in the struggle against Ferrara. Despite all his antipathy for the Estes, the Pope was anything but a war-monger for its own sake, and in January he made proposals for peace which involved leaving Ferrara to Alfonso but keeping Modena and its territory, which had just been conquered, for himself. But Alfonso and above all his French allies mistakenly thought that these proposals were dictated by fear, and rejected them. The Pope's answer was to lay siege to Mirandola, which was one of the most important and best-defended of the Este fortresses.

The siege of Mirandola is famous in the history of the art of war, both for the obstinacy of the besieged and the patience and implacability of the besiegers. The stronghold was stormed magnificently by the Pontifical forces in wind and snow, and the Pope, forgetful of his age and ill-health, insisted on entering the fortress before the gates were open, which he did by pulling himself up a ladder.

But Mirandola was in an advanced position and left the flank of the Pontifical army exposed to danger, so Julius II's advisers dissuaded him from remaining there. Leaving a substantial garrison, Julius returned to Bologna, escaping a Ferrarese ambush by a miracle. From Bologna he proceeded to the interior of Romagna, to Cesare Borgia's former headquarters in Imola. The government of Bologna was left in the hands of Cardinal Alidosi, a young man as handsome and vicious as he was idle and incompetent. At the first rumour of a revolt in Bologna, this Cardinal fled to Castel del Rio and then on to Ravenna where the Pope's nephew, Francesco Maria della Rovere, struck him dead with the shout of 'Traitor!' Meanwhile inside Bologna all was chaos. The revolt spread and the Bentivoglio took advantage of the confusion to fall on the city with French help and scatter its few defenders. The jubilation of the people was such that they pulled down Michelangelo's great bronze statue of Julius II and welcomed the Bentivoglio once more as tyrants of their city.

Nor was this all. In France Louis XII had got the dangerous

idea into his head that what was needed was a new Pope, a Frenchman, and he fell to attacking Julius II on the spiritual level, disputing the legitimacy of his election to office and his suitability for the priestly life. The King instigated a search throughout Italy for women who had had carnal relations with the Pope, with the intention of gathering material for the prosecution in a future immorality trial of the head of the Church. Three such women were found. But though this news may have upset a monk here and there, it had no effect in Italy or abroad. More important was the establishment of a council of schismatic Cardinals at Pisa to discuss the accusations and depose the Pope, and Bulls of convocation appeared on the walls of cathedrals signed by Cardinals Brissonet, Sanseverino, Francesco Borgia, Ippolito of Este, and Carvahal. But Julius II was too able a man to be shaken by all this, and he knew too much about ecclesiastical affairs not to have his answer ready. He attacked the weak points of the Bull and gave such a dazzling display of majesty that when the little group of half-convinced accusers gathered at Pisa it was obvious that the schism would have no outcome. The guttersnipes jeered at the men who had had the presumption to depose a Pope of such stature.

On the very brink of the disaster that had been foreseen when Mirandola fell, the Ferrarese plucked up their courage. 'And so Mars and Venus are venerated amongst us as the planets that now dominate the world', Bernardo dei Prosperi put it with no fear of exaggeration.

The French had now arrived. The soldiers were adventurers who were not over-scrupulous about raping women and other forms of disorderly conduct, but their leaders included the flower of the nobility of France. Gallant men they were, such as inspired the legends of medieval chivalry and the traditions of the courts of love, ready to move from battlefield to ballroom with an ease that looked like light-heartedness and was really moral courage. To the civilized manners of the Italians – to be described a little later in Baldassare Castiglione's *The Courtier* – and to the humanist splendour of the court in which an extreme freedom was tempered by measure, the French brought the fire and vitality of their temperament in matters of courtly life. The Duchess gave balls and receptions and they could not resist responding with demonstrations of exuberant delight. When the Bentivoglio returned to Bologna there were further celebrations which spread to the people. The burghers in new clothes and the women with flowers in their hair streamed along the wide streets towards the ducal palace waving fresh green branches. Under Lucrezia's balcony there were flowers and leaves brought from the countryside which gave a holiday appearance to the ordered perspectives of the piazza.

The importance of the Duchess was increasing from day to day and Alfonso must have appreciated this, for he tried to keep her free from preoccupations and from becoming a mother once more. If the Este family knew that Lucrezia was corresponding with the Marquis of Mantua, then this was the moment to cherish her so as to use her to enmesh Gonzaga. There was no danger of the two meeting. So Lorenzo Strozzi's journeys were stepped up and he was allowed to come and go with letters and messages pretty well as he wished.

Francesco Gonzaga felt a fresh renewal of love. It was now Lucrezia who was a prisoner, confined to her city by the encircling movements of the Venetian and Church forces. She implored his protection with the tone that he knew so well, and believed in him with gentle and blind devotion. He had to follow his wife's advice because he was caught in the net of her calculations, but deep down, though Isabella did not suspect it, his rancour was growing. And while pretending to be ill he was able to continue his romance with Lucrezia. He begged her to write a few words in her own hand to console him. The lovers still used their symbolic language – the words 'hawk' and 'hawker' recur over and over again in their letters and in their intermediary's. Lucrezia let him know that she would write in her own hand as soon as he asked her to do so in his own hand, for in that case she could deny him nothing. During his period of enforced leisure Gonzaga wrote her his most loving letter. Lucrezia waited a little before answering for she felt some slight and agreeable scruples: Easter was approaching when it was her custom to retire to a convent, and possibly she took his letter with her; certainly she took a lively memory of it.

Lucrezia did not go to Corpus Domini now, for after 1510 she had a convent of her own, founded, protected and privileged by herself. In it she established the nuns she liked best, the faces that smiled when she smiled and were heart-broken when she was heart-broken. This second home, in which no one could violate her repose, was in the ancient aristocratic little palace of the casa Romei, outside the walls of which Ercole Strozzi's body had been found in June 1508. Perhaps this in some way influenced her choice and she was making a mysterious act of retribution or at least of remembrance. The building has preserved its old familiar contours, but at that time, in the fine fifteenth-century cortile that opens out beyond the entrance, there was a flaming rose, emblem of San Bernardino to whom the convent was dedicated. Lucrezia had appointed Suor Laura Boiardo from Corpus Domini as Abbess, and amongst the first novices was the other Lucrezia Borgia, Cesare's illegitimate daughter, who had come from Rome in 1507. There, overlooking the two sunny courtyards where it seemed impossible to think of war, Lucrezia wrote to Gonzaga as soon as Easter and the holy ceremonies were over.

She apologized for not having written earlier, but felt sure that he would understand her scruples and her desire not to 'disturb your Lordship during these holy days'. How, for instance, while she was doing penance, could she mention the 'falcon'? But Francesco should rest assured that the 'falcon' was very well and indeed had improved 'and is often examined by others than a confessor about certain things of the past'. But Lucrezia hastened to add, so as to tranquillize her own conscience, that this could be said 'without offence to God or harm to one's neighbour', 'because I desire as much as my own salvation that your

Lordship should be entirely renewed in the fear of God, and as a good son of Saint Francis, as I am, though unworthy'. Then came a pause. The little homily sounded impressive. And Lucrezia went on to laugh gracefully at her sermon and put the blame on her friends, Suor Laura and Suor Eufrosina, who wished that 'to spite the world I should turn preacher and martyr'. Finally came a playful and affectionate reproof for the 'all too human terms' that Francesco had used when writing to her. They were too full of earthly love; she loved him, of course, but as 'Lord and brother'.

The intention of the writer was strengthened by the atmosphere of the convent and the sun in the garden, while the scent of incense gave her letter a tender if doubtful chastity. For her refusal to accept his love gave her the occasion to refer to it and let him know that she had understood what he meant, and though she replied as duty dictated she was really delighted. What she said cannot have displeased Gonzaga for he, too, was turning to religious devotion. He could not be displeased at a love that would infuse life into his old age while preserving the rules of religion and piety. When he thought of Lucrezia as a young girl, he felt that physically and spiritually all his male qualities were renewed, and the fact that he knew her to be in danger exalted him still more, for his hope that he would one day have her at Mantua entirely for himself seemed possible of realization. Indeed, acting as if it were a certainty, he had already pondered how the booty should be divided, and had asked the Pope to give him full power over Duke Alfonso's wife.

Such a request would seem incredible but that there exists a letter, dated January 23, 1511, in which it is expressed in the clearest terms. After assuring the Pope's private adviser, the Archdeacon of Gabbionetta, that if Alfonso of Este were ever caught in Mantuan territory he would be handed over to the Pope immediately, Gonzaga adds an appeal that the maximum of clemency should be exercised for 'the lady Duchess formerly of Ferrara (the Pope had declared Alfonso's title to be forfeit), and give her safety into our hands, and this because of the loving and loyal terms that she alone, amongst our many relatives, used to us at the time when we were prisoner in Venice, and which oblige us in these days to show her gratitude; for had the providence of your Holiness not helped us, there was no one else who showed that they held us in compassion as much as this poor girl'. We can feel Gonzaga's emotion especially in the eager and grateful expression 'this poor girl'. (It is from this letter that we know that Lucrezia helped Gonzaga during his imprisonment.)

The Pope must have promised him the Duchess, or let it be understood, for Francesco began preparing an apartment in a palace near the church of San Sebastiano by the meadows of the Te. He chose pictures, tapestries and furniture for it and wrote to tell her about it – not referring to the frightening contingency against which he had prepared it, but merely describing what she would find when she came on a future visit. A house made specially for her. 'Let us hope that we shall enjoy it together after so much tribulation', answered Lucrezia in her letter of thanks. This was exactly what the Marquis of Mantua was thinking, and his imagination must have dwelt on being with his mistress under a sky of painted ceilings, and having long conversations in which he, the saviour, would bend down towards the woman he had rescued. His life was now complete and the warm and murmuring spring of 1511 left nothing to be desired. The echoes of battle, if real enough, were far away, and Francesco Gonzaga spent his best hours watching the painters and decorators who were touching up the great cornices or painting friezes on the walls. And when the tapestry-makers spread out their many-coloured brocades which were shot through with Lucrezia's favourite brown, he could hear the echo of the courtly verse by Niccolò da Correggio:

E chi veste morel secreto sia

And they who wear brown must secret be

which seemed written on purpose to explain to him and Lucrezia the meaning of that colour and of their friendship.

Summer passed, and when enthusiasm for the war was diminished by Pope Julius II falling grievously ill, Lucrezia set out for Reggio to take the medicinal waters for her health. But perhaps the waters were only allegorically health-giving, and she really hoped to see her brother-in-law arriving from Borgoforte. Reggio meant hope, and the gentle sensuous landscape made her feel that anything could happen: if there was a knock at the door at an unusual hour she would grow pale and imagine a cavalier was riding from the north. Lucrezia loved Reggio, so much so that on October 4, 1511, though the annual plague had ceased for some while in Ferrara, she sent a message to Ostellato, where Alfonso was hunting, to ask if she could remain at Reggio and have the children, Ercole and Ippolito, sent there (Ippolito had been born in the year 1509). But the answer from Prosperi was: 'the children will remain, for that is his Lordship's will'. In Rome the Pope had recovered, and war would soon begin again, so it was not proper for the little Este boys to be outside the walls of the castle. Lucrezia returned to Ferrara where she found things exciting and gay, as there were many new and distinguished people there.

Now that she had had a good rest and was in good health, her spirits revived to meet the new situation. With the help of her hairdressers, Maestro Gerardo and Maestro Bartolomeo, she devised 'unheard-of' fashions that showed how much she had developed her taste along the lines suggested by Ercole Strozzi. With her gentlemen (the only man of letters she now retained was Tebaldeo), her musicians, her singers and dancers, she planned balls and supper parties which the French found infinitely preferable to the plays that they could hardly understand. One day Alfonso launched an attack against the Pontifical forces at La Bastia and, armed with only a stick, performed feats of valour for which he was compared to Hercules with his club. When he came back to Ferrara his hair had to be shaved off because of a wound on the head, and the whole court and city were set talking perhaps more about his tonsure than his valour. And when a number of the courtiers sacrificed their own hair so as to be like the Duke, a little revolution took place and the girls could not help laughing to see this 'shaven company' after so many centuries of hairy heads. The Cardinal of Este had now returned to Ferrara with a beard, which caused comment even in the Mantuan court where Isabella amused herself by satirizing it in writing. But her joke fell flat. The proud Cardinal answered: 'Your excellency (Isabella) can bear in mind that I will govern myself over the beard as my mood takes me.' But this tiff did not prevent him from enlisting his sister's help in getting back some of his belongings that had fallen into enemy hands – especially some flutes 'because they are of surpassing excellence and it would pain me very much to lose them'. It could hardly be said that life at court was dull with all these fashions in hair and clothes, with jokes, love-intrigues, masked festivals, flutes, violas, open-air suppers, and the fooleries of clowns – such as those of Fritella, which were watched by the whole ducal court. Laura Gonzaga Bentivoglio and Lucrezia d'Este Bentivoglio passed through Ferrara on their way back to reconquered Bologna, and they were welcomed like queens and looked very different from a few months earlier. The populace cheered them and sang a special little song made for the occasion, of which the chorus ran:

> Il Papa se sogna
> che volendo Ferrara
> perderà Bologna

> Let the Pope think over
> that by wanting Ferrara
> he will lose Bologna.

The French officers who came to and fro across the Alps gleaned news of the war and descriptions of the Ferrara revelries, and were so full of praise for the Duchess that their tales aroused the curiosity of Queen Anne of France and she asked to see

Lucrezia. So a project was formed in Ferrara of visiting France after the war. Isabella, who had been the first to hear of this, asked Alfonso whether it was true and when they would be setting out and what following would he and the Duchess take with them, and so on. Alfonso answered as best he might, saying that the subject would come up in due course. But in Ferrara the names of the ladies who would accompany Lucrezia were already being mentioned. They included Cassandra and Mamma da Correggio, and Jeronima, the quiet wife of doctor Ludovico Bonaciolo, the only survivor of those who had originally come from Rome. But the visit never took place. Among those who praised the Duchess most enthusiastically was a certain captain Fondraglia and, above all, the great warrior Bayard. The famous encomium on Lucrezia written by the Loyal Serviteur reveals the heart of the *chevalier sans peur et sans reproche*:

Sur toutes personnes, la bonne duchesse qui était une perle de ce monde, leur (that is to the French) fit singulier recueil et tous les jours leur faisait banquets et festins à la mode d'Italie, tant beaux que merveilles. Bien ose dire que, de son temps, ni de beaucoup d'avant, ne s'est point trouvé de plus triomphante princesse, car elle était belle, bonne, douce et courtoise à toutes gens. Elle parlait espagnol, grec, italien et français, quelque peu très bon latin, et composait en toutes ces langues: et n'est rien si certain que combien son mari fût sage et hardi prince, ladite dame, par sa bonne grâce, a été cause de lui avoir fait de bons et loyaux services.[1]

---

[1] 'To all the people the good duchess, who was a pearl of this world, gave special welcome and every day gave banquets and festivities after the Italian fashion which were alike fine and marvellous. I dare to say that neither in her time nor often before was ever to be found a more triumphant princess for she was beautiful, good, sweet, and courteous to all. She spoke Spanish, Greek, Italian and French, excellent Latin a little, and composed in all these languages; and nothing is so sure as that just as her husband was a wise and bold prince, the same lady, by her good grace, has been the cause of doing him good and loyal services.'

This, of course, is not the sort of testimony that Borgia historians in love with the treacherous craft of 'rehabilitating' would like: it is not a testimony to virtue but, better still, a testimony to the fact that Lucrezia had managed to find her own way of holding dominion – through the sheer grace of her personality. She exercised her sovereignty, as the French observed, by making everyone feel – by a smile here, a gesture there – that they were being lifted up to her level, admitted for a moment into private communion with her. Now that she was happy and free and lit up within by the thought of the Marquis, she ceased to feel the shadow of the Estes' watchfulness; as never before in Ferrara she could breathe really freely and she had a sensation of independence that she had lacked even in Rome. She could not fail to feel grateful to the charming Frenchmen, and they for their part could let their romantic imagination play round the mysteries she presented: the contrast, for example, between her almost sacrilegious parentage and her innocent face, between her obvious goodness and the sombre tales of her past, between her slightness and nordic fairness and the heavy languor of her eyelids. At court the talk was of poetry, music and love; there were choice concerts and people exchanged French, Spanish and Italian dancing lessons. Lucrezia's conversation had overtones deriving from the ever-remembered tutelage of Bembo and Ercole Strozzi. And what court could boast more dignified chivalry than the one whose Duchess was surrounded by the most beautiful women of the city, who was dressed in the inimitable velvets of Venice and Florence, whose hands and hair glistened with gems, and who always turned the conversation to the praise of Francesco Gonzaga, Captain-General of the enemy army? For Lucrezia could not resist extolling her friend in the great court gatherings, and to the French this seemed the very metaphysics of chivalry, the epitome of the courteous usages of Roland and King Arthur. Let us admit that it would have been a little excessive had not the extent to which Gonzaga was secretly helping Ferrara been known, but nevertheless everything took on an heroic air and both the French and the Ferrarese awaited the hour of battle enthralled by the Duchess's sweet voice and the smiles of her ladies.

The next event was the arrival of Gaston de Foix, grand *Ecuyer* and Generalissimo of the French army, young and handsome, valiant and amorous. His achievements and valour were already famous, and the women were transported with admiration when they saw him take the field with his right arm unprotected, in obedience to a love vow. After a sojourn in Ferrara during which he participated in the festivities at the castle, he marched on Bologna then besieged by the pontifical army, relieved the Bentivoglio family, and returned. Lucrezia appealed to his imagination. He surrendered with child-like trust to the magnificence of the court and introduced an atmosphere of vigour there, rather like that which Alexander VI brought to the halls of the Vatican. The fame of the Este court spread through the whole of Italy.

By February 20, 1520, news reached Ferrara that the French had recaptured Brescia from the Venetians, and it gave fresh impetus to Carnival. The Duke gave a magnificent – exclusively male – supper, and the Duchess a reception followed by a ball. That year, which marked the beginning of the foreign domination of Italy, was more famous for festivities and love-adventures than any other. While the French were in Ferrara, the Pope's allies, the Spaniards, were disembarking at Naples where they were welcomed to the luxury and decorum of the Neapolitan court whose queens and duchesses preserved if not the power, at least the pomp, of their rank. The newcomers divided their time between military training and merry-making, competing in love, chivalry, witticisms and verses. The most important thing to those gentlemen awaiting the battles ahead was to please the ladies, and as they took themselves seriously in everything, they ended up by making themselves ridiculous. Thus the Marquis of Pescara, husband of Vittoria Colonna, dressed in yellow velvet trimmed with silver bearing a triple motto, or alternatively a suit of white brocade trimmed and lined with yellow satin and embroidered with pens and a sentence pointing out that so great a love as his could not be put into words.

But the sojourn in Naples was followed by war, and the Pontifical and Spanish army, commanded by Raimondo de Cardona (Francesco Gonzaga was left to his illness in Mantua), moved forward. It was a splendid spectacle of magnificent arms, of pourpoint embroidered with gold, silver caparisons resplendent with precious stones, velvet, brocade, ribbons, feathers and steeds – for the most part Arab. From Ferrara another army set out, less brilliant but laden with artillery that included the cannon called 'Giulia', forged from the bronze of Michelangelo's statue of Julius II. Duke Alfonso, or 'Earthquake' as his followers called him, was in charge of the guns under the supreme command of Gaston de Foix.

The two armies met on April 11, 1512, near Ravenna, and the ensuing battle lasted from the morning until four o'clock in the afternoon to the rhythm of Alfonso's cannon – for this battle provided the first great test for artillery in war. As Jacopo Guicciardini wrote to Francesco his brother: 'It was a frightful thing ... for at every stroke a path was cleared through the enemy ranks, helmets shot into the air with the heads inside, and shoulder pieces, and halves of men flew up.' But though the French and Ferrarese army was valiant, the Spanish-Pontifical one was even braver and held out heroically under the ordeal of fire. The combatants fought with a sense of intoxication that put them outside life and with the sort of warlike euphoria that makes heroes die with a smile on their lips. Gaston de Foix was the first to fall among the 10,000 dead of that bloody day. On the evening of April 11 the Spaniards were beaten and Ravenna experienced the horrors of sacking. All the wealth of the Pontifical army, the silverware, horses, arms, jewels and 300,000 ducats fell as booty into the hands of the French survivors – survivors because their ranks had been decimated, and, as Ariosto was soon to write:

in veste bruna e lagrimosa guancia
le vedovelle fan per tutta Francia

In mourning, with tear-stained cheeks
Widows make their way throughout all France.

The body of Gaston de Foix was borne into Ferrara on April
12 preceded by eighteen flags seized from the enemy and under a
triumphal canopy, and was given a funeral that was the very
apotheosis of chivalry. But with his death the fortunes of the
French changed. The new Generalissimo, Monseigneur de la
Palisse, was unable to establish his supreme authority in face of
party discord. There was continual bickering between the
French and the Lanzknechts, whom the Emperor Maximilian
had sent to help Alfonso. And while in Rome there reigned
alarm and confusion and Julius II prepared to defend Castel
Sant' Angelo, the Swiss under the command of Cardinal
Schinner were already crossing the Alps to defend the Pope.

The anti-French revolt began to extend throughout Italy. First
Genoa, then Rimini, and then Ravenna itself set themselves free.
The Swiss and the Spaniards and the Italians who hurried to
their help united and quickly conquered Parma, Piacenza, Pavia
and even Asti, which was part of the patrimony of the French
crown. Scarcely two months after the victory at Ravenna, the
French recrossed the Alps. They left a garrison behind them in
Milan, and the fame of their achievements. Julius II, who had
inspired and directed the whole movement of resistance, was
radiant as the sun. The Roman populace which had trembled at
the defeat of Ravenna rushed through the streets crying 'Giulio!
Giulio! Giulio!'

There were stormy times ahead for Ferrara. Alfonso had his
cannons and many illustrious prisoners and a large part of his
army which, being composed of artillerymen, was still intact. He
retired behind his walls as soon as he knew that he stood alone,
and remained quiet so as not to irritate the Pope. But as the days
passed the policy of marking time became inadequate. A

decision had to be taken before the Pope took the initiative
himself, which at this point might have spelt disaster. Alfonso
weighed the alternatives and concluded that the best line would
be that of repentance. He would go to Rome in person, beg
pardon and make an act of submission. Isabella of Este made
herself responsible for asking the Pope for Alfonso's safe-conduct,
and had the satisfaction of taking it to him personally in Ferrara
where she was hailed by the whole city as almost a saviour.

On June 24, 1512, having liberated all his prisoners and left the
affairs of State in the hands of Lucrezia and the Cardinal, the
Duke of Ferrara rode towards Rome in the company of Fabrizio
Colonna. They reached the city on July 1 and Alfonso lodged in
the palace of Sigismondo Gonzaga and was met and welcomed
by his nephew Federico Gonzaga, the family hostage, who had
reassuring news about the attitude of Julius II. Thus at the outset
the going seemed good; but even so that very night the Colonna
family, who knew a great deal about Vatican affairs and were
grateful to Alfonso for the friendship he had shown the head of
their house when a prisoner, introduced five hundred armed
infantrymen into the city. With these up his sleeve Alfonso,
dressed as a penitent, went to the consistory on June 9 to present
himself to the Pope. There followed one of those scenes of
pardon which are made in the name of divine power and hence
do not hurt people's pride. After his long weary days of suffering
and uncertainty, Alfonso wept with relief and the Papal
absolution descended upon his tears. The pain of excommunication was removed from all the members of the Este family and
the Duchy. Masino del Forno had the singular privilege of being
excluded from it on grounds that he was guilty of aiding and
abetting the schismatic Cardinal Sanseverino. The ceremony
was followed by a grand supper at the house of Cardinal Luigi of
Aragon, and Alfonso waited for the Pope to lay down his peace
terms.

When these arrived it was plain that Julius II had no intention
of loosening his hold. The easiest of the terms was the immediate
liberation of Don Giulio and Don Ferrante of Este – a condition

which Isabella, despite her desire to see her younger brother set free, judged to be 'unbecoming' for reasons of State. But this was nothing compared with the first and principal condition which was that Alfonso should abandon Ferrara to the Pope and accept Asti in exchange. This would have meant the ruin of the Este dynasty, and Alfonso could never accept it. It was time to bring the five hundred Colonna infantrymen into play and under their escort, without even giving the Pope an official answer, the Duke fled from Rome and took refuge at the Colonna fortress of Marino – a place well-known to the Pope himself for he too had often had to take refuge there in the reign of Alexander VI. And, while in Rome Julius II blustered with rage, the Colonna family paid back the hospitality that Alfonso had offered their chief in Ferrara, and alleviated his sojourn with hunts and rustic revelries in the cyclamen-strewn woods round about. Alfonso never lost his calm and readiness for all eventualities during his compulsory holiday, but soon wrote to Ferrara that they could count on his early return.

Meanwhile Lucrezia had heard the news that her son Rodrigo of Aragon, Duke of Bisceglie, had died of a sickness in Bari towards the end of August 1512, at the age of thirteen. On September 7 she hurried to the convent of San Bernardino where she was met by Suor Laura Boiardo with all the comforts of religion. But the wound did not heal easily.

Lucrezia had never forgotten her little son and only the psychologically slow-witted Gregorovius could blame her for abandoning and forgetting this unique witness of the loving and ill-starred adventure she had shared with the Duke of Bisceglie. A woman with such warm feelings as Lucrezia must have been a tender if not a passionate mother. And this is shown by documents that have now come to light in the Este archives which prove Lucrezia's never-failing affection for Rodrigo. In her coffers she preserved long documents describing the quantity and quality and sites of the possessions depending from the

Duchy of Bisceglie, and the annual changes of administrators prove how Lucrezia managed those territories.

Besides looking after the household, Lucrezia also acted as we would expect of a mother. From his earliest youth the child had been entrusted to the care of a cheerful and homely governess or nurse called Caterina. When Lucrezia sent gifts to Bari for her child she never failed to add frocks and linen for Caterina. There are many descriptions of such gifts in Lucrezia's account books and their variety is a proof of her loving and imaginative spirit. There were fine embroidered shirts, doublets of velvet and gold and crimson damask, little gold hats lined with silk, toys and above all swords of gilded wood and velvet-lined scabbards. Lucrezia sent gifts to everyone who had to do with the child, and frequent gifts to Isabella of Aragon, Duchess of Bari, who kept the child at her court. This magnificent ex-Duchess of Milan eased her mind about the child's present condition and future prospects. She was energetic and straightforward and held a celebrated court at Bari, where she boldly defied the oncoming years. She often went to Naples where she was much sought after, and she must have taken Lucrezia's son with her. There, too, Lucrezia's presents arrived. The most original, perhaps, was one for Isabella's daughter – the lovely Bona Sforza who was later to become Queen of Poland. This was a doll – 'a little wooden girl, provided with all her limbs' and jointed and painted. Small replicas of Lucrezia's famous dresses were sent for it to wear, like the doll that Francis I sent a few years later to Isabella of Este which was 'dressed like her, both on top and underneath'.

But Lucrezia's greatest longing had always been to see the little Duke once more. In 1504 she had tried in vain to have him sent to Ferrara. An informant tells us that on July 24, 1506, she planned to go to Loreto to meet the Duchess of Bari and little Rodrigo and would have taken the child back to Ferrara with her. But this was the summer in which Don Giulio's plot was discovered and nothing more was heard of the plan. Possibly the informants neglected to mention Lucrezia's journey owing to the tragic events taking place, but it is more likely that these events prevented Lucrezia's departure.

And now that he had gone for ever Lucrezia wanted to do nothing but weep and pray. Cardinal Ippolito, however, descended on her at the convent and there was no way of escaping him. She had to listen to his icy condolences and pretend to be cheered by the marvellous news that Alfonso was shortly returning. Next came dressmakers and tailors to see about her mourning and she was obliged to try on clothes. Finally she had the task of dispersing the little Duke's court in Bari and taking over the inheritance.

Lucrezia did not dare to keep up strict mourning for long, and when she heard that Alfonso was really on his way back she dressed in brown. He had set out from Marino on September 20 under the protection of Prospero Colonna, Fabrizio's cousin, who was on his way to join up with the Spanish army in northern Italy. When he reached Tuscany Alfonso separated from Colonna's soldiers and took a zigzag route in disguise so as to put the nearby Pontifical forces off the scent. Ariosto, as Catalano rightly shows, went to meet him in Tuscany with a few Ferrarese gentlemen and was kept awake at night by the suggestive noises of darkness, so that every time he heard a horse pawing the ground the nervous poet imagined that the enemy was upon them. During these exhausting nights Alfonso proved the solid quality of his nerves by sleeping like a log fully-dressed on chance palliasses, with Masino del Forno by his side. Once beyond Tuscany they again joined up with the Colonna soldiers and were accompanied by a group of horse almost all the way to Ferrara. There Alfonso changed his clothes because he had 'rags on' and entered the city.

The populace gathered in the square to acclaim him, bells were rung and there were shouts of triumph as he mounted the stairway of the palace and met his wife in the second room of the ducal apartments. There were embraces and congratulations and Alfonso, on the verge of displaying emotion, stayed for a while in the family circle while joyfully receiving visitors who came to pay their respects. The two children Ercole and Ippolito (the latter was later to be made a Cardinal and found the Villa d'Este at Tivoli) gazed at their father in adoring stupefaction. And yet all the while Alfonso was facing the hardest of all his tasks as Duke and making up his mind to wage war against the Pope to the death. That same day he had a long consultation with Cardinal Ippolito from which both emerged with a look of decision on their faces.

Ippolito was concerned about his Cardinal's hat which he had kept by a miracle through the maelstrom of the schismatic council, and now decided to hand over Ferrara to his brother and adopt a position of neutrality by withdrawing to his far-away bishopric in Hungary. Alfonso's time was fully taken up in enrolling and arming his militia, and Lucrezia's in pawning her famous jewellery. The new Captain-General of the Pontifical army was the Pope's nephew Francesco Maria della Rovere, Duke of Urbino, who, being a son-in-law of the Gonzagas of Mantua, conveyed to Alfonso that he would proceed against him 'as mildly as possible'. But people who had seen the Pope at the storming of Mirandola and knew how active he was, viewed the fall of Ferrara as imminent. Armed forces were hurrying through Italy when at the end of February, just after embarking on the war, Julius II died.

During the ten years of his pontificate he had shown greatness of character even in his intemperance. His magnanimity must be included with the achievements by which his reign was dignified. These latter included the laying of the foundation stone of the new St Peter's, the Raphael *Stanze* in the Vatican, Michelangelo's Moses and the painting of the Sistine Chapel, the great oecumenical movement which led ultimately to the reform of the Church, and the struggle against the foreigner in Italy. His death was as courageous as his life. He was concerned about the future of his enterprises in which he believed morally as well as politically. He did not forget the schismatic Cardinals who were a thorn in the side of the Papacy and the influence they might exercise at the next conclave, and he recommended in a weak voice, but with a fiery expression, that the forces of the Church should not be weakened and divided by that council of failures. He exhorted the Cardinals to choose his successor in a lawful manner, he accused himself of his sins and declared that he sincerely forgave all his enemies. He died on the evening of February 21, 1513. Rome wept, and the populace showed its grief by queuing patiently in St Peter's so as to see for the last time the face in which it had put its trust.

But in Ferrara the people were tempted to ring the bells for a Te Deum. The nightmare of war had been averted. Despite Duke Alfonso's insistence on wisdom and moderation in the demonstrations of joy, Lucrezia journeyed from one altar to another to thank God for freeing the world 'from this Holofernes' by sending him 'to wage his wars elsewhere'. When it became known that a friend of the Estes had been elected Pope under the name of Leo X, joy increased. The new Pope was Giovanni dei Medici, son of Lorenzo the Magnificent, who later gave his name to a whole age of humanist splendour and annexed the generous inheritance of Julius II for himself. Leo X later became a secret and persistent enemy of Ferrara though he lacked the courage to come out into the open: nor was equanimity restored by the knowledge that they could count on the help of Lucrezia's ally, Pietro Bembo, who, with Sadoleto, was summoned by Leo X to be his secretary. But Bembo never forgot Ferrara and had the pleasure of being of assistance to Lucrezia and of obtaining for her a confirmation of the right to all the indulgences that she had enjoyed under Alexander VI. He also arranged for the Pope to be little Ercole's godfather at his confirmation. On that occasion Leo X sent the child a medal representing Hercules vanquishing the hydra, an allegory easily translated into Christian terms.

Yet from the outset the Pope aroused apprehension in Ferrara by his slowness in absolving the Duke from the accusations made by Julius II. But, as Lucrezia knew, the delays were dictated to the new Pope by motives of temporary prudence, and her opinion was shared by the merchants who returned her pawned jewellery before receiving the money they had lent on it, on grounds that 'the affairs of Ferrara' were now 'in another state than they were when the pledge was made'. So at last the bitter peril of war was over. Lucrezia's life had come to the end of an epoch as she went to hear Lauds, moving from church to church, light-footed and majestic. It is thus that she is represented by the goldsmith who engraved her and Alfonso's image on a silver plaque dedicated to the protector of the city, San Maurelio. This work, with its long tapering lines, may well not be a life-portrait of Lucrezia, as it was held to be until a few years ago. To those familiar with portraits of the Duchess it is plain that her profile in this instance is an identical repetition of the one on the medal that portrays her with her hair plaited and gathered together in a fine net. It is almost certainly a copy, then, and not taken from a direct pose, and this explains the slight yet noticeable difference between the Duchess's large and heavy head and the tiny curled heads of the ladies-in-waiting behind her. The artist made a slight mistake in proportions but found an intelligent solution for the figure of little Ercole.

Though this rather ungainly portrait cannot be taken as a real and significant likeness of Lucrezia, it helps our imaginations to evoke her surroundings and the refinement and wealth characteristic of the tyrannies at the beginning of the sixteenth century. Ferrara and the Este family saw that she bent to their will, yet their victory was due more to the circumstances of the time than to her fundamental consent. Henceforward State problems were to become rarer. Now that Alfonso had assuaged his military ardour by nearly losing his Duchy, he began to return to his father's policy of balance of power which he adapted to the new epoch – though he never abandoned military exercises. Lucrezia had no active part to play other than that of Duchess; she had only to accept what she had already acquired. Francesco Gonzaga thought that he was cured of syphilis and told his courtiers that he was ready to 'consummate marriage'. His desires could turn either in the direction of his wife or to fresh love affairs – and he could shut up the apartment in the palace overlooking the meadows of the Te and try to forget the dreams and light-headed plans his love had once inspired.

AN ERA OF PEACE

When we come to Lucrezia's last years we notice at the outset
the extent to which her existence was filled with active love (this,
of course, excludes conjugal habits). She never tired of public
office and as a particular task she had the important matter of
examining the appeals of her subjects. We will not stop here to
argue with the historians who belittle her ability in such matters
and dismiss as pure adulation the '*acerrimum judicium*', the
prudence and integrity that Aldo Manuzio attributed to her in
the dedication of the complete poetic works of Ercole Strozzi in
1513. Obviously Lucrezia was not another Isabella of Este, but
for all that she fulfilled her office conscientiously and only
abandoned it towards the end of 1518 when Alfonso took on the
burden himself to save her when she was tired and ill.

She was always ready for public gatherings, whether of duty
or pleasure. Perhaps indeed she was now readier than before, for
she could amuse herself with more detachment than in her early
years at Ferrara. On festival days she would withdraw from the
ducal hall to take the slight repast ordered by the doctor at a
regular hour, and then return to witness the end of the play or
dance. At one period dancing and play-acting went rather out of
fashion to be replaced by guessing games – 'secrets', and other
games. Men such as Ariosto and Bembo (alas, how far away they
were) were clever at the art of making use of the liberties allowed
in these games, slipping in words of love for the ears of the ladies;
and the courtiers of Ferrara must have done the same though
without the masters' literary grace. Probably these games owed
their popularity to the fact that they gave scope for such
agreeable verbal licence. Nor was music forgotten. There were

excellent concerts every day and Lucrezia's taste for fine voices and schools of dancing never declined. As well as Tromboncino and Niccolò of Padua there were Dalida de Putti and the musical lady Graziosa Pio; and the principal dancers were the Valencian girl Caterina, the Sienese Nicola, and a Slav or possibly Russian dancer called Dimitria: the Duchess loved to be surrounded by these little harem figures dressed in golden veils and jewels and silks. The long winter evenings, and the town and country festivities, were enlivened by dwarfs and jesters such as the famous Santino, mentioned by Ariosto, who was clever both at epigrams and stories. In the evening after supper they would place a little bench on the square court table and the little dwarf would quickly slip up and sit on it, turn his lively little eyes from side to side and begin to tell a tale based on Aesop. Lucrezia, her girls-in-waiting and her children would lift up their bright faces in attentive amusement and he would act his parts looking – in the words of a courtier – for all the world like 'a wolf preaching to sheep'.

From Santino's fables the Duchess would proceed to sermons by friars who were famed for their oratory. The Convent of San Bernardino was still her favourite religious house and she retired there to follow the exercises that preceded the great feast days, and to seek solitude whenever she could think of a valid pretext. The courtyards of casa Romei were quiet and cheerful, and there was sun in the loggia in winter and shade under arches in summer, and there was protection from the wind and rain in the intermediary seasons. In the smaller courtyard which is fourteenth-century there may well have been the clusters of light four-petalled flowers with a pungent smell that are there today and with which the nuns decorate the statue of the Madonna in May. Such scents inspired confidence and in this they resembled the view that Lucrezia could see from her room – convent gardens and houses of simple people. There was no break in the harmony as long as she refrained from lowering her eyes to the road below and seeing in her mind's eye a group of cloaked figures lifting up the corpse of Ercole Strozzi (on a night like other death-bringing nights in the shadows of Roman churches).

Thoughts of this kind could be driven away by prayer. Suor Laura and Suor Eufrosina would call on her accompanied by Valentinois' daughter who may have resembled her father in feature as she resembled him in the ability and flexibility of her mind. In June the air was transparent. There would be a knocking at the convent gate and the lay sister, who was a bundle of good intentions from her veil to the hem of her skirt, would rustle off and open the door to the ladies who had dropped in to visit the Duchess. The doorway would be suddenly filled with fashionable figures, and Laura Gonzaga would mount the little stairway to Lucrezia's room and find her resting on her bed dressed in light black silk, and Lucrezia would beg pardon for her weakness with a faint smile. They would talk about clothes: Laura would describe the recent creations of Isabella of Este and her account would be warmly received.

Lucrezia's wardrobe was a product of international influences, a conscious and fanciful mingling of Spanish, Roman, Neapolitan, Ferrarese, French, Lombard and Mantuan themes; and she also liked foreign jewellery. To the Borgia character pomp and riches were an essential means for setting free the inner personality. Through Aldobrandino del Sacrato, the French ambassador, she was sent some golden chains of the finest possible gothic mesh which she ran through her fingers like a glistening river: if she read one of the very few books in her personal library, such as her Petrarch, or Bembo's *Asolani*, Strozzi's Poems, her Spanish songs, an adventure story or a pious work, or if she began to read a book of philosophy – going over the opening phrase 'the surface of things in which we live' for the hundredth time – she would leave to mark her place a book-marker sewn with 'ninety pearls of medium size': the fans that kept the lazy air in motion in summertime were made of beaten gold and black and white feathers. All the objects around her were of fine material and workmanship. We need only mention her many necklaces heavy with gems, cascades of pearls, the dozens of rings and bracelets, the forty tuckers, the hundred buckles and clasps of gold and enamel, the medals, emeralds, rubies, sapphires, the diamonds cut flat to wear on the forehead, the earrings, chains, belts with or without purses, rubies, pearls, cornelians and corals. Then there were the useful objects such as the inkstand of silver and black velvet, the garters of beaten gold and cord, grey like St Francis's, but made of silk with four knots of beaten gold, the little boxes and vessels of massive gold and silver full of rare ointments, the pestles for grinding some cosmetic to a secret formula, the ivory and silver combs, the mirrors such as the one framed with silver leaf-work, enamelled with green and scattered with little pearls suggestive of dew in a cold and sylvan light.

When the time came for saying the rosary Lucrezia's pale fingers would fumble with beads of gold, of silver gilt, or rubies, cornelian, mother of pearl and gold. When she opened her prayer-books her thoughts would rise to God with the help of miniatures like the one found in 'a book of the office of the Madonna handwritten on parchment, with lovely miniatures and covered with green velvet and clasps of beaten gold'. In the chapel were vessels brought from Rome but enriched in Ferrara, the bejewelled crosses, medallions, chalices and reliquaries. One of the chaplains, Don Rainaldo or Don Bartolomeo, dressed in a chasuble of golden linen, velvet and brocade, would handle with cautious reverence the gold and jewels that shone to the glory of God, and while the scent of incense mingled with that of flowers and rare cosmetics, Lucrezia's thoughts would relax into prayer.

Lucrezia never felt that she was Ferrarese. She gave the city children and service and in return received esteem, but never affection. She had become accustomed to the climate; but she was never able to understand the great tradition of Ferrarese art as exemplified in the grim paintings of Cosimo Tura and the rough spirituality of Ercole de Roberti; when decorating her apartment she had turned to the smartness of Garofano and his school. Nor was she ever able to understand Ariosto but preferred poets who followed the graces and conceits of Serafino

Aquilano. So it was only by indirect allusion that she could grasp the passionate force of the city and the robust fantasy of the wide Ferrara sky, of the bright bewitched landscape, and the magic transformations of the swollen coloured clouds – all of which recalls the genius of Ariosto.

To this fantasy Lucrezia opposed the more familiar fantasy of Spain. Anyone connected with the homeland of the Borgias could count on Lucrezia's protection and favour. This applied alike when Don Enrico Enriques, father of the Duchess of Gandia and cousin of the King of Spain, passed through Ferrara and she presented him with one of her bejewelled cups, as when other Spanish ambassadors, important people or prelates came through. The account books of her wardrobe record daily gifts to Spaniards – to the chevalier of Santa Cruz, to Count Stabella, to the chevalier Gabanyllas, and many others. She kept as many Spaniards around her as she could without offending Alfonso's nationalism – such as Miguel the goldsmith, Baldassar the groom, Sancho the carver and Messer Francisco the gold spinner. Lucrezia had summoned the latter from afar with some of his fellow-artisans and had sent ducal horses and carriages to meet him at the border of Ferrara.

Lucrezia always remained in friendly correspondence with the Duchess of Gandia while never transgressing the rules of the most rigid etiquette. In February 1515 one of Ippolito's informants wrote to him from Rome: 'There is here a Spaniard who has come from Spain with two chests of material for our Lady Duchess in the name of the Duchess of Gandia, one being full of scents and oils and the other of sweetmeats and sugar.' The bergamot and jasmine and sweets of sugar, almonds and honey must have brought the taste and smell of Spain to Lucrezia, and she responded with gifts such as a coral rosary which was well suited to her sister-in-law who, now that the legitimate heir, Juan II, had reached his majority, retired to a convent with her daughter Isabella. The informants must all have known something of Lucrezia's love of Spain for one of them wrote from Florence saying that the chevalier Cavriana, when in Spain at the court of the Catholic King, had seen the young Duke of Gandia and had had 'suddenly present to his mind the face and likeness of the Lady Duchess, saying that he resembled her much in this respect'. The Borgia blood must have risen when these words were read. Lucrezia, like everyone who looks to a wonderful destiny in early life and then realizes that it will never be achieved, contrived to find balance and harmony with the help of whatever came to hand – doubtful friendships, mental reservations, false reasoning. But even when she had found stability she could not shed the illusory conviction that, had she been able to go to Catalonia, she would have found perfect happiness there.

Lucrezia was always fond of flowers, gardens and the country. As soon as Alfonso's manner betokened relaxation and ease, and the weather became warm, they would get the river boat ready with the usual baggage and the women-in-waiting, not forgetting Dalida de Puti the singer (if not delayed by Cardinal Ippolito), Dimitria the dancer, and the woman jester Caterina Matta, and they would set out on the long vacation that lasted from the spring to the autumn. Then came the joy of sailing along the narrow channels of the river under a milky springtime sky and with the strong light breeze that blew from the plain. The flat-keeled boat would move slowly on the shallow waters drawn by mules or horses, and the only tragedy would be plump geese breaking their ranks and seeking shelter in the rushes. Usually the company went to Belriguardo – '*O Belriguardo d'amore*', as Gian Battista Guarini was later to sing – and Lucrezia must have felt much the same as they reached the end of their journey, undusty and unwearied, and saw the loveliest of the Este summer houses rise from the restful green around it. The crawling barge came to a standstill by the entrance tower. Lucrezia must have seen the Este shield upheld by two angels, as we still see it today, and beyond the great gate as it turned on its hinges, the immense courtyard, the gothic windows of the central edifice, the great avenue, the bright fountain, the ordered perspectives, and she must have felt consoled for all her melancholy. Once inside the halls and loggias and galleries, they passed between works of art, paintings of the time of Leonello, Lazzaro Grimaldi's story of Psyche, and Ercole de Roberti's frescoes for which even Duke Ercole laid aside the affairs of state. And in the chapel there were the hundred and forty-five angels, doctors of the Church, and evangelists, for the painting of which Cosimo Tura had gone to Brescia to study the magic manner of Gentile da Fabbriano.

But Lucrezia's real pleasure at Belriguardo must have been the great park with its airy splendour artfully ordered by gardeners, painters and architects, with its fish-ponds, fountains, waterfalls, avenues, woods, shrubberies and flowers. The pleasure she derived from these things was not a naturalistic one which might have ultimately led her to a return to the earth in the spirit of the *Georgics*. Her formation had been too literary and princely for her ever to rid herself of a certain pride and a scrupulously hierarchical awareness of her social rank. Lucrezia's arcadia, if it existed, consisted of a polite little grass lawn on which ladies and gentlemen dressed in satin and velvet would gather in the shade of a fine beech tree, while at their feet would run a little stream as like as possible to the 'clear, fresh and sweet waters' of Petrarch's verse. They would reread Bembo's *Asolani* and discuss the problems and examples of Platonic love. One of the gentlewomen would take up the lute and sing softly – perhaps Lucrezia's intimate friend Graziosa Pio, a famous Milanese beauty of the House of Maggi. The painted towers of Belriguardo nearby would attract their gaze and suggest thoughts of the court, and the conversation would change to plans for balls and *fêtes champêtres*. Lucrezia would be in a good humour, she would want to please her favourites and see everyone around her happy. She would give jewels to Graziosa Pio, and for her daughter Beatrice she would give dances and supper parties to celebrate her betrothal. The three hundred rooms of Belriguardo would all be full to overflowing. Between music and dancing someone would note that the betrothed was late and murmur ironically '*Lungi fia dal becco l'erba*' – 'there's many a slip twixt the cup and the lip'. The speaker would, of course, be a friend of Isabella of Este.

Gossip about events in Ferrara was now provided not only by the ever-faithful Bernardino de Prosperi but also by a courtier who was a friend of the Marchesa of Mantua, Battista Stabellino, a mediocre humanist but a witty courtier who signed his letters 'Demogorgon' or even 'Apollo' and belonged to a comic sect based on a philosophical system of elementary epicureanism. This system was three-quarters a joke and one-quarter due to a natural terror of anything sad, and the underlying principle was 'to cultivate happy things so as not to die of melancholy'. All its adherents adopted amorous pseudonyms with an element of comedy in them. Thus illustrious ladies at Ferrara and Mantua – including Isabella of Este herself – disguised themselves under the names of Madonna Blanda, Madonna Amata and Madonna Risibile. Only light and gay conversation and amusing anecdotes were permitted among the members, but their elegant small talk was salted with a good deal of irony and a strong dash of satire when the Duchess of Ferrara was under discussion. There was malicious laughter, for instance, about the card game Lucrezia played with her favourites, using little marzipan tarts and young stuffed chickens as stakes which winners and losers ate together afterwards at an improvised lunch. The players would have joined in the laughter, too. It was the countryside that inspired lunches and games of this kind, and when the Duchess was unable to take her court as far as Belriguardo she would go to Belfiore, the great villa just outside Ferrara which was frescoed by the vigorous Ferrarese artists of the fourteenth century and surrounded by a famous park containing every kind of game from hares to goats, foxes, boars and even wolves. From there she would go out to the 'castellina' built on the ruins of a fortress and planted over with high pine trees reached through an avenue of cypresses and a large garden. The 'castellina's' greatest attraction was an underground nymphaeum where there was a great scooped-out bath supplied by the waters of the Po, and there we would like to imagine the Duchess and her girls bathing and playing in the water far from the sight of the courtiers.

But winter came bringing with it the official festive season. Lucrezia had to be in residence in the castle and her longest journey would be a drive through the city streets. During the winter she spent her periods of repose at the convent of San Bernardino. It was in 1516 at a supper party in the magnificent Costabili palace that Lucrezia met Giulia's brother Cardinal Farnese again, who had now grown mature in wisdom and experience and showed promise of his future majesty as Pope Paul III. During the supper and afterwards Lucrezia and the Cardinal were able to converse about events of long ago regarding which they alone knew the truth. They spoke of Giulia (Lucrezia kept up relations with her and wrote to her as late as 1518), and they spoke of Rome. If they shut their eyes, the fourteen years that had passed would roll away with all the changes they had wrought on people and things, and they could imagine that Alexander VI might appear at any moment announced by the voice of his Cardinal Treasurer.

There were still survivors from the scattered world of Alexander VI and one was the lively Vannozza Cattanei. Clinging strongly to life and rooted now in Rome, Lucrezia's mother had for some time past devoted herself to good works. She helped the churches; but her solid maternal instincts made her give yet more help to hospitals and we know that she had to do specially with the hospital of the Consolazione. Here she made them keep a massive silver bust of Valentinois as if to preserve him from future oblivion (though probably the bust ended up in the bag of one of Frundsberg's lanzknechts at the sack of Rome in 1527). Vannozza had loved ornaments dearly, but now that they could have no further significance for her she had them made into religious objects by her gold- and silver-smiths. She ordered a marble tabernacle from Andrea Bregno which was to be identical in all respects to that of San Giacomo degli Spagnuoli, with candelabras and friezes and arabesques that followed the florid designs of the Lombard decorators and suited perfectly the fussy taste of ageing women. For the church of St John Lateran Vannozza had a metal tabernacle made, possibly of silver and decorated with the pearls, diamonds and turquoises which in the days of Alexander VI had enhanced the pink and whiteness of her skin. She quarrelled with a goldsmith, Nardo Antoniazzo, who said she ought to have paid him more for making a silver cross. She kept up her place in life despite the fall of the Borgias, and was judged an estimable and excellent woman even by a historian such as Giovio who only got to know her late in life. For though she had lost all her children she had a flourishing old age of resignation and noble piety.

Vannozza knew her limitations and never went beyond them, and the tone of her correspondence with Lucrezia never shows any lack of respect. The all too few letters to be found in the Este archives date only from 1515 and may well be less interesting than others; the most revealing phrase contained in them is 'your happy and unhappy mother' immediately preceding the signature. Vannozza's letters contained recommendations or appeals, rarely for herself but often for some protégé, and she would add in a postscript that she wrote out of obligation, thereby abstracting herself (the school of Alexander VI) from all responsibility for any trouble she caused. On only one occasion do we find her asking for help in another spirit; then the conventional expressions take on a fresh life and her aged heart warms with anxiety and affection. The matter in question was the family. Jofre, living the quiet life of a little provincial lord at Squillace, had sent an illegitimate son of his to his mother in Rome, a boy of ten. Vannozza had received him with open arms and was devoted to him, but she foresaw that her life would not last much longer and therefore wrote to Lucrezia and Cardinal Ippolito asking that the child might be taken to Ferrara after her death where 'he should be brought up to serve your most illustrious House'. We do not know whether Lucrezia promised to do this or not. In 1517 Jofre died at Squillace when he was only just thirty-six and Lucrezia was duly informed by his eldest son, Don Francesco. Not a year had elapsed before Vannozza herself died. News of her death was announced in the streets of Rome on November 24, 1518:

'Messer Paolo,' said the herald, 'informs you that Vannozza, mother of the Duke of Gandia, has died; the deceased belonged to the Gonfalone confraternity.'

When they heard the announcement – which made no mention of Valentinois, Lucrezia or Jofre – members of the confraternity prepared for the funeral. It was all very respectful and performed in the presence of the Pope's *Cubicolari*. She was buried in Santa Maria del Popolo under a stone which described her as venerable because the mother of Duke Valentinois, the Duke of Gandia, the Prince of Squillace and the Duchess of Ferrara, and illustrious because pious, good, wise and old. In accordance with the dispositions of Vannozza's will, Masses were said for her at Santa Maria del Popolo for two hundred years. Then prayers ceased, and in the end even the stone was taken away; the memory of Alexander VI's woman was handed over to the historians.

Lucrezia took refuge in San Bernardino and gave orders that no one should speak to her of her bereavement. It would have served no purpose talking to people who had no idea what her mother had meant to her. This would have been the moment to take in Jofre's son, but we find no reference to the boy in the archives of Ferrara. True, in the account book of Lucrezia's wardrobe for 1518 we do find mention of a 'Hyeronimo Borgia, regazo', that is to say a page. But a later document refers to him as a son of Cesare Borgia. Little Jeronimo was a lively boy who was cherished not only by Lucrezia but – a trickier matter altogether – by Duke Alfonso, 'for his worth'. He set up house at Ferrara, lived, married and died there. Thus of the great new dynasty, intended by Alexander VI to have Europe for its stage, the heirs were few and divided. There was Luisa Borgia, who grew up to be ugly and intelligent in France, there was Juan Borgia, third Duke of Gandia, who became the father of St Francis Borgia, fourth general of the Jesuits, and there were Jofre's children in a remote part of South Italy. Alexander VI's last son, Rodrigo, was an obscure ecclesiastic in Campania, and in Ferrara, besides Lucrezia, there were Valentinois' daughter the nun, the boy Jeronimo and the Roman Infante.

Readers will remember the complicated circumstances surrounding the Infante's birth, his ambiguous legitimization and the affair of the two Pontifical Bulls. But interest in the person of Giovanni Borgia begins and ends with his birth. If we want to explain the failure, and hence tragedy, of his life, we shall have to examine the origins of his blighted psychology, for the Infante's upbringing must have contributed to his moral retardedness. Historians could find no trace of him between the death of Alexander VI and 1518 and supposed him to be living with one of the Borgia Cardinals in Naples or Rome; but actually documents of 1506 and 1508 now reveal that he had arrived in Ferrara in 1505 and was put in charge of Alberto Pio da Carpi, whence he was taken away again in October 1506 when a henchman of the Duchess 'went to Carpi to remove the Lord Giovanni Borgia with his things'. This is what is written in Lucrezia's account book; and shortly afterwards we find a note of the expenses incurred on that occasion 'for a pilot who has brought the Lord Don Giovanni Borgia from Finale to Ferrara' by river.

At that time the Don Giulio conspiracy was only just over and though Pio had remained outside it, he gave many indications of his animus against the House of Este. So the Infante was removed to Ferrara and lodged either at the castle or elsewhere. He had a court of his own, an outstanding tutor – the humanist Bartolomeo Grotto – an agent, a groom, and even a jester whom Lucrezia dressed at her own expense. Lucrezia's account book tells us day by day of the Infante's life. We find that he wore out stockings in an appalling way, as well as shirts, waistcoats and caps. One day he asked Lucrezia's permission to give some clothes to a poor Spaniard and she naturally allowed him to do so. On another day his tutor asked for books, a Virgil and a Donatus – i.e. a Latin grammar – an inkstand and other writing materials. The fact that the Este family tolerated the presence of the Roman Infante in Ferrara may seem to testify to the normality of his birth. But we must remember that he was protected by Alexander VI's two Bulls of legitimization and nobody dared to indulge in conjectures concerning the Duchess of Ferrara. Moreover, taking all into account, the Este toleration was pretty limited, and first Alfonso and then his children gave ample proof that they detested the Infante. In other words Lucrezia was allowed to keep him with her but a ban of silence was imposed around his name which applied even to the Marchesa of Mantua's most gossipy informants. Apart from two references by Prosperi who termed the little Borgia 'son of Duke of Valentinois', he was never mentioned even on the occasion of the death of Cesare who, by the first Bull of legitimization, was held to be his father.

An order concerning him – tacitly understood rather than verbally given – must have run from court to court like the order forbidding people to mention the names of Don Ferrante and Don Giulio after their imprisonment. And Giovanni Borgia, whom nature had not endowed with much personality, resented his humiliation and was not compensated by Lucrezia's love. Her love became increasingly mingled with feelings of pity and alarm when she saw that the mortifications of his social and economic position were arousing the arrogance and insolence of the Borgias in him. No one will ever know the memories she looked for in his face, what resemblances she saw, what remorse she felt.

At twenty he began to cause Lucrezia more anxiety still. He was frequently seen about in the streets of Ferrara and was unable to apply his brain to any solid discipline; he was at once weak and turbulent and entirely lacked the warmth and charm that had made even the vices of the Borgias irresistible. He was surrounded by rowdy servants, encouraged their insolence and egged them on to provoke other servants, especially those of little Ercole of Este: in fact on one occasion there was a scuffle in the piazza del Duomo in which a man was killed. There were arrests and worries for Lucrezia who may herself have abetted the

Infante's flight from Ferrara before Alfonso of Este returned from Venice and punished him, as everyone – including the Infante himself – expected. It was considered urgent to give the boy some status in life including duties of no matter what kind.

Lucrezia left no stone unturned. To raise money for the boy she wrote to Rome to enlist the help of Agostino Chigi, the great banker of Christendom. But her letter cannot have been very clear for Chigi, who was the Maecenas of Raphael and the Roman humanists and artists, as well as a very acute man of business, answered that he had not quite understood how he could 'give or lend two hundred ducats and get them back at fifty a month from he knows not where, and he begs the Duchess to write more explicitly what she has in mind'. This loan or another must subsequently have been made, for Lucrezia remained on very friendly terms with Chigi and at the next Carnival sent him a gift of twenty-six masks with and without beards made by a famous artisan, Giovanni da Brescia. But the loan, though helpful, did not solve the problem. Lucrezia sent an envoy in the person of Jerolamo Nasello of Cervia to Naples – to no avail, however – and finally, encouraged by the courteous and cordial attitude of the women of the French royal family, she decided to send the Infante to seek his fortunes in France. Alfonso of Este was himself setting out for the court of Francis I towards the end of 1518 and he agreed to take the Infante with him, doubtless so as to get him out of Ferrara. Lucrezia now hoped she had found a solution. She provided letters of introduction for the young man, chose two highly distinguished Ferrarese noblemen, Del Sacrato and Trotti, to be his companions, and gave him gold bracelets and jars of rare scented creams for Queen Charlotte (Francis I later observed that the perfumes left a very pleasant smell on the Queen's nightdress 'when she goes to bed, which is very pleasing'). As Alfonso also took gifts to the King, the Queen and Madame the King's sister, there seemed every expectation of launching the Infante satisfactorily at the French court.

Giovanni Borgia arrived in Paris in Alfonso's suite and was duly presented to the King and Queen and great ladies at court.

But when the moment came to show a modicum of wit or civility or gallantry he became tongue-tied and ineffectual. Though the Ferrarese ambassador and gentlemen of the suite did their best to shake him out of his inertia, they could not move him; nor was he moved by any desire to show affection and gratitude to Lucrezia, who was tireless in her efforts to find him a career. Indeed, when the Ferrarese ambassador asked him if he wished to add a line in a letter to the Duchess, he answered that he had nothing to say – which is a fool's answer. The ambassador himself even went so far as to write to Spain in an attempt to raise money for the Infante, and actually obtained some – he did not say from whom but probably from the young Duke of Gandia, Juan II. He also tried to liven up the young man and get him to show some vestige of intelligence and vitality, for the King of France and the women of the court could hardly fail to wonder why on earth they should give French honour to such an uncouth fellow. In the end all concerned lost patience. Alfonso of Este returned to Ferrara soon followed by Del Sacrato and Trotti who left the Infante in the charge of the ambassador; but he in his turn was driven crazy by the burden. We do not know what Lucrezia answered to the ambassador's letter begging her to write to young Borgia to tell him to get down to something, but Giovanni soon returned from France empty-handed and lived the life of a wastrel in Italy, though he never set foot in Ferrara after Lucrezia's death. At one time he had the unfortunate idea of claiming the Duchy of Camerino on the grounds that he had been invested with it by Alexander VI, and his court case against the heir of the estate, Giulia Vanaro, continued until the Pope told him peremptorily to keep quiet. We see him for the last time in Rome in 1548 in a lawsuit with a woman creditor over a handful of ducats. By then he had an esteemed and safe post as a Papal functionary. Thus the most puzzling person in Lucrezia's life, who has even been suspected of being the monstrous outcome of incest, had no idea what to do with himself and sought refuge with the Church – the Church which was too lofty to be sullied even by men's worst errors.

Towards the end of her life, Lucrezia appears to have discovered in herself a flame of youth that struggled against death. Once more she attempted to pick up her friendship with Bembo that had never entirely ceased. She also had Francesco Gonzaga, of course, but he was so wretched and ill that their relationship had reached the stage of prayers only. The vitality of Lucrezia's heart and mind asked for more than that.

'The more I think of that remedy of despair that that friend of yours suggested to you, the more it pleases me and seems to me always appropriate', she wrote to Bembo in the old allusive style in an undated letter. Another letter, full of affectation and mannerisms, is dated August 7, 1517. 'My dearest Messer Pietro,' she begins, adopting the familiar tone of affection and trust, 'as I know that the expectation of an expected thing is a great part of our satisfaction with it, since the hope of possessing the same thing kindles our desire and makes it seem not as it is but more beautiful than it is, I have thought to postpone answering until now, so that you, by awaiting the fine reward for your beautiful (letters), shall be yourself the cause of your satisfaction and at once payer and debtor.' It would be difficult to be more graciously artificial. Her letter suggests that Bembo wrote 'beautiful' letters and at fairly frequent intervals. Despite the lapse of the years he had not forgotten her, though, with the passage of time and the increase of his power and the flattery which now surrounded him, he had become a stranger to her. Messer Pietro was still a very handsome man and the elegance of his wit had grown into a pose, but a pose ideally adapted for magnificence and refinement. He was a good talker and, as he loved talking on his favourite subjects, he sometimes grew ecstatic in the closed circle of his thoughts – so much so that he would experience an intellectual rapture that seemed to cut him off from the world around him. But his raptures and intoxications did not deprive him of his wit for, as Castiglione tells us, when Emilia Pio heard a peroration by him on platonic love and saw him in an attitude of ecstasy, she pulled at his coat and whispered in a small mordant voice: 'Take care, messer Pietro, that with these thoughts your soul does not leave your body entirely!' to which he straightway answered: 'Lady, that would not be the first miracle that love has performed in me.'

Bembo enjoyed a viceroy's power in Rome, and so the Este family availed themselves of every opportunity to send messengers and friends to pay their respects to him. He once told Ariosto that he retained the liveliest memories of Ferrara. When Duke Alfonso heard this he sent him a message warmly pressing him to come at any time he pleased and stay at any villa he liked for as long as he liked. If Bembo recalled the autumn of 1503, when he had been obliged to flee hungry from Ostellato because Alfonso's court had requisitioned all the food, he must have smiled a melancholy smile. But when Lucrezia repeated her husband's offer he answered with compliments and thanks; he would surely go, he said, to enjoy her sweet company. But Lucrezia must have read between the lines and realized that she would never see him again. The perfect lover would find it intolerable to see the woman he had crowned with the glory of love diminished in any way. It was less the fact that her once great beauty was now dimmed – for her body had thickened with years of child-bearing – that frightened him, as the fear of finding that something had died within himself, leaving him without reaction, empty. 'His' Duchess was the woman who once appeared by his sick-bed, radiant with love – let her remain so. Indeed it is possible that Lucrezia did not really wish to see Bembo either, and was satisfied if she could bring herself to his mind and perform acts of courtesy, sending letters and gifts with Alfonso's approval. The friendship with Pope Leo's powerful secretary was well worth keeping up.

Alfonso of Este now realized that he had no further reason to fear his wife's deserting him; indeed he had kept her physically and morally subjected by repeated child-bearing, and had succeeded in taming her without destroying the appearances of domestic harmony. He had never loved her with his heart, but esteemed her and, though he bore her no gratitude for the offspring she had given him (that, for him, was a matter of duty), her position as the mother of Este children gave her dignity in the eyes of all including himself.

Alfonso was a man of robust temperament and slow wit, and these two qualities in combination produced a massive figure in whom the lack of psychological understanding was a natural phenomenon rather than a defect. If we start from this premise, the history of his relationship with Lucrezia can be summed up without difficulty. He had not wanted her as a wife, but once she had been given him he had accepted her and had found her more docile and pliant than he expected. Later he realized that she was not easily driven and he was forced into a struggle against the feminine passivity and flexibility that is the bane of strong men. He thundered against the Spanish-style court, against the toadying poets, against the things that made his wife a foreigner in Ferrara. With Cardinal Ippolito's help he had managed to some extent to get rid of the threats to proper order. Of course Alfonso had grown physically accustomed to his wife. Fidelity apart (it will be remembered that during the first weeks of his marriage he had gone for solace to prostitutes with the approval of his father-in-law), he maintained continual conjugal relations with her and probably considered this to be a strict duty. Hence Lucrezia had one pregnancy after another, only interrupted during the hazardous war against Julius II. We may well wonder why, when he saw how ill his wife was, it never occurred to him to spare her. Possibly he never even realized that she did all she could to escape from him on the pretext of visits to convents or to the country or of taking cures. In Alfonso of Este's character there must have been a hint of strangeness whose origin is not very clear. To set a high price on a woman's fertility is to be expected in a prince who has to think of his successors, but in Alfonso's case this became less natural when fertility was valued, not only in his wife, but also in a mistress of plebeian origin such as Laura Dianti, who later became his favourite. In his enthusiasm for pregnancy he nicknamed Laura 'Eustochia' or 'good-conceiver', though she only gave him two children whereas Lucrezia, counting dead and living, gave him at least seven. True, in that age bastards were treated much as legitimate children; but the example of Don Giulio had shown Alfonso what disorders a mixture of blood could bring to a family, and he cannot have wanted to try the experiment again. His satisfaction may have had other origins. If we remember the gross sensualities of his youth, we may be tempted to think that his feeling for progeny may have been tied up with sexual perversion.

In the beginning of 1519 Lucrezia was pregnant and in very bad health. She was so weak that she could only just drag herself around. Yet she was patient and cheerful, she took care of her health and she hoped to have a successful confinement. At the same time she was taken up with State affairs (Alfonso being in France), was anxiously following the fortunes of the Roman Infante in Paris, and was corresponding with Gonzaga, whose life was rapidly drawing to a close. On January 24, 1519, she wrote Gonzaga an affectionate letter of comfort. On March 29 he died – finished off by syphilis. She wrote a conventional letter of condolence to Isabella of Este showing her emotion only when she said: 'I, too, have need of consolation.' Though this was a common formula in letters of that time, it must have been particularly apt in this case. Isabella on her side had no need for excessive sympathy. She took the power into her own hands, dismissed all her husband's councillors – beginning with the hated Tolomeo Spagnuoli – and solaced herself by a second period of holding the reins. She failed to realize that her son, Federico, the new Marquis of Mantua, would soon want to rule alone.

Lucrezia felt confusedly that something was changing. There were no apparent signs. The days followed each other as usual and even the panic about existence, which at times had made her long for the dissolution of death, was appeased. Now that she had ceased to feel her passions so strongly, she saw things in a new and truer light. The hierarchy of morals was no longer confused in her mind in such a way as to make it impossible to choose an example or model.

Strange, that in the past she had failed to understand that her examples and models were to be found at the altar and in the lives of the saints. The path of divine love now opened up for her. This was logical enough given the formal and assiduous religious formation she had received in Rome. Lucrezia now indulged in penance, fasting and prayer, which bring to the faithful the hope of an incorrupt and glorious future at the moment of human decline. Belief in the immortality of the soul was for her belief in life. But Lucrezia's religion brought her the sweets of love as well as the strength of hope, as we can see from her tender devotion to St Francis of Assisi. In 1518 she joined the Third Order of St Francis under the direction of Fra Ludovico della Torre. She took to wearing a hair shirt under her court dresses, she went to daily confession – she had always enjoyed discussing her weaknesses with a discreet confidante – and she received Communion frequently. And then, unexpectedly, the order and balance she felt she had reached were rudely upset.

At the beginning of 1519, when she knew she was pregnant again, she may have had a presentiment. Certainly by May she was uneasy. The assurances of her religious advisers and confessors no longer satisfied her. She wanted something more – a stronger pledge and the most powerful protection possible. Perhaps someone else suggested to her (unless the idea was due to her own tortuous way of harking back to her beginnings) that she should appeal to the Pope for a special blessing which would serve as a safe-conduct through the dark days ahead. At the end of May she sent for Niccolò Maria of Este, Bishop of Adria, and with his help drew up a letter in which the pious phrases conceal the writer's uneasiness. When the ambassador in Rome read it he described it as 'full of all possible feelings that prove her (i.e. Lucrezia's) humility and devotion' to the Pope, and the 'holy obligation that she feels every day' in his regard. The letter was dispatched by special messenger who rode hot from Ferrara to

Rome, and as in the old days Lucrezia's name was pronounced in the Vatican before the pontifical throne by the Ferrarese ambassador, now no longer Costabili but Alfonso Paulucci.

'Holiness,' said the ambassador, 'the Lady Duchess who is pregnant and in bad health begs pardon that she is unable to write to your Holiness in her own hand.' The ambassador went on to expound the character of Lucrezia's illness and, while listening to the contents of the letter, the Pope's mind wandered over some of the strange by-ways of Borgia history. Finally with a cheerful face, as Paulucci puts it, and with great solicitude, he said: 'We are pleased; may God preserve her', and he traced a gesture of benediction in the air.

We do not know whether Lucrezia's mind was set at rest. Her pregnancy was being difficult and the doctors, Maestro Palmarino and Maestro Ludovico Bonacciuolo, realizing that complications were arising, began to consider hastening the birth. Finally, on the evening of June 15, Lucrezia gave birth to a pinched and lean baby, a girl who refused to take nourishment and seemed not to want to live. It was decided to baptize the baby without delay. It was night. Lucrezia was lying in an unhealthy torpor. There was a weary coming and going of people, and a few candles were lit to prepare for the ceremony. Eleanora Pico, who happened at that moment to be on duty, was godmother and the first gentlemen discovered near the ducal apartments acted as godfathers – Alessandro Ferrufino and Masino del Forno. The baby was christened Isabella Maria.

Lucrezia put up a strong resistance to the ravages of her fever. It was said afterwards that her religious life during the last years had made her ready for death, but this was not true for she showed a great desire for life. She was encouraged by every proof of her remaining strength, even by her ability to breathe. Her head ached, and its weight was so intolerable to her, that they cut off her hair. While the scissors were busy, her nose began to bleed. But she still held out for another week and it was only on the evening of June 22 that it became known that she was really dying and had lost both her sight and her hearing. But she survived even that abyss, regained the use of her eyes and ears and, breathless and exhausted, she held on just this side of life's frontier. Outside, the month of June was glorious, the sun was hot, the earth warm and the fruit ripening. Why did Alfonso of Este look so cast down, so frightened? She had confessed her sins and received Communion. She had made her will, which included handsome bequests for convents, and perhaps she knew that a courtier had written to the Vatican to ask for the blessing *in extremis* on her behalf. In spite of these things she was unable to resign herself. The courtiers noted that she, who was so affectionate, made no request to see her children. All she asked was a day, an hour, a minute of grace. On the evening of June 22 she took a little broth and was so tranquil that everyone thought she might pull through after all. But on the following day her agony began. 'The poor woman is having great difficulty in departing', said the courtiers.

The day of the 23rd passed and the 24th dawned in clear gay sunlight. Lucrezia was quiet and seemed to have lost consciousness. Yet down in the depths where she lay some image must still have reached her. The colour of the sky at Subiaco, the sound of the river Aniene rolling below, Vannozza's full-throated laugh and motherly kiss; the Cardinals' purple outshone by the dazzling white of the pontifical robes, the great face of Alexander VI lit up by the August light, the Vatican ceilings fresh from the brush of Pinturicchio, the Duke of Gandia's little silver bells, Cesare's dangerous glance; Rome dissolving in rosy dusk at evening, the bell on the Campidoglio chiming for Borgia festivals. Perhaps with that magic chime, coming from such a remote past, a human eternity, there came serenity; perhaps her terrors dissolved and gave place to an infinite weariness, like peace. The moment had come when fear was over. Lucrezia looked into her father's face as on the snowy morning of their separation on January 6, 1502. And she gave a sigh, as she had sighed when told that it was time to leave.

BIBLIOGRAPHY

Acton, Lord. *The Borgias and their latest Historian*. Historical Essays and studies, 1907

Ademollo, A. *Alessandro VI, Giulio II e Leone X nel carnevale di Roma, doc. ined.*, Florence, 1886, Lucrezia Borgia e la verità. *Arch. Stor. Prov. Roma*, 1887

Adinolfi, P. *Il canale di Ponte*, Narni, 1860. *La torre dei Sanguigni e S. Apollinare*. Rome, 1863

Albertazzi, A. Un romanzo per Lucrezia Borgia, *La Lettura*, 1902

Alvisi, E. *Cesare Borgia duca di Romagna*. Imola, 1878

Ancona, A. D'. *Origini del teatro italiano*. 2 vols. Turin, 1891

Antonelli, G. Lucrezia Borgia. *Archivio Veneto*, II, 2, 1871

Apollinaire, G. *La Rome des Borgia*. Paris, 1914

Arco, C. D'. Notizie su Isabella Estense. *Arch. Stor. Ital.*, App. 2, 1845

Bacchelli, R. *La congiura di don Giulio d'Este*. 2 vols. Milan, 1931

Balan, P. *Roberto Boschetti e gli avvenimenti italiani dei suoi tempi* (1494–1529). 2 vols., Modena 1884. *Storia d'Italia*. Modena, 1894–99

Bembo, Pietro. *Gli Asolani*, with dedication to Lucrezia Borgia. Venice, 1505, *Lettere giovanili di Messer Pietro Bembo*. Milan, 1558

Bendeldei, N. *Lettera al pontefice Alessandro VI per gli sponsali di Lucrezia Borgia con Alfonso d'Este*. Ferrara, 1889

Bérence, F. *Lucrèce Borgia*. Paris, 1937

Bernardi, Andrea. *Cronache forlivesi dal 1476 al 1517*, ed. D. Mazzantini, 2 vols. Bologna, 1895–97

Bertaux, E. *Les Borgia dans le royaume de Valence*. Paris, 1911

Bertoni, G. *La biblioteca estense e la cultura ferrarese al tempo di Ercole I*. Turin, 1903. *L'Orlando Furioso e la Rinascenza a Ferrara*. Modena, 1919. 'Una putina de legno' di Lucrezia Borgia. *Archivum Romanicum*, II, 1918, pp. 91–93

Berzeviczy, A. *Beatrice d'Ungheria*. ed. R. Mosca. Milan, 1931

Béthencourt, Fernandez De, *Historia genealógica y heráldica de la Monarquia Española, Casa Real y Grandes de España*, Vol. IV. *Gandia*. Madrid, 1902. Alejandro VI Sumo Pontifice, *Rivista del Collegio Araldico*, VI, 1908

Blaze, H. De Bury. Les Borgia, *Revue des Deux Mondes*, 1877

Boschi, G. *Lucrezia Borgia*. Bologna, 1923

Brann, H. A. The Borgias' myth, *Catholic World*, XLIV, I, 1886

Brom, G. Einige Briefe von R. Brandolinus Lippus, *Romische Quartalschrift*, II, 1888

Brosch, J. Alexander VI und Lucrezia Borgia, *Historische Zeitschrift*, XXXIII, 1875

Buggelli, U. *Lucrezia Borgia*. Milan, 1929

Burchardi, Joh. *Diarium sive rerum urbanarum commentarii 1483–1506*. Ed. L. Thuasne, 3 vols. Paris, 1883–85. *Liber notarum ab anno LXXXIII usque ad annum MDVI*, ed. E. Celani, *Rerum Italicarum Scriptores*, Città di Castello, 1901–11

Cabanés, A. *Dans les coulisses de l'histoire*: Le journal des couches de Lucrèce Borgia. First series, Paris, 1929

Campori, G. Una vittima della storia – Lucrezia Borgia. *Nuova Antologia*. II, 1866

Cappelletti, L. *Lucrezia Borgia e la storia*. Pisa, 1876

Cappelli, A. *Lettere di Ludovico Ariosto*. Milan, 1887

Cartwright, J. *Isabella d'Este, Marchioness of Mantua 1474–1539*. 2 vols. London, 1903

Castiglione, Baldesar. *Il Cortigiano*, ed. with notes and biographical dictionary by V. Cian. Florence, 1919

Catalano, M. *Lucrezia Borgia duchessa di Ferrara*. Ferrara, 1920. *Vita di Ludovico Ariosto*, 2 vols. Geneva, 1930

Célier, L. Alexandre VI et ses enfants en 1493. *Mélanges d'archéologie et d'histoire*. XXVI, 1906

Cerri, D. *Borgia, ossia Alessandro VI papa e suoi contemporanei*. Turin, 1858

Chabas, R. Alejandro VI y el duque de Gandia. *El Archivo*, VII. Valencia, 1893. Don Jofré de Borja y Doña Sancha de Aragón. *Revue Hispanique*, IX. 1902

Chroniques du Monastère de San Domenico e Sisto à Rome. ed. G. J. Berthier. Levanto, 1919

Clan, V. *Un decennio della vita di Pietro Bembo*. Turin, 1885. Pietro Bembo e Isabella d'Este. *Giorn. Stor. Lett. Ital.*, IX. 1887. p. 92ff

Cionini, Niccolo. *Angela Borgia e una pagina della storia sassolese del sec. XVI*. Modena, 1907. Reprinted from *Atti e memorie della R. Dep. Storia patria per le province modenesi*. Series V, vol. VI

Cittadella, L. N. *Notizie amministrative storiche artistiche di Ferrara*. Ferrara, 1868. *Saggio di Albero genealogico e di memorie su la famiglia Borgia, specialmente in relazione a Ferrara*. Turin, 1872

Clément, L'abbé. *Les Borgia*. Paris, 1882

Collison-Morley, L. *The Story of the Borgias*. London, 1932

Conti, Sigismondo Dei. *Le storie dei suoi tempi dal 1475 al 1510*. Rome, 1883

Corio, B. *Storia di Milano*. 3 vols. Milan, 1855–57

Corvo, F. Baron *Chronicles of the House of Borgia*. London, 1901

Creighton, M. *A History of the Papacy*, 5 vols. London, 1887

Croce, Benedetto. *La Spagna nella vita italiana durante la Rinascenza*. Bari, 1922. *Versi spagnoli in lode di Lucrezia Borgia duchessa di Ferrara e delle sue damigelle*. Naples, 1884

Cronaca di Napoli di Notar Giacomo. Ed. P. Garzilli. Naples, 1845

Dal Re. Discorso critico sui Borgia con l'aggiunta di documenti ined. rel. al. pontificato di Alessandro VI. *Archivio R. Società Romano Storia Patria*. IV, 1881

Davidsohn, R. Lucrezia Borgia suora di penitenza. *Arch. Stor. Ital.* 1901

Delaborde, H. *L'expédition de Charles VIII en Italie*. Paris, 1888

Dell'oro, I. *Il segreto dei Borgia*. Milan, 1938. *Papa Alessandro VI*. Milan, 1940

Dennistoun, G. *Memoirs of the Dukes of Urbino, from 1540–1640*. London, 1851

De Roo, P. *Material for a history of Pope Alexander VI*, 5 vols., Bruges, 1924

Diario Ferrarese dal 1409 al 1502 di autori incerti. ed. G. Pardi, *Rerum Italicarum Scriptores*, Bologna, 1933

Epinois, H. De L', Alexandre VI. *Revue des questions historiques*, 1881

Errera, C. *Il passaggio per Forli di Lucrezia Borgia sposa ad Alfonso d'Este*. Florence, 1892

Farinelli, A. *Italia e Spagna*. Turin, 1929

Fedele, P. I gioielli di Vannozza. *Archivio R. Società Romana Storia Patria*, 1905

Feliciangeli, B. *Il matrimonio di Lucrezia Borgia con G. Sforza signore di Pesaro*. Turin, 1901. Isabella d'Este Gonzaga a Camerino e a Pioraco. *Atti e Memorie della R. Dep. storica marchigiana*. 1912

Fernandez y Gonzales. *Lucrecia Borja*. Madrid, n.d.

Forcella, V. *Iscrizioni delle chiese e d'altri edifizi di Roma*. 14 vols. Rome, 1869–85

Frizzi, A. *Memorie per la storia di Ferrara*. 5 vols., Ferrara, 1791–1805

Fumi, L. *Alessandro VI e il Valentino in Orvieto*, Siena, 1877

Funk, Brentano F. Lucrèce Borgia. *Nouvelle Revue critique*. 1930

Gagnière, A. Le journal des médecins de Lucrèce Borgia. *La Nouvelle Revue*. LIV, 1888

Gallari, U. *Carteggio tra i Bentivoglio e gli Este dal 1401 al 1542*. Bologna,

1902. Un vescovo di Reggio. *Atti e Mem. della R. Dep. Storia Patria per le province modenesi.* Series IV, vol. IX

Gallier, A. De *César Borgia, Duc de Valentinois, et documents inédits sur son séjour en France.* Paris, 1895

Gandini, L. A. Lucrezia Borgia nell'imminenza delle sue nozze con Alfonso d'Este. *Atti e Memorie della Dep. Storia Patria per la Romagna,* 1902. *Una cuna del secolo XVI* (nozze Tacoli-Ronchetti). Modena, 1894

Garner, J. L. *Caesar Borgia. A study of the Renaissance.* London, 1912

Gastine, L. *César Borgia.* Paris, 1911

Gatti, B. *Lettere di Lucrezia Borgia a M. Pietro Bembo dagli autografi conservati in un codice della Biblioteca Ambrosiana.* Milan, 1859

Gebhart, E. Un problème de morale et d'histoire. Les Borgia. *Revue des Deux Mondes.* 1888–89

Gherardi, Jacopo (da Volterra). *Diario Romano dal VII settembre* 1479 *al XII agosto* 1494 de. E. Carusi, *Rerum Italicarum Scriptores.* Citta di Castello, 1904

Ghirardacci, cherubino. *Historia di Bologna. Rerum Italicarum Scriptores.* 1915

Gilbert, W. *Lucrezia Borgia Duchess of Ferrara.* London, 1869

Giovio, Paolo. *La vita di Alfonso da Este duca di Ferrara tradotta in lingua toscana da G.B. Gelli.* Venice, 1597. *Le vite del Gran Capitano e del Marchese di Pescara.* Bari, 1931

Giustinian, Antonio. *Dispacci.* Ed. P.Villari. 3 vols. Florence, 1886

Gori, F. Fortificazioni dei Borgia nella Rocca di Subiaco. *Archivio Storica Artistica Archeologico e letterario della città e provincia di Roma.* Vol. IV. Roma-Spoleto, 1875–83

Gregorovius, F. *Lucrezia Borgia.* Stuttgart, 1874. *Geschichte der Stadt Rom im Mittelalter.* Stuttgart, 1859–72

Grimaldi, N. *Reggio, Lucrezia Borgia e un romanzo d'amore della duchessa di Ferrara.* Reggio Emilia, 1926

Guicciardini, F. *Storia d'Italia.* 5 vols. Bari, 1929. *Storie Fiorentine dal* 1378 *al* 1509. Bari, 1931

Hagen, T. H. Alexander VI, Caesar Borgia und die Ermordung des Herzogs von Biselli, *Zeitscshrift für Katholische Theologie.* X, 1886

Heuer, O. Zur Heirat der Lucrezia Borgia mit Alfons von Este, *Deutsche Zeitschrift für Geschichtswissenschaft.* I, 1889

Hofler, C. *Don Rodrigo de Borja (Papst Alexander VI) und seine Sohne Don Pedro Luis, erster, und Don Juan zweiter Herzog von Gandia aus dem Hause Borja.* Vienna, 1889

Infessura, Stefano. *Diario della città di Roma.* Rome, 1890

La Torre, F. *Del conclave di Alessandro VI.* Florence, 1933

Leonetti, A. *Papa Alessandro VI secondo documenti e carteggi del tempo.* 3 vols. Bologna, 1880

Luzio, A. *Federico Gonzaga ostaggio alla corte di Giulio II.* Rome, 1887. I preliminari della lega di Cambray concordati a Milano ed a Mantova. *Arch. Stor. Lombardo*, 4th series, XVI, 1911. Isabella d'Este di fronte a Giulio II negli ultimi tre anni del suo pontificato. *Arch. Stor. Lombardo*, 4th series, XVII–XVIII. Isabella d'Este e Giulio II (1503–5). *Rivista d'Italia*, XII, 2. 1909. *Isabella d'Este e Francesco Gonzaga promessi sposi.* Milan, 1908. *Isabella d'Este e i Borgia. Con nuovi documenti.* Milan, 1916. Isabella d'Este e la corte sforzesca. *Arch. Stor. Lombardo*, 3rd series, XV. Isabella d'Este nei primordi del papato di Leone X. *Arch. Stor. Lombardo*, VI. Isabella d'Este nelle tragedie della sua casa. *Atti e Memorie della R. Accademia Virgiliana di Mantova.* New series, vol. V, 1912. I ritratti di Isabella d'Este. *Emporium*, May–June 1900. La 'Madonna della Vittoria' del Mantegna. *Emporium*, November 1899. La reggenza d'Isabella d'Este durante la prigionia del marito. *Arch. Stor. Lombardo*, 4th series, XVI, 1911. *Pietro Aretino nei primi suoi anni a Venezia, e la corte dei Gonzaga*, Turin, 1888. *Precettori di Isabella d'Este.* Ancona, 1887

Luzio, A. Renier R. Buffoni nani schiavi dei Gonzaga, ai tempi di I. d'Este. *Nuova Antologia*, August–September 1891. Francesco Gonzaga alla battaglia di Fornovo secondo documenti mantovani. *Arch. Stor. Ital.* Series V, Vol. VI. Il lusso di Isabella d'Este. *Nuova Antologia*, Vols. 63–65, 1896. La cultura e le relazioni letterarie di Isabella d'Este ed Elisabetta Gonzaga. I) La cultura. *Giorn. Stor. Lett. Ital.*, XXXIII 1899. II) Le relazioni letterarie: 1. Gruppo mantovano, *ibid.* XXXIV, 1899. 2. Gruppo ferrarese, *ibid.* XXXV, 1900. 3. Gruppo lombardo, *ibid.* XXXVI, 1900. 4. Gruppo veneto, *ibid.* XXXVII, 1901. 5. Gruppo emiliano, *ibid.* XXXVIII, 1901. 6. Gruppo dell'Italia centrale, *ibid.* XXXIX, 1902. 7. Gruppo meridionale, *ibid.* XL, 1902. Appendici, *ibid.* XLII, 1903. *Mantova e Urbino*, Turin, 1893. Niccolò da Correggio. *Giorn. Stor. Lett. Ital.* XXI, XXII, 1893. Gara di viaggi fra due celebri dame del Rinascimento. *Intermezzo*, vol. I, Alessandria, 1890

Machiavelli, Niccolo. *Tutte le opere storiche e letterarie di N.M.* ed. Guido Mazzoni e Mario Casella. Florence, 1929

Malipiero, D. Annali veneti dall'anno 1457 al 1500 ordinati dal sen. F. Longo. *Arch. Stor. Ital.* VII, 1843

Mantagne, H. (R. P.) Une réhabilitation d'Alexandre VI. *Revue des questions historiques.* XI, 1870, p. 466. See also 1872, p. 180

Mariana, J. de. *Historiae de rebus Hispaniae.* Toledo, 1572

Maricourt, R. de. *Le procès des Borgia consideré au point de vue de l'histoire naturelle et sociale*. Poitiers-Paris, 1883

Martelli, U. *Lucrezia Borgia e la valle siciliana da un manoscritto del secolo XVI*. Spoleto, 1931

Matarazzo, Francesco. Cronaca della città di Perugia 1492–1503. *Arch. Stor. Ital.*, XVI, II, 1851

Mathew, A. H. *The Life and Times of Rodrigo Borgia*. London, n.d.

Medin, A. Il duca Valentino nella mente di Niccolò Machiavelli, *Rivista Europea*. Florence, 1885

Menotti, M. *I Borgia, storia ed iconografia*. Rome, 1917. *I Borgia. Documenti inediti sulla famiglia e la corte di Alessandro VI*. Rome, 1917

Morsolin, B. Pietro Bembo e Lucrezia Borgia. *Nuova Antologia*. 52, 1885

Muntz, E. *Les arts à la cour des papes Innocent VIII, Alexandre VI, Pie III*. 1484–1503. Paris, 1898

Oliver y Hurtado J. M. Rodrigo de Borja. Sus hijos y descendientes. *Bulletin de la Real Academia de la historia*. December, 1886

Olivier, P. *Le pape Alexandre VI et les Borgia*. Paris, 1870

Pardi, G. Il teatro classico a Ferrara. *Atti e Memorie della R. Dep. ferrarese Storia Patria*, XV, 1904

Pasini, Frassoni. Un ritratto di Lucrezia Borgia nella collezione Antonelli in Ferrara. *Rivista Araldica*, XV. I Borgia in Ferrara. *Giornale Araldico Genealogico Diplom*. Rome, January–February 1880 Appunti vari sui Borgia. *Riv. Collegio Araldico*, 1910. Lo stemma di Vannozza Borgia de Cathaneis, *Rivista Araldica*. June 1909. Lucrezia Borgia duchessa di Ferrara. Invenzione del suo sepolcro. *Riv. Collegio Araldico*, 1904. Ritratto di Lucrezia Borgia. *Rassegna d'arte*. XVII. 1917

Pasolini, P. D. *Caterina Sforza*. 3 vols. Rome, 1893. *Caterina Sforza. Nuovi documenti*, Bologna, 1897

Pastor, L. Von. Geschichte der Päpste seit dem Ausgang des Mittelalters, vol. II and III, 3rd–4th ed., Freiburg i. Br., 1901–4

Pazzi, Gianna. *Le delizie estensi e l'Ariosto*. Pescara Riviera, 1933

Pélicier, P. *Lettres de Charles VIII roi de France*. Vols. 1–5. Paris, 1898–1905

Picotti, G. B. *La giovinezza di Leone X*. Milan, 1928

Pistofilo, Bonaventura. Vita di Alfonso d'Este. *Atti e Memorie della R. Dep. Storia Patria per le province modenesi*. Series I, vol. III, 1865

Polifilo, L. Beltrami. *Le guardaroba di Lucrezia Borgia*. (Milan) 1903

Portigliotti, G. *I Borgia*. Milan, 1913. Un ritratto tizianesco di Lucrezia Borgia?, *Rivista d'Italia* X, 1915

Priuli, Girolamo. *I Diarii. Rerum Italicarum Scriptores*, 1912, 1919

Rajna, P. I versi spagnoli di mano di Pietro Bembo e di Lucrezia

Borgia, serbati in un codice ambrosiano. *In Homenaje ofrecido a Menendez Pidal.* Vol. II. Madrid, 1925

Reumont, A. *Vittoria Colonna.* Turin, 1883

Ricci, C. Il figlio di Cesare Borgia. *Rassegna Contemporanea* 2, 1909, p. ii

Ricci, E. *Vita di Suor Colomba da Rieti,* Perugia, 1912

Rodocanachi, E. *La femme italienne à l'époque de la Renaissance. Sa vie privée et mondaine. Son influence sociale.* Paris, 1907

Ronchini, A. Documenti borgiani. *Atti e Memorie delle RR. Dep. Storia Patria per le province dell'Emilia,* I, 1877

Roscoe, W. *The Life and Pontificate of Leo the Tenth,* 4 vols. Liverpool, 1805

Sabatini, R. *The life of Cesare Borgia. A History and some Criticism.* London, 1912

Sanchis, y Sivera J. *Algunos documentos y cartas privadas que pertenecieron al segundo Duque de Gandia don Juan de Borja.* Valencia, 1919

Sanudo Marino. *I Diari dal* 1496 *al* 1532 ed. Nicolò Boroni, Venice, 1879

Schnitzer, G. *Savonarola.* 2 vols., Munich, 1924. Zur Geschichte Alexanders VI. *Histor. Jahrbuch,* XXI, 1900

Strozzi Poetae (Pater et Filius). Simon Colinaeus. Paris, 1530. Poems of Ercole Strozzi and Tito Vespasiano Strozzi

Tedallini (Sebastiano Di Branca). *Diario Romano dal maggio* 1485 *al giugno* 1524. ed. P. Piccolomini. In the appendix to *Diario Romano* of Jacopo da Volterra. *Rerum Italicarum Scriptores,* Città di Castello, 1907

Tiraboschi, G. *Biblioteca Modenese.* 6 vols. Modena, 1781–86

Tomasi, Tomaso. *La vita del duca Valentino.* Montechiaro, 1655

Tommasini, O. *Vita e scritti di Niccolò Machiavelli,* 2 vols. Turin, 1883, 1911. E. Maddaleni dei Capodiferro. *Atti della R. Accademia dei Lincei.* Series IV, 10, 1893

Tommaso, Di Silvestro. *Diario.* Orvieto, 1891

Trinchera, F. *Codice aragonese. Lettere dei sovrani aragonesi in Napoli.* Naples, 1866

Truc, G. *Rome et les Borgia.* Paris, 1939

Ugolini, F. *Storia dei conti e duchi d'Urbino.* 2 vols. Florence, 1859

Uhagón, F. R. de. *Relación de los festines que se celebraron en el Vaticano con motivo de las bodas de Lucrecia Borja con Alonso de Aragón.* Madrid, 1896

Vattasso, M. *Antonio Flaminio e le principali poesie dell'autografo Vaticano* 2870. (Studi e testi, I) Rome, 1900

Venturi, A. *Galleria Estense in Modena.* Modena, 1882. Lavori di Dosso nel castello di Ferrara. *Arch. Stor. dell'Arte,* 1889

Villari, P. *Arte, storia e filosofia:* Nuovi studi sui Borgia, Florence, 1884

Villa-Urrutia, Marqués de. *Lucrecia Borja.* Madrid, 1922

Wirtz, M. Ercole Strozzi poeta ferrarese. *Atti e Memorie della R. Dep. ferrarese Storia Patria.* XVI, 1906

Woodward, W. H. *Cesare Borgia, a biography with documents and illustrations.* London, 1913

Yriarte, Charles. *César Borgia. Sa vie, sa captivité, sa mort.* 2 vols. Paris, 1889. *Autour des Borgia.* Paris, 1891

Zaccarini, D. Un ritratto di Lucrezia Borgia. *La Domenica dell' operaio.* Ferrara, 27 April 1919

Zambotti, Bernardino. *Diario ferrarese dal 1476 al 1504.* ed. G. Pardi, *Rerum Italicarum Scriptores.* Bologna, 1937

Zucchetti, G. *Lucrezia Borgia duchessa di Ferrara.* Mantua, 1860. Reprinted from *Gazzetta di Mantova.* 44–49

Zurita, G. *Anales de la corona de Aragón,* vols. IV and V. Saragossa, 1610

INDEX